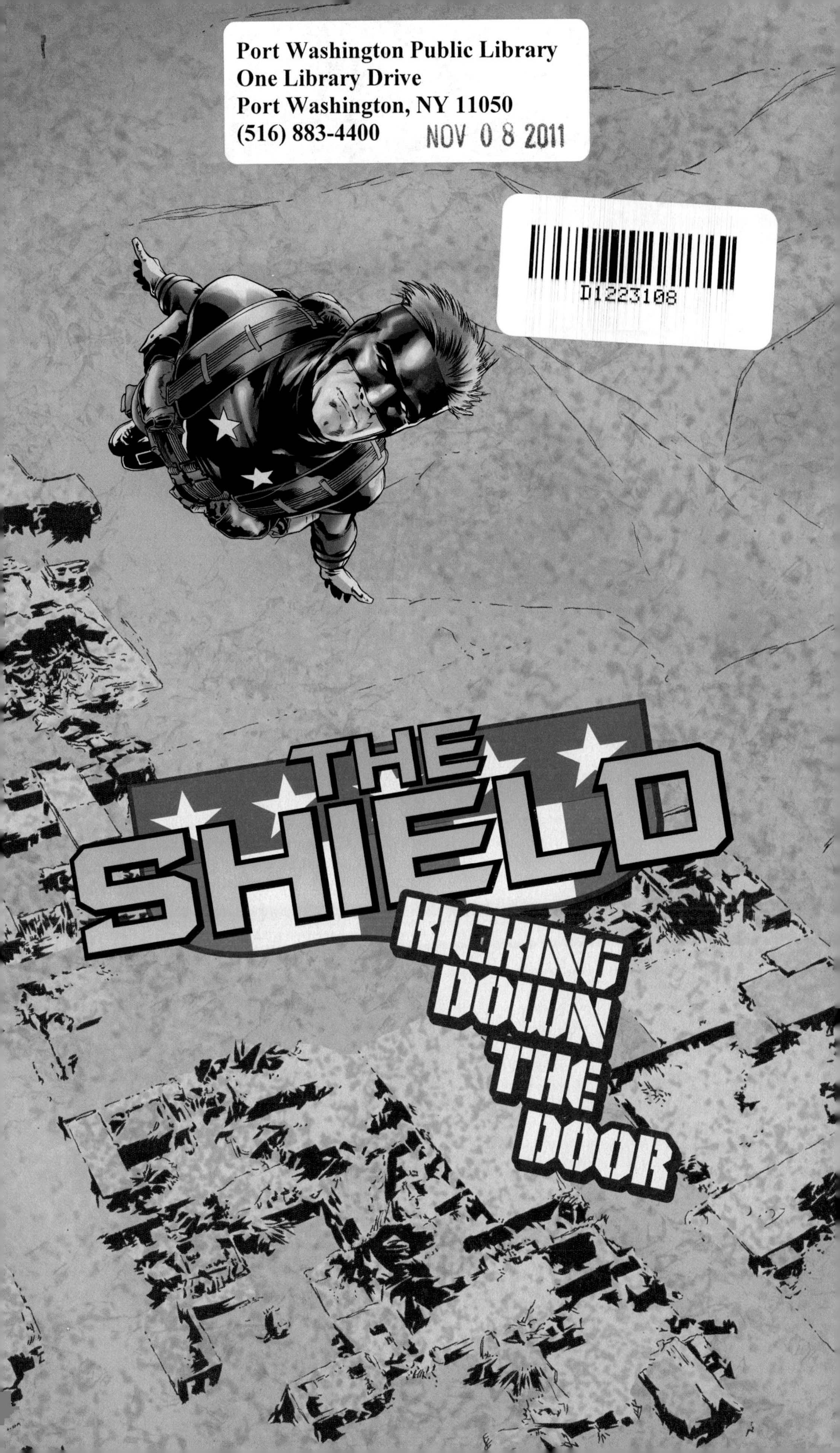
THE SHIELD
KICKING DOWN THE DOOR

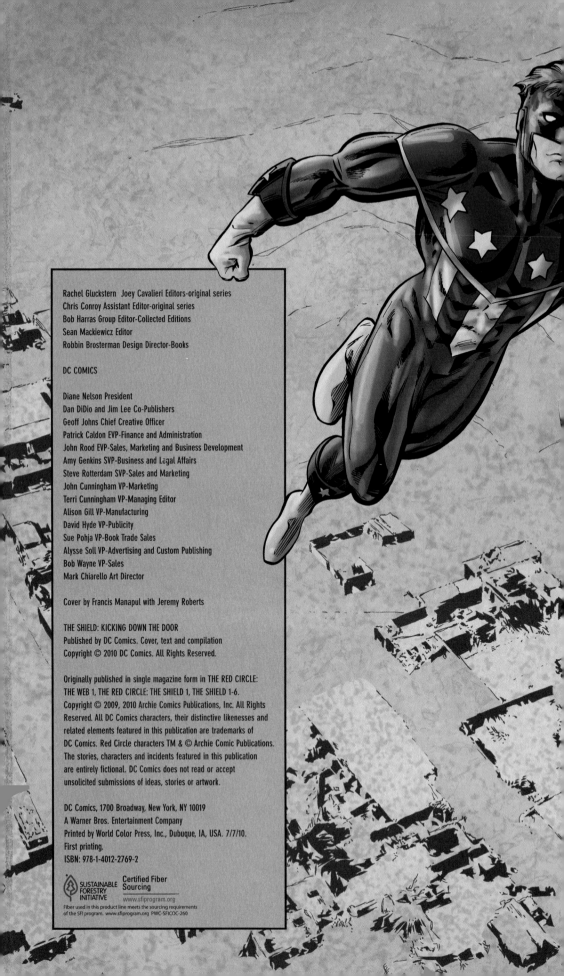

Rachel Gluckstern Joey Cavalieri Editors-original series
Chris Conroy Assistant Editor-original series
Bob Harras Group Editor-Collected Editions
Sean Mackiewicz Editor
Robbin Brosterman Design Director-Books

DC COMICS

Diane Nelson President
Dan DiDio and Jim Lee Co-Publishers
Geoff Johns Chief Creative Officer
Patrick Caldon EVP-Finance and Administration
John Rood EVP-Sales, Marketing and Business Development
Amy Genkins SVP-Business and Legal Affairs
Steve Rotterdam SVP-Sales and Marketing
John Cunningham VP-Marketing
Terri Cunningham VP-Managing Editor
Alison Gill VP-Manufacturing
David Hyde VP-Publicity
Sue Pohja VP-Book Trade Sales
Alysse Soll VP-Advertising and Custom Publishing
Bob Wayne VP-Sales
Mark Chiarello Art Director

Cover by Francis Manapul with Jeremy Roberts

THE SHIELD: KICKING DOWN THE DOOR

DC Comics, 1700 Broadway, New York, NY 10019
A Warner Bros. Entertainment Company
Printed by World Color Press, Inc., Dubuque, IA, USA. 7/7/10.
First printing.
ISBN: 978-1-4012-2769-2

SUSTAINABLE FORESTRY INITIATIVE
Certified Fiber Sourcing
www.sfiprogram.org
Fiber used in this product line meets the sourcing requirements of the SFI program. www.sfiprogram.org PWC-SFICOC-260

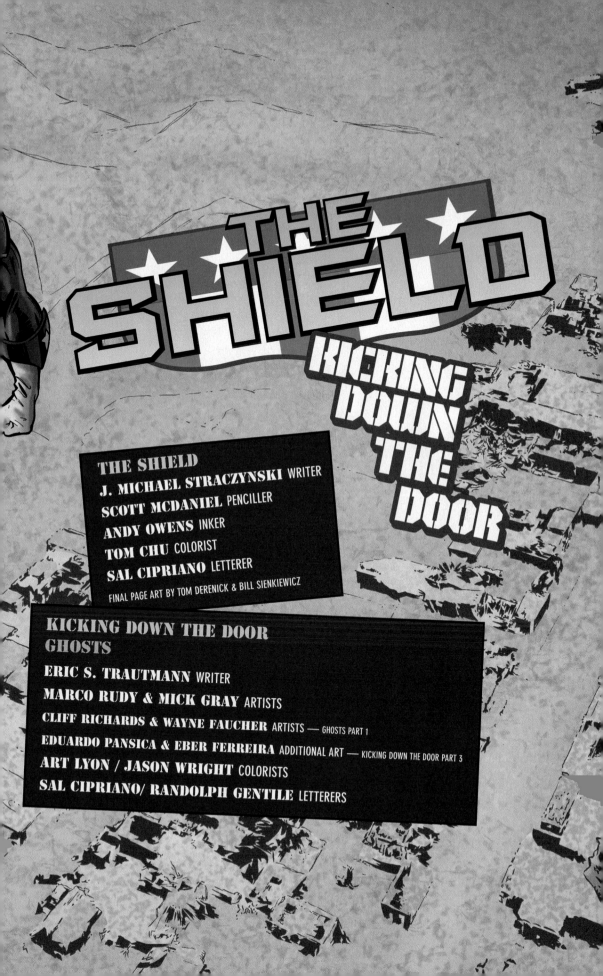

THE SHIELD

KICKING DOWN THE DOOR

THE SHIELD

J. MICHAEL STRACZYNSKI WRITER

SCOTT MCDANIEL PENCILLER

ANDY OWENS INKER

TOM CHU COLORIST

SAL CIPRIANO LETTERER

FINAL PAGE ART BY TOM DERENICK & BILL SIENKIEWICZ

KICKING DOWN THE DOOR
GHOSTS

ERIC S. TRAUTMANN WRITER

MARCO RUDY & MICK GRAY ARTISTS

CLIFF RICHARDS & WAYNE FAUCHER ARTISTS — GHOSTS PART 1

EDUARDO PANSICA & EBER FERREIRA ADDITIONAL ART — KICKING DOWN THE DOOR PART 3

ART LYON / JASON WRIGHT COLORISTS

SAL CIPRIANO / RANDOLPH GENTILE LETTERERS

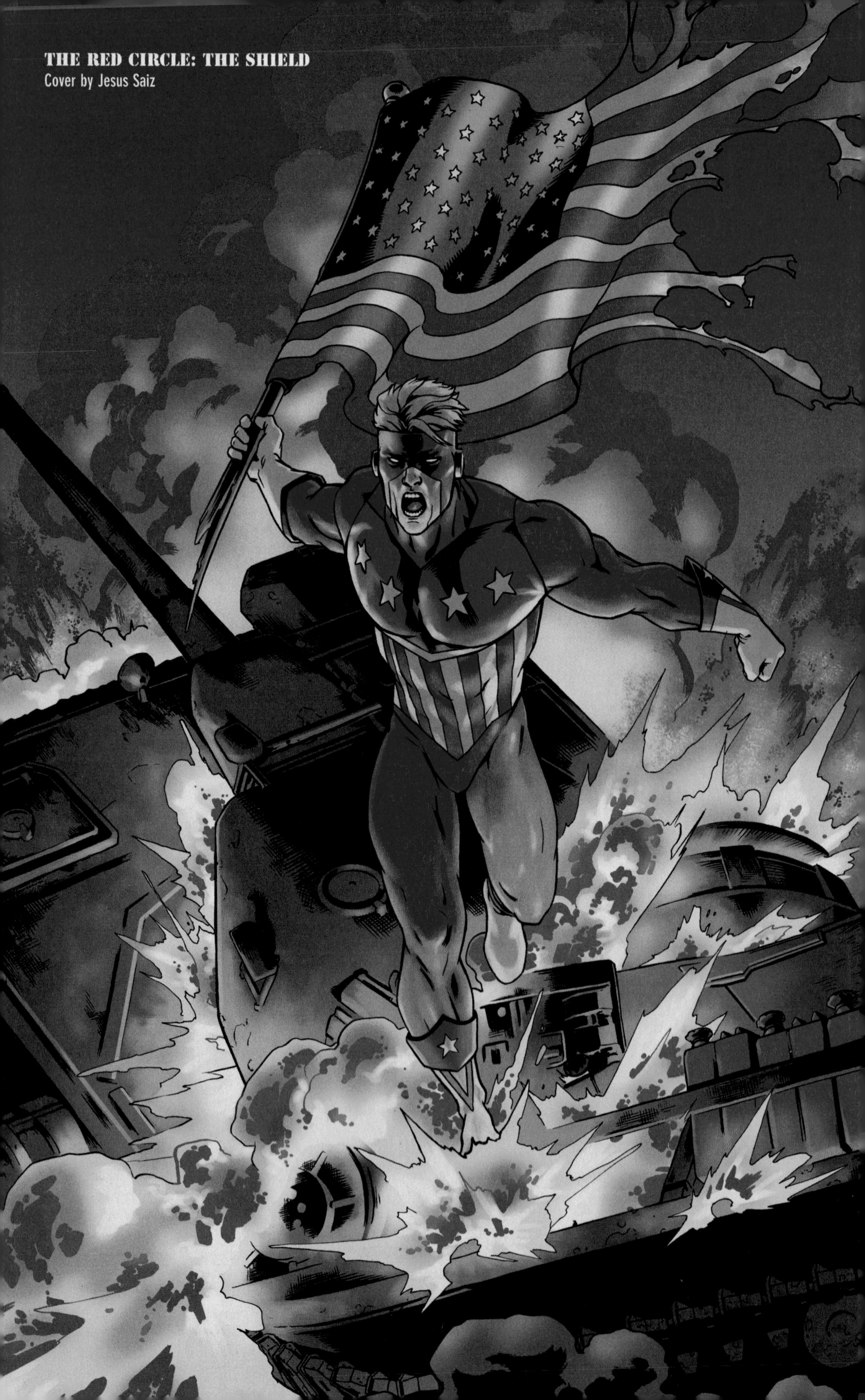

THE RED CIRCLE: THE SHIELD
Cover by Jesus Saiz

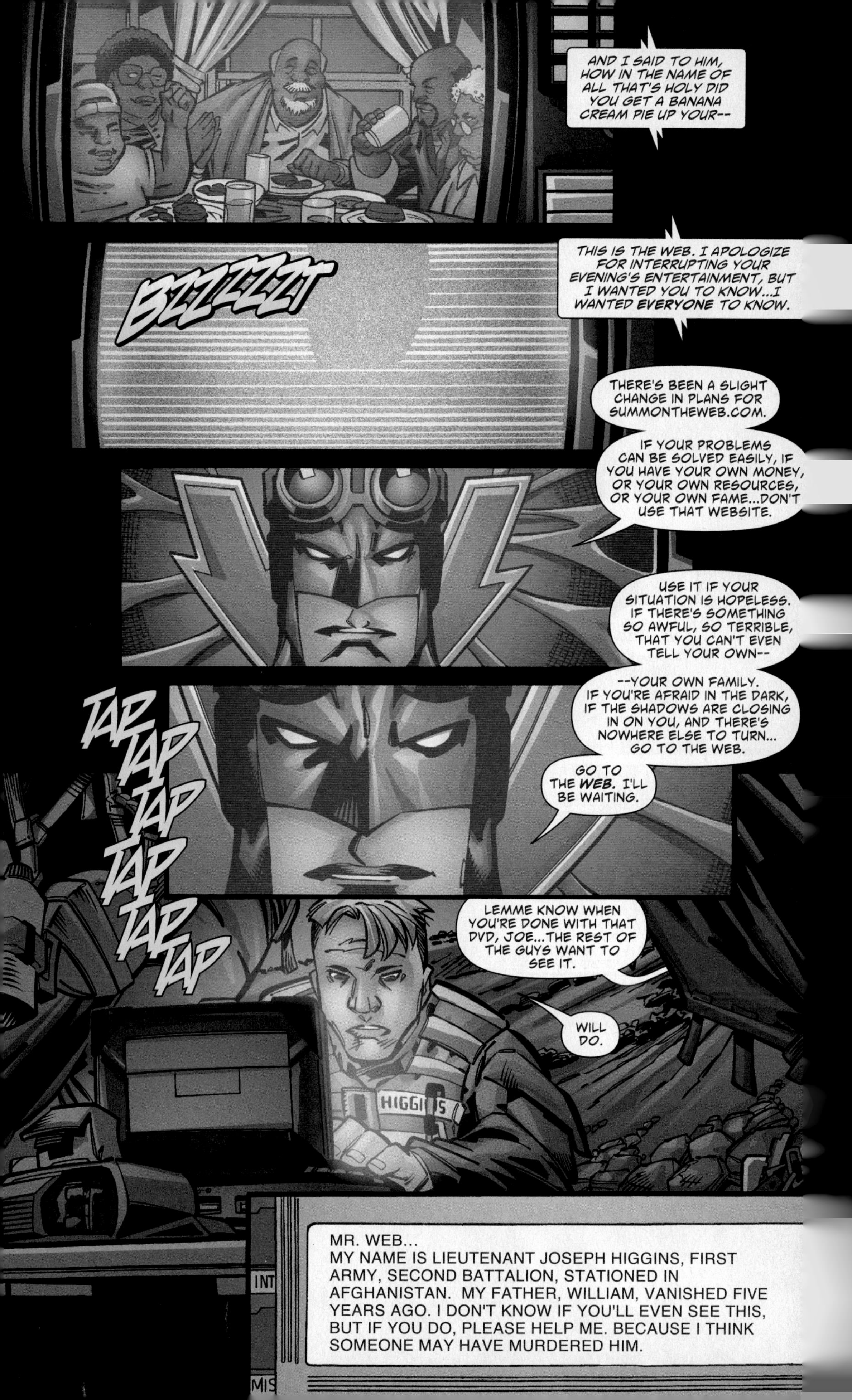
AND I SAID TO HIM, HOW IN THE NAME OF ALL THAT'S HOLY DID YOU GET A BANANA CREAM PIE UP YOUR--
BZZZZZZT
THIS IS THE WEB. I APOLOGIZE FOR INTERRUPTING YOUR EVENING'S ENTERTAINMENT, BUT I WANTED YOU TO KNOW...I WANTED EVERYONE TO KNOW.
THERE'S BEEN A SLIGHT CHANGE IN PLANS FOR SUMMONTHEWEB.COM.
IF YOUR PROBLEMS CAN BE SOLVED EASILY, IF YOU HAVE YOUR OWN MONEY, OR YOUR OWN RESOURCES, OR YOUR OWN FAME...DON'T USE THAT WEBSITE.
USE IT IF YOUR SITUATION IS HOPELESS. IF THERE'S SOMETHING SO AWFUL, SO TERRIBLE, THAT YOU CAN'T EVEN TELL YOUR OWN--
--YOUR OWN FAMILY. IF YOU'RE AFRAID IN THE DARK, IF THE SHADOWS ARE CLOSING IN ON YOU, AND THERE'S NOWHERE ELSE TO TURN... GO TO THE WEB.
GO TO THE WEB. I'LL BE WAITING.
TAP TAP TAP TAP TAP TAP
LEMME KNOW WHEN YOU'RE DONE WITH THAT DVD, JOE...THE REST OF THE GUYS WANT TO SEE IT.
WILL DO.
HIGGINS
INT
MIS
MR. WEB...
MY NAME IS LIEUTENANT JOSEPH HIGGINS, FIRST ARMY, SECOND BATTALION, STATIONED IN AFGHANISTAN. MY FATHER, WILLIAM, VANISHED FIVE YEARS AGO. I DON'T KNOW IF YOU'LL EVEN SEE THIS, BUT IF YOU DO, PLEASE HELP ME. BECAUSE I THINK SOMEONE MAY HAVE MURDERED HIM.

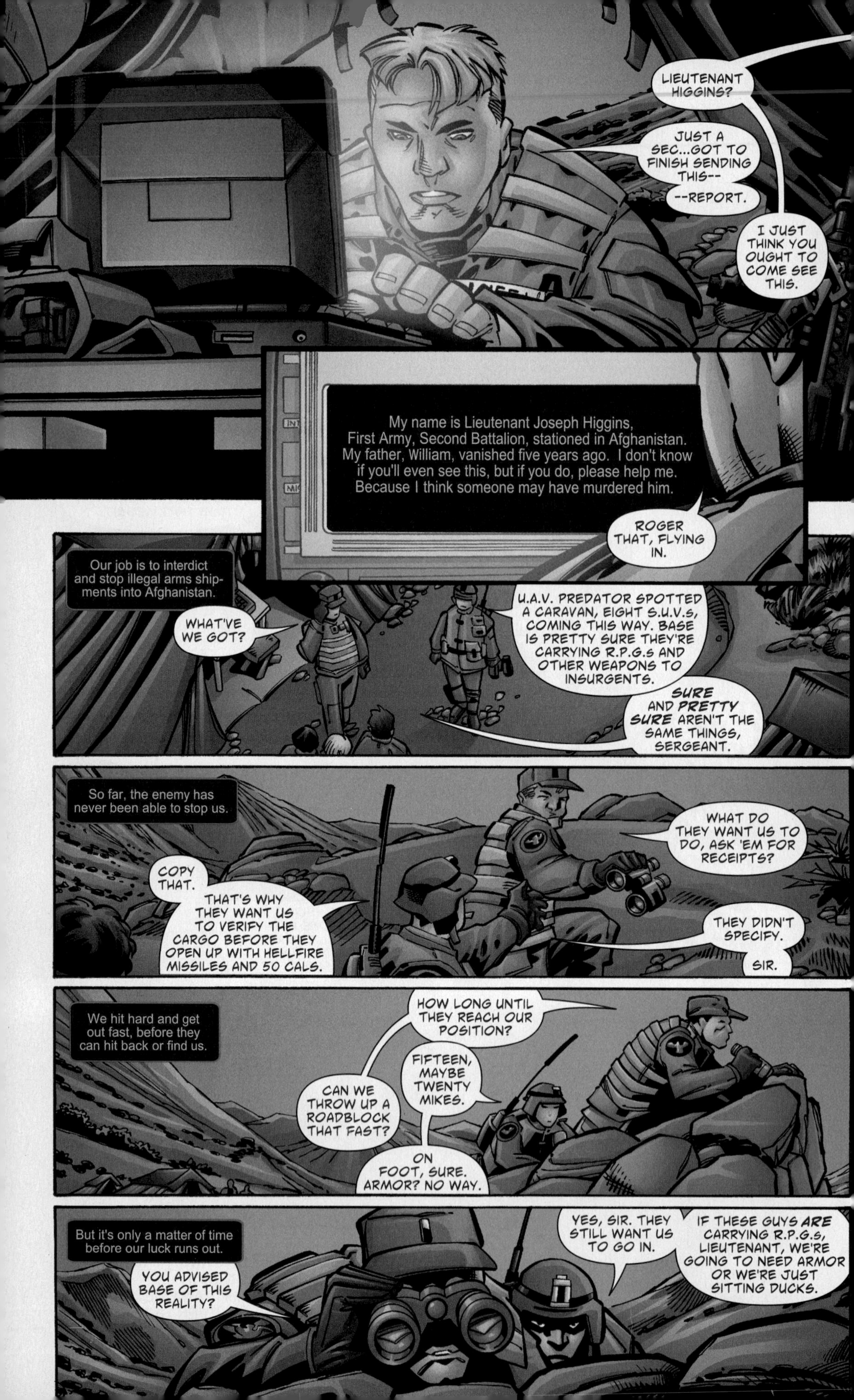
LIEUTENANT HIGGINS?
JUST A SEC...GOT TO FINISH SENDING THIS--
--REPORT.
I JUST THINK YOU OUGHT TO COME SEE THIS.
My name is Lieutenant Joseph Higgins, First Army, Second Battalion, stationed in Afghanistan. My father, William, vanished five years ago. I don't know if you'll even see this, but if you do, please help me. Because I think someone may have murdered him.
ROGER THAT, FLYING IN.
Our job is to interdict and stop illegal arms shipments into Afghanistan.
WHAT'VE WE GOT?
U.A.V. PREDATOR SPOTTED A CARAVAN, EIGHT S.U.V.s, COMING THIS WAY. BASE IS PRETTY SURE THEY'RE CARRYING R.P.G.s AND OTHER WEAPONS TO INSURGENTS.
SURE AND PRETTY SURE AREN'T THE SAME THINGS, SERGEANT.
So far, the enemy has never been able to stop us.
WHAT DO THEY WANT US TO DO, ASK 'EM FOR RECEIPTS?
COPY THAT.
THAT'S WHY THEY WANT US TO VERIFY THE CARGO BEFORE THEY OPEN UP WITH HELLFIRE MISSILES AND 50 CALS.
THEY DIDN'T SPECIFY.
SIR.
We hit hard and get out fast, before they can hit back or find us.
HOW LONG UNTIL THEY REACH OUR POSITION?
FIFTEEN, MAYBE TWENTY MIKES.
CAN WE THROW UP A ROADBLOCK THAT FAST?
ON FOOT, SURE. ARMOR? NO WAY.
But it's only a matter of time before our luck runs out.
YOU ADVISED BASE OF THIS REALITY?
YES, SIR. THEY STILL WANT US TO GO IN.
IF THESE GUYS ARE CARRYING R.P.G.s, LIEUTENANT, WE'RE GOING TO NEED ARMOR OR WE'RE JUST SITTING DUCKS.

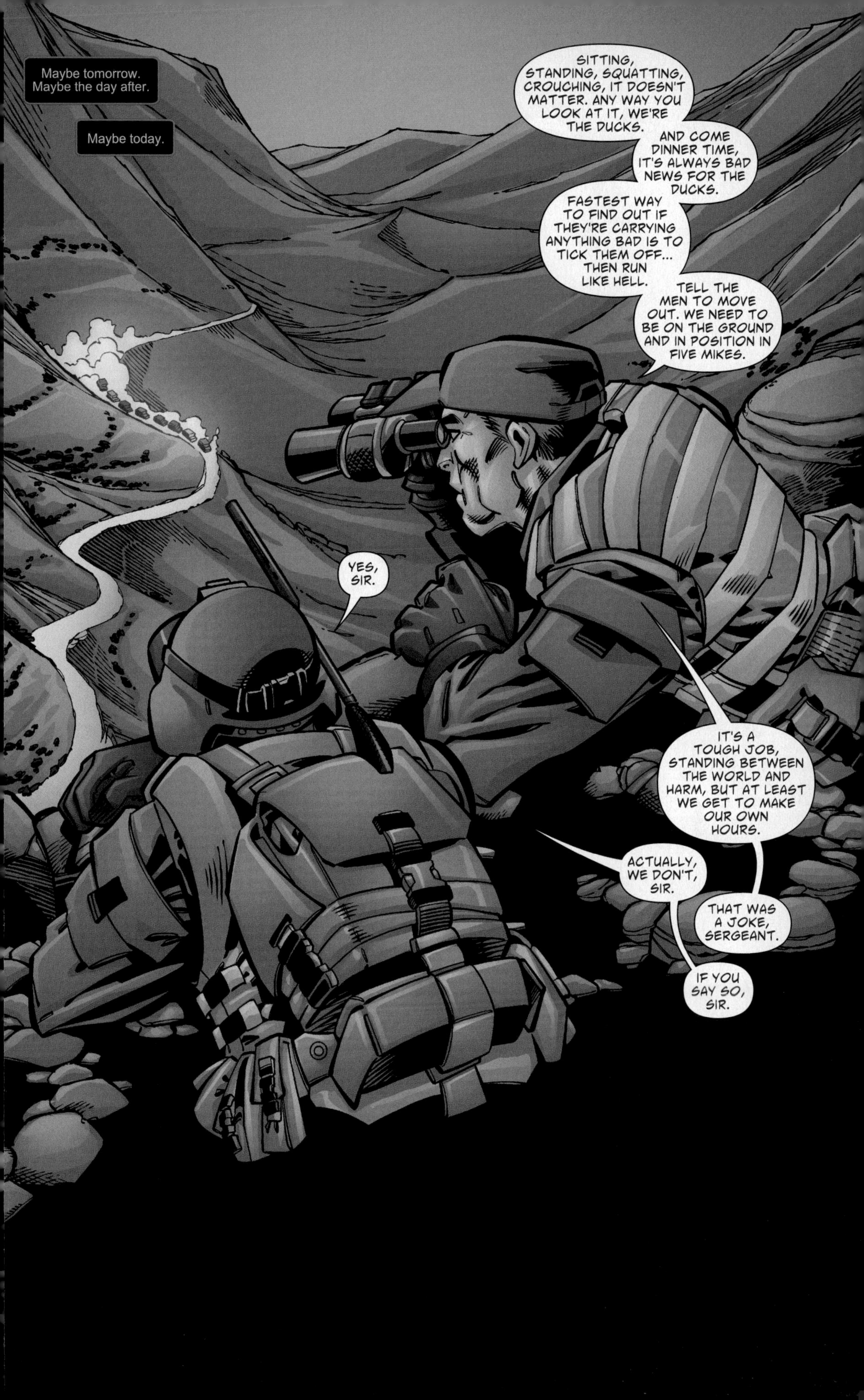
Maybe tomorrow. Maybe the day after.
Maybe today.
SITTING, STANDING, SQUATTING, CROUCHING, IT DOESN'T MATTER. ANY WAY YOU LOOK AT IT, WE'RE THE DUCKS.
AND COME DINNER TIME, IT'S ALWAYS BAD NEWS FOR THE DUCKS.
FASTEST WAY TO FIND OUT IF THEY'RE CARRYING ANYTHING BAD IS TO TICK THEM OFF... THEN RUN LIKE HELL.
TELL THE MEN TO MOVE OUT. WE NEED TO BE ON THE GROUND AND IN POSITION IN FIVE MIKES.
YES, SIR.
IT'S A TOUGH JOB, STANDING BETWEEN THE WORLD AND HARM, BUT AT LEAST WE GET TO MAKE OUR OWN HOURS.
ACTUALLY, WE DON'T, SIR.
THAT WAS A JOKE, SERGEANT.
IF YOU SAY SO, SIR.

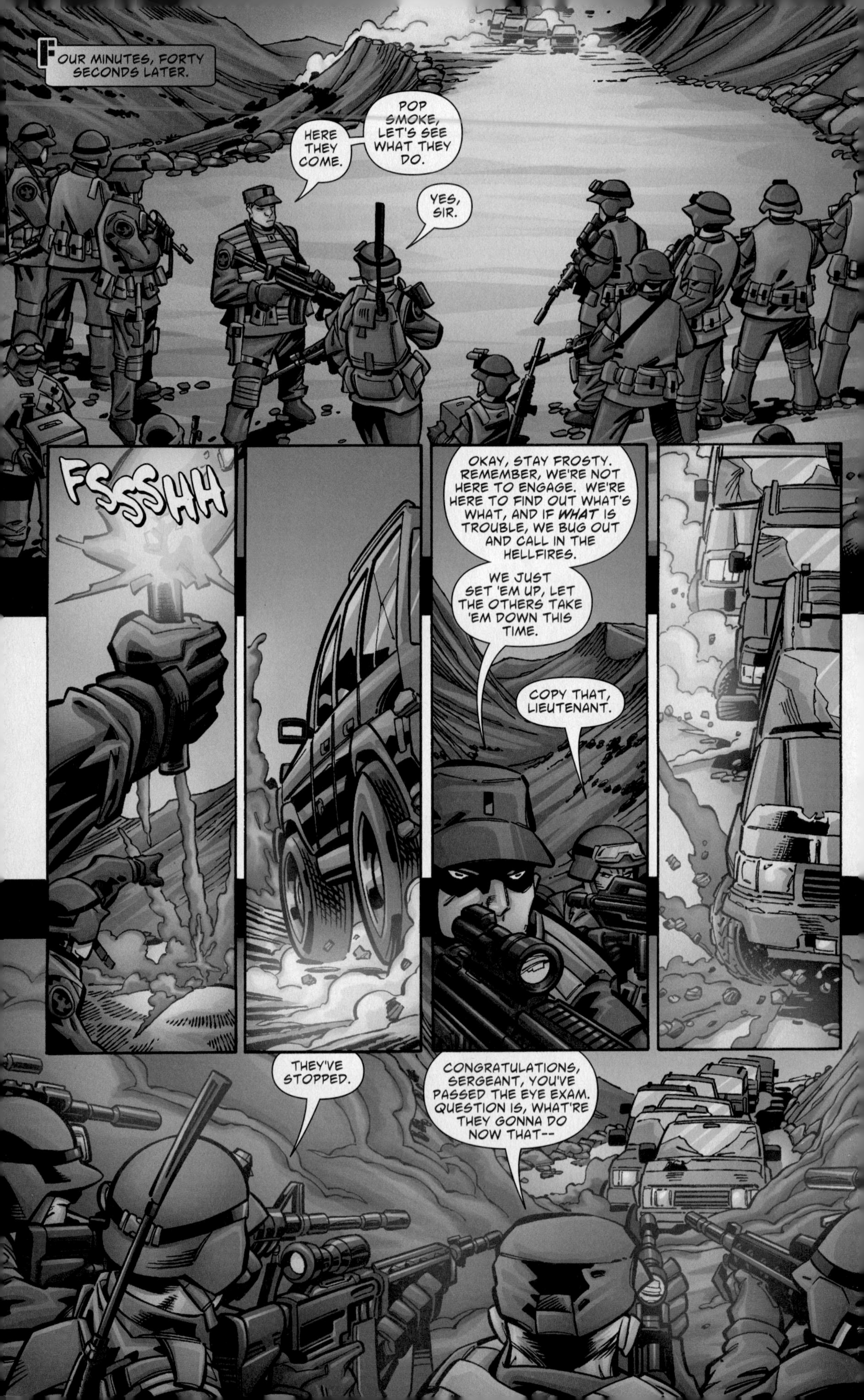
FOUR MINUTES, FORTY SECONDS LATER.
HERE THEY COME.
POP SMOKE, LET'S SEE WHAT THEY DO.
YES, SIR.
FSSSHH
OKAY, STAY FROSTY. REMEMBER, WE'RE NOT HERE TO ENGAGE. WE'RE HERE TO FIND OUT WHAT'S WHAT, AND IF WHAT IS TROUBLE, WE BUG OUT AND CALL IN THE HELLFIRES.
WE JUST SET 'EM UP, LET THE OTHERS TAKE 'EM DOWN THIS TIME.
COPY THAT, LIEUTENANT.
THEY'VE STOPPED.
CONGRATULATIONS, SERGEANT, YOU'VE PASSED THE EYE EXAM. QUESTION IS, WHAT'RE THEY GONNA DO NOW THAT--

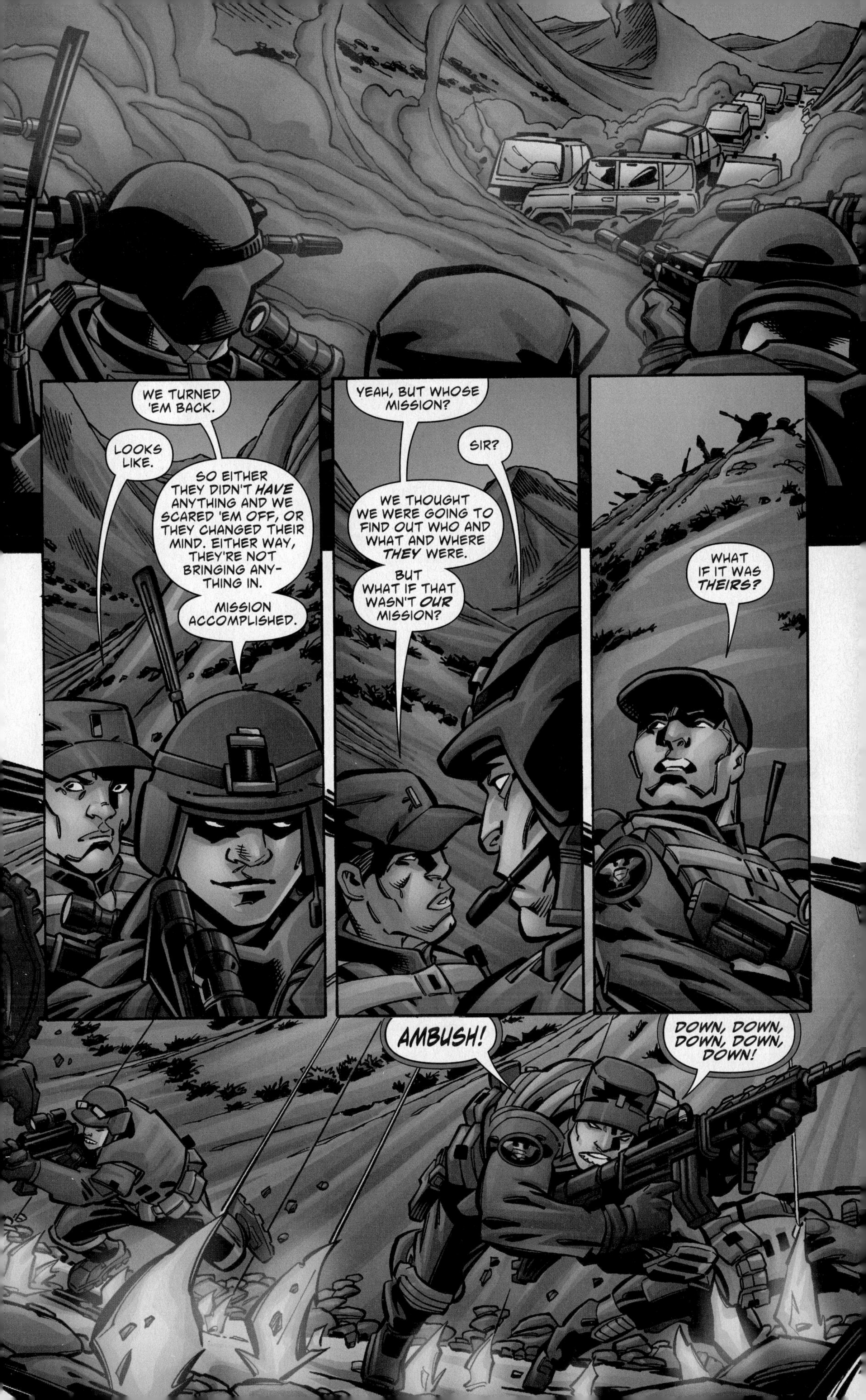
WE TURNED 'EM BACK.
LOOKS LIKE.
SO EITHER THEY DIDN'T HAVE ANYTHING AND WE SCARED 'EM OFF, OR THEY CHANGED THEIR MIND. EITHER WAY, THEY'RE NOT BRINGING ANY-THING IN.
MISSION ACCOMPLISHED.
YEAH, BUT WHOSE MISSION?
SIR?
WE THOUGHT WE WERE GOING TO FIND OUT WHO AND WHAT AND WHERE THEY WERE.
BUT WHAT IF THAT WASN'T OUR MISSION?
WHAT IF IT WAS THEIRS?
AMBUSH!
DOWN, DOWN, DOWN, DOWN, DOWN!

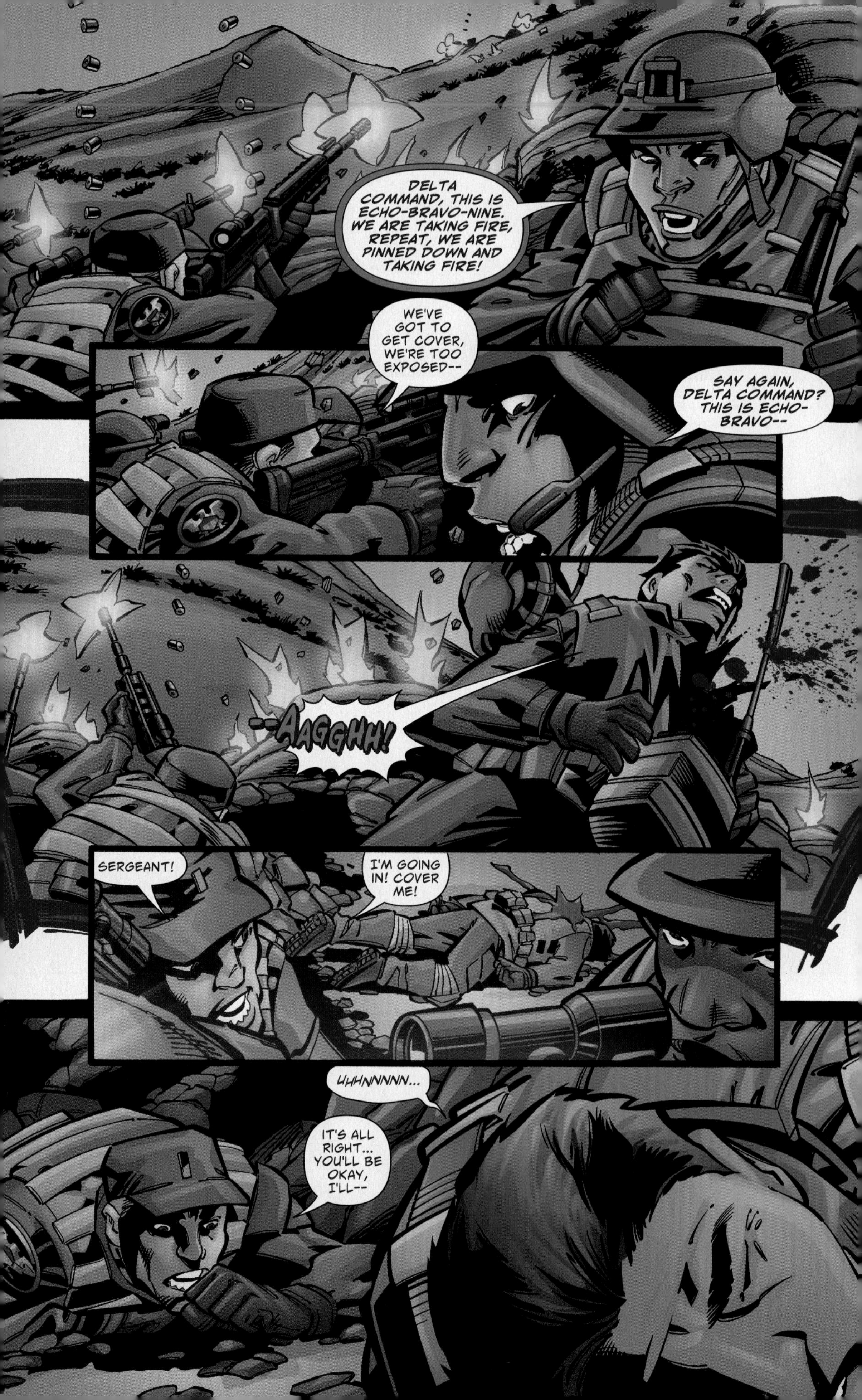
DELTA COMMAND, THIS IS ECHO-BRAVO-NINE. WE ARE TAKING FIRE, REPEAT, WE ARE PINNED DOWN AND TAKING FIRE!
WE'VE GOT TO GET COVER, WE'RE TOO EXPOSED--
SAY AGAIN, DELTA COMMAND? THIS IS ECHO-BRAVO--
--AAGGHH!
SERGEANT!
I'M GOING IN! COVER ME!
UHHNNNNN...
IT'S ALL RIGHT... YOU'LL BE OKAY, I'LL--

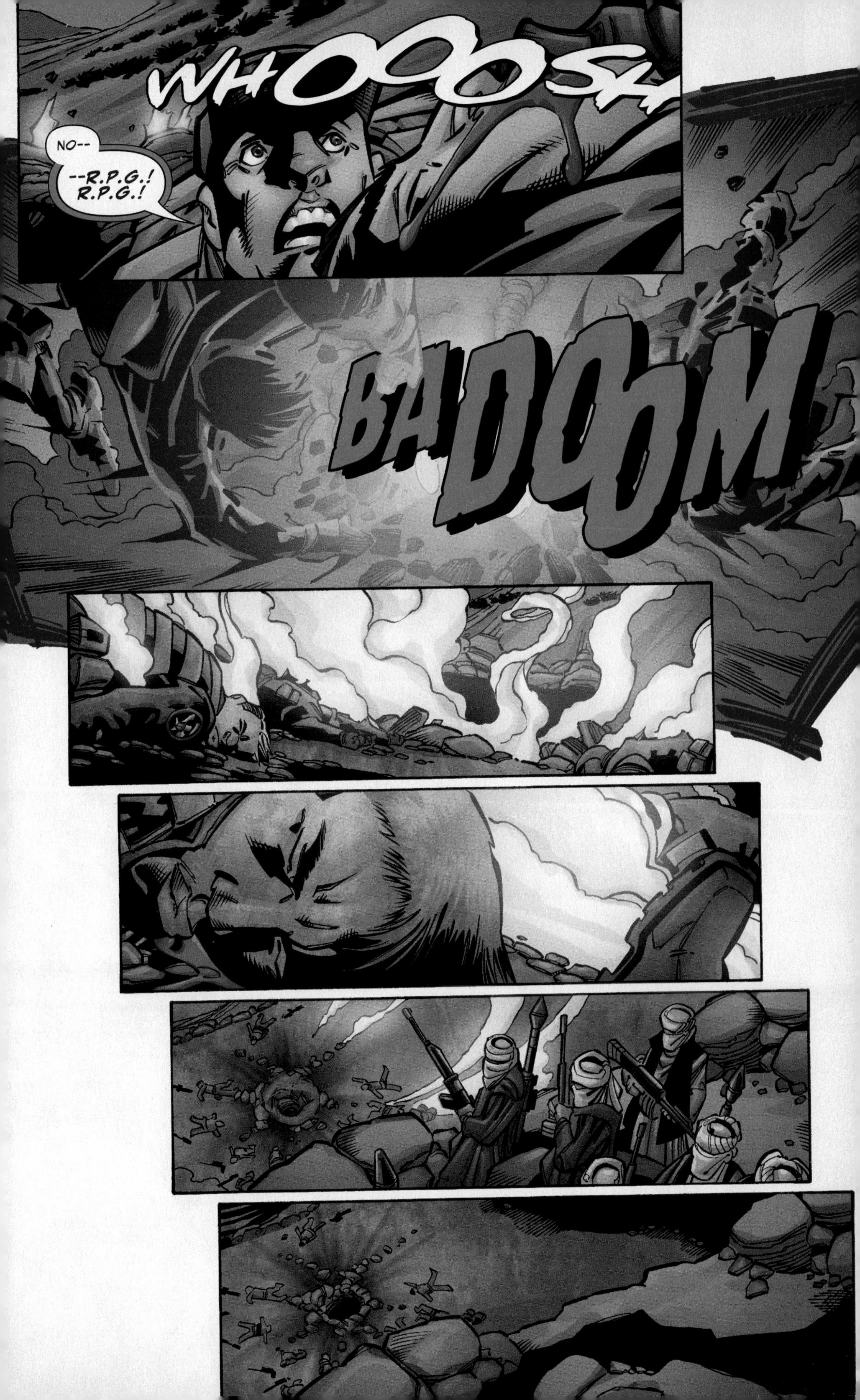
WHOOOOSH
NO--
--R.P.G.! R.P.G.!
BADOOM

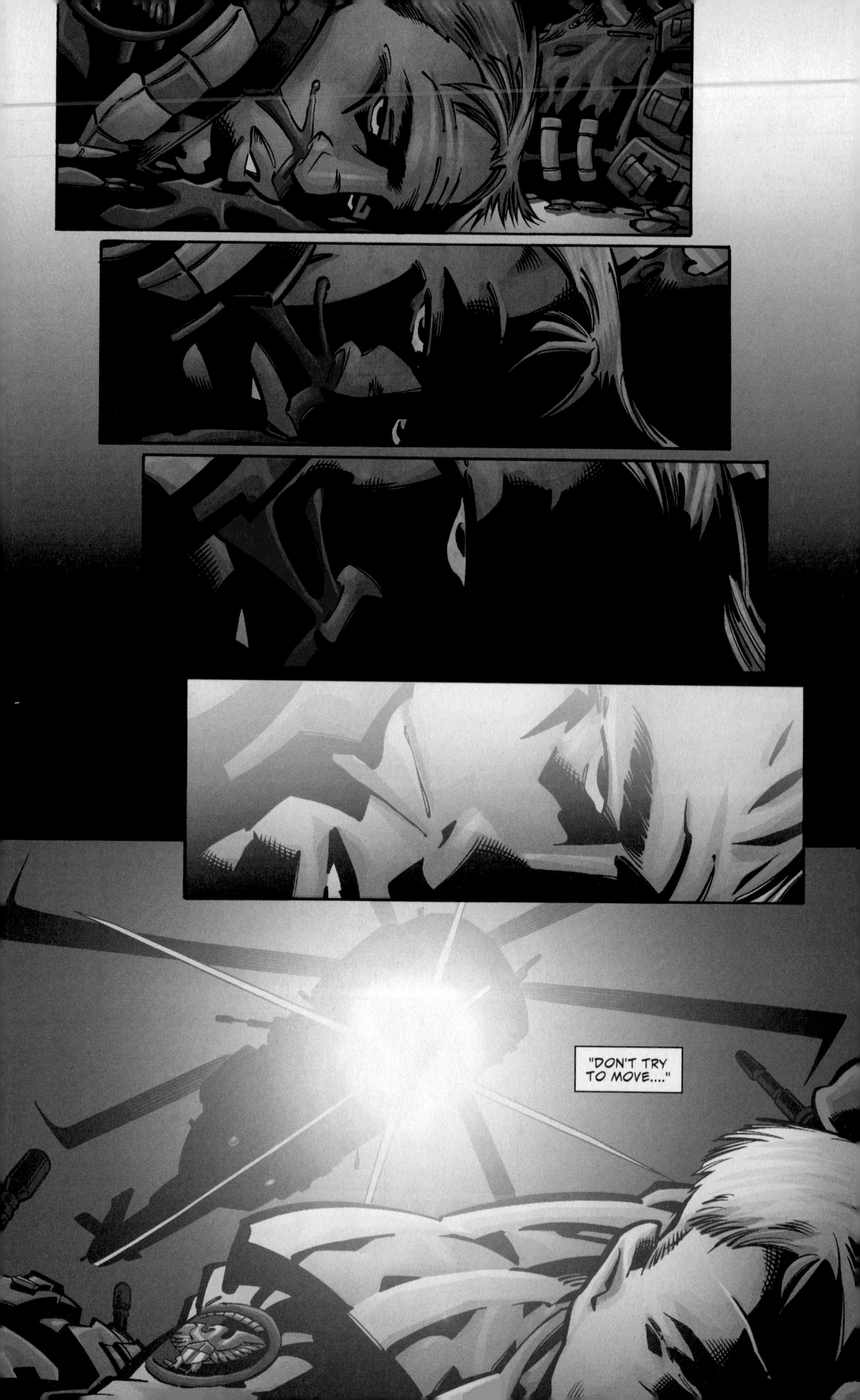
"DON'T TRY TO MOVE...."

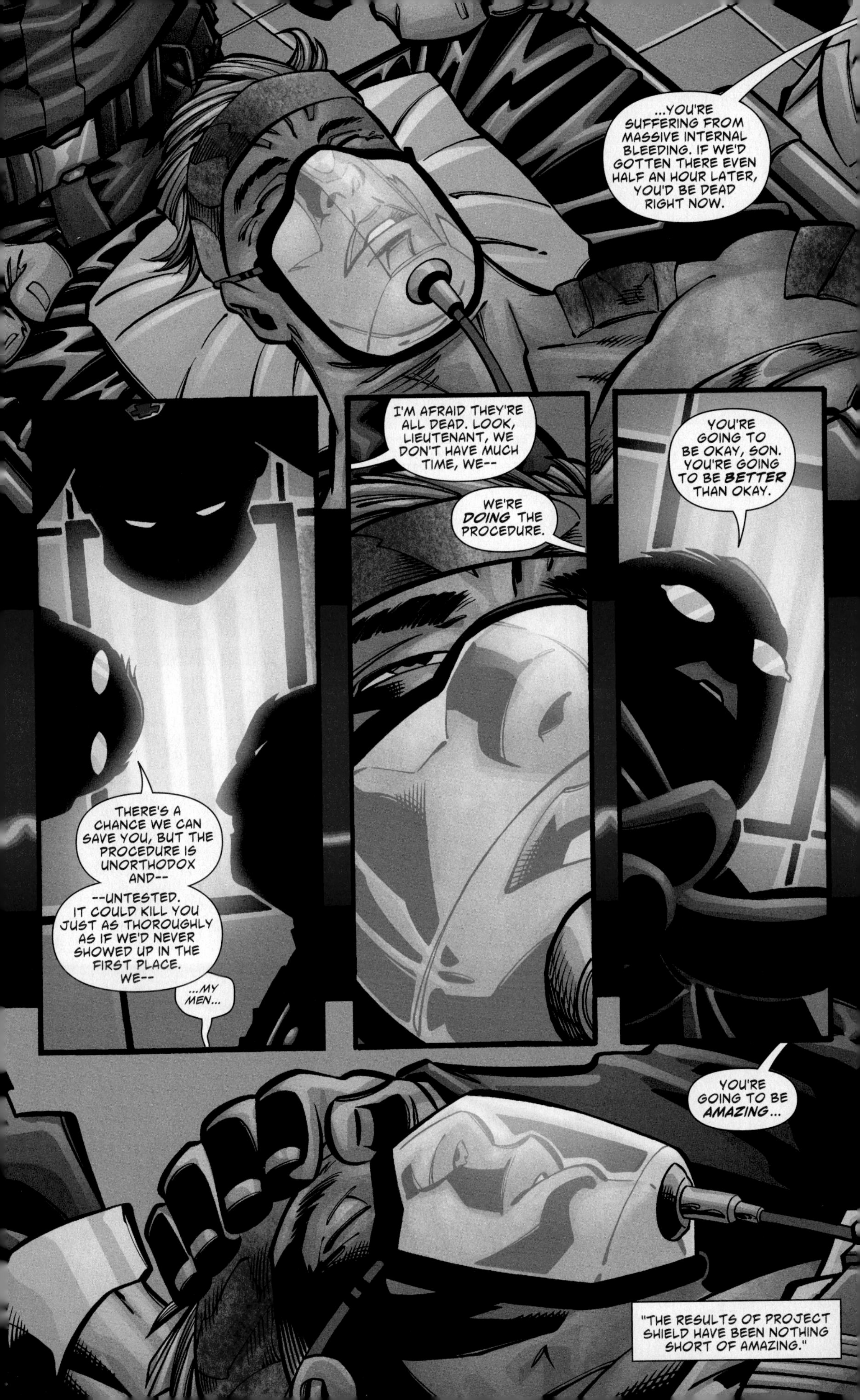
...YOU'RE SUFFERING FROM MASSIVE INTERNAL BLEEDING. IF WE'D GOTTEN THERE EVEN HALF AN HOUR LATER, YOU'D BE DEAD RIGHT NOW.
THERE'S A CHANCE WE CAN SAVE YOU, BUT THE PROCEDURE IS UNORTHODOX AND--
--UNTESTED. IT COULD KILL YOU JUST AS THOROUGHLY AS IF WE'D NEVER SHOWED UP IN THE FIRST PLACE. WE--
...MY MEN...
I'M AFRAID THEY'RE ALL DEAD. LOOK, LIEUTENANT, WE DON'T HAVE MUCH TIME, WE--
WE'RE DOING THE PROCEDURE.
YOU'RE GOING TO BE OKAY, SON. YOU'RE GOING TO BE BETTER THAN OKAY.
YOU'RE GOING TO BE AMAZING...
"THE RESULTS OF PROJECT SHIELD HAVE BEEN NOTHING SHORT OF AMAZING."

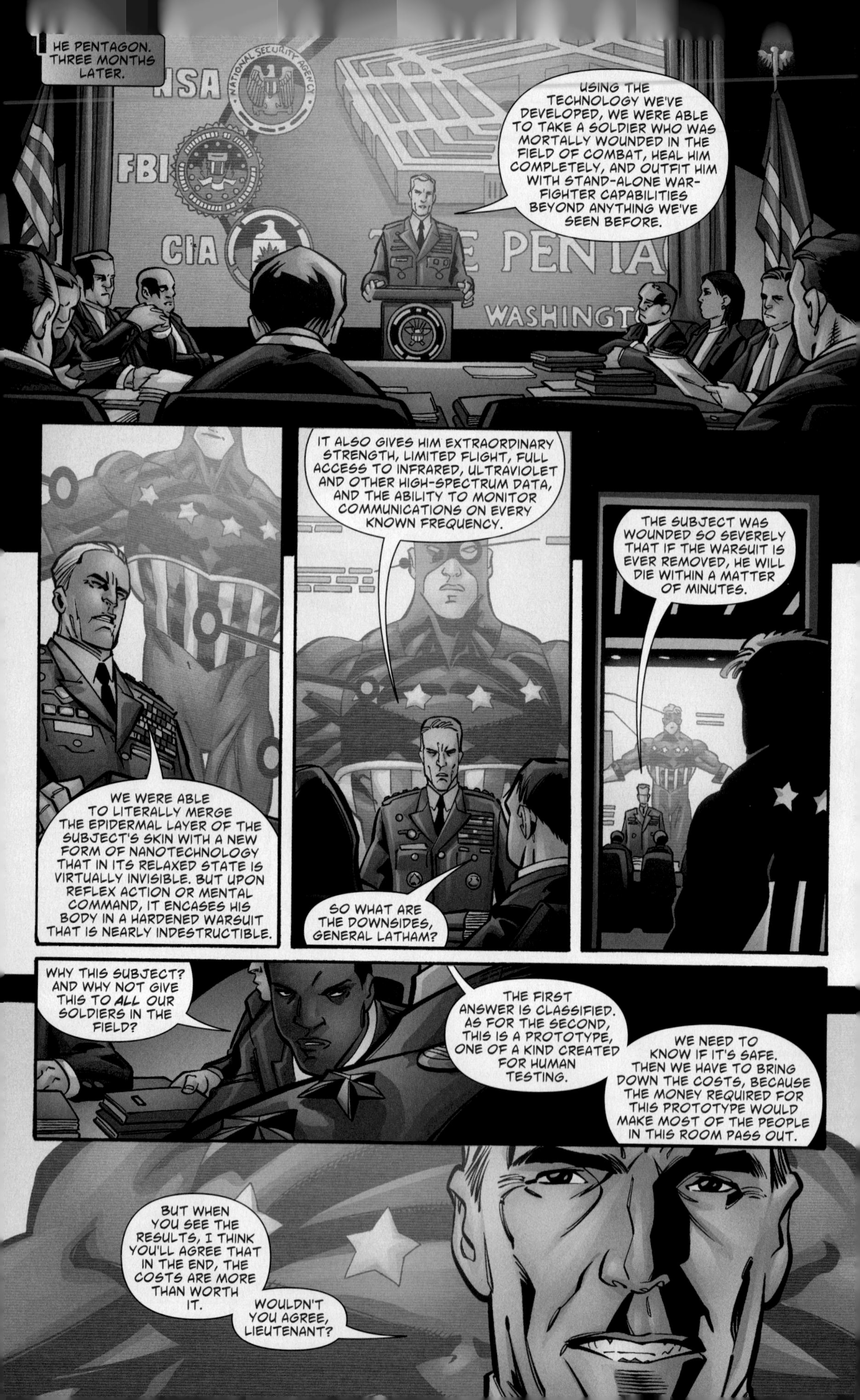
HE PENTAGON. THREE MONTHS LATER.
NSA
NATIONAL SECURITY AGENCY
FBI
CIA
WASHINGTO
USING THE TECHNOLOGY WE'VE DEVELOPED, WE WERE ABLE TO TAKE A SOLDIER WHO WAS MORTALLY WOUNDED IN THE FIELD OF COMBAT, HEAL HIM COMPLETELY, AND OUTFIT HIM WITH STAND-ALONE WAR-FIGHTER CAPABILITIES BEYOND ANYTHING WE'VE SEEN BEFORE.
WE WERE ABLE TO LITERALLY MERGE THE EPIDERMAL LAYER OF THE SUBJECT'S SKIN WITH A NEW FORM OF NANOTECHNOLOGY THAT IN ITS RELAXED STATE IS VIRTUALLY INVISIBLE. BUT UPON REFLEX ACTION OR MENTAL COMMAND, IT ENCASES HIS BODY IN A HARDENED WARSUIT THAT IS NEARLY INDESTRUCTIBLE.
IT ALSO GIVES HIM EXTRAORDINARY STRENGTH, LIMITED FLIGHT, FULL ACCESS TO INFRARED, ULTRAVIOLET AND OTHER HIGH-SPECTRUM DATA, AND THE ABILITY TO MONITOR COMMUNICATIONS ON EVERY KNOWN FREQUENCY.
SO WHAT ARE THE DOWNSIDES, GENERAL LATHAM?
THE SUBJECT WAS WOUNDED SO SEVERELY THAT IF THE WARSUIT IS EVER REMOVED, HE WILL DIE WITHIN A MATTER OF MINUTES.
WHY THIS SUBJECT? AND WHY NOT GIVE THIS TO ALL OUR SOLDIERS IN THE FIELD?
THE FIRST ANSWER IS CLASSIFIED. AS FOR THE SECOND, THIS IS A PROTOTYPE, ONE OF A KIND CREATED FOR HUMAN TESTING.
WE NEED TO KNOW IF IT'S SAFE. THEN WE HAVE TO BRING DOWN THE COSTS, BECAUSE THE MONEY REQUIRED FOR THIS PROTOTYPE WOULD MAKE MOST OF THE PEOPLE IN THIS ROOM PASS OUT.
BUT WHEN YOU SEE THE RESULTS, I THINK YOU'LL AGREE THAT IN THE END, THE COSTS ARE MORE THAN WORTH IT.
WOULDN'T YOU AGREE, LIEUTENANT?

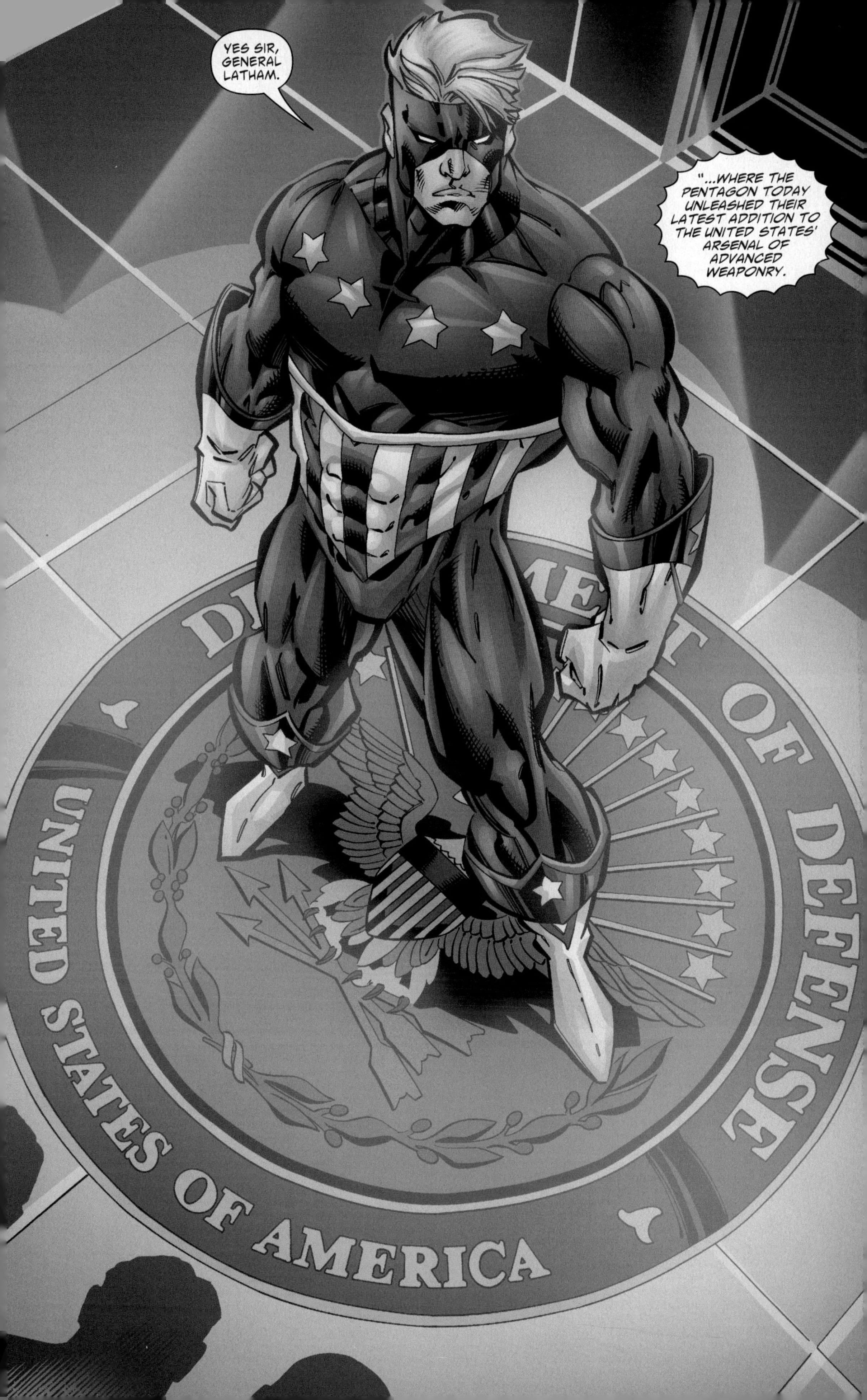
YES SIR, GENERAL LATHAM.
"...WHERE THE PENTAGON TODAY UNLEASHED THEIR LATEST ADDITION TO THE UNITED STATES' ARSENAL OF ADVANCED WEAPONRY.
DEPARTMENT OF DEFENSE
UNITED STATES OF AMERICA

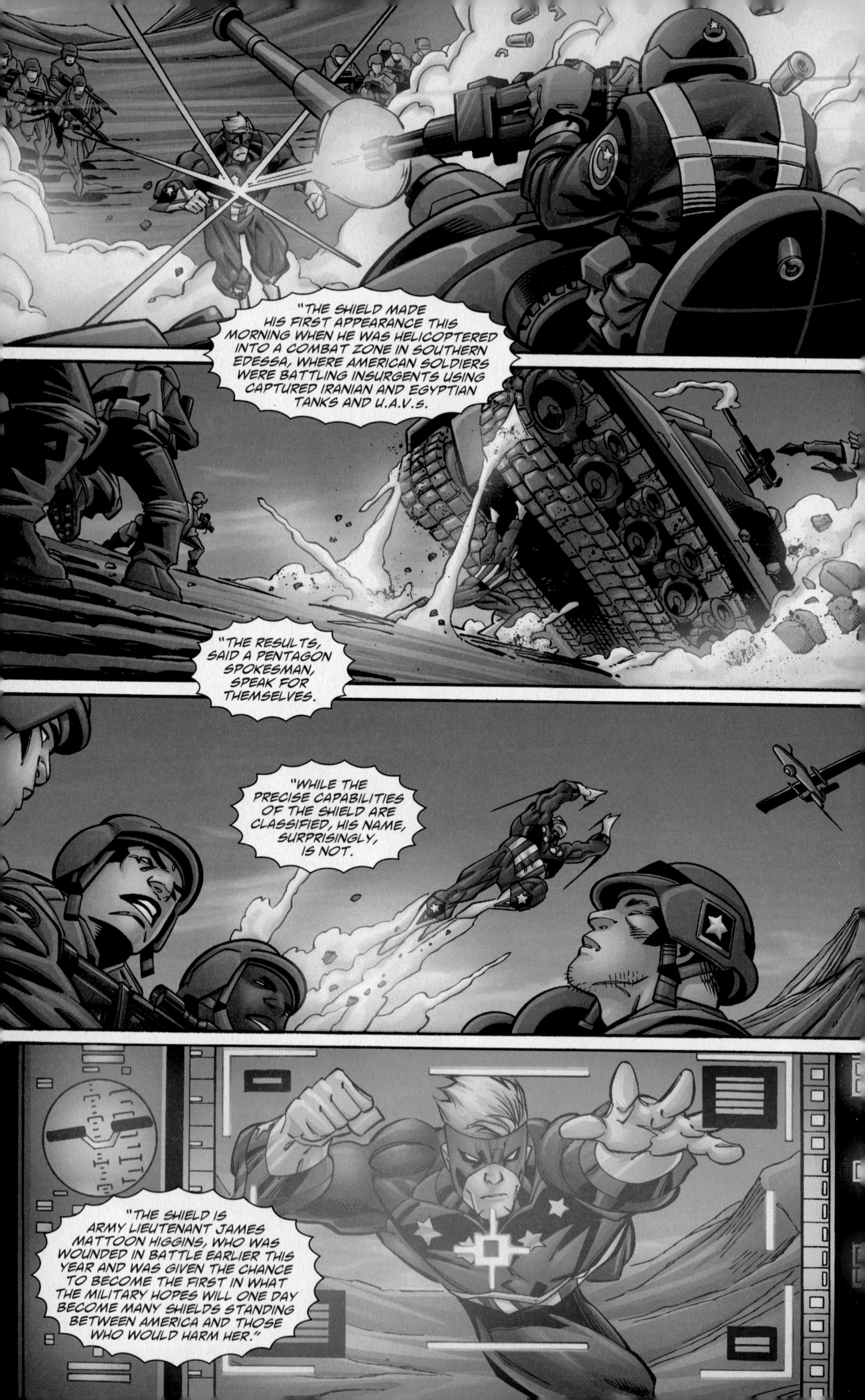
"THE SHIELD MADE HIS FIRST APPEARANCE THIS MORNING WHEN HE WAS HELICOPTERED INTO A COMBAT ZONE IN SOUTHERN EDESSA, WHERE AMERICAN SOLDIERS WERE BATTLING INSURGENTS USING CAPTURED IRANIAN AND EGYPTIAN TANKS AND U.A.V.s.
"THE RESULTS, SAID A PENTAGON SPOKESMAN, SPEAK FOR THEMSELVES.
"WHILE THE PRECISE CAPABILITIES OF THE SHIELD ARE CLASSIFIED, HIS NAME, SURPRISINGLY, IS NOT.
"THE SHIELD IS ARMY LIEUTENANT JAMES MATTOON HIGGINS, WHO WAS WOUNDED IN BATTLE EARLIER THIS YEAR AND WAS GIVEN THE CHANCE TO BECOME THE FIRST IN WHAT THE MILITARY HOPES WILL ONE DAY BECOME MANY SHIELDS STANDING BETWEEN AMERICA AND THOSE WHO WOULD HARM HER."

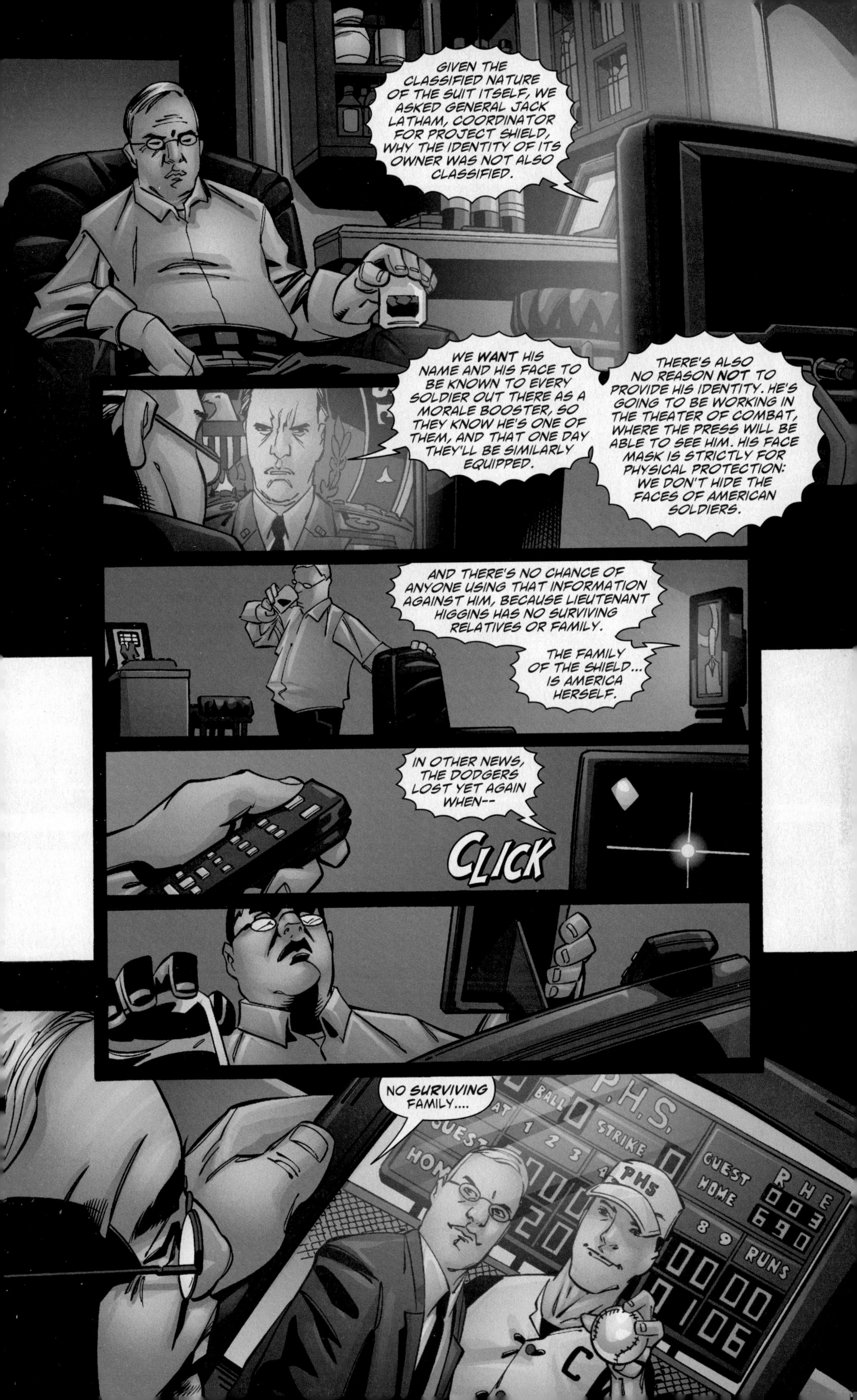
GIVEN THE CLASSIFIED NATURE OF THE SUIT ITSELF, WE ASKED GENERAL JACK LATHAM, COORDINATOR FOR PROJECT SHIELD, WHY THE IDENTITY OF ITS OWNER WAS NOT ALSO CLASSIFIED.
WE WANT HIS NAME AND HIS FACE TO BE KNOWN TO EVERY SOLDIER OUT THERE AS A MORALE BOOSTER, SO THEY KNOW HE'S ONE OF THEM, AND THAT ONE DAY THEY'LL BE SIMILARLY EQUIPPED.
THERE'S ALSO NO REASON NOT TO PROVIDE HIS IDENTITY. HE'S GOING TO BE WORKING IN THE THEATER OF COMBAT, WHERE THE PRESS WILL BE ABLE TO SEE HIM. HIS FACE MASK IS STRICTLY FOR PHYSICAL PROTECTION: WE DON'T HIDE THE FACES OF AMERICAN SOLDIERS.
AND THERE'S NO CHANCE OF ANYONE USING THAT INFORMATION AGAINST HIM, BECAUSE LIEUTENANT HIGGINS HAS NO SURVIVING RELATIVES OR FAMILY.
THE FAMILY OF THE SHIELD... IS AMERICA HERSELF.
IN OTHER NEWS, THE DODGERS LOST YET AGAIN WHEN--
CLICK
NO SURVIVING FAMILY....
P.H.S.
BALL
STRIKE
GUEST
HOME
PHS
R H E
RUNS

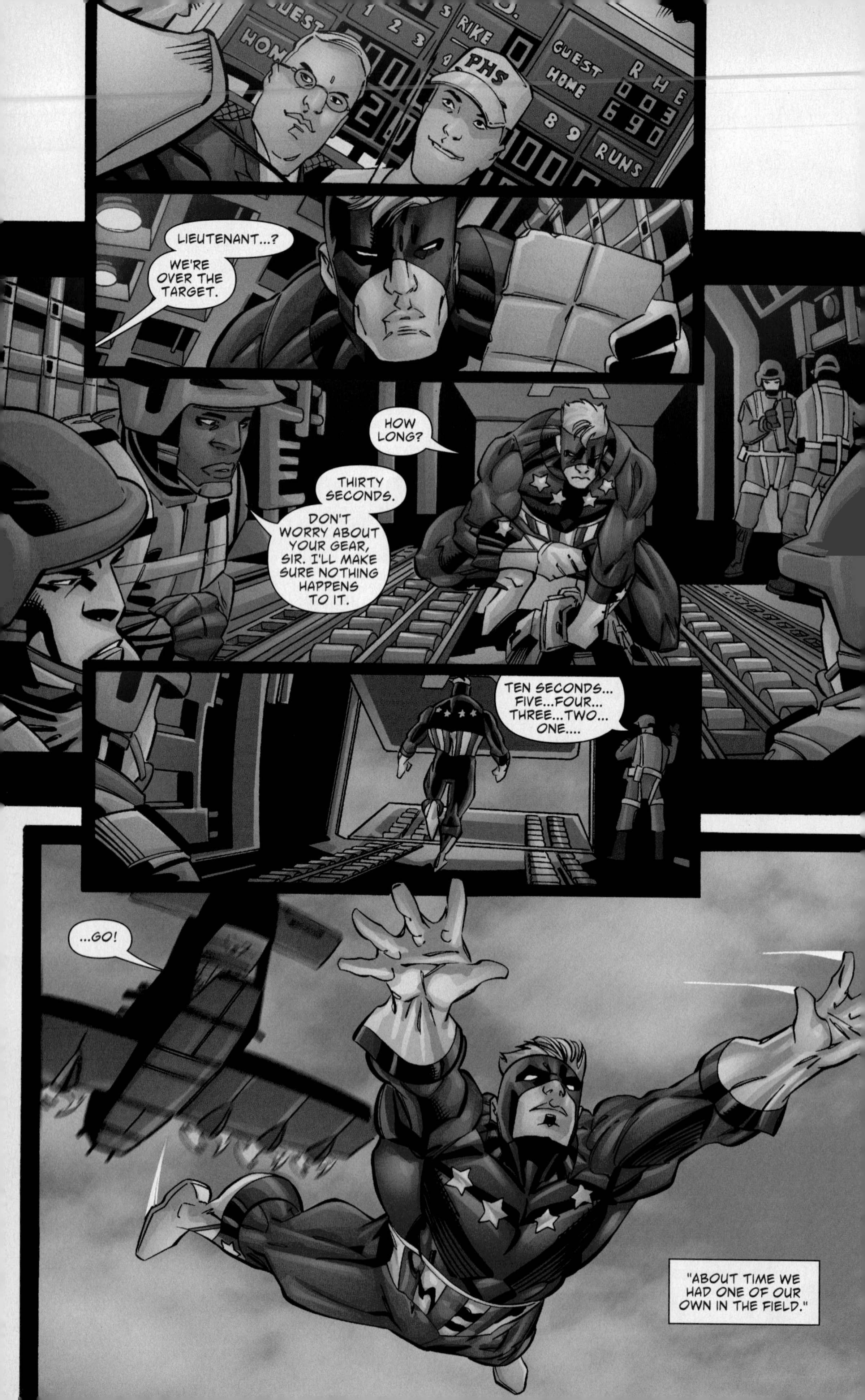
GUEST
HOME
STRIKE
PHS
GUEST
HOME
R H E
RUNS
LIEUTENANT...?
WE'RE OVER THE TARGET.
HOW LONG?
THIRTY SECONDS.
DON'T WORRY ABOUT YOUR GEAR, SIR. I'LL MAKE SURE NOTHING HAPPENS TO IT.
TEN SECONDS... FIVE...FOUR... THREE...TWO... ONE....
...GO!
"ABOUT TIME WE HAD ONE OF OUR OWN IN THE FIELD."

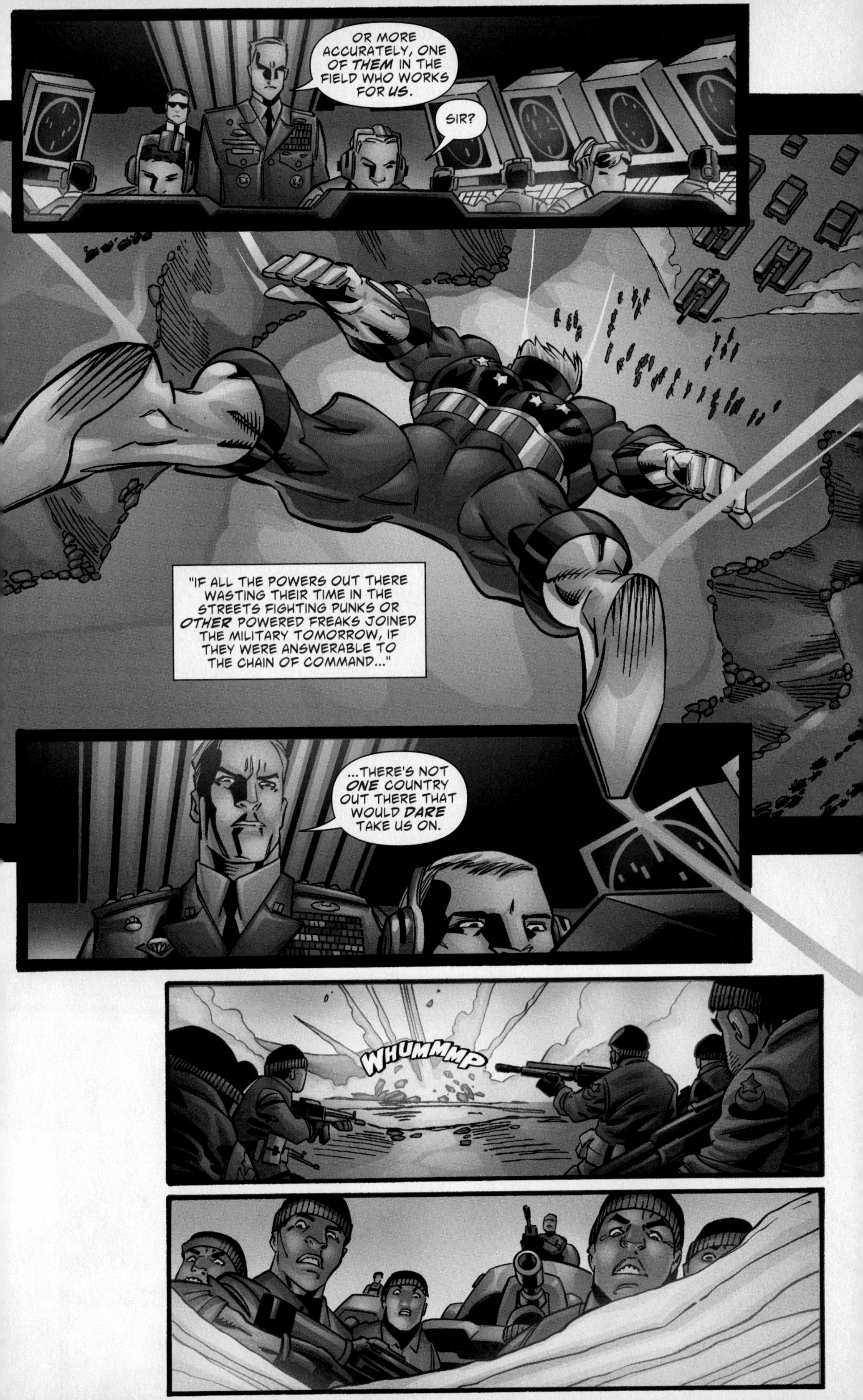
OR MORE ACCURATELY, ONE OF THEM IN THE FIELD WHO WORKS FOR US.
SIR?
"IF ALL THE POWERS OUT THERE WASTING THEIR TIME IN THE STREETS FIGHTING PUNKS OR OTHER POWERED FREAKS JOINED THE MILITARY TOMORROW, IF THEY WERE ANSWERABLE TO THE CHAIN OF COMMAND..."
...THERE'S NOT ONE COUNTRY OUT THERE THAT WOULD DARE TAKE US ON.
WHUMMMP

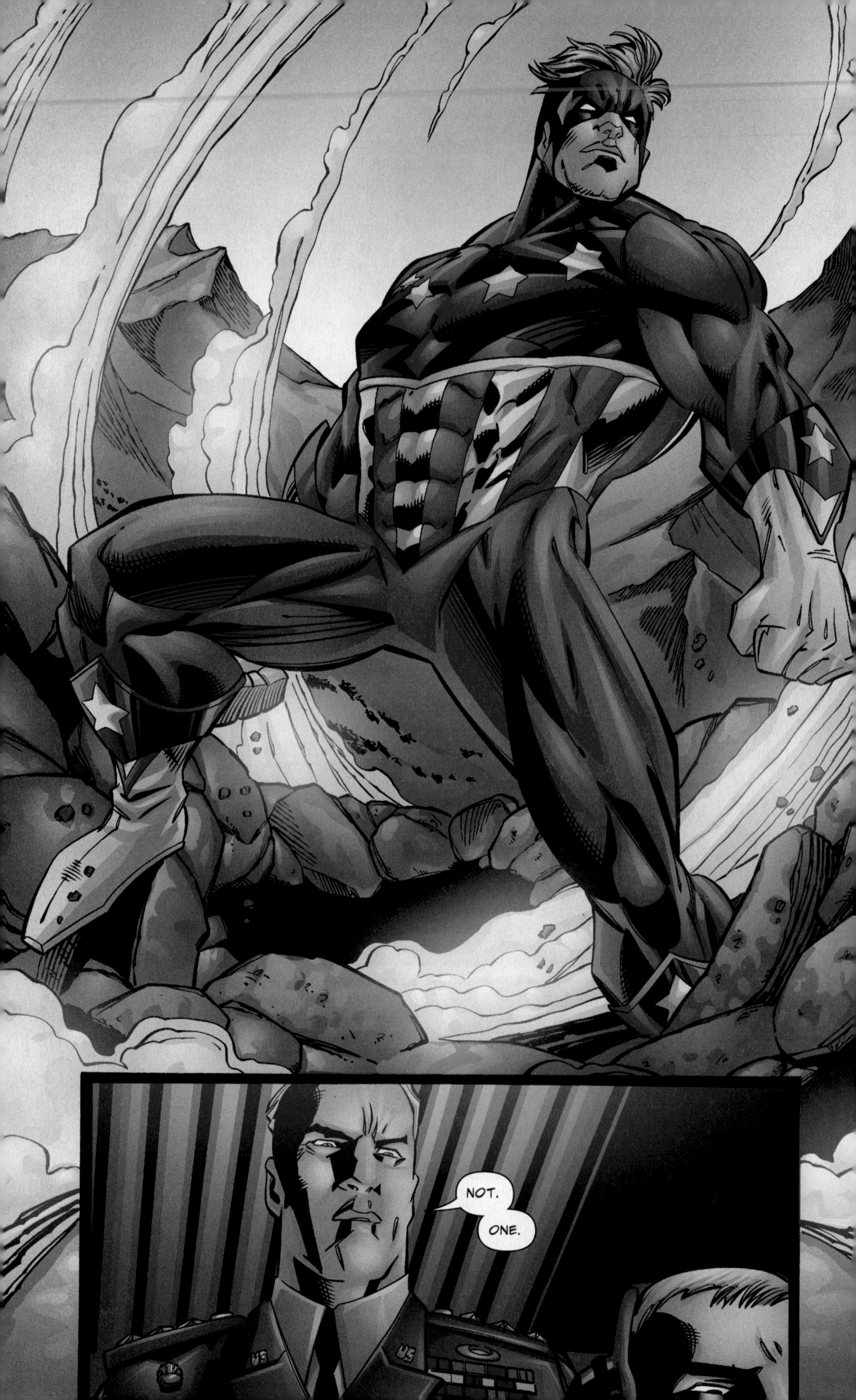
NOT.
ONE.

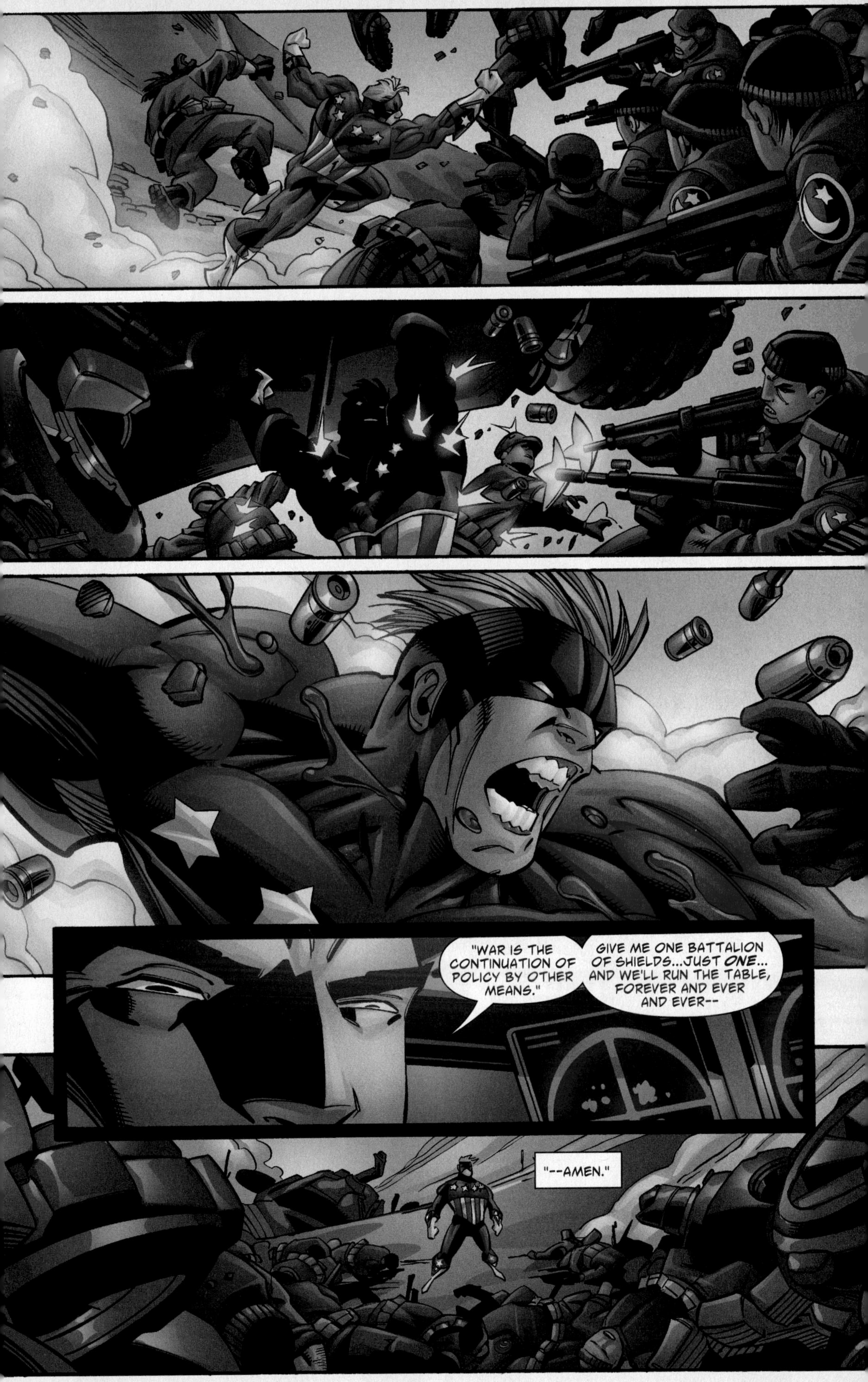
"WAR IS THE CONTINUATION OF POLICY BY OTHER MEANS."
GIVE ME ONE BATTALION OF SHIELDS...JUST ONE... AND WE'LL RUN THE TABLE, FOREVER AND EVER AND EVER--
"--AMEN."

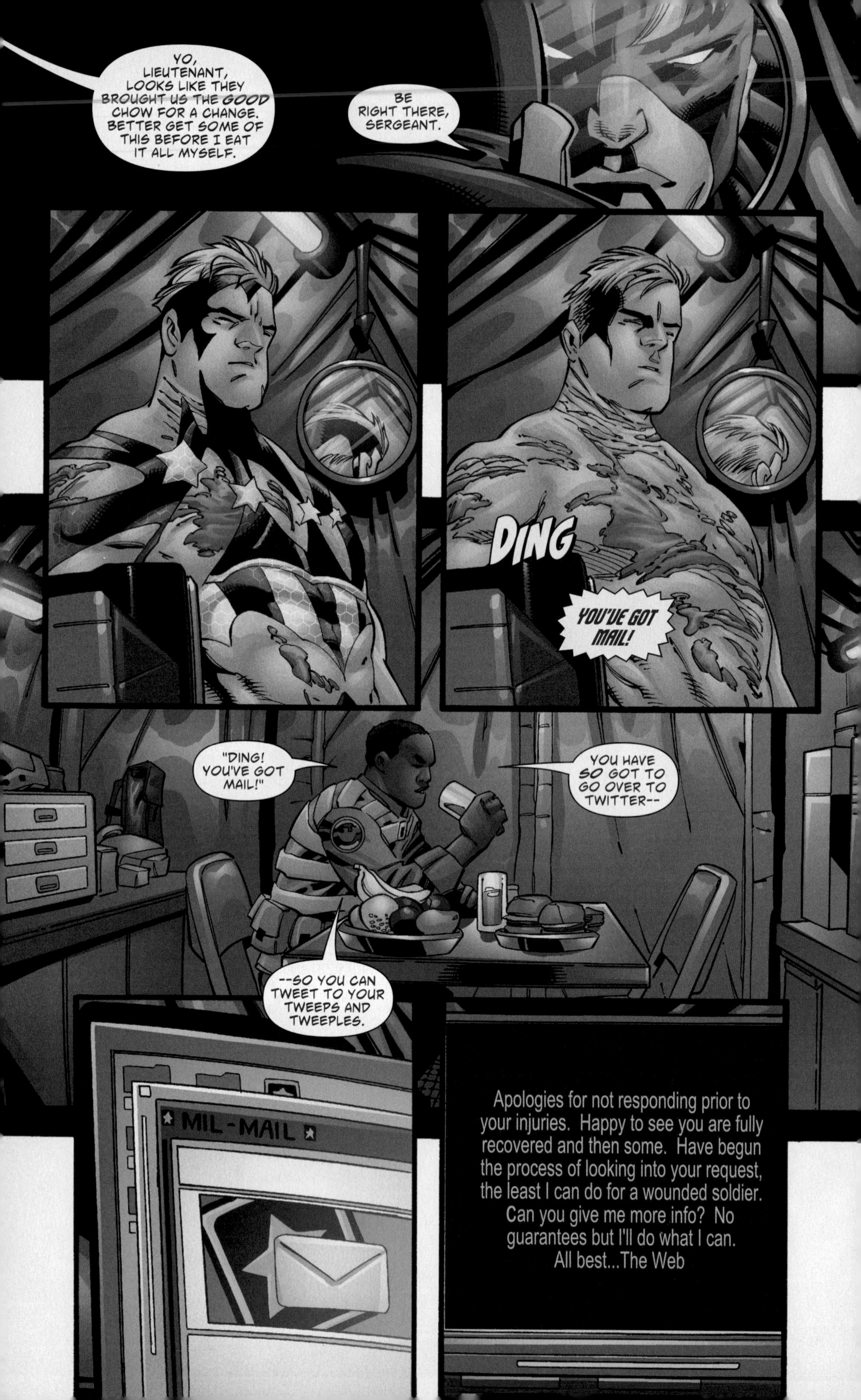

YO, LIEUTENANT, LOOKS LIKE THEY BROUGHT US THE *GOOD* CHOW FOR A CHANGE. BETTER GET SOME OF THIS BEFORE I EAT IT ALL MYSELF.
BE RIGHT THERE, SERGEANT.
DING
YOU'VE GOT MAIL!
"DING! YOU'VE GOT MAIL!"
YOU HAVE *SO* GOT TO GO OVER TO TWITTER--
--SO YOU CAN TWEET TO YOUR TWEEPS AND TWEEPLES.
MIL-MAIL
Apologies for not responding prior to your injuries. Happy to see you are fully recovered and then some. Have begun the process of looking into your request, the least I can do for a wounded soldier. Can you give me more info? No guarantees but I'll do what I can. All best...The Web

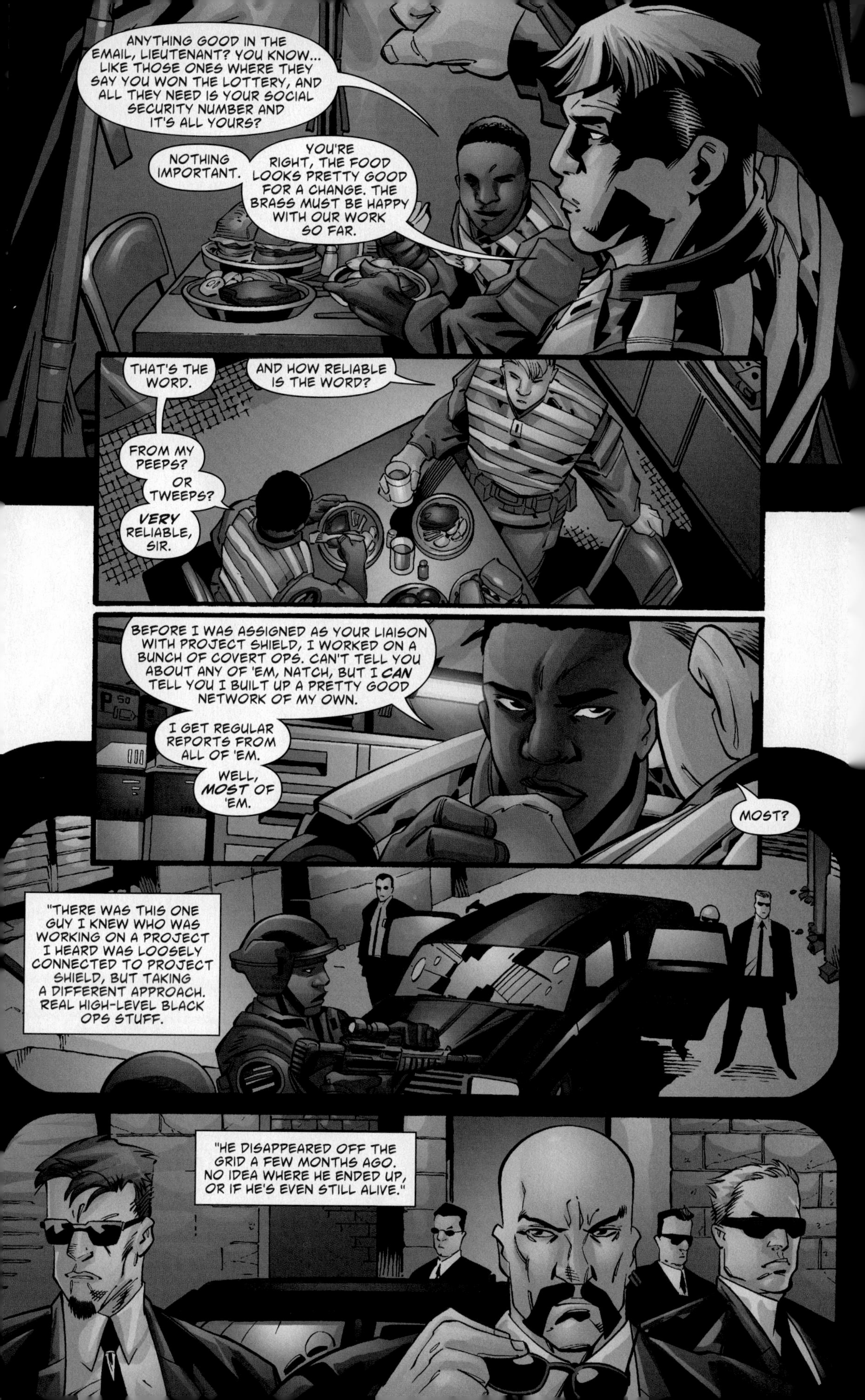
ANYTHING GOOD IN THE EMAIL, LIEUTENANT? YOU KNOW... LIKE THOSE ONES WHERE THEY SAY YOU WON THE LOTTERY, AND ALL THEY NEED IS YOUR SOCIAL SECURITY NUMBER AND IT'S ALL YOURS?
NOTHING IMPORTANT.
YOU'RE RIGHT, THE FOOD LOOKS PRETTY GOOD FOR A CHANGE. THE BRASS MUST BE HAPPY WITH OUR WORK SO FAR.
THAT'S THE WORD.
AND HOW RELIABLE IS THE WORD?
FROM MY PEEPS?
OR TWEEPS?
VERY RELIABLE, SIR.
BEFORE I WAS ASSIGNED AS YOUR LIAISON WITH PROJECT SHIELD, I WORKED ON A BUNCH OF COVERT OPS. CAN'T TELL YOU ABOUT ANY OF 'EM, NATCH, BUT I *CAN* TELL YOU I BUILT UP A PRETTY GOOD NETWORK OF MY OWN.
I GET REGULAR REPORTS FROM ALL OF 'EM.
WELL, *MOST* OF 'EM.
MOST?
"THERE WAS THIS ONE GUY I KNEW WHO WAS WORKING ON A PROJECT I HEARD WAS LOOSELY CONNECTED TO PROJECT SHIELD, BUT TAKING A DIFFERENT APPROACH. REAL HIGH-LEVEL BLACK OPS STUFF.
"HE DISAPPEARED OFF THE GRID A FEW MONTHS AGO. NO IDEA WHERE HE ENDED UP, OR IF HE'S EVEN STILL ALIVE."

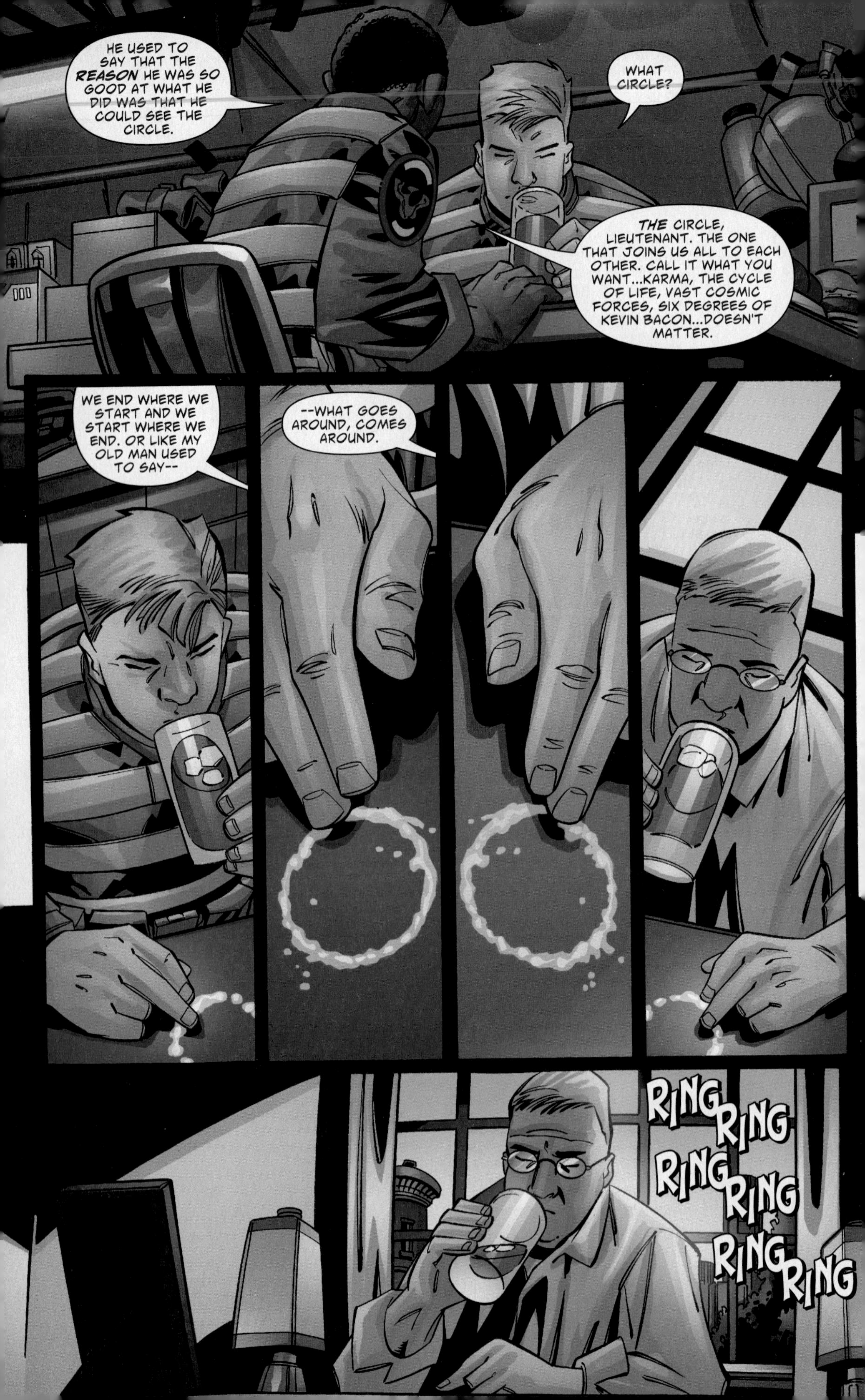
HE USED TO SAY THAT THE *REASON* HE WAS SO GOOD AT WHAT HE DID WAS THAT HE COULD SEE THE CIRCLE.
WHAT CIRCLE?
THE CIRCLE, LIEUTENANT. THE ONE THAT JOINS US ALL TO EACH OTHER. CALL IT WHAT YOU WANT...KARMA, THE CYCLE OF LIFE, VAST COSMIC FORCES, SIX DEGREES OF KEVIN BACON...DOESN'T MATTER.
WE END WHERE WE START AND WE START WHERE WE END. OR LIKE MY OLD MAN USED TO SAY--
--WHAT GOES AROUND, COMES AROUND.
RING RING
RING RING
RING RING

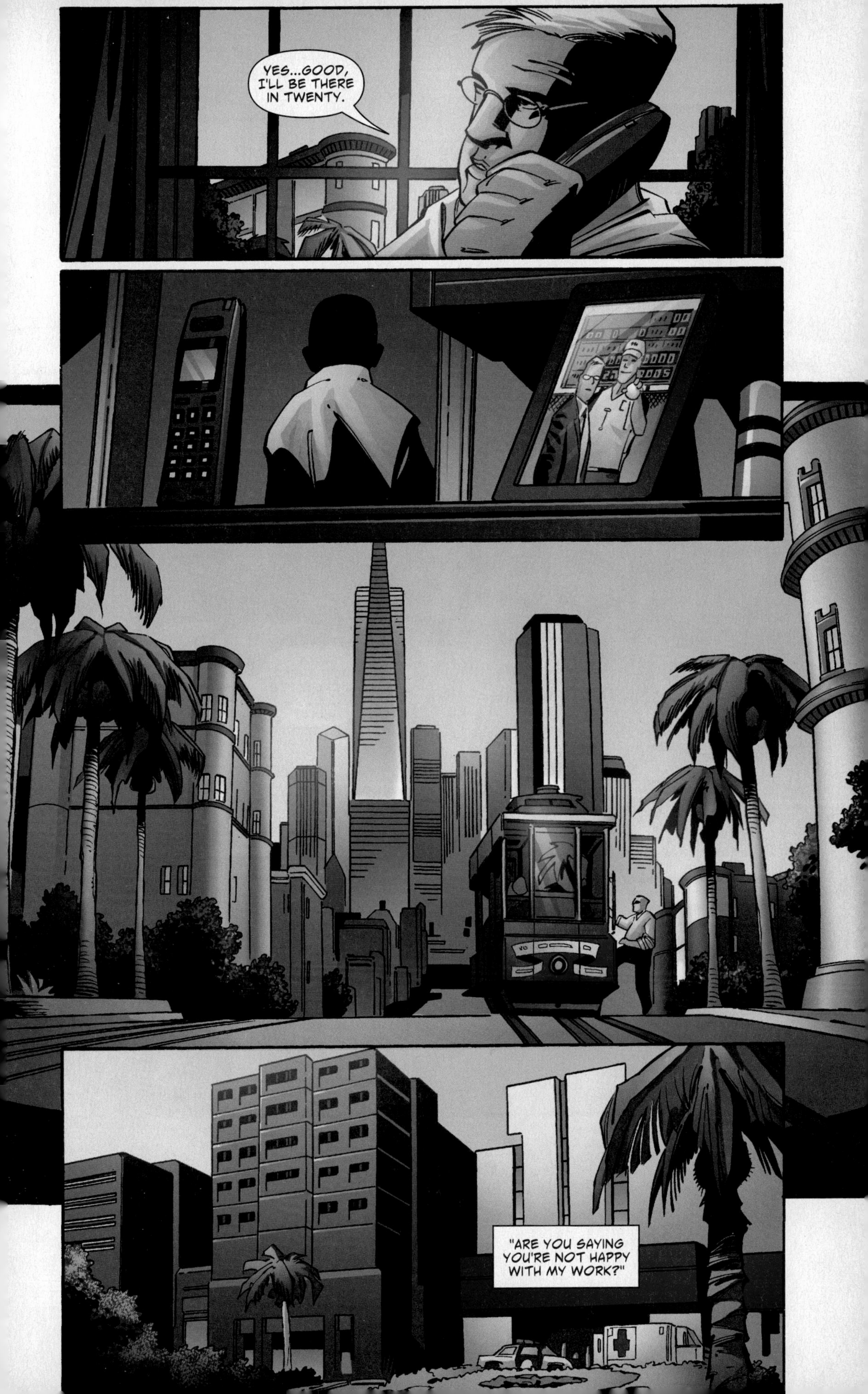
YES...GOOD, I'LL BE THERE IN TWENTY.
"ARE YOU SAYING YOU'RE NOT HAPPY WITH MY WORK?"

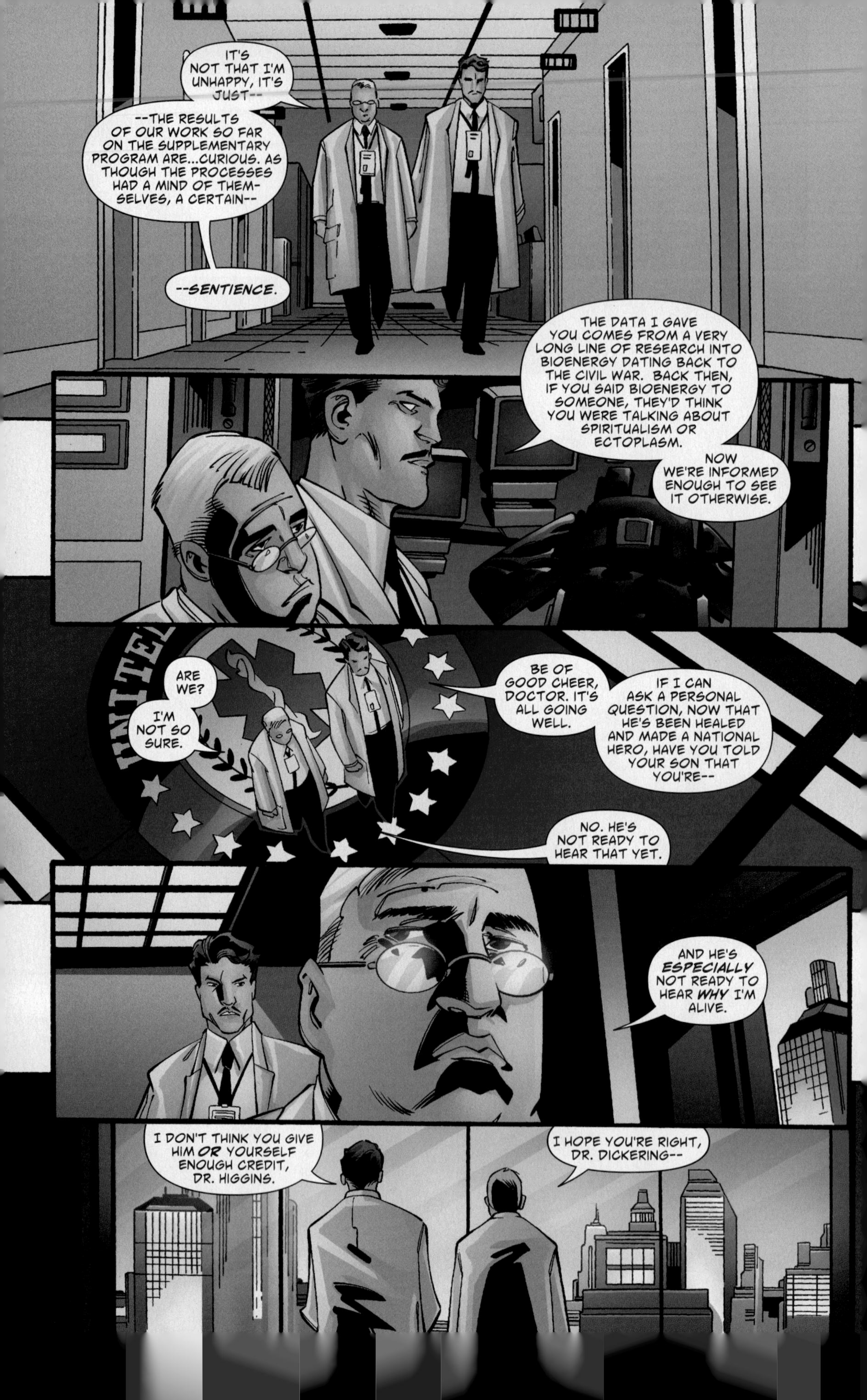
IT'S NOT THAT I'M UNHAPPY, IT'S JUST--
--THE RESULTS OF OUR WORK SO FAR ON THE SUPPLEMENTARY PROGRAM ARE...CURIOUS. AS THOUGH THE PROCESSES HAD A MIND OF THEMSELVES, A CERTAIN--
--SENTIENCE.
THE DATA I GAVE YOU COMES FROM A VERY LONG LINE OF RESEARCH INTO BIOENERGY DATING BACK TO THE CIVIL WAR. BACK THEN, IF YOU SAID BIOENERGY TO SOMEONE, THEY'D THINK YOU WERE TALKING ABOUT SPIRITUALISM OR ECTOPLASM.
NOW WE'RE INFORMED ENOUGH TO SEE IT OTHERWISE.
ARE WE?
I'M NOT SO SURE.
BE OF GOOD CHEER, DOCTOR. IT'S ALL GOING WELL.
IF I CAN ASK A PERSONAL QUESTION, NOW THAT HE'S BEEN HEALED AND MADE A NATIONAL HERO, HAVE YOU TOLD YOUR SON THAT YOU'RE--
NO. HE'S NOT READY TO HEAR THAT YET.
AND HE'S *ESPECIALLY* NOT READY TO HEAR *WHY* I'M ALIVE.
I DON'T THINK YOU GIVE HIM *OR* YOURSELF ENOUGH CREDIT, DR. HIGGINS.
I HOPE YOU'RE RIGHT, DR. DICKERING--

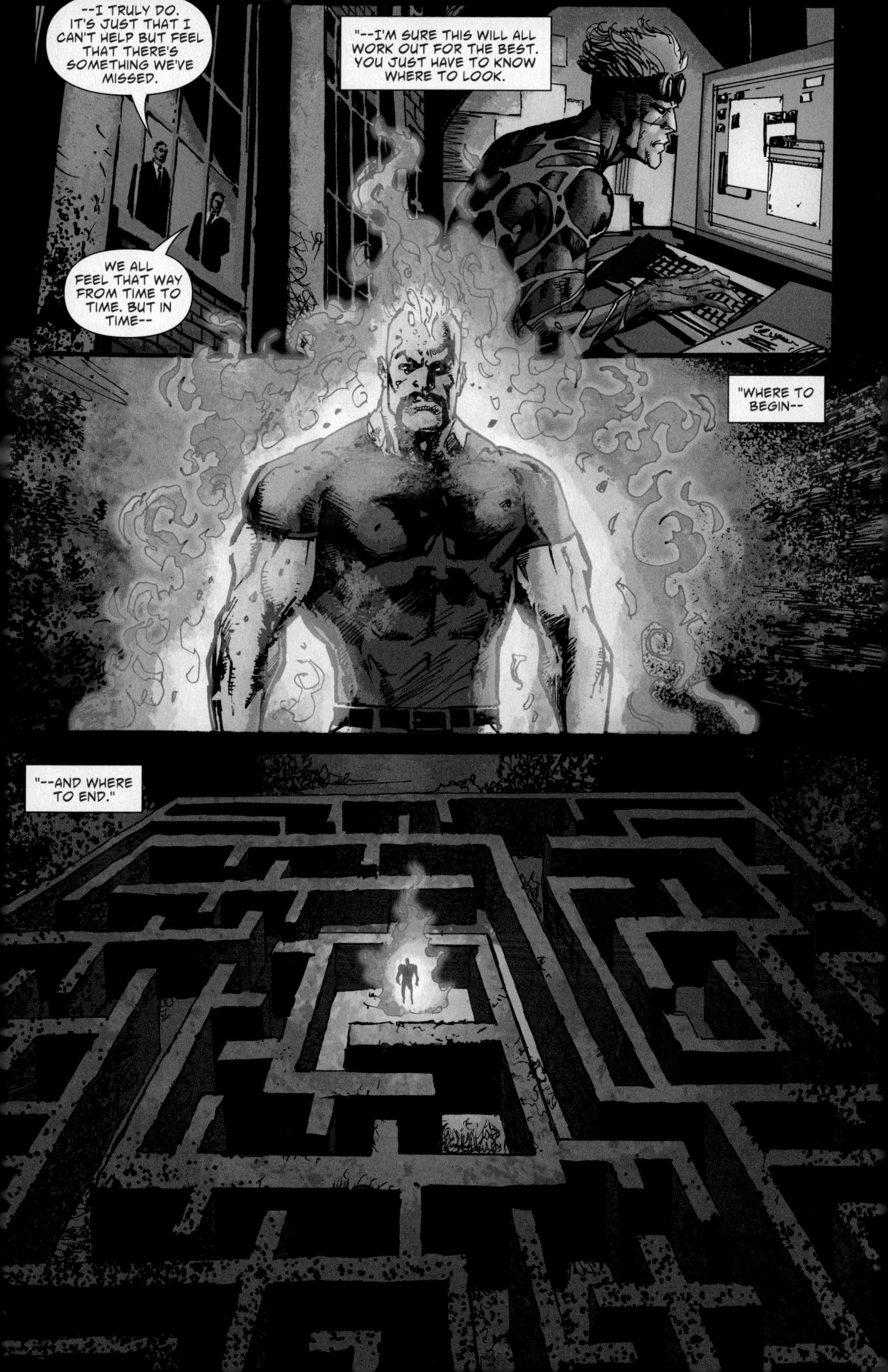
--I TRULY DO. IT'S JUST THAT I CAN'T HELP BUT FEEL THAT THERE'S SOMETHING WE'VE MISSED.
WE ALL FEEL THAT WAY FROM TIME TO TIME. BUT IN TIME--
"--I'M SURE THIS WILL ALL WORK OUT FOR THE BEST. YOU JUST HAVE TO KNOW WHERE TO LOOK.
"WHERE TO BEGIN--
"--AND WHERE TO END."

KICKING DOWN THE DOOR PART 1

Cover by Francis Manapul with Jeremy Roberts

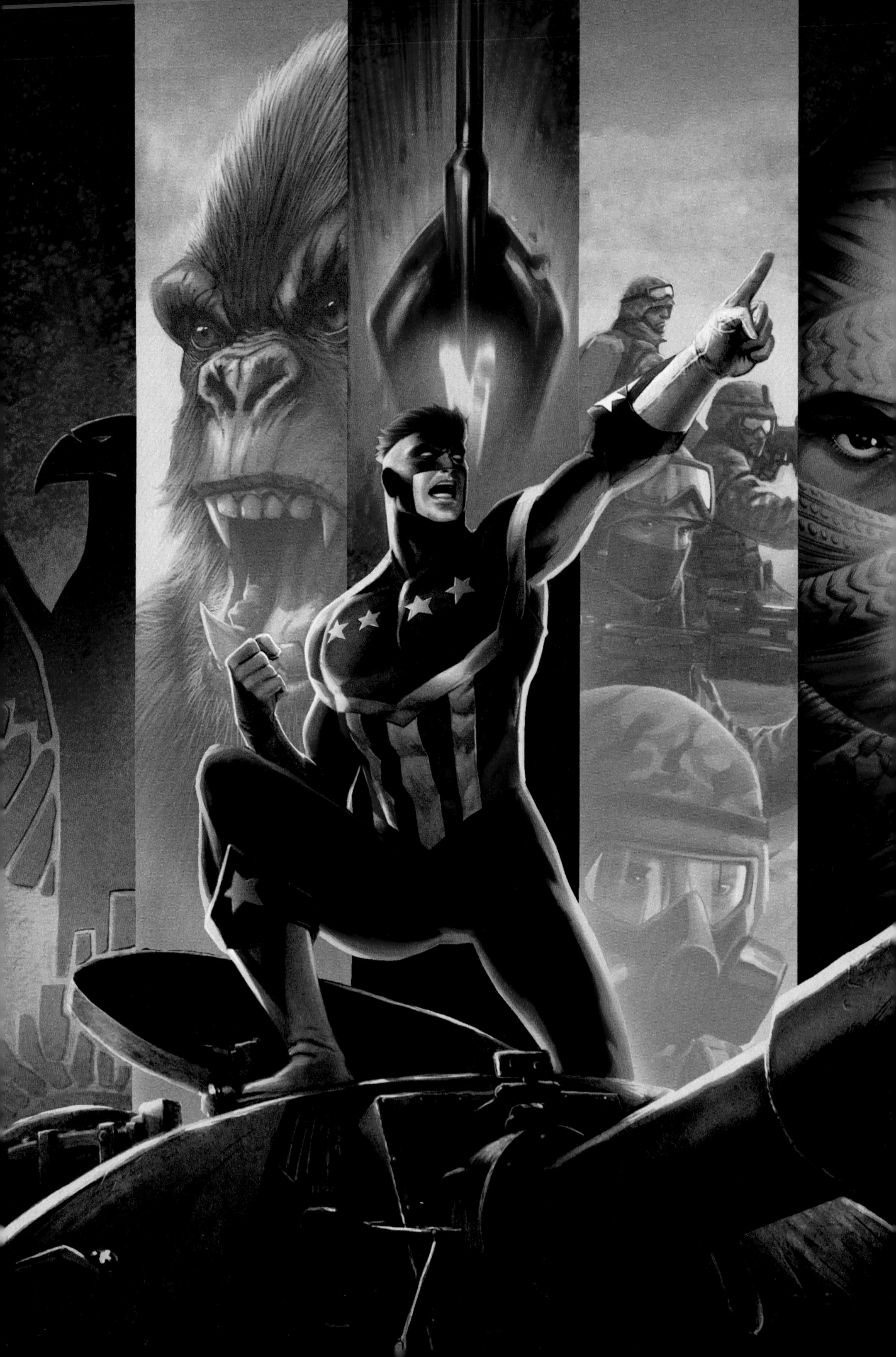

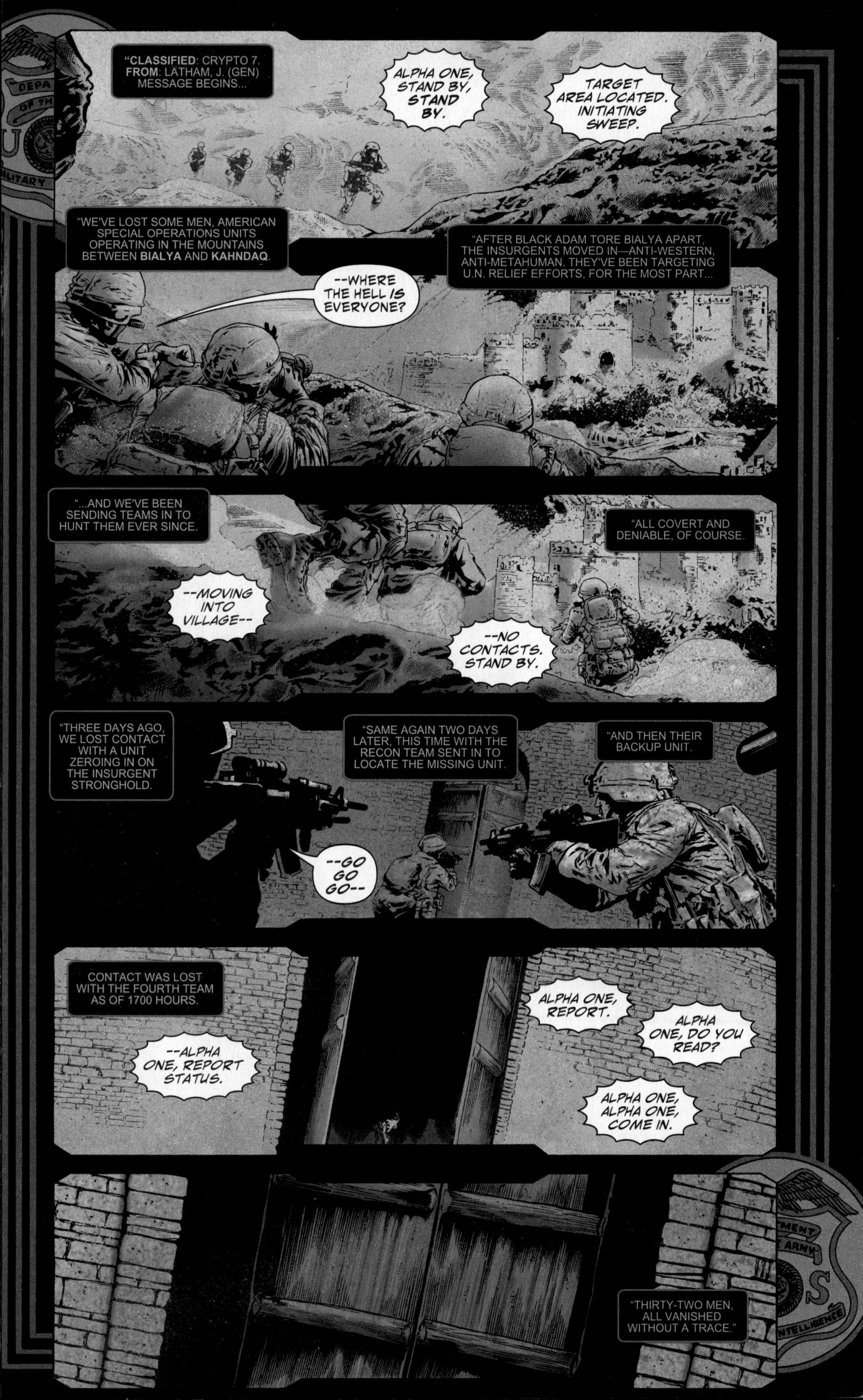

"CLASSIFIED: CRYPTO 7. FROM: LATHAM, J. (GEN) MESSAGE BEGINS...
ALPHA ONE, STAND BY, STAND BY.
TARGET AREA LOCATED. INITIATING SWEEP.
"WE'VE LOST SOME MEN, AMERICAN SPECIAL OPERATIONS UNITS OPERATING IN THE MOUNTAINS BETWEEN BIALYA AND KAHNDAQ.
"AFTER BLACK ADAM TORE BIALYA APART, THE INSURGENTS MOVED IN—ANTI-WESTERN, ANTI-METAHUMAN. THEY'VE BEEN TARGETING U.N. RELIEF EFFORTS, FOR THE MOST PART...
--WHERE THE HELL IS EVERYONE?
"...AND WE'VE BEEN SENDING TEAMS IN TO HUNT THEM EVER SINCE.
"ALL COVERT AND DENIABLE, OF COURSE.
--MOVING INTO VILLAGE--
--NO CONTACTS. STAND BY.
"THREE DAYS AGO, WE LOST CONTACT WITH A UNIT ZEROING IN ON THE INSURGENT STRONGHOLD.
"SAME AGAIN TWO DAYS LATER, THIS TIME WITH THE RECON TEAM SENT IN TO LOCATE THE MISSING UNIT.
"AND THEN THEIR BACKUP UNIT.
--GO GO GO--
CONTACT WAS LOST WITH THE FOURTH TEAM AS OF 1700 HOURS.
--ALPHA ONE, REPORT STATUS.
ALPHA ONE, REPORT.
ALPHA ONE, DO YOU READ?
ALPHA ONE, ALPHA ONE, COME IN.
"THIRTY-TWO MEN, ALL VANISHED WITHOUT A TRACE."

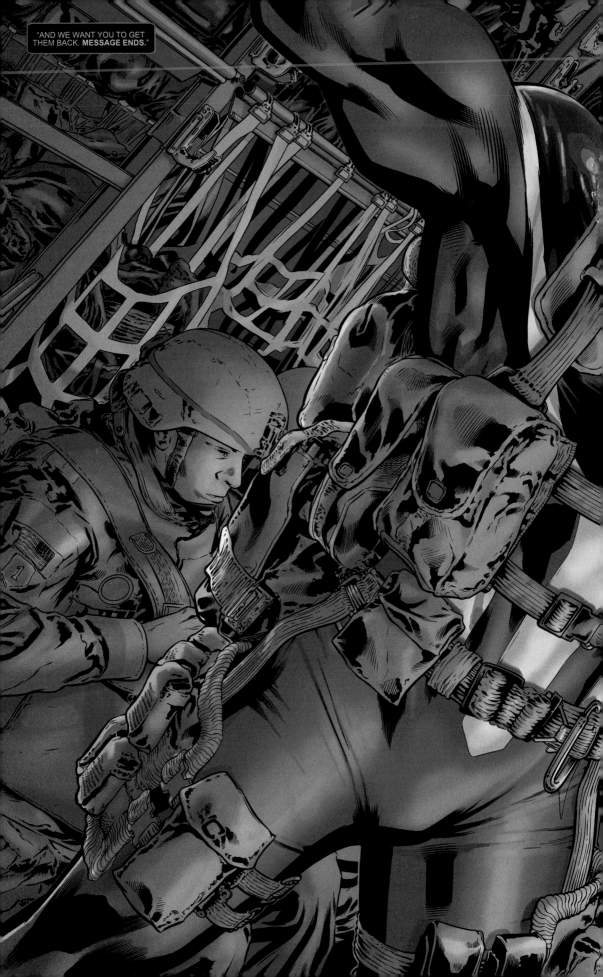

"AND WE WANT YOU TO GET THEM BACK. **MESSAGE ENDS.**"

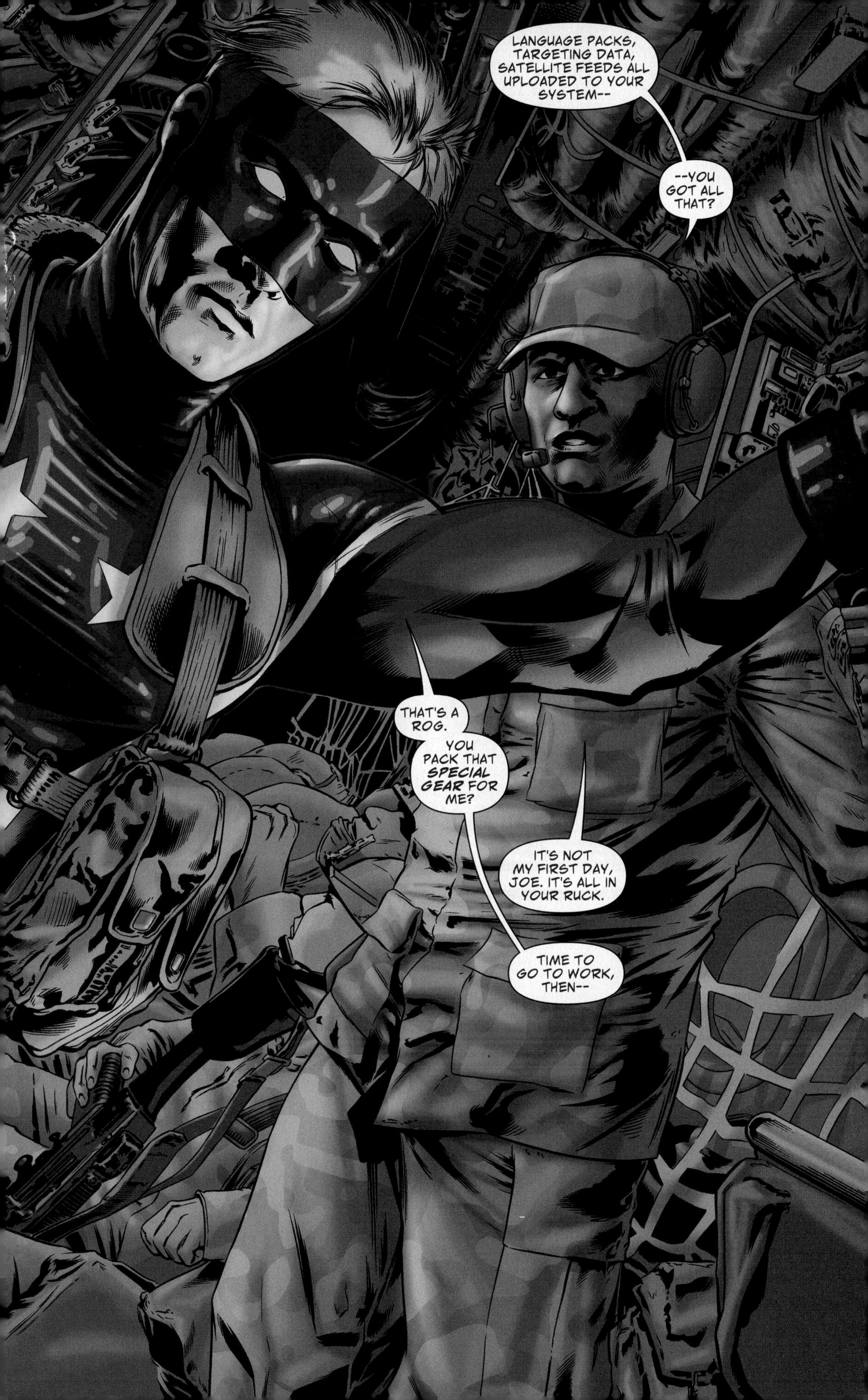
LANGUAGE PACKS, TARGETING DATA, SATELLITE FEEDS ALL UPLOADED TO YOUR SYSTEM--
--YOU GOT ALL THAT?
THAT'S A ROG.
YOU PACK THAT SPECIAL GEAR FOR ME?
IT'S NOT MY FIRST DAY, JOE. IT'S ALL IN YOUR RUCK.
TIME TO GO TO WORK, THEN--

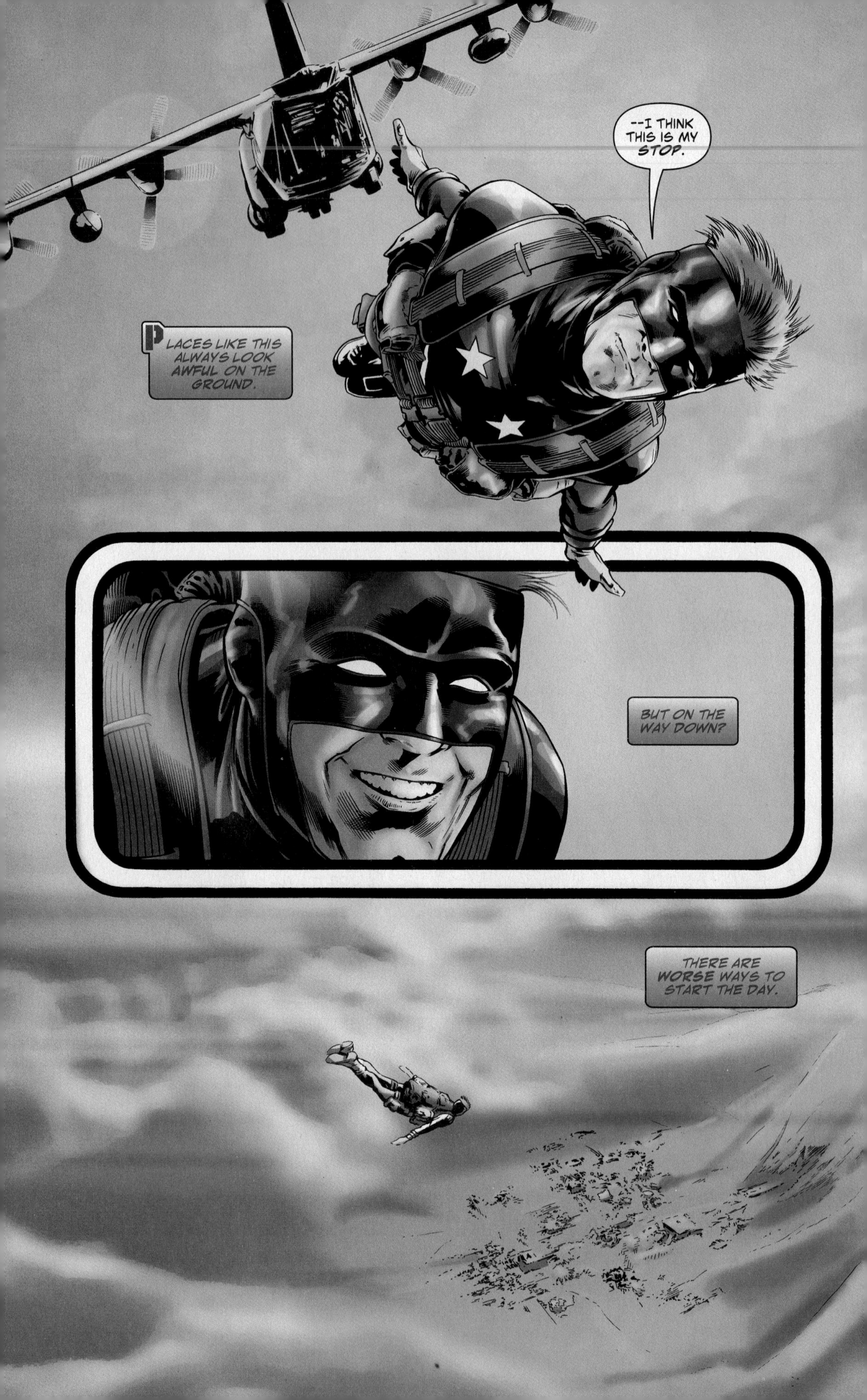
--I THINK THIS IS MY STOP.
PLACES LIKE THIS ALWAYS LOOK AWFUL ON THE GROUND.
BUT ON THE WAY DOWN?
THERE ARE WORSE WAYS TO START THE DAY.

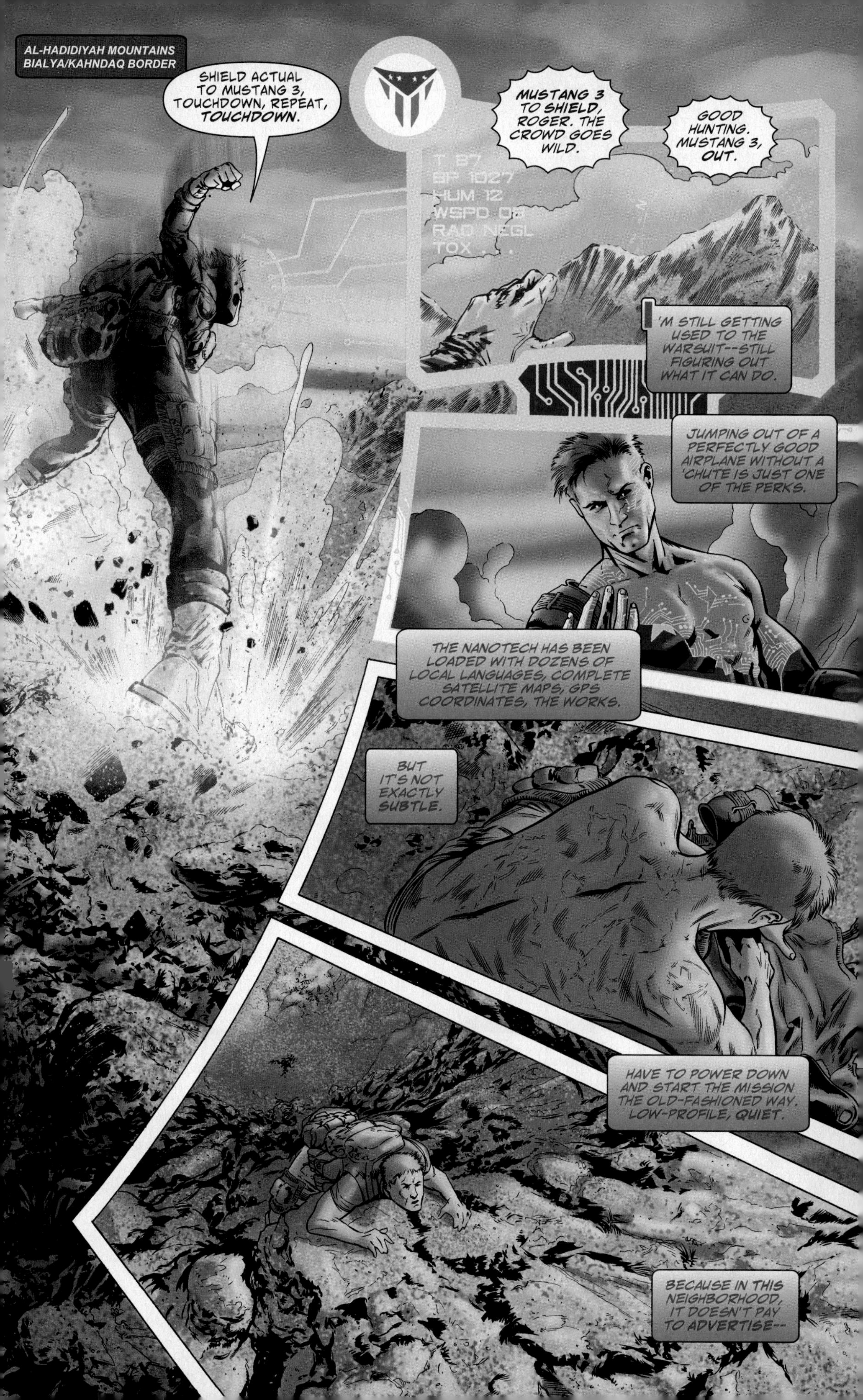
AL-HADIDIYAH MOUNTAINS
BIALYA/KAHNDAQ BORDER
SHIELD ACTUAL TO MUSTANG 3, TOUCHDOWN, REPEAT, TOUCHDOWN.
MUSTANG 3 TO SHIELD, ROGER. THE CROWD GOES WILD.
GOOD HUNTING. MUSTANG 3, OUT.
T 87
BP 1027
HUM 12
WSPD 08
RAD NEGL
TOX . . .
I'M STILL GETTING USED TO THE WARSUIT--STILL FIGURING OUT WHAT IT CAN DO.
JUMPING OUT OF A PERFECTLY GOOD AIRPLANE WITHOUT A 'CHUTE IS JUST ONE OF THE PERKS.
THE NANOTECH HAS BEEN LOADED WITH DOZENS OF LOCAL LANGUAGES, COMPLETE SATELLITE MAPS, GPS COORDINATES, THE WORKS.
BUT IT'S NOT EXACTLY SUBTLE.
HAVE TO POWER DOWN AND START THE MISSION THE OLD-FASHIONED WAY. LOW-PROFILE, QUIET.
BECAUSE IN THIS NEIGHBORHOOD, IT DOESN'T PAY TO ADVERTISE--

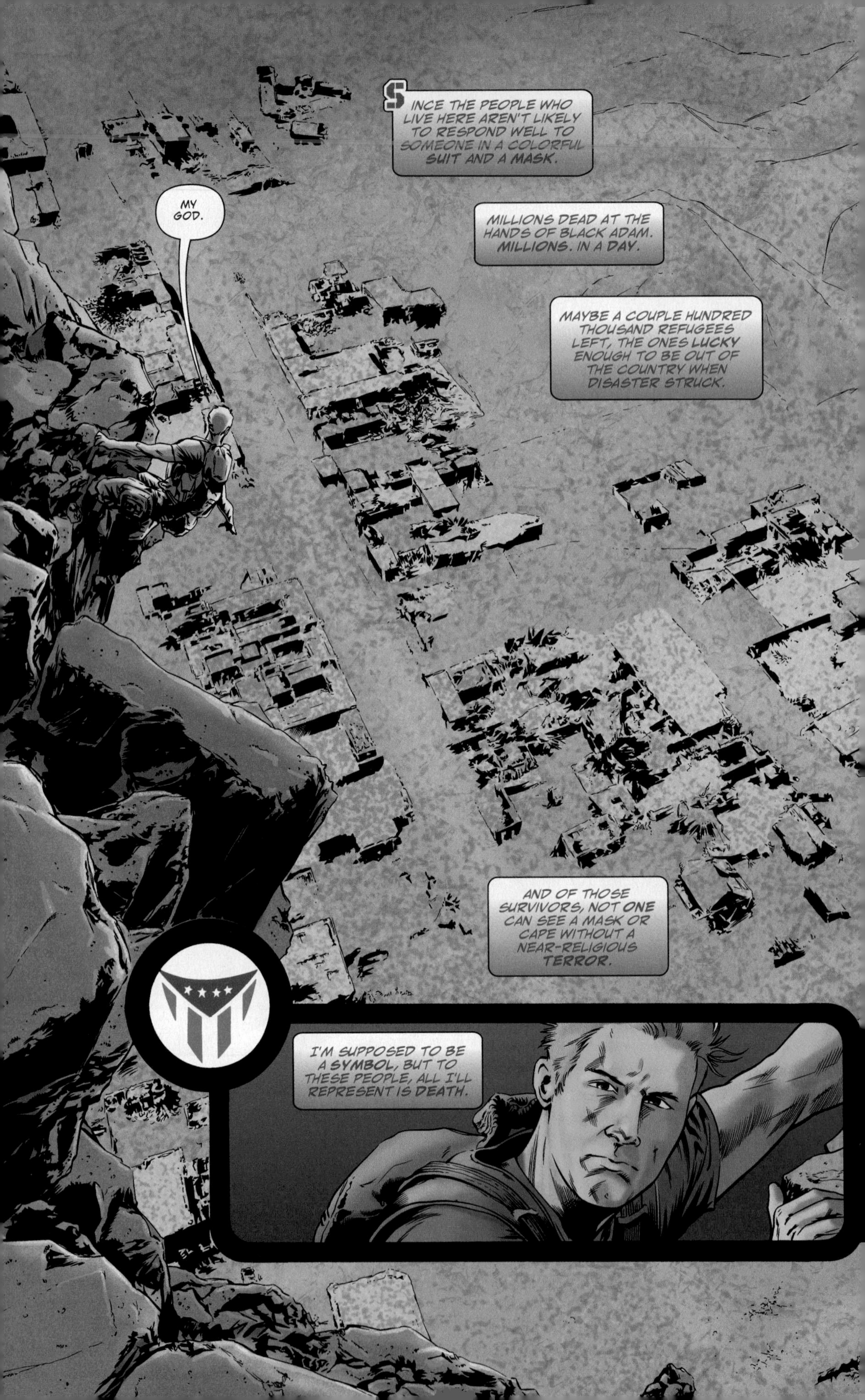
SINCE THE PEOPLE WHO LIVE HERE AREN'T LIKELY TO RESPOND WELL TO SOMEONE IN A COLORFUL SUIT AND A MASK.
MY GOD.
MILLIONS DEAD AT THE HANDS OF BLACK ADAM. MILLIONS. IN A DAY.
MAYBE A COUPLE HUNDRED THOUSAND REFUGEES LEFT, THE ONES LUCKY ENOUGH TO BE OUT OF THE COUNTRY WHEN DISASTER STRUCK.
AND OF THOSE SURVIVORS, NOT ONE CAN SEE A MASK OR CAPE WITHOUT A NEAR-RELIGIOUS TERROR.
I'M SUPPOSED TO BE A SYMBOL, BUT TO THESE PEOPLE, ALL I'LL REPRESENT IS DEATH.

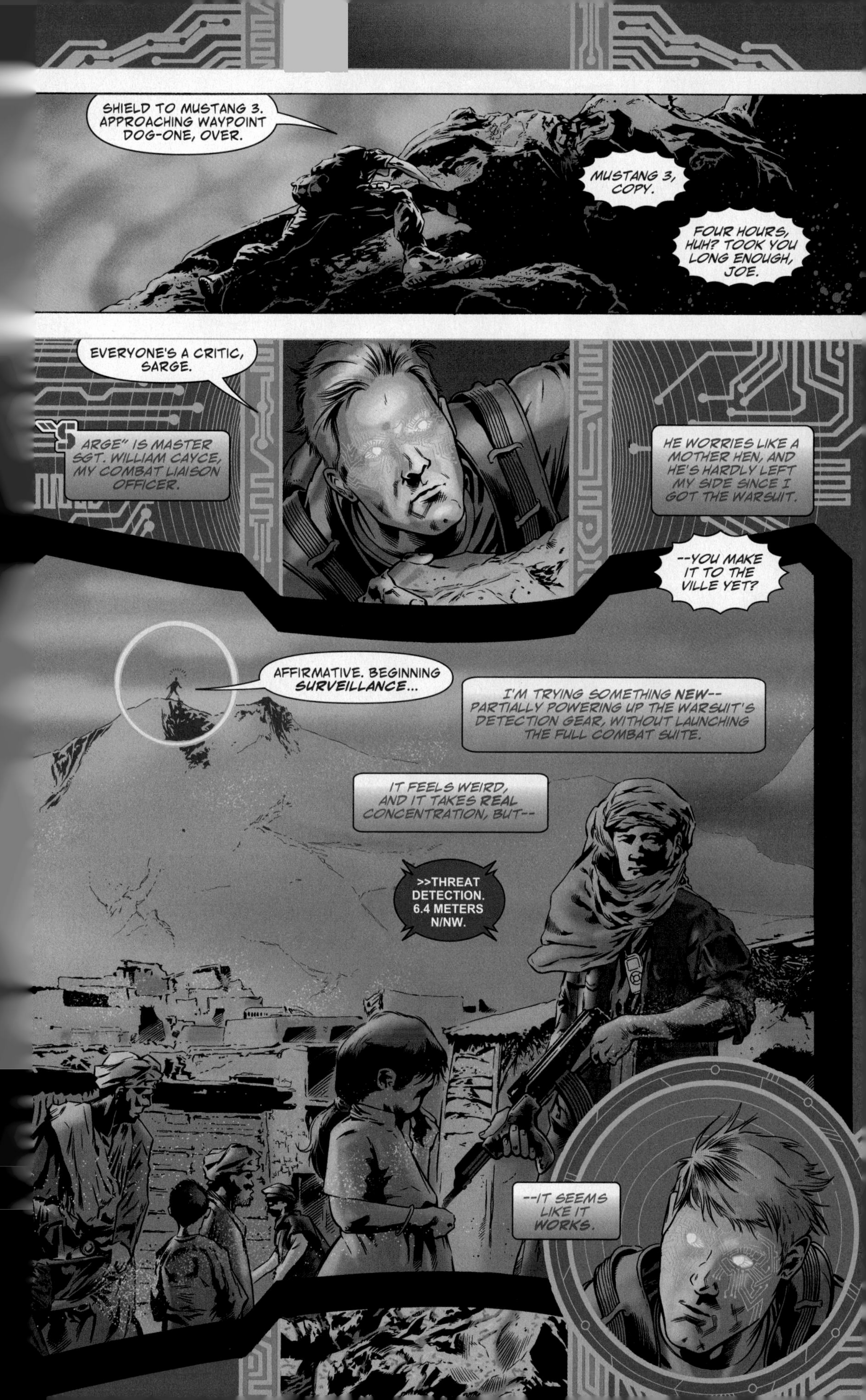
SHIELD TO MUSTANG 3. APPROACHING WAYPOINT DOG-ONE, OVER.
MUSTANG 3, COPY.
FOUR HOURS, HUH? TOOK YOU LONG ENOUGH, JOE.
EVERYONE'S A CRITIC, SARGE.
"SARGE" IS MASTER SGT. WILLIAM CAYCE, MY COMBAT LIAISON OFFICER.
HE WORRIES LIKE A MOTHER HEN, AND HE'S HARDLY LEFT MY SIDE SINCE I GOT THE WARSUIT.
--YOU MAKE IT TO THE VILLE YET?
AFFIRMATIVE. BEGINNING SURVEILLANCE...
I'M TRYING SOMETHING NEW--PARTIALLY POWERING UP THE WARSUIT'S DETECTION GEAR, WITHOUT LAUNCHING THE FULL COMBAT SUITE.
IT FEELS WEIRD, AND IT TAKES REAL CONCENTRATION, BUT--
>>THREAT DETECTION. 6.4 METERS N/NW.
--IT SEEMS LIKE IT WORKS.

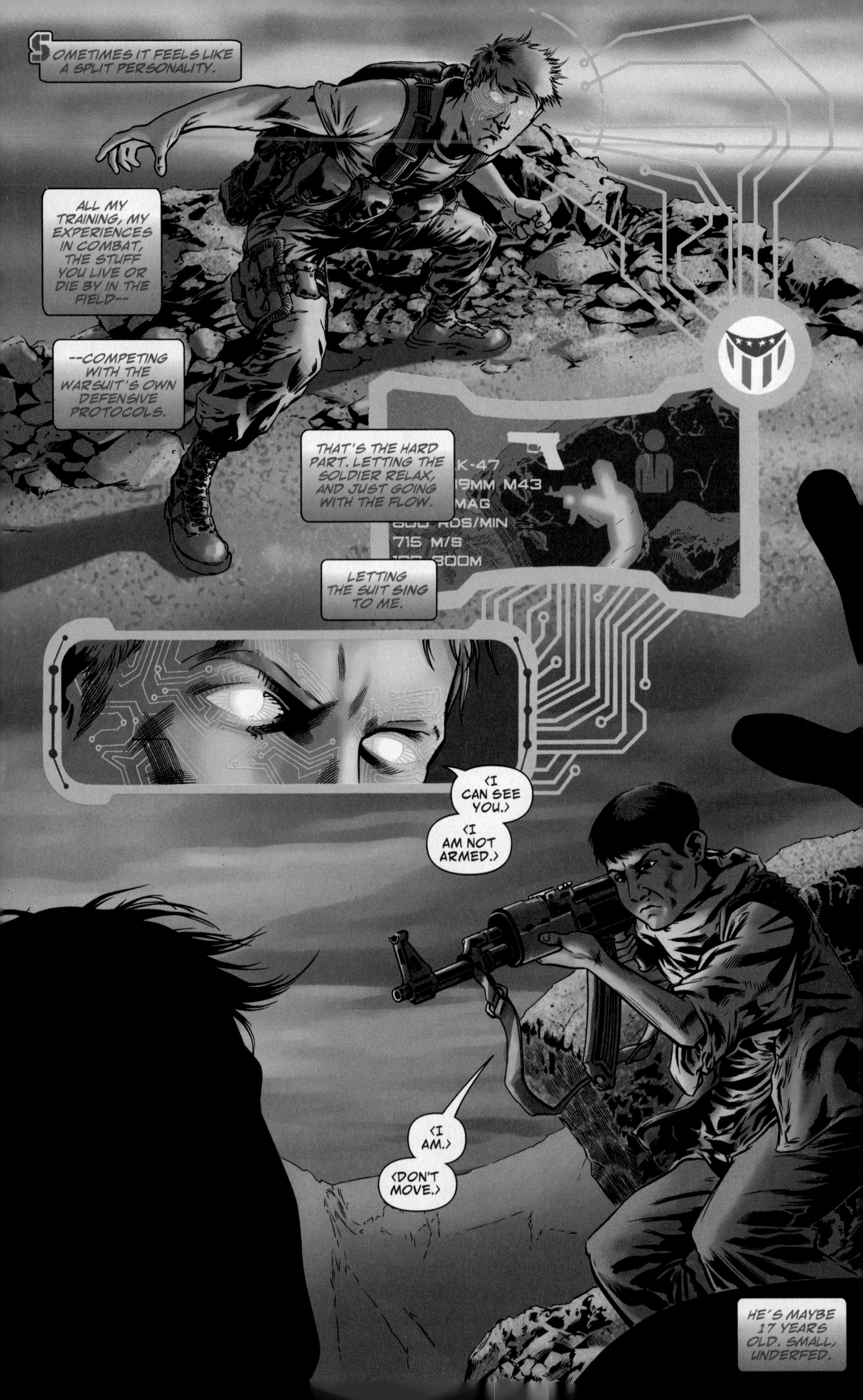
SOMETIMES IT FEELS LIKE A SPLIT PERSONALITY.
ALL MY TRAINING, MY EXPERIENCES IN COMBAT, THE STUFF YOU LIVE OR DIE BY IN THE FIELD--
--COMPETING WITH THE WARSUIT'S OWN DEFENSIVE PROTOCOLS.
THAT'S THE HARD PART. LETTING THE SOLDIER RELAX, AND JUST GOING WITH THE FLOW.
715 M/S
LETTING THE SUIT SING TO ME.
‹I CAN SEE YOU.›
‹I AM NOT ARMED.›
‹I AM.›
‹DON'T MOVE.›
HE'S MAYBE 17 YEARS OLD. SMALL, UNDERFED.

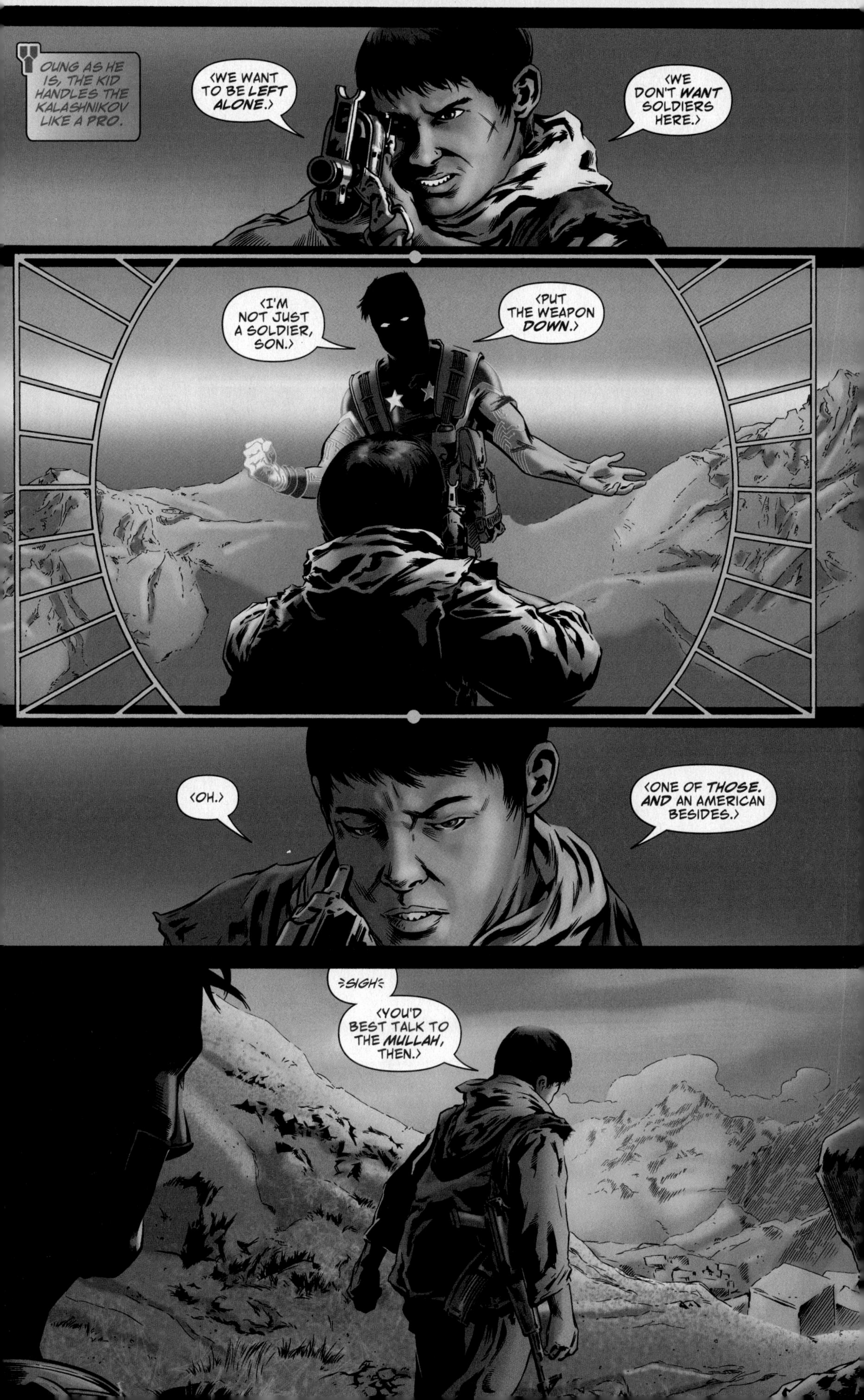
YOUNG AS HE IS, THE KID HANDLES THE KALASHNIKOV LIKE A PRO.
<WE WANT TO BE LEFT ALONE.>
<WE DON'T WANT SOLDIERS HERE.>
<I'M NOT JUST A SOLDIER, SON.>
<PUT THE WEAPON DOWN.>
<OH.>
<ONE OF THOSE. AND AN AMERICAN BESIDES.>
SIGH
<YOU'D BEST TALK TO THE MULLAH, THEN.>

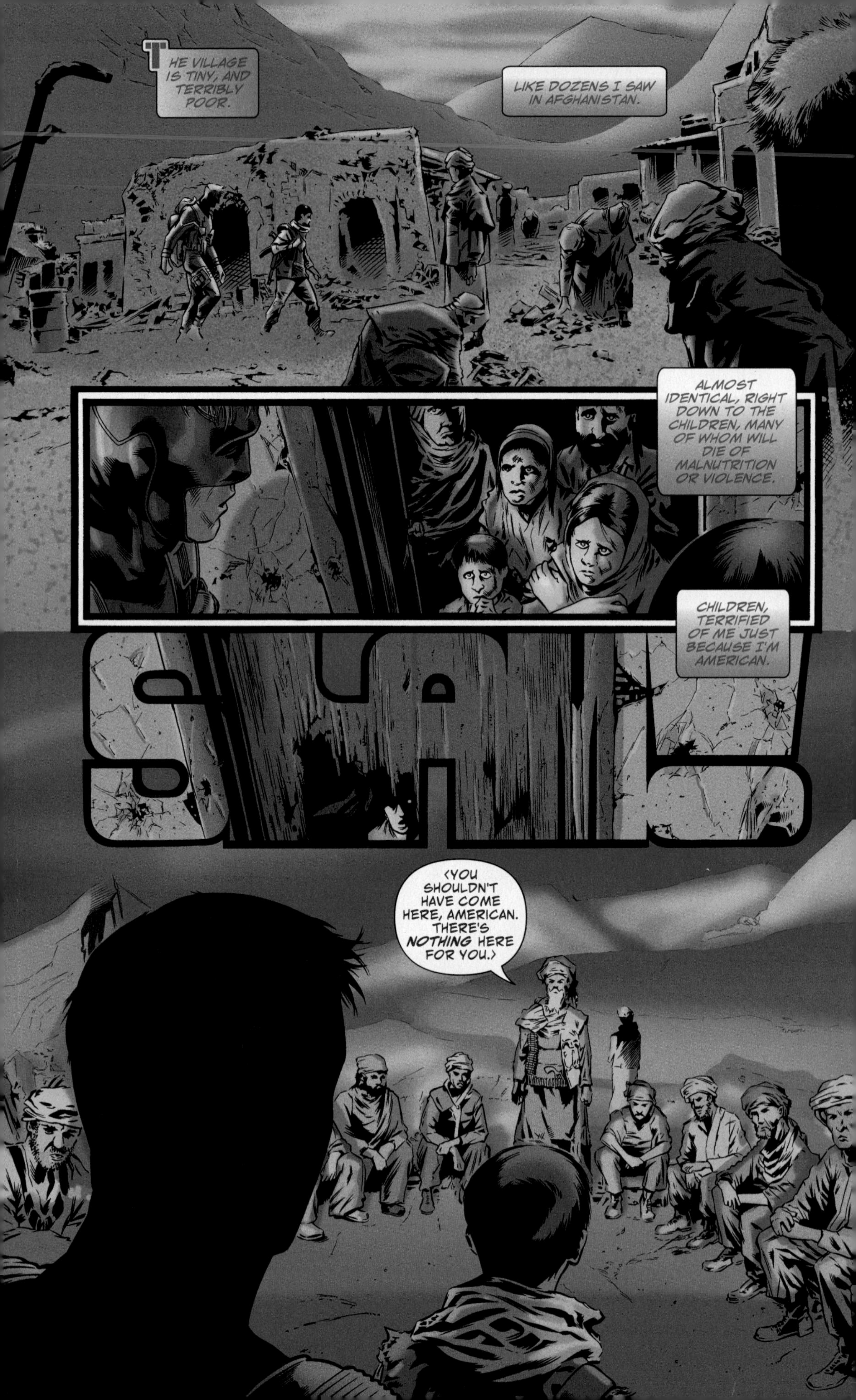
THE VILLAGE IS TINY, AND TERRIBLY POOR.
LIKE DOZENS I SAW IN AFGHANISTAN.
ALMOST IDENTICAL, RIGHT DOWN TO THE CHILDREN, MANY OF WHOM WILL DIE OF MALNUTRITION OR VIOLENCE.
CHILDREN, TERRIFIED OF ME JUST BECAUSE I'M AMERICAN.
SLAM!
<YOU SHOULDN'T HAVE COME HERE, AMERICAN. THERE'S NOTHING HERE FOR YOU.>

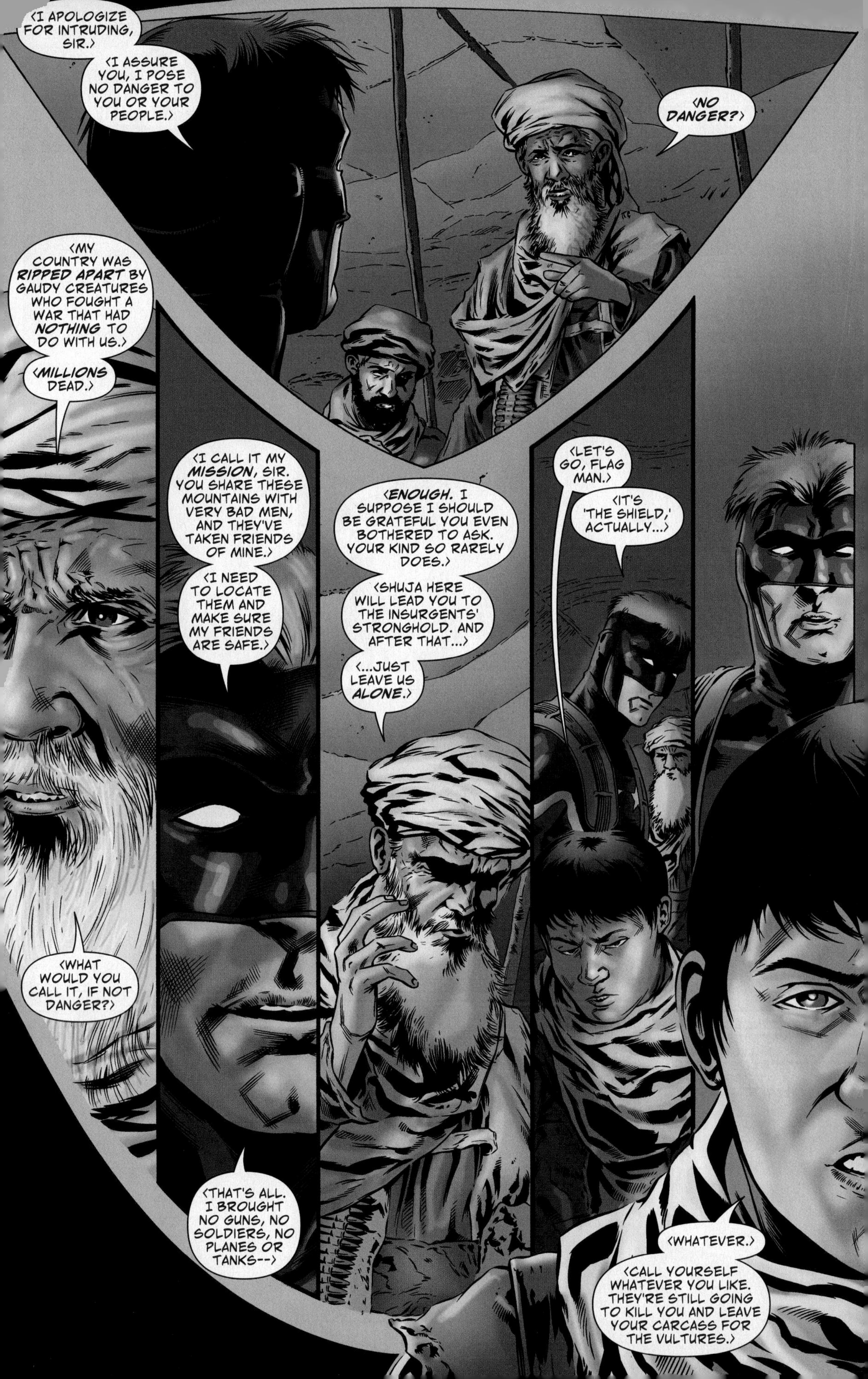

<I APOLOGIZE FOR INTRUDING, SIR.>
<I ASSURE YOU, I POSE NO DANGER TO YOU OR YOUR PEOPLE.>
<NO DANGER?>
<MY COUNTRY WAS RIPPED APART BY GAUDY CREATURES WHO FOUGHT A WAR THAT HAD NOTHING TO DO WITH US.>
<MILLIONS DEAD.>
<WHAT WOULD YOU CALL IT, IF NOT DANGER?>
<I CALL IT MY MISSION, SIR. YOU SHARE THESE MOUNTAINS WITH VERY BAD MEN, AND THEY'VE TAKEN FRIENDS OF MINE.>
<I NEED TO LOCATE THEM AND MAKE SURE MY FRIENDS ARE SAFE.>
<THAT'S ALL. I BROUGHT NO GUNS, NO SOLDIERS, NO PLANES OR TANKS-->
<ENOUGH. I SUPPOSE I SHOULD BE GRATEFUL YOU EVEN BOTHERED TO ASK. YOUR KIND SO RARELY DOES.>
<SHUJA HERE WILL LEAD YOU TO THE INSURGENTS' STRONGHOLD. AND AFTER THAT...>
<...JUST LEAVE US ALONE.>
<LET'S GO, FLAG MAN.>
<IT'S 'THE SHIELD,' ACTUALLY...>
<WHATEVER.>
<CALL YOURSELF WHATEVER YOU LIKE. THEY'RE STILL GOING TO KILL YOU AND LEAVE YOUR CARCASS FOR THE VULTURES.>

I HAD A SERGEANT WITH ME IN AFGHANISTAN. TOUGH OLD BASTARD, KNEW THE TERRAIN LIKE YOU WOULDN'T BELIEVE.

HE HATED THAT COUNTRY BUT LOVED ITS PEOPLE, AND HE TOLD ME A STORY ONCE THAT STUCK WITH ME.

HE SAID THAT AS MUCH AS THE INSURGENTS AND DRUG RUNNERS AND BAD GUYS HATED AMERICANS, THEY SURE LOVE AMERICAN CULTURE.

ONCE, WE EVEN RAN ACROSS A BUNCH OF THEM HUDDLED AROUND AN OLD TV, WATCHING "TITANIC."

THEIR COMMANDER SAID LATER THAT IT WAS THEIR FAVORITE MOVIE.

EVER SINCE, I MAKE A POINT OF PACKING OUT SOME SPECIAL GEAR. JUST IN CASE.

SOMETHING TO SHOW WE'RE NOT JUST MEN WITH GUNS AND BOMBS AND TANKS.

SOMETHING TO SHOW WE LOVE CHILDREN, TOO.

SOMETHING TO DULL THE MISDIRECTED HATE.

THEY'RE TOO YOUNG TO UNDERSTAND, YOU KNOW.

NO CONCEPT OF WHAT IT WAS LIKE...*BEFORE.* NO INKLING OF WHAT WE'VE LOST. NO IDEA WHAT PEOPLE LIKE *YOU* REPRESENT.

OUR CULTURE IS IN RUINS...

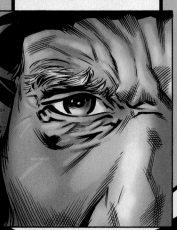

...BUT AT LEAST THE AMERICANS HAVE BROUGHT US *COMIC BOOKS.*

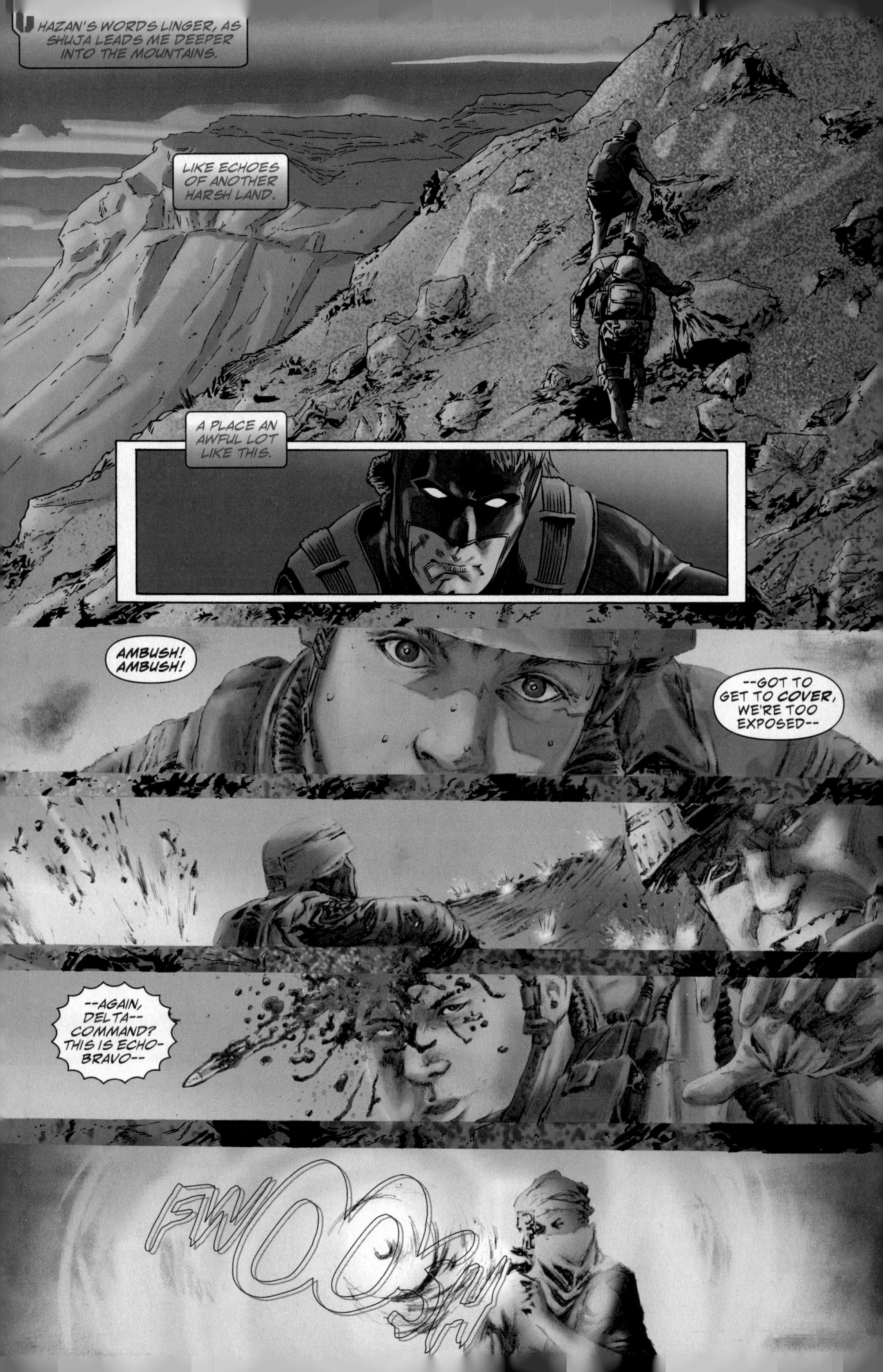
HAZAN'S WORDS LINGER, AS SHUJA LEADS ME DEEPER INTO THE MOUNTAINS.
LIKE ECHOES OF ANOTHER HARSH LAND.
A PLACE AN AWFUL LOT LIKE THIS.
AMBUSH! AMBUSH!
--GOT TO GET TO COVER, WE'RE TOO EXPOSED--
--AGAIN, DELTA--COMMAND? THIS IS ECHO-BRAVO--
FWOOSH

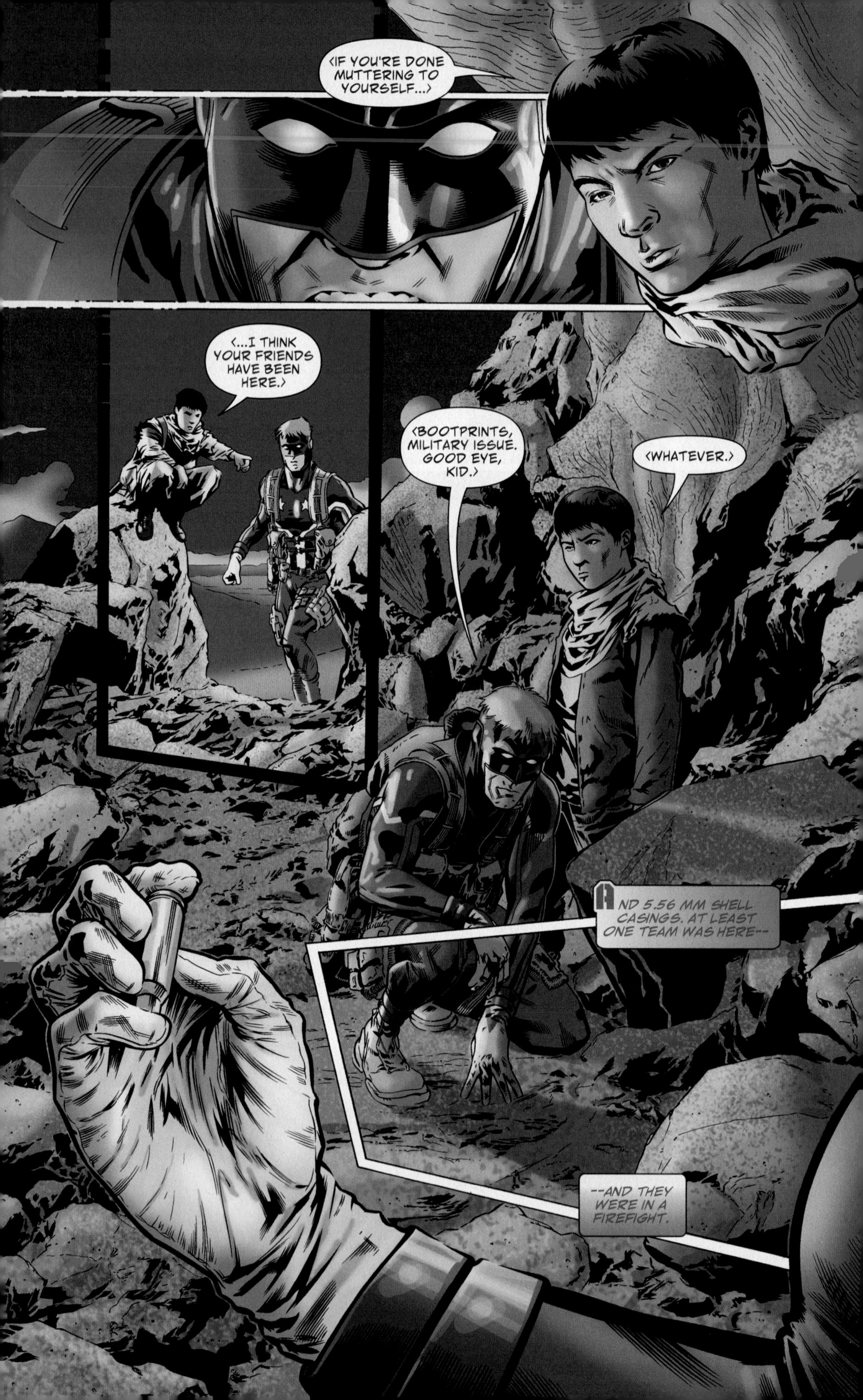

<IF YOU'RE DONE MUTTERING TO YOURSELF...>
<...I THINK YOUR FRIENDS HAVE BEEN HERE.>
<BOOTPRINTS, MILITARY ISSUE. GOOD EYE, KID.>
<WHATEVER.>
AND 5.56 MM SHELL CASINGS. AT LEAST ONE TEAM WAS HERE--
--AND THEY WERE IN A FIREFIGHT.

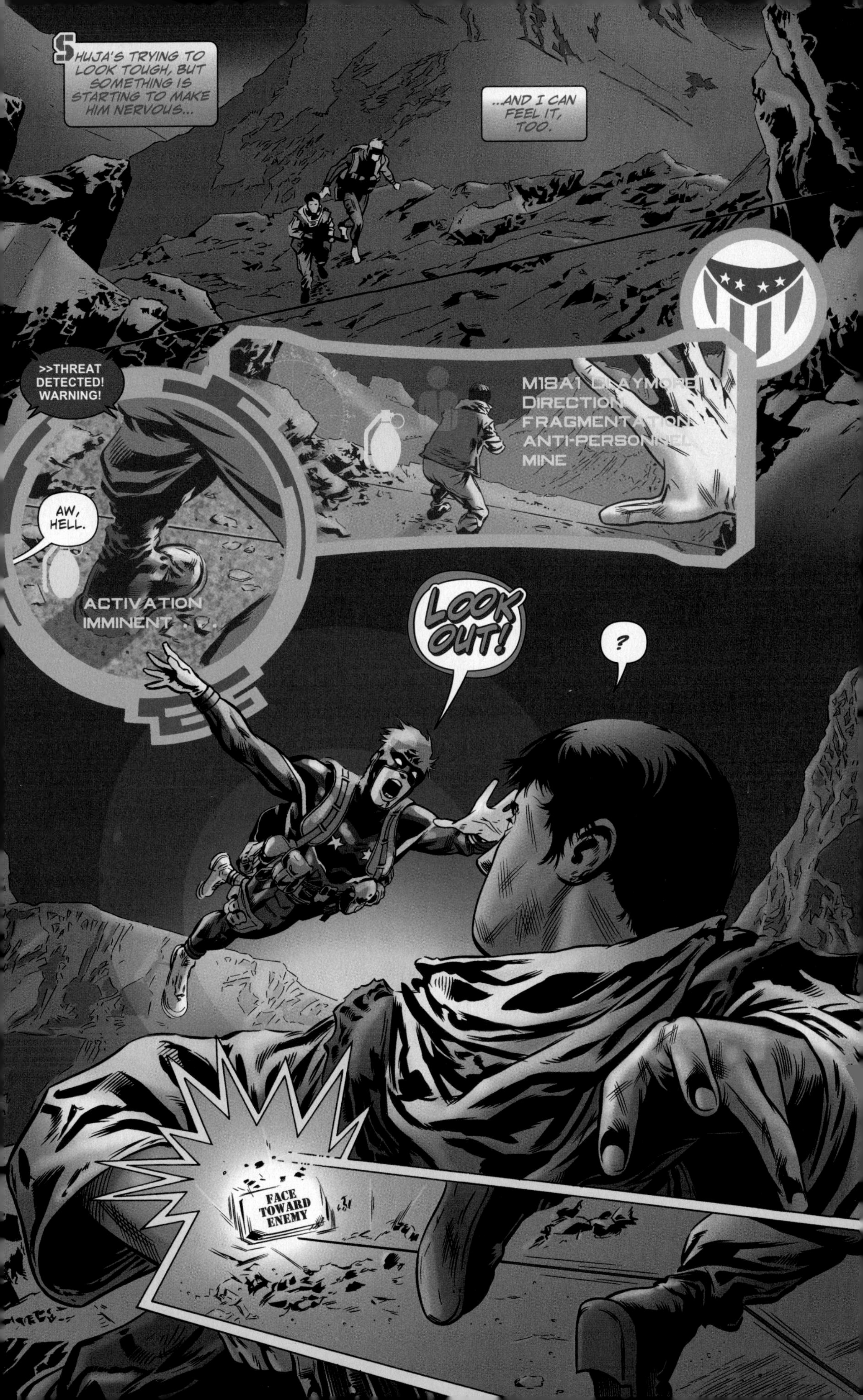
SHUJA'S TRYING TO LOOK TOUGH, BUT SOMETHING IS STARTING TO MAKE HIM NERVOUS...
...AND I CAN FEEL IT, TOO.
>>THREAT DETECTED! WARNING!
M18A1 CLAYMORE DIRECTION FRAGMENTATION ANTI-PERSONNEL MINE
AW, HELL.
ACTIVATION IMMINENT . . .
LOOK OUT!
?
FACE TOWARD ENEMY

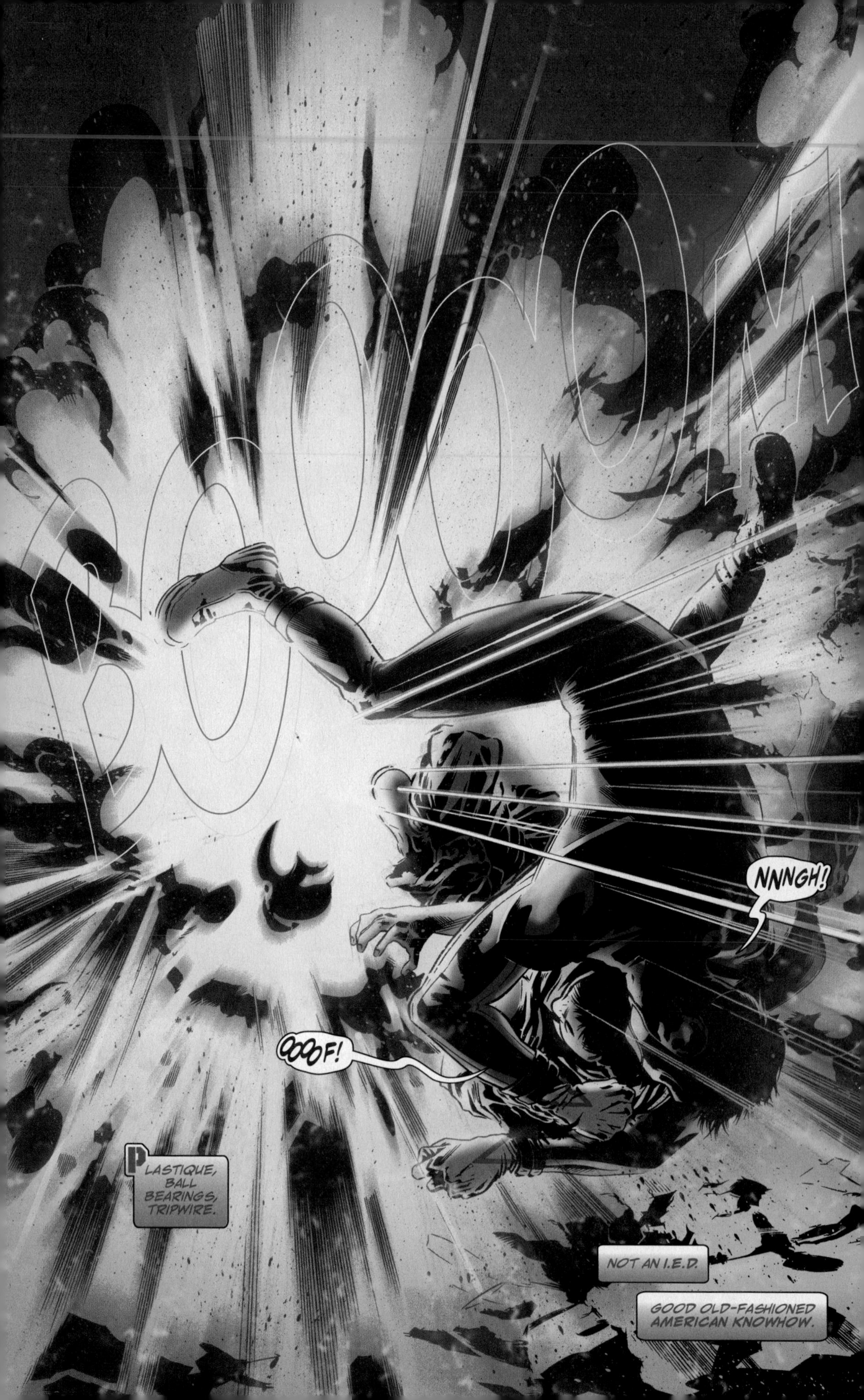
BOOOOOM
NNNGH!
OOOOF!
PLASTIQUE, BALL BEARINGS, TRIPWIRE.
NOT AN I.E.D.
GOOD OLD-FASHIONED AMERICAN KNOWHOW.

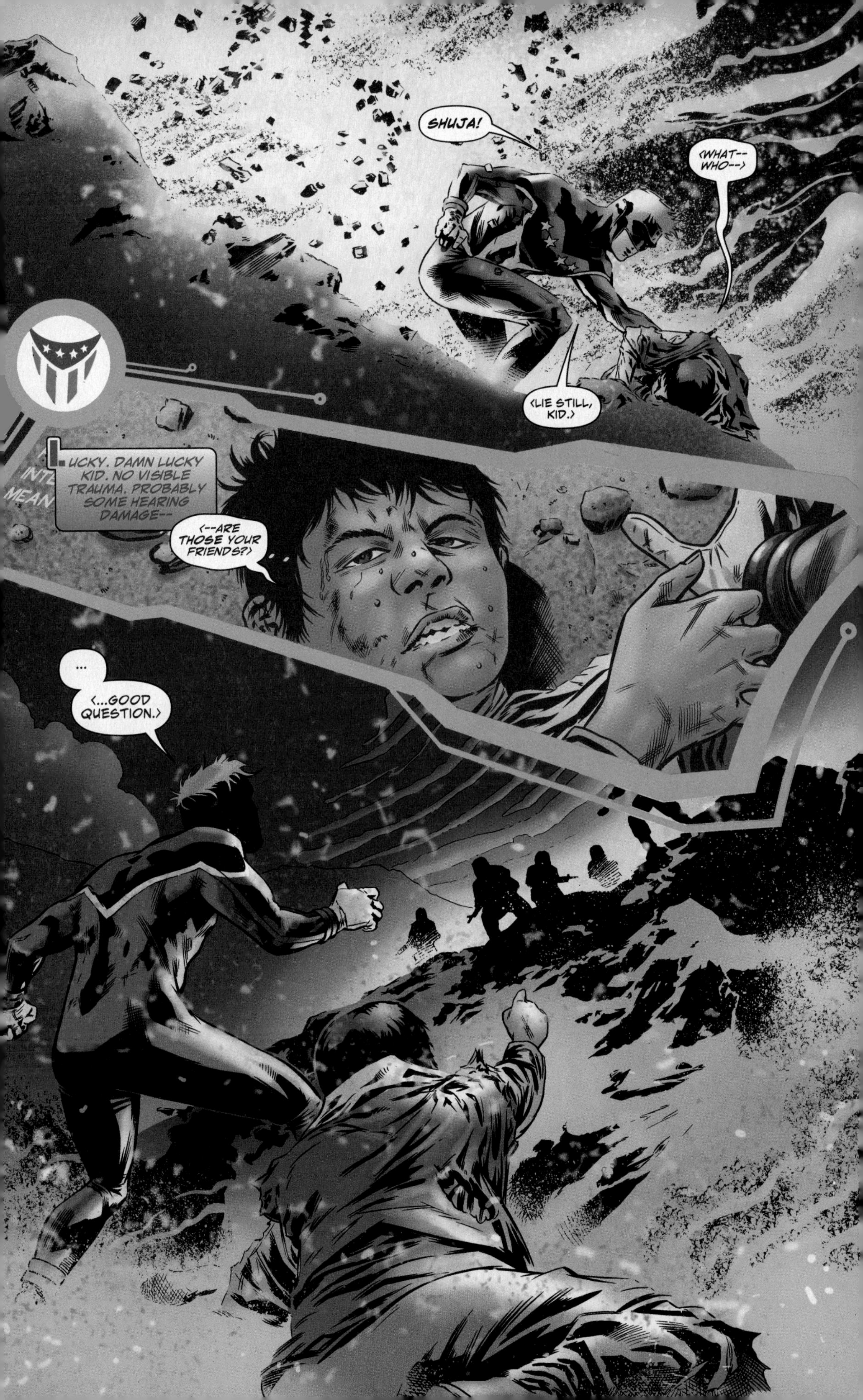
SHUJA!
<WHAT-- WHO-->
<LIE STILL, KID.>
LUCKY. DAMN LUCKY KID. NO VISIBLE TRAUMA. PROBABLY SOME HEARING DAMAGE--
<--ARE THOSE YOUR FRIENDS?>
...
<...GOOD QUESTION.>

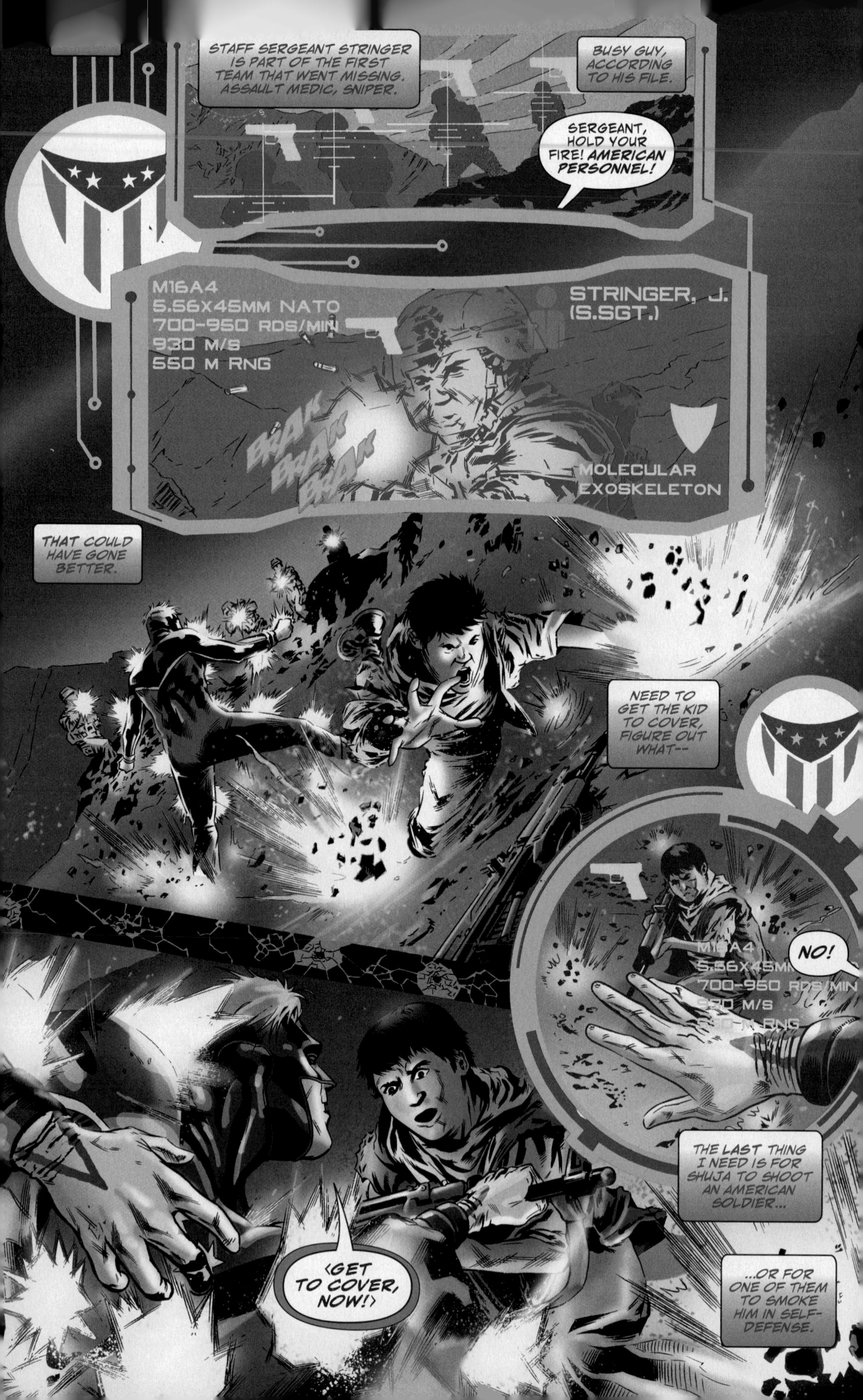
STAFF SERGEANT STRINGER IS PART OF THE FIRST TEAM THAT WENT MISSING. ASSAULT MEDIC, SNIPER.
BUSY GUY, ACCORDING TO HIS FILE.
SERGEANT, HOLD YOUR FIRE! AMERICAN PERSONNEL!
M16A4
5.56X45MM NATO
700-950 RDS/MIN
930 M/S
550 M RNG
STRINGER, J.
(S.SGT.)
BRAK BRAK BRAK
MOLECULAR
EXOSKELETON
THAT COULD HAVE GONE BETTER.
NEED TO GET THE KID TO COVER, FIGURE OUT WHAT--
NO!
THE LAST THING I NEED IS FOR SHUJA TO SHOOT AN AMERICAN SOLDIER...
‹GET TO COVER, NOW!›
...OR FOR ONE OF THEM TO SMOKE HIM IN SELF-DEFENSE.

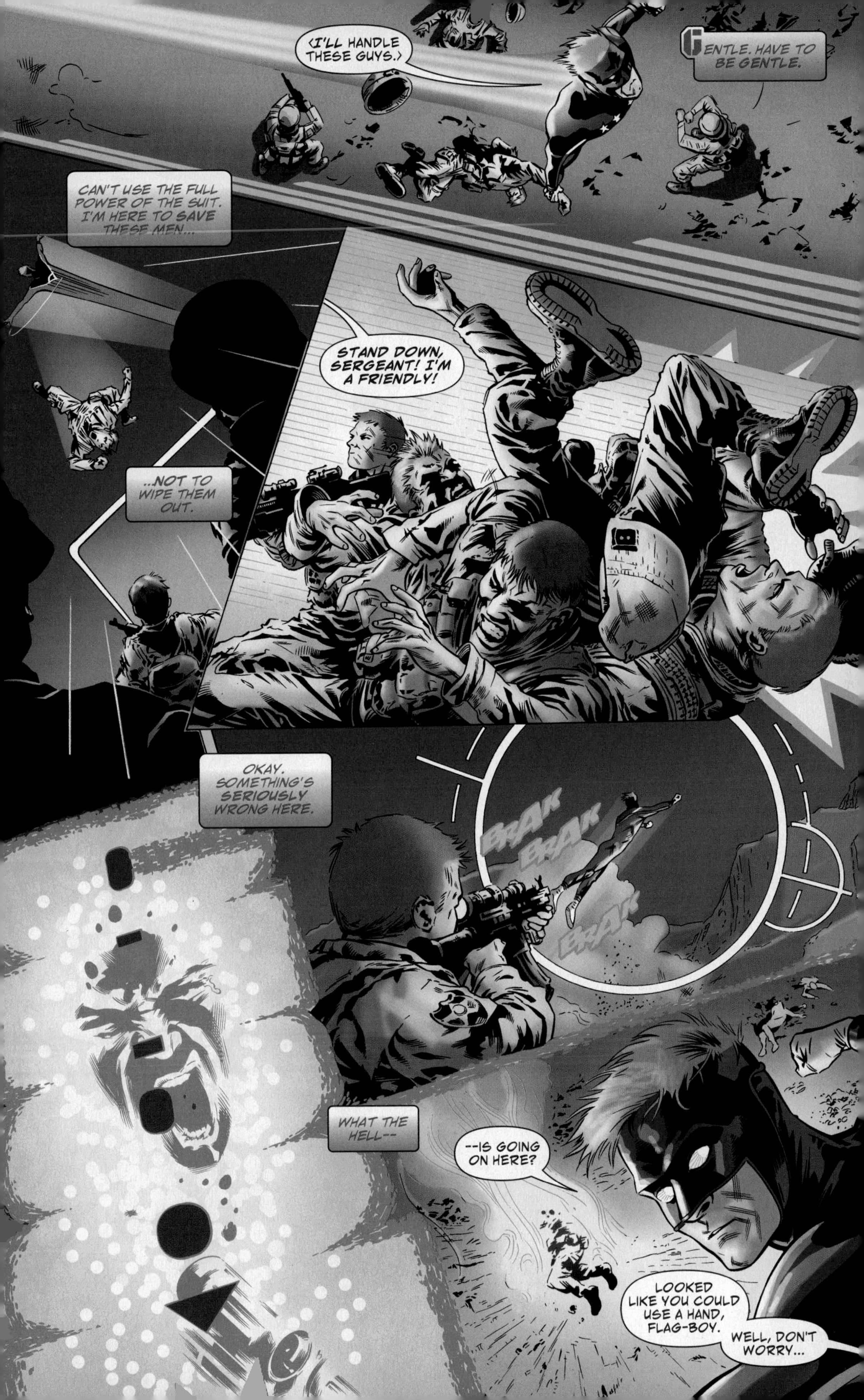

‹I'LL HANDLE THESE GUYS.›
GENTLE. HAVE TO BE GENTLE.
CAN'T USE THE FULL POWER OF THE SUIT. I'M HERE TO SAVE THESE MEN...
STAND DOWN, SERGEANT! I'M A FRIENDLY!
...NOT TO WIPE THEM OUT.
OKAY. SOMETHING'S SERIOUSLY WRONG HERE.
BRAK
BRAK
BRAK
WHAT THE HELL--
--IS GOING ON HERE?
LOOKED LIKE YOU COULD USE A HAND, FLAG-BOY.
WELL, DON'T WORRY...

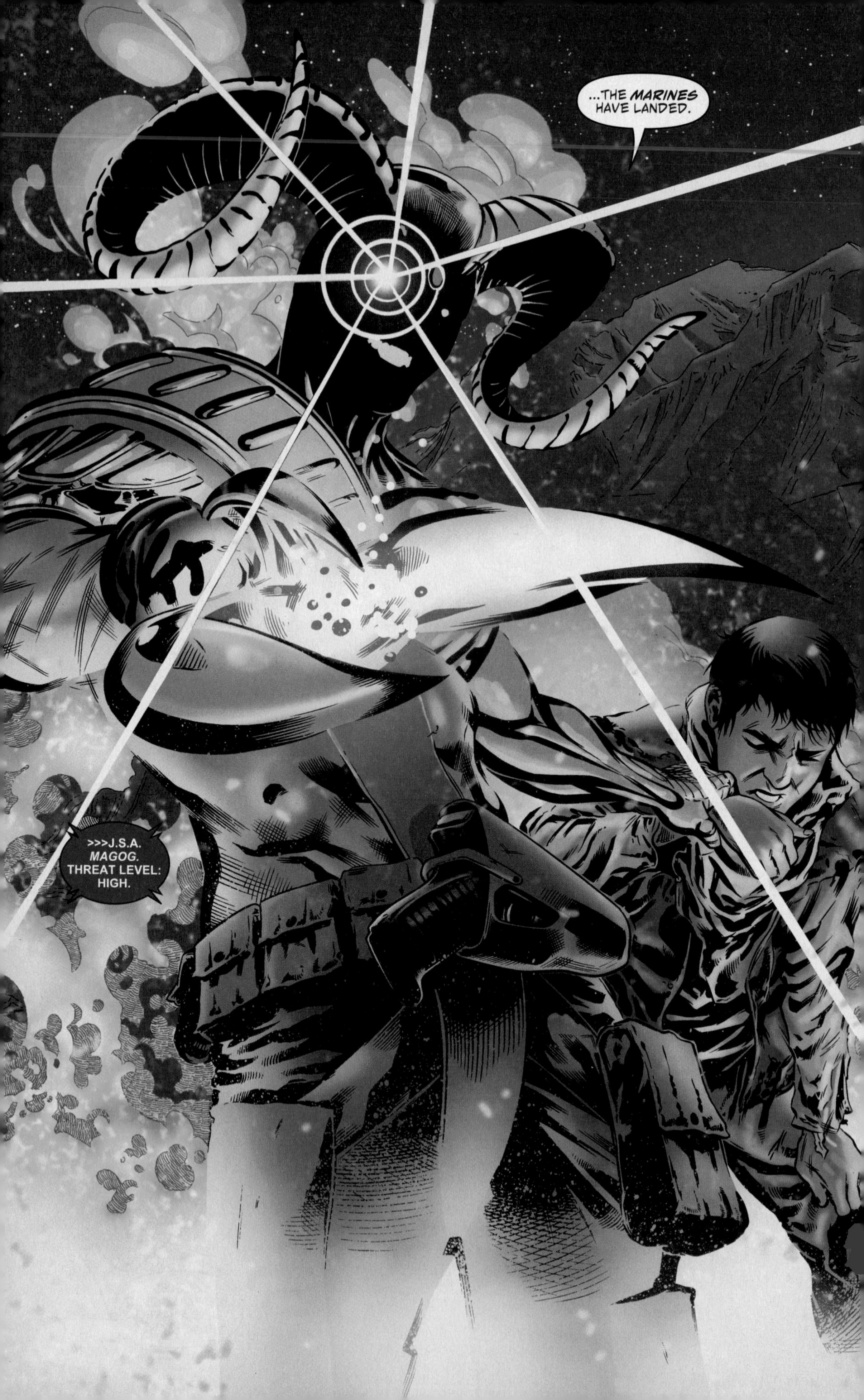
...THE *MARINES* HAVE LANDED.
>>>J.S.A. *MAGOG.* THREAT LEVEL: HIGH.

KICKING DOWN THE DOOR PART 2: ALPHA DOGS
Cover by Francis Manapul

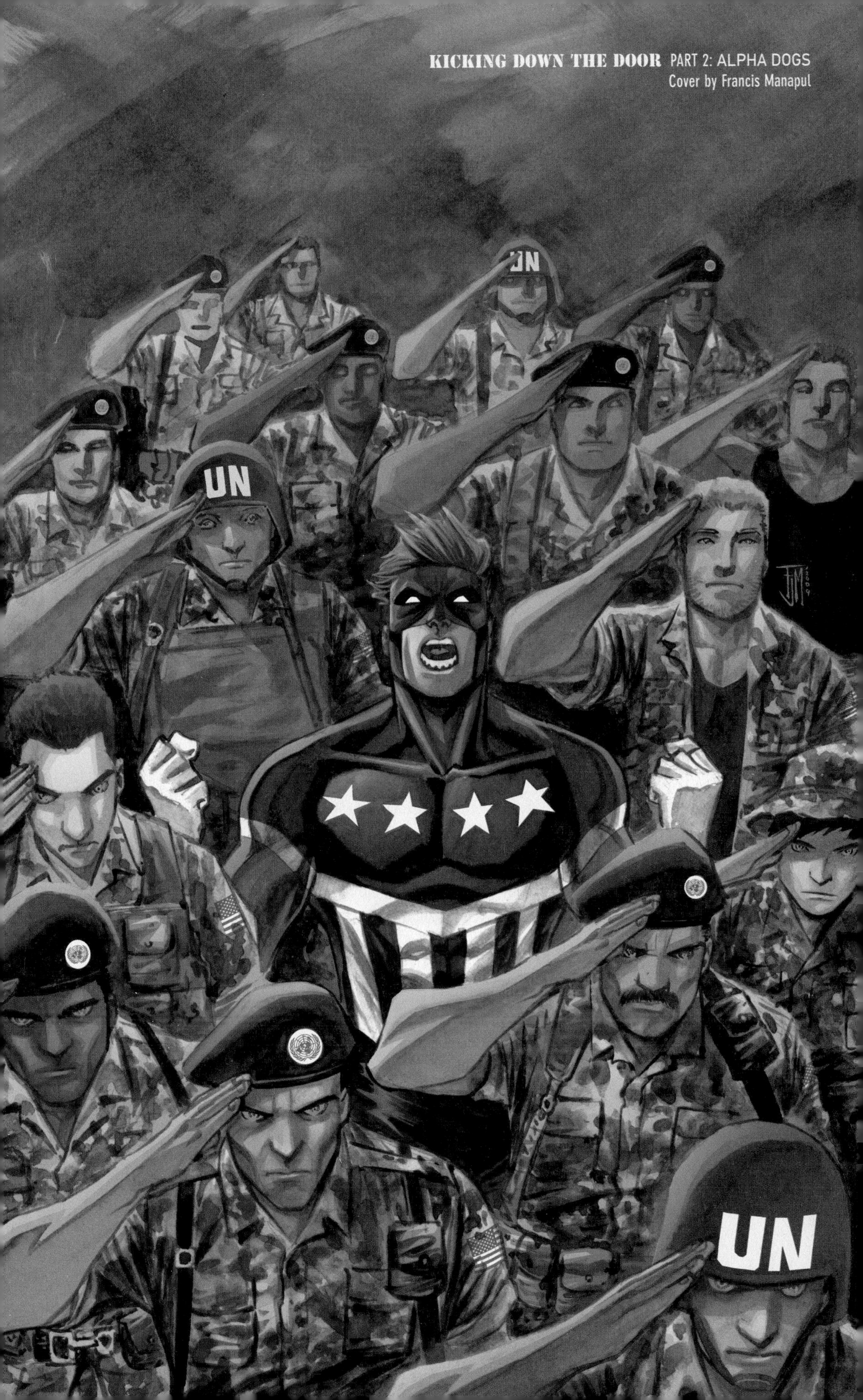
UN
UN
UN

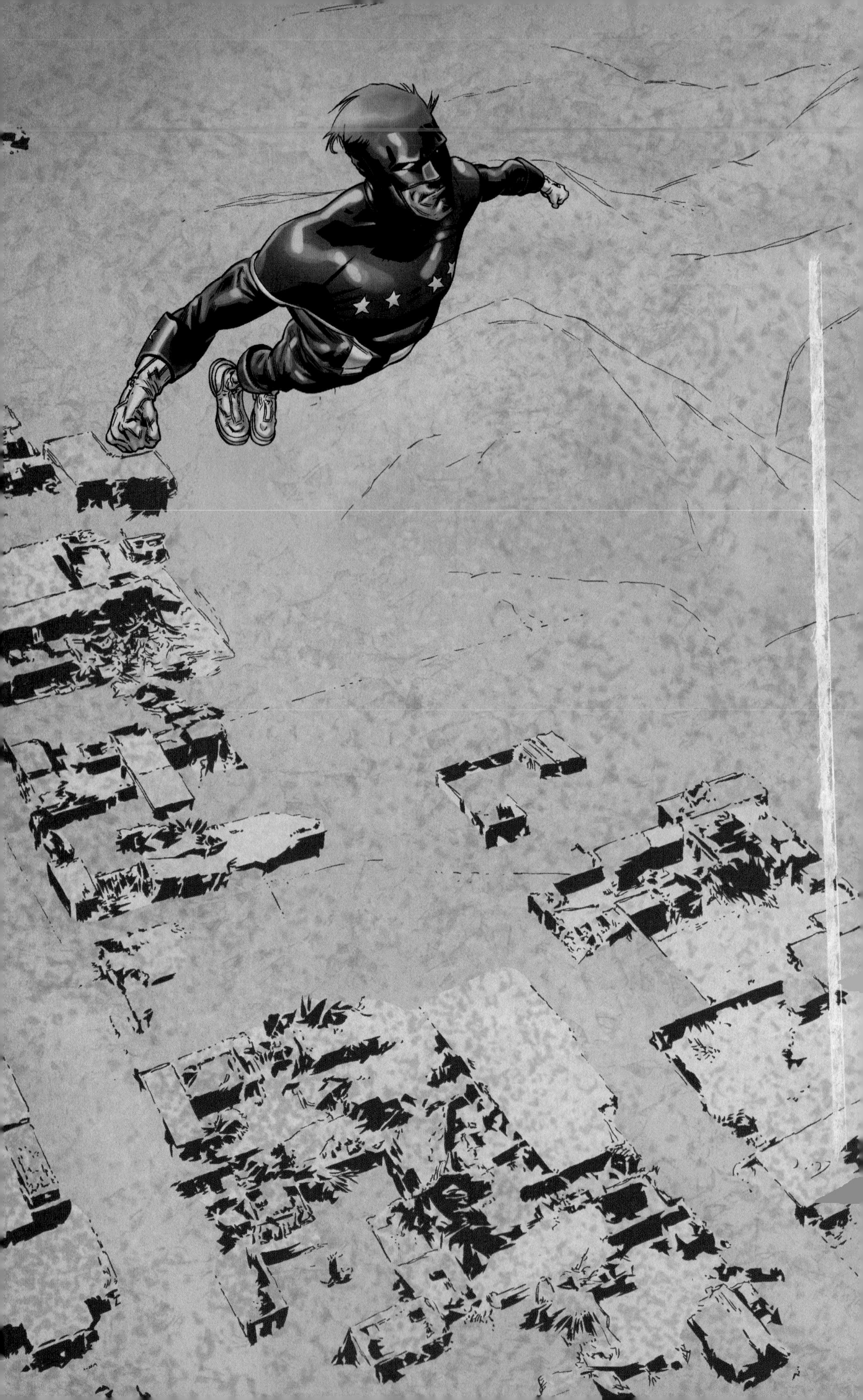

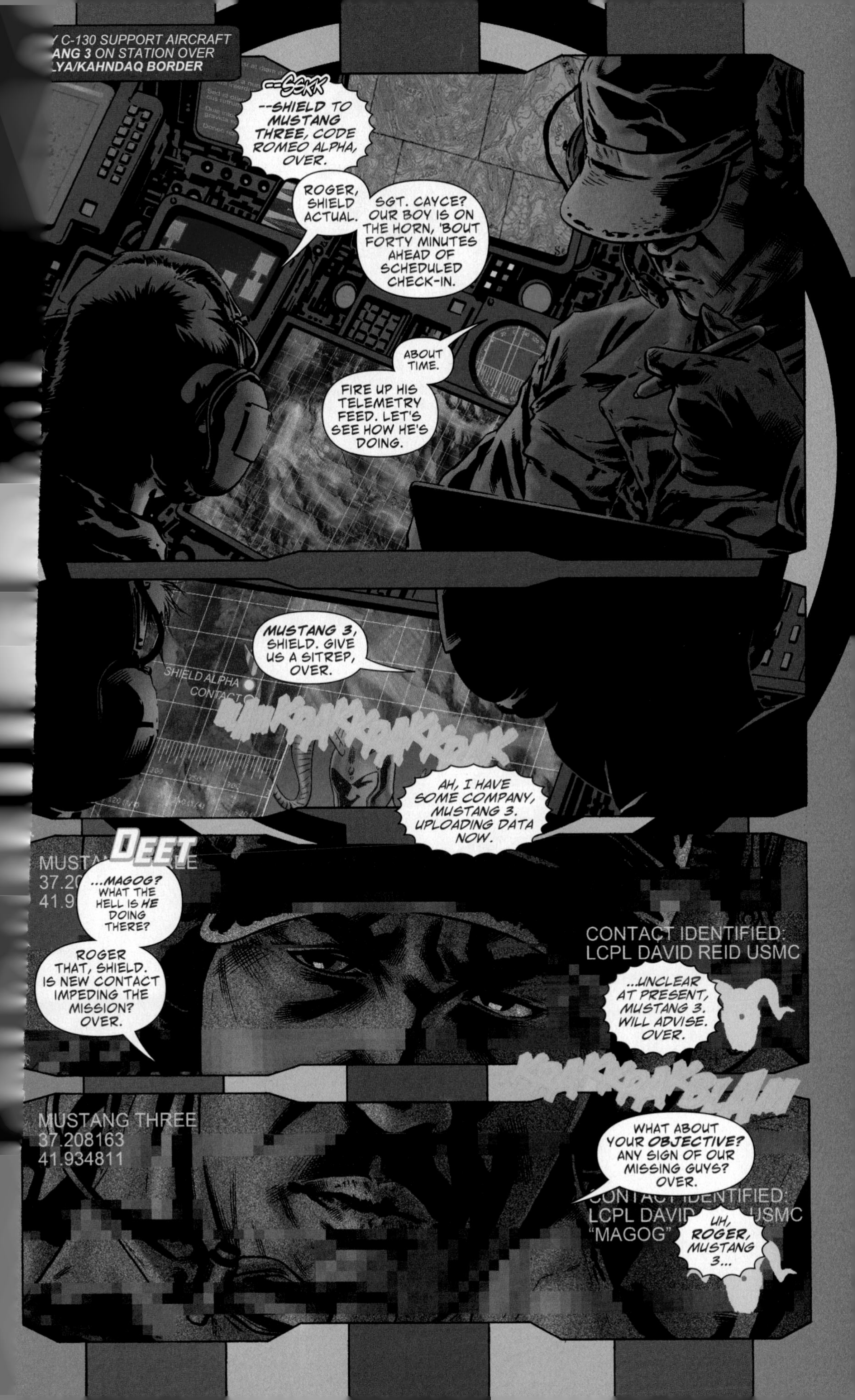
Y C-130 SUPPORT AIRCRAFT
ANG 3 ON STATION OVER
LYA/KAHNDAQ BORDER
--SSKK
--SHIELD TO MUSTANG THREE, CODE ROMEO ALPHA, OVER.
ROGER, SHIELD ACTUAL.
SGT. CAYCE? OUR BOY IS ON THE HORN, 'BOUT FORTY MINUTES AHEAD OF SCHEDULED CHECK-IN.
ABOUT TIME.
FIRE UP HIS TELEMETRY FEED. LET'S SEE HOW HE'S DOING.
MUSTANG 3, SHIELD. GIVE US A SITREP, OVER.
SHIELD ALPHA
CONTACT
AH, I HAVE SOME COMPANY, MUSTANG 3. UPLOADING DATA NOW.
DEET
...MAGOG? WHAT THE HELL IS HE DOING THERE?
ROGER THAT, SHIELD. IS NEW CONTACT IMPEDING THE MISSION? OVER.
CONTACT IDENTIFIED:
LCPL DAVID REID USMC
...UNCLEAR AT PRESENT, MUSTANG 3. WILL ADVISE. OVER.
MUSTANG THREE
37.208163
41.934811
WHAT ABOUT YOUR OBJECTIVE? ANY SIGN OF OUR MISSING GUYS? OVER.
"MAGOG"
UH, ROGER, MUSTANG 3...

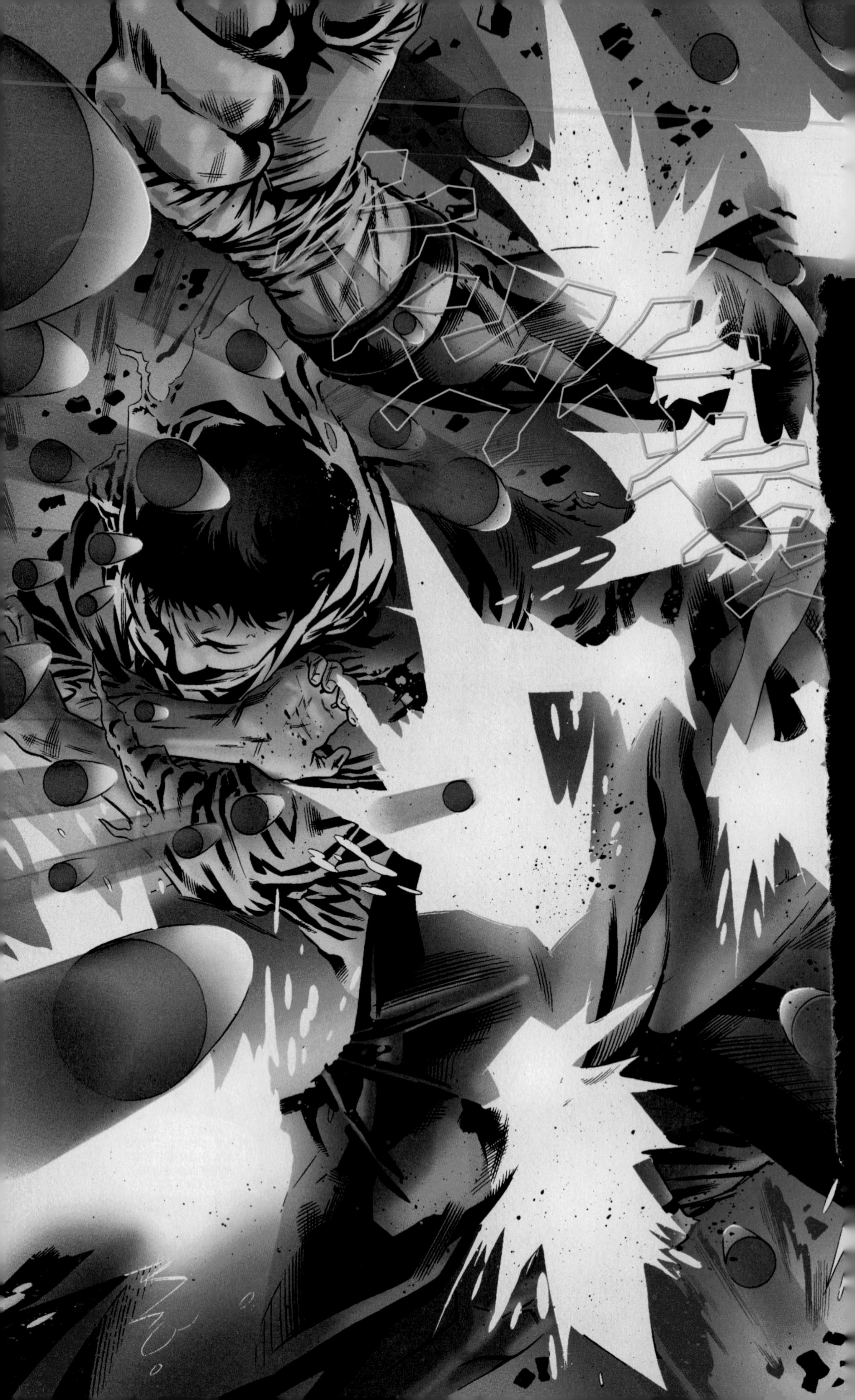

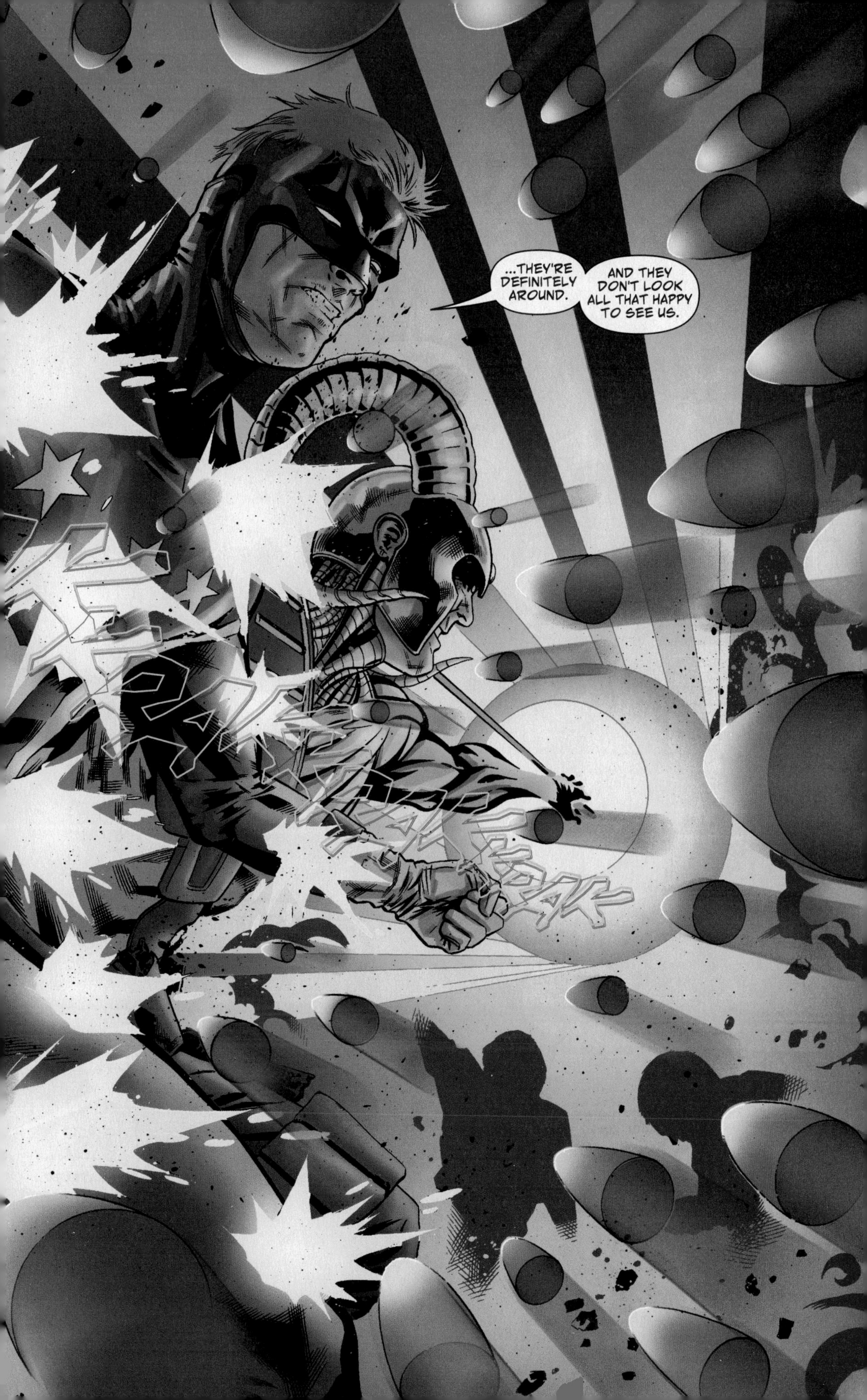
...THEY'RE DEFINITELY AROUND.
AND THEY DON'T LOOK ALL THAT HAPPY TO SEE US.

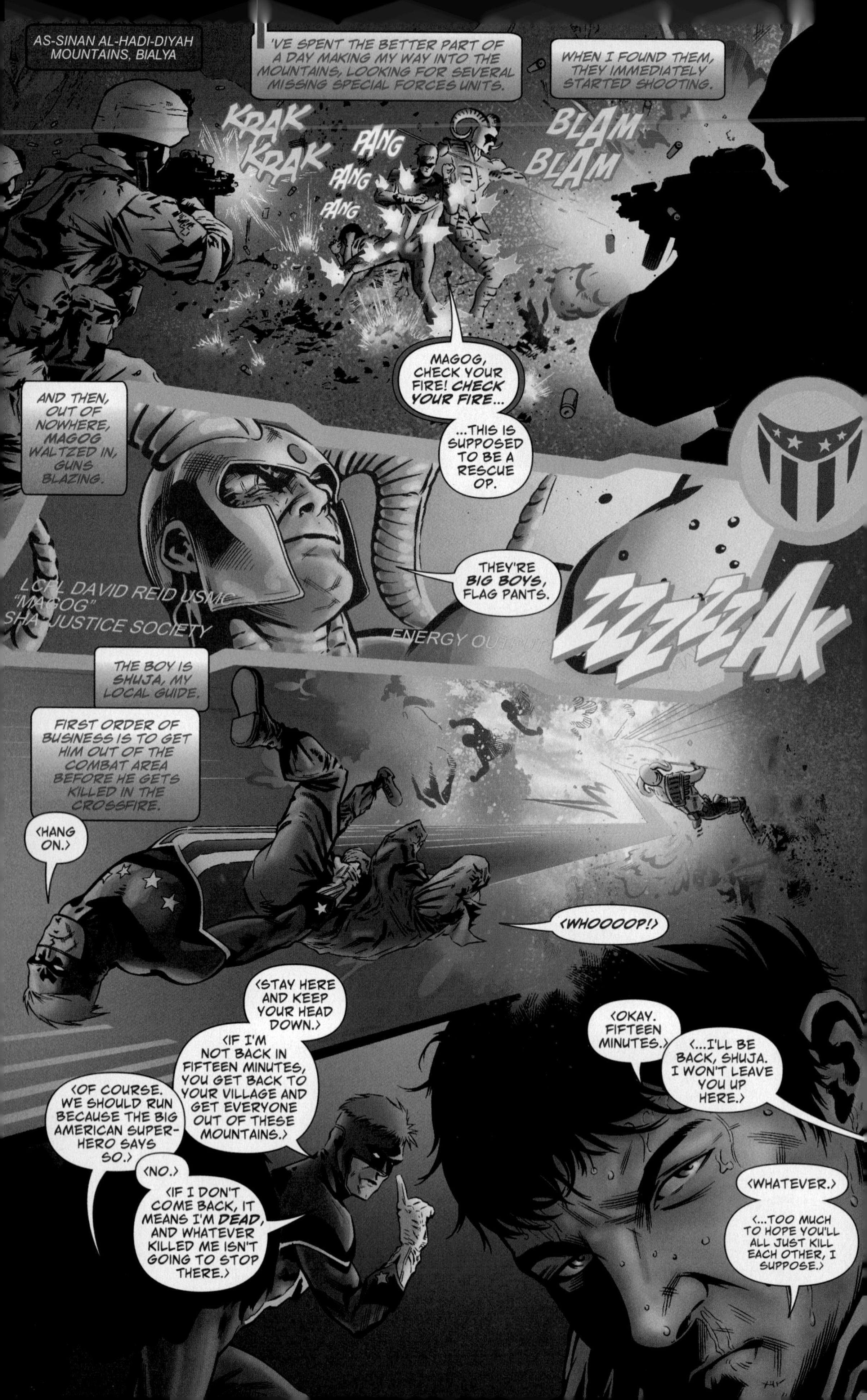
AS-SINAN AL-HADI-DIYAH MOUNTAINS, BIALYA
I'VE SPENT THE BETTER PART OF A DAY MAKING MY WAY INTO THE MOUNTAINS, LOOKING FOR SEVERAL MISSING SPECIAL FORCES UNITS.
WHEN I FOUND THEM, THEY IMMEDIATELY STARTED SHOOTING.
KRAK KRAK
PANG PANG PANG
BLAM BLAM
MAGOG, CHECK YOUR FIRE! CHECK YOUR FIRE...
...THIS IS SUPPOSED TO BE A RESCUE OP.
AND THEN, OUT OF NOWHERE, MAGOG WALTZED IN, GUNS BLAZING.
THEY'RE BIG BOYS, FLAG PANTS.
ZZZZZAK
THE BOY IS SHUJA, MY LOCAL GUIDE.
FIRST ORDER OF BUSINESS IS TO GET HIM OUT OF THE COMBAT AREA BEFORE HE GETS KILLED IN THE CROSSFIRE.
<HANG ON.>
<WHOOOOP!>
<STAY HERE AND KEEP YOUR HEAD DOWN.>
<IF I'M NOT BACK IN FIFTEEN MINUTES, YOU GET BACK TO YOUR VILLAGE AND GET EVERYONE OUT OF THESE MOUNTAINS.>
<OF COURSE. WE SHOULD RUN BECAUSE THE BIG AMERICAN SUPER-HERO SAYS SO.>
<NO.>
<IF I DON'T COME BACK, IT MEANS I'M DEAD, AND WHATEVER KILLED ME ISN'T GOING TO STOP THERE.>
<OKAY. FIFTEEN MINUTES.>
<...I'LL BE BACK, SHUJA. I WON'T LEAVE YOU UP HERE.>
<WHATEVER.>
<...TOO MUCH TO HOPE YOU'LL ALL JUST KILL EACH OTHER, I SUPPOSE.>

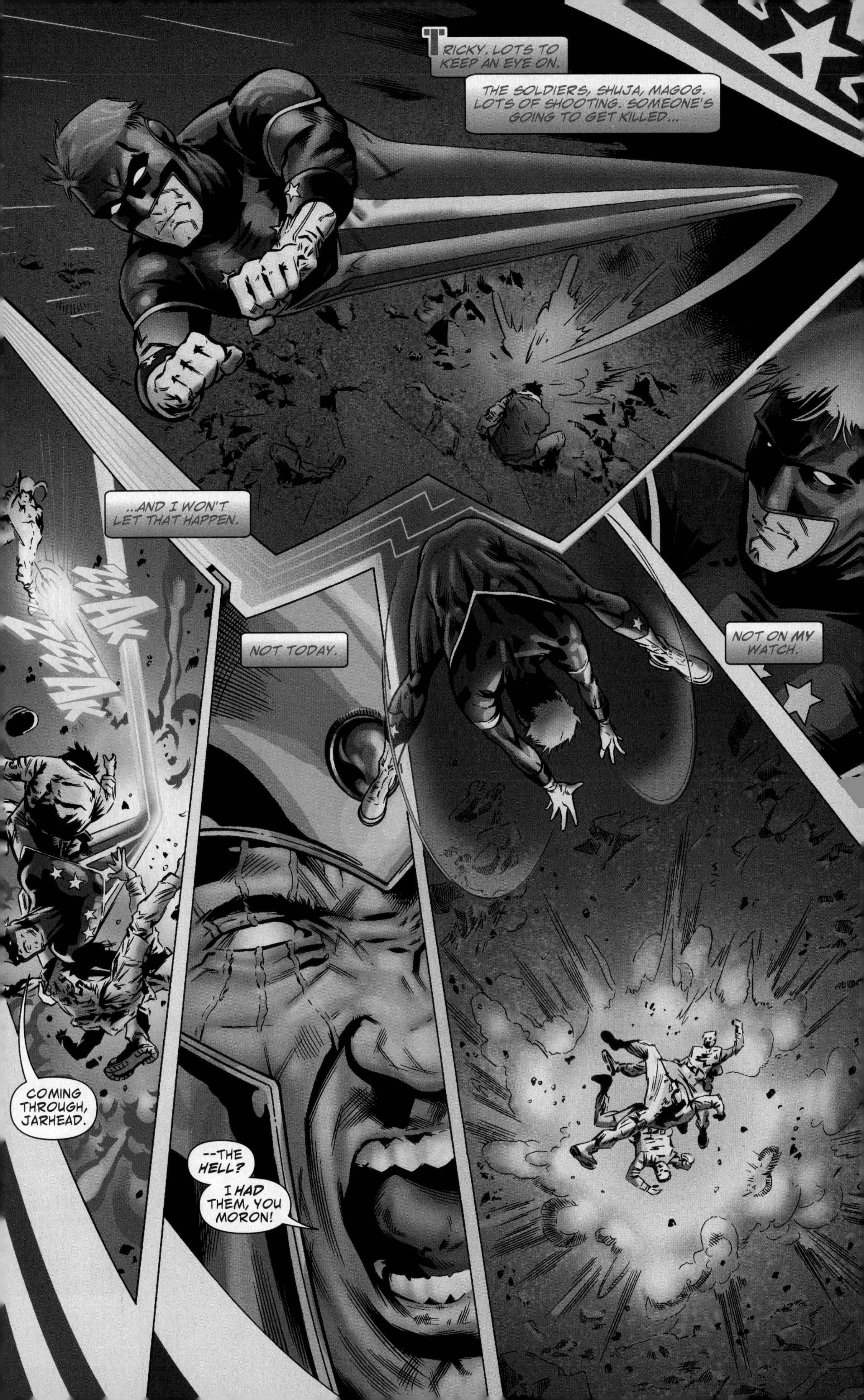
TRICKY. LOTS TO KEEP AN EYE ON.
THE SOLDIERS, SHUJA, MAGOG. LOTS OF SHOOTING. SOMEONE'S GOING TO GET KILLED...
...AND I WON'T LET THAT HAPPEN.
ZZAK
ZZZAK
NOT TODAY.
NOT ON MY WATCH.
COMING THROUGH, JARHEAD.
--THE HELL? I HAD THEM, YOU MORON!

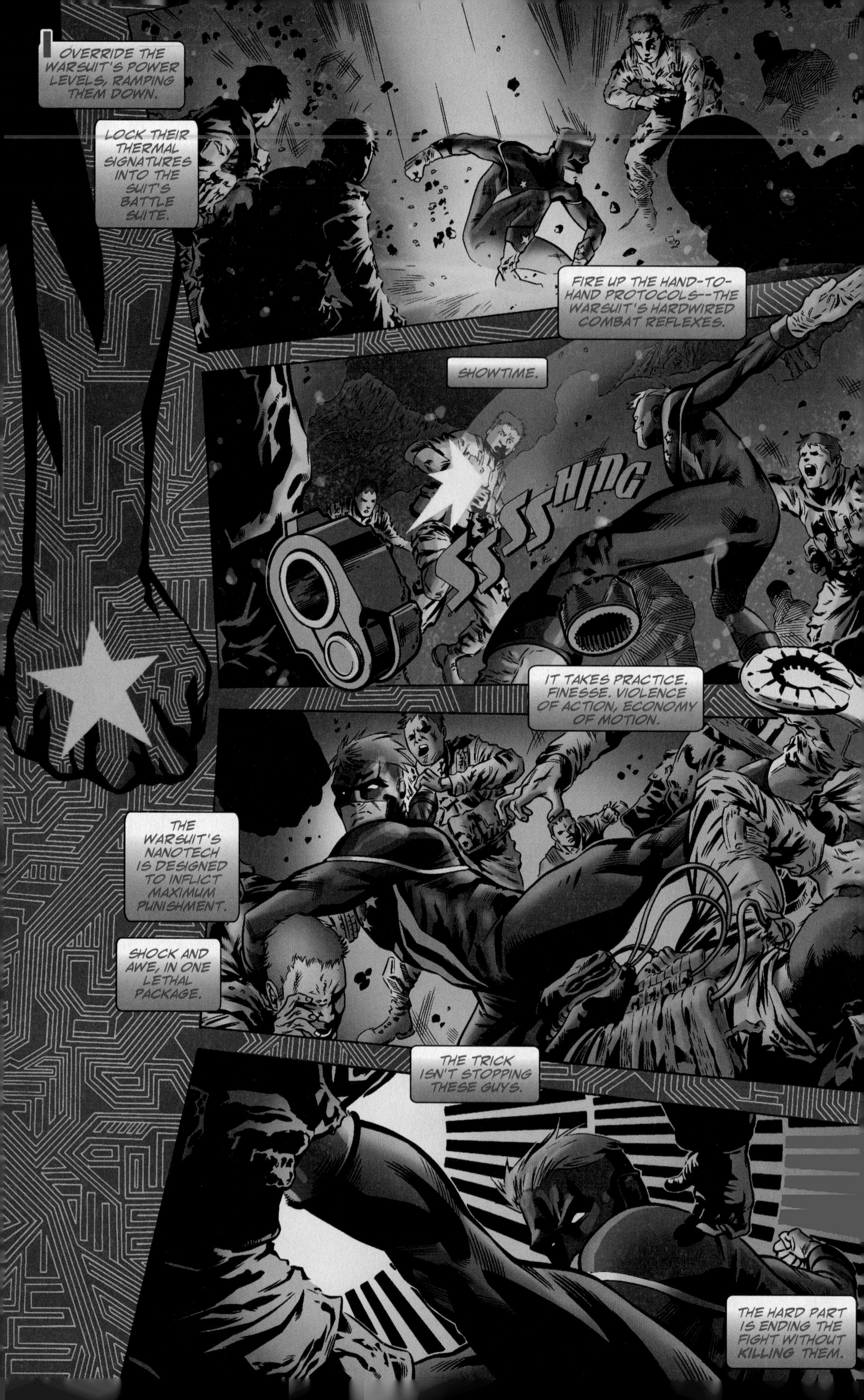
OVERRIDE THE WARSUIT'S POWER LEVELS, RAMPING THEM DOWN.
LOCK THEIR THERMAL SIGNATURES INTO THE SUIT'S BATTLE SUITE.
FIRE UP THE HAND-TO-HAND PROTOCOLS--THE WARSUIT'S HARDWIRED COMBAT REFLEXES.
SHOWTIME.
SSSHING
IT TAKES PRACTICE. FINESSE. VIOLENCE OF ACTION, ECONOMY OF MOTION.
THE WARSUIT'S NANOTECH IS DESIGNED TO INFLICT MAXIMUM PUNISHMENT.
SHOCK AND AWE, IN ONE LETHAL PACKAGE.
THE TRICK ISN'T STOPPING THESE GUYS.
THE HARD PART IS ENDING THE FIGHT WITHOUT KILLING THEM.

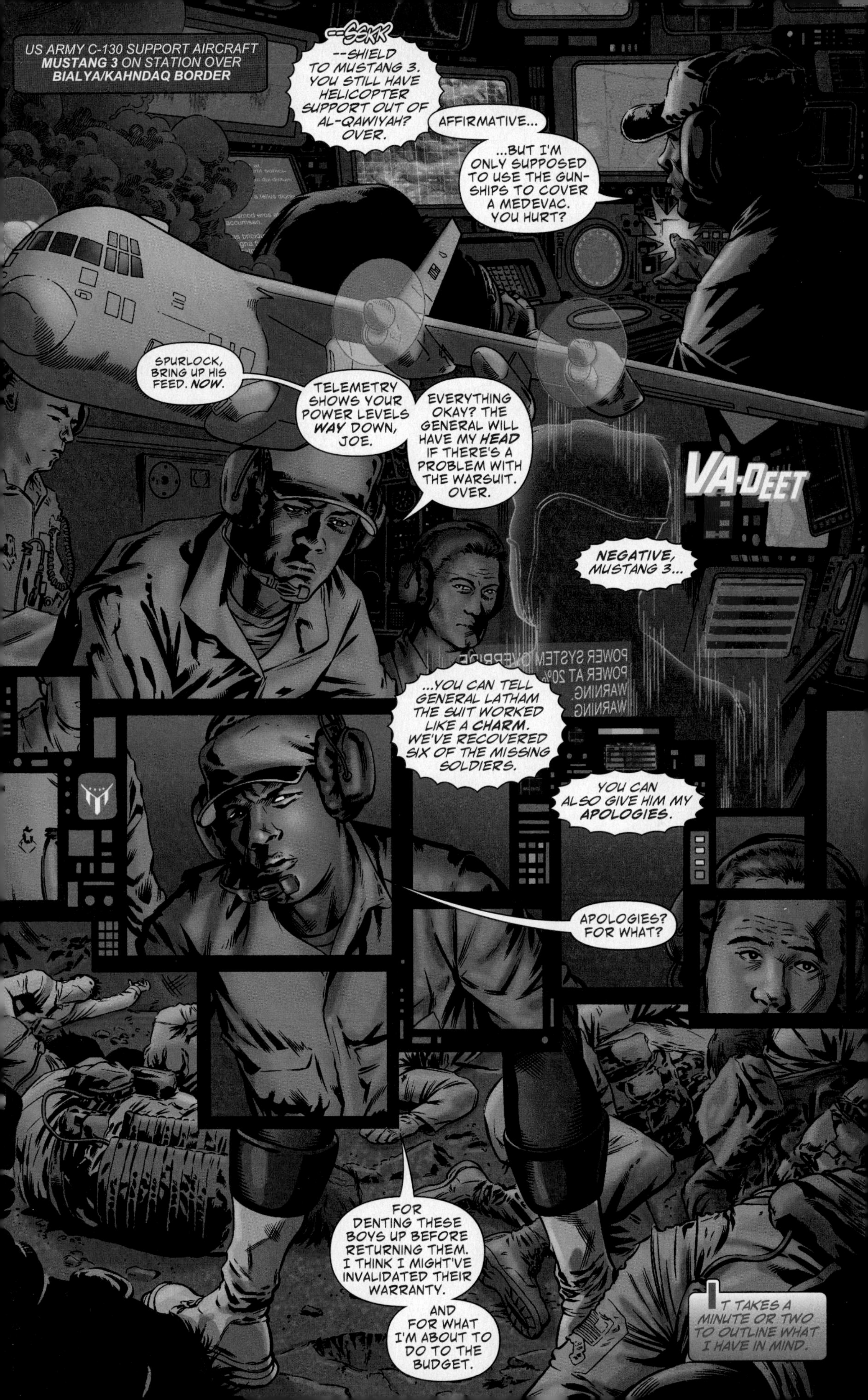
US ARMY C-130 SUPPORT AIRCRAFT
MUSTANG 3 ON STATION OVER
BIALYA/KAHNDAQ BORDER
--SSKK
--SHIELD TO MUSTANG 3. YOU STILL HAVE HELICOPTER SUPPORT OUT OF AL-QAWIYAH? OVER.
AFFIRMATIVE...
...BUT I'M ONLY SUPPOSED TO USE THE GUNSHIPS TO COVER A MEDEVAC. YOU HURT?
SPURLOCK, BRING UP HIS FEED. NOW.
TELEMETRY SHOWS YOUR POWER LEVELS WAY DOWN, JOE.
EVERYTHING OKAY? THE GENERAL WILL HAVE MY HEAD IF THERE'S A PROBLEM WITH THE WARSUIT. OVER.
VA-DEET
NEGATIVE, MUSTANG 3...
...YOU CAN TELL GENERAL LATHAM THE SUIT WORKED LIKE A CHARM. WE'VE RECOVERED SIX OF THE MISSING SOLDIERS.
YOU CAN ALSO GIVE HIM MY APOLOGIES.
APOLOGIES? FOR WHAT?
FOR DENTING THESE BOYS UP BEFORE RETURNING THEM. I THINK I MIGHT'VE INVALIDATED THEIR WARRANTY.
AND FOR WHAT I'M ABOUT TO DO TO THE BUDGET.
IT TAKES A MINUTE OR TWO TO OUTLINE WHAT I HAVE IN MIND.

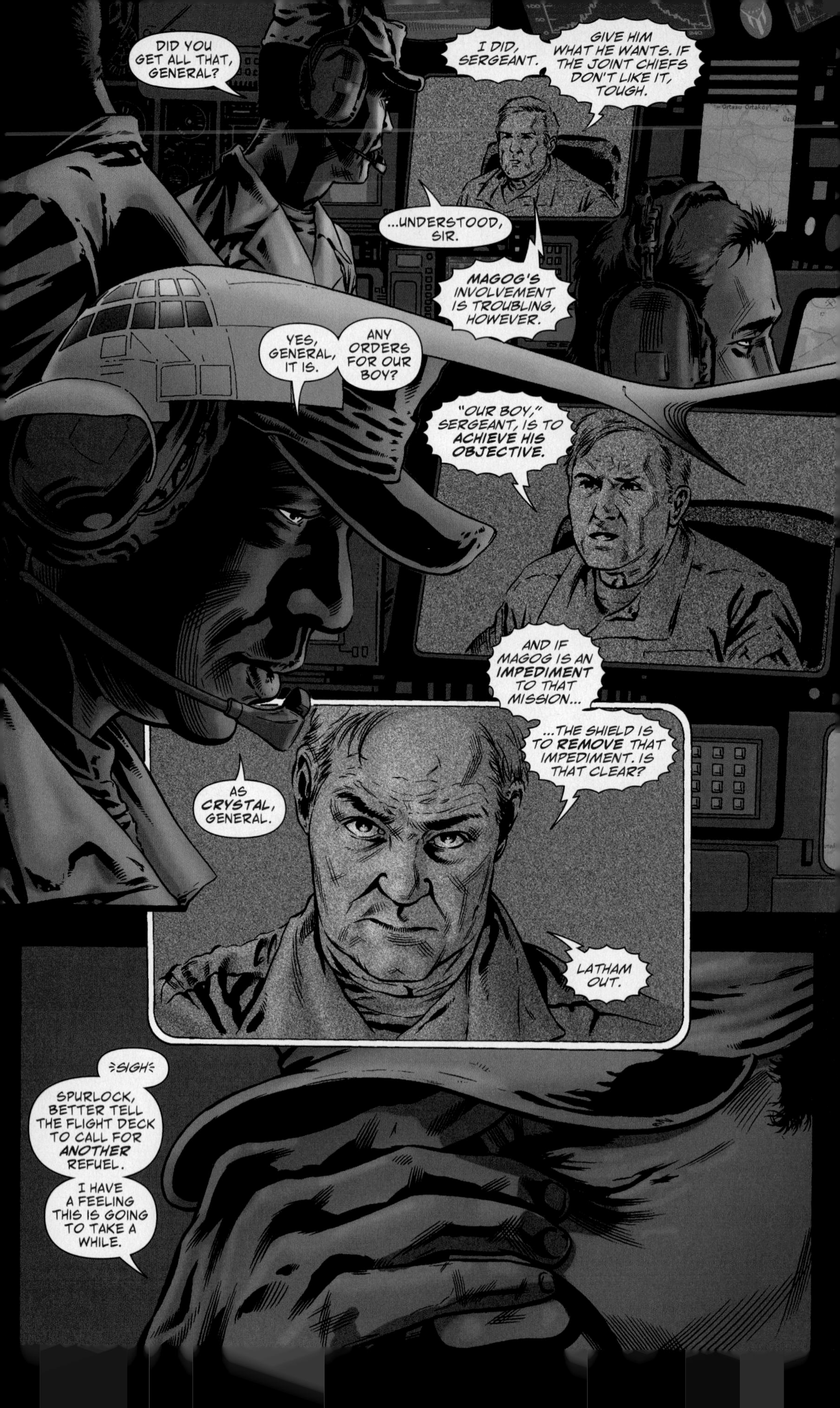
DID YOU GET ALL THAT, GENERAL?
I DID, SERGEANT.
GIVE HIM WHAT HE WANTS. IF THE JOINT CHIEFS DON'T LIKE IT, TOUGH.
...UNDERSTOOD, SIR.
MAGOG'S INVOLVEMENT IS TROUBLING, HOWEVER.
YES, GENERAL, IT IS.
ANY ORDERS FOR OUR BOY?
"OUR BOY," SERGEANT, IS TO ACHIEVE HIS OBJECTIVE.
AND IF MAGOG IS AN IMPEDIMENT TO THAT MISSION...
...THE SHIELD IS TO REMOVE THAT IMPEDIMENT. IS THAT CLEAR?
AS CRYSTAL, GENERAL.
LATHAM OUT.
SIGH
SPURLOCK, BETTER TELL THE FLIGHT DECK TO CALL FOR ANOTHER REFUEL.
I HAVE A FEELING THIS IS GOING TO TAKE A WHILE.

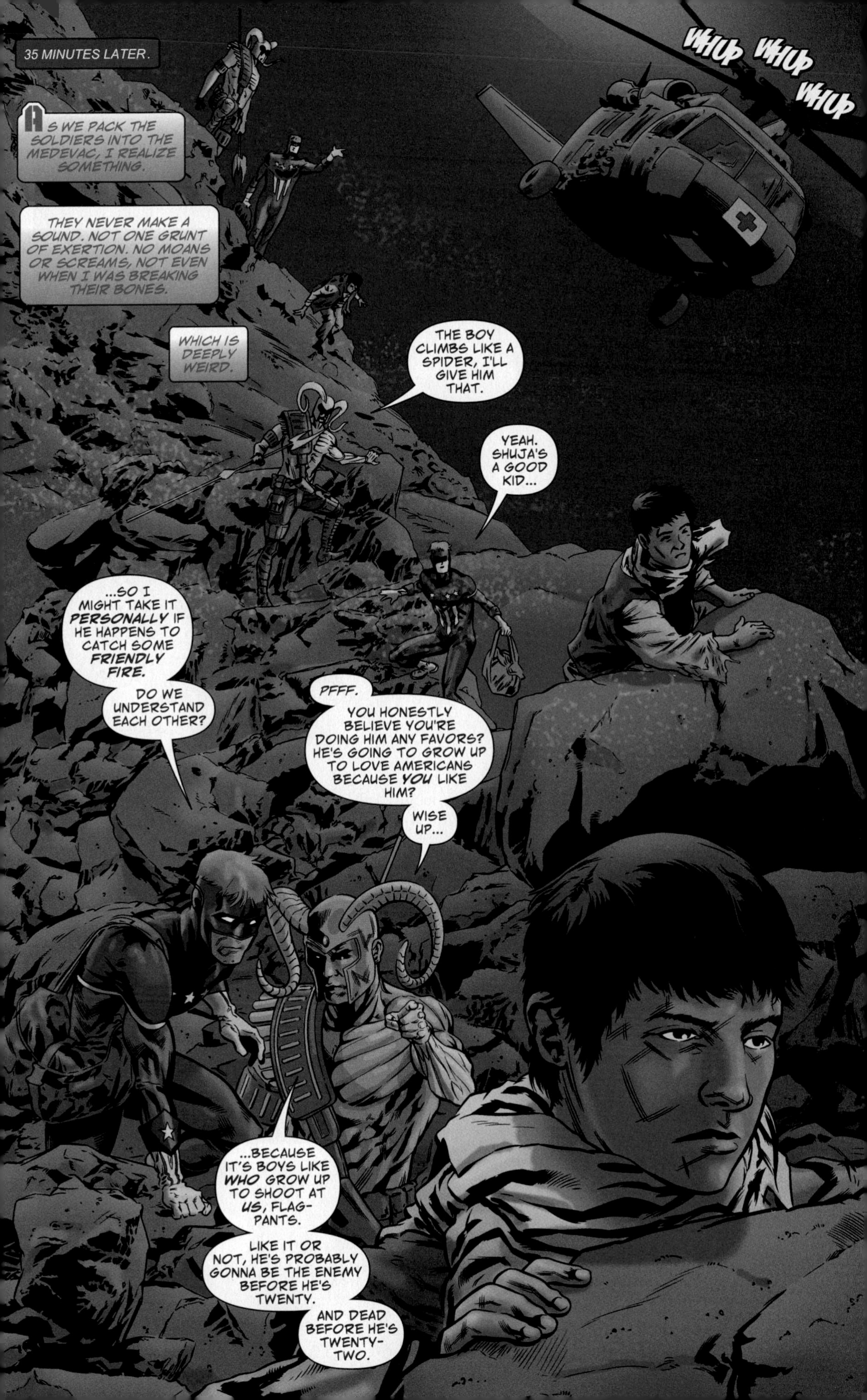
35 MINUTES LATER.
WHUP WHUP WHUP
AS WE PACK THE SOLDIERS INTO THE MEDEVAC, I REALIZE SOMETHING.
THEY NEVER MAKE A SOUND. NOT ONE GRUNT OF EXERTION. NO MOANS OR SCREAMS, NOT EVEN WHEN I WAS BREAKING THEIR BONES.
WHICH IS DEEPLY WEIRD.
THE BOY CLIMBS LIKE A SPIDER, I'LL GIVE HIM THAT.
YEAH. SHUJA'S A GOOD KID...
...SO I MIGHT TAKE IT PERSONALLY IF HE HAPPENS TO CATCH SOME FRIENDLY FIRE.
DO WE UNDERSTAND EACH OTHER?
PFFF.
YOU HONESTLY BELIEVE YOU'RE DOING HIM ANY FAVORS? HE'S GOING TO GROW UP TO LOVE AMERICANS BECAUSE YOU LIKE HIM?
WISE UP...
...BECAUSE IT'S BOYS LIKE WHO GROW UP TO SHOOT AT US, FLAG-PANTS.
LIKE IT OR NOT, HE'S PROBABLY GONNA BE THE ENEMY BEFORE HE'S TWENTY.
AND DEAD BEFORE HE'S TWENTY-TWO.

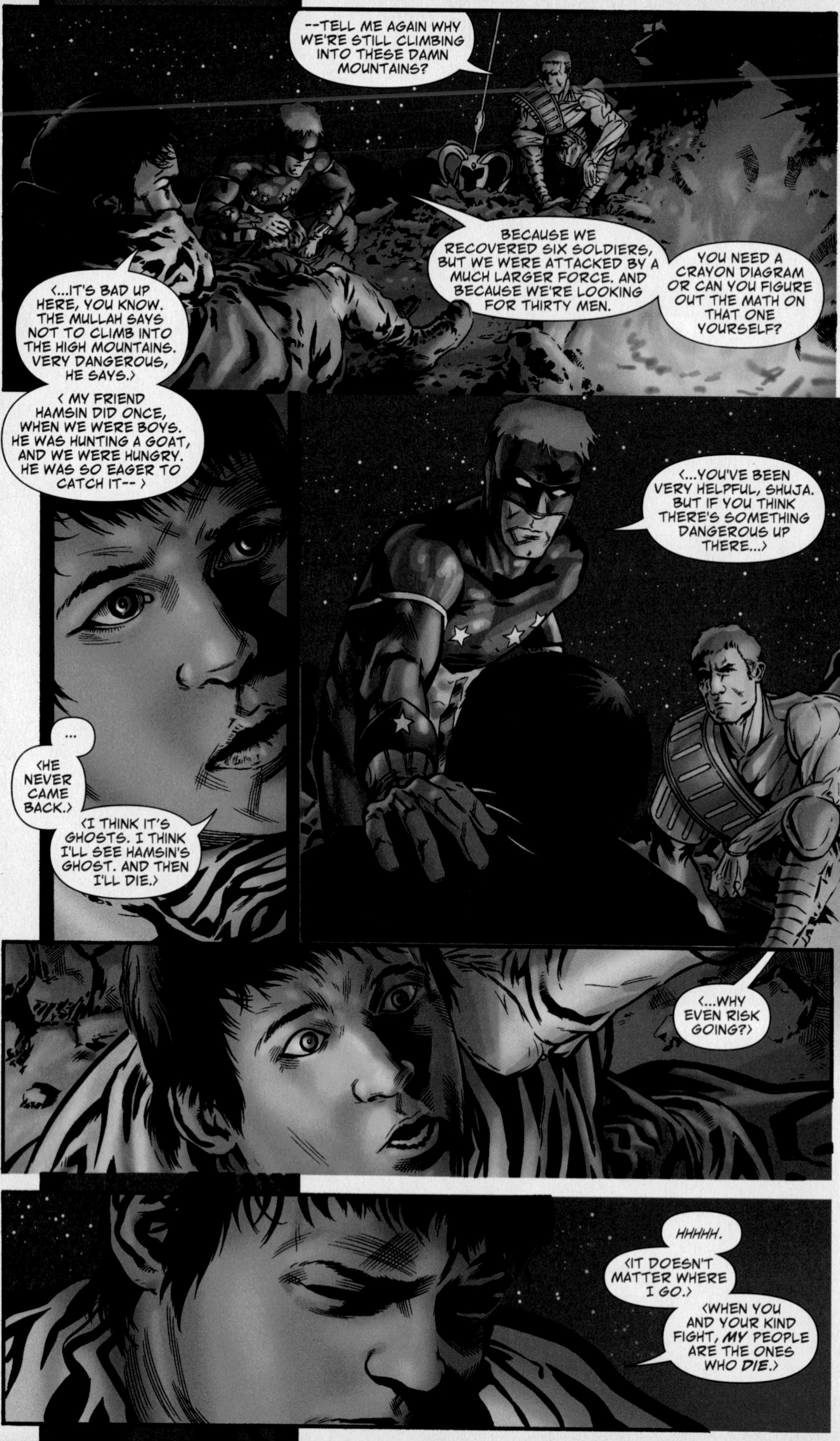
--TELL ME AGAIN WHY WE'RE STILL CLIMBING INTO THESE DAMN MOUNTAINS?
BECAUSE WE RECOVERED SIX SOLDIERS, BUT WE WERE ATTACKED BY A MUCH LARGER FORCE. AND BECAUSE WE'RE LOOKING FOR THIRTY MEN.
YOU NEED A CRAYON DIAGRAM OR CAN YOU FIGURE OUT THE MATH ON THAT ONE YOURSELF?
<...IT'S BAD UP HERE, YOU KNOW. THE MULLAH SAYS NOT TO CLIMB INTO THE HIGH MOUNTAINS. VERY DANGEROUS, HE SAYS.>
< MY FRIEND HAMSIN DID ONCE, WHEN WE WERE BOYS. HE WAS HUNTING A GOAT, AND WE WERE HUNGRY. HE WAS SO EAGER TO CATCH IT-- >
<...YOU'VE BEEN VERY HELPFUL, SHUJA. BUT IF YOU THINK THERE'S SOMETHING DANGEROUS UP THERE...>
...
<HE NEVER CAME BACK.>
<I THINK IT'S GHOSTS. I THINK I'LL SEE HAMSIN'S GHOST. AND THEN I'LL DIE.>
<...WHY EVEN RISK GOING?>
HHHHH.
<IT DOESN'T MATTER WHERE I GO.>
<WHEN YOU AND YOUR KIND FIGHT, *MY* PEOPLE ARE THE ONES WHO *DIE*.>

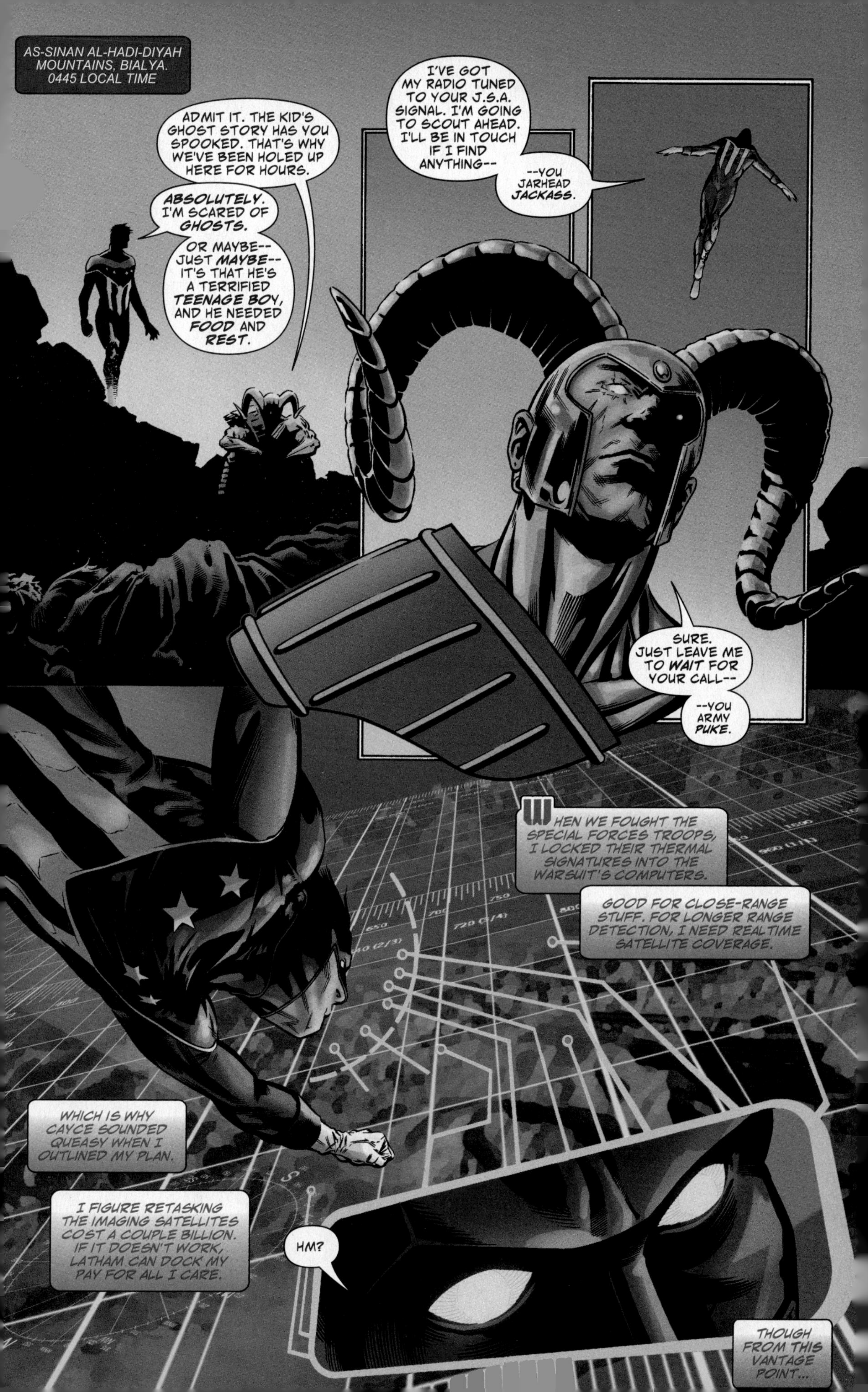
AS-SINAN AL-HADI-DIYAH MOUNTAINS, BIALYA. 0445 LOCAL TIME
ADMIT IT. THE KID'S GHOST STORY HAS YOU SPOOKED. THAT'S WHY WE'VE BEEN HOLED UP HERE FOR HOURS.
ABSOLUTELY. I'M SCARED OF GHOSTS.
OR MAYBE-- JUST MAYBE-- IT'S THAT HE'S A TERRIFIED TEENAGE BOY, AND HE NEEDED FOOD AND REST.
I'VE GOT MY RADIO TUNED TO YOUR J.S.A. SIGNAL. I'M GOING TO SCOUT AHEAD. I'LL BE IN TOUCH IF I FIND ANYTHING--
--YOU JARHEAD JACKASS.
SURE. JUST LEAVE ME TO WAIT FOR YOUR CALL--
--YOU ARMY PUKE.
WHEN WE FOUGHT THE SPECIAL FORCES TROOPS, I LOCKED THEIR THERMAL SIGNATURES INTO THE WARSUIT'S COMPUTERS.
GOOD FOR CLOSE-RANGE STUFF. FOR LONGER RANGE DETECTION, I NEED REALTIME SATELLITE COVERAGE.
WHICH IS WHY CAYCE SOUNDED QUEASY WHEN I OUTLINED MY PLAN.
I FIGURE RETASKING THE IMAGING SATELLITES COST A COUPLE BILLION. IF IT DOESN'T WORK, LATHAM CAN DOCK MY PAY FOR ALL I CARE.
HM?
THOUGH FROM THIS VANTAGE POINT...

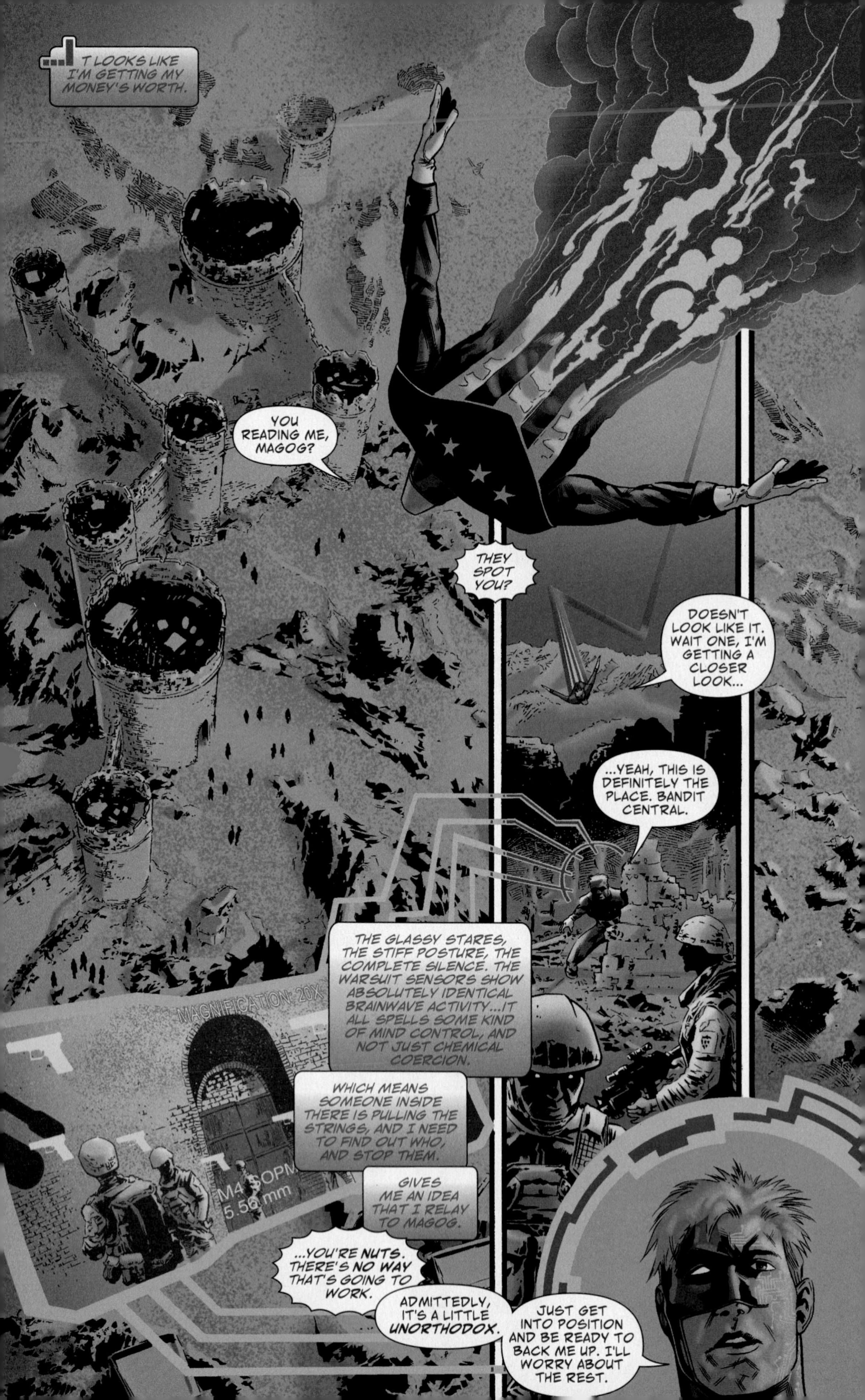
IT LOOKS LIKE I'M GETTING MY MONEY'S WORTH.
YOU READING ME, MAGOG?
THEY SPOT YOU?
DOESN'T LOOK LIKE IT. WAIT ONE, I'M GETTING A CLOSER LOOK...
...YEAH, THIS IS DEFINITELY THE PLACE. BANDIT CENTRAL.
MAGNIFICATION: 20X
THE GLASSY STARES, THE STIFF POSTURE, THE COMPLETE SILENCE. THE WARSUIT SENSORS SHOW ABSOLUTELY IDENTICAL BRAINWAVE ACTIVITY...IT ALL SPELLS SOME KIND OF MIND CONTROL, AND NOT JUST CHEMICAL COERCION.
WHICH MEANS SOMEONE INSIDE THERE IS PULLING THE STRINGS, AND I NEED TO FIND OUT WHO, AND STOP THEM.
GIVES ME AN IDEA THAT I RELAY TO MAGOG.
...YOU'RE NUTS. THERE'S NO WAY THAT'S GOING TO WORK.
ADMITTEDLY, IT'S A LITTLE UNORTHODOX.
JUST GET INTO POSITION AND BE READY TO BACK ME UP. I'LL WORRY ABOUT THE REST.

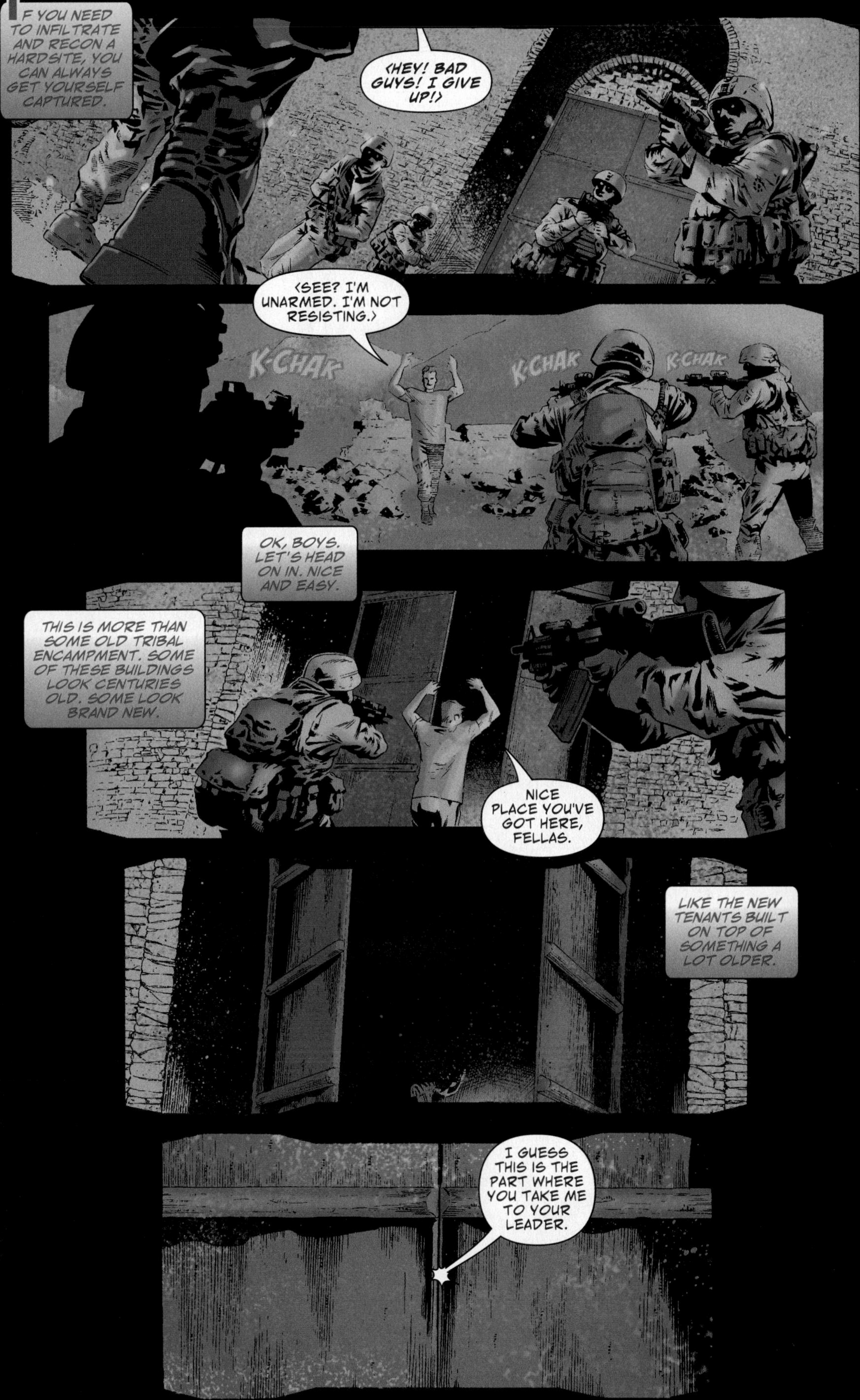
IF YOU NEED TO INFILTRATE AND RECON A HARDSITE, YOU CAN ALWAYS GET YOURSELF CAPTURED.
‹HEY! BAD GUYS! I GIVE UP!›
‹SEE? I'M UNARMED. I'M NOT RESISTING.›
K-CHAK
K-CHAK
K-CHAK
OK, BOYS. LET'S HEAD ON IN. NICE AND EASY.
THIS IS MORE THAN SOME OLD TRIBAL ENCAMPMENT. SOME OF THESE BUILDINGS LOOK CENTURIES OLD. SOME LOOK BRAND NEW.
NICE PLACE YOU'VE GOT HERE, FELLAS.
LIKE THE NEW TENANTS BUILT ON TOP OF SOMETHING A LOT OLDER.
I GUESS THIS IS THE PART WHERE YOU TAKE ME TO YOUR LEADER.

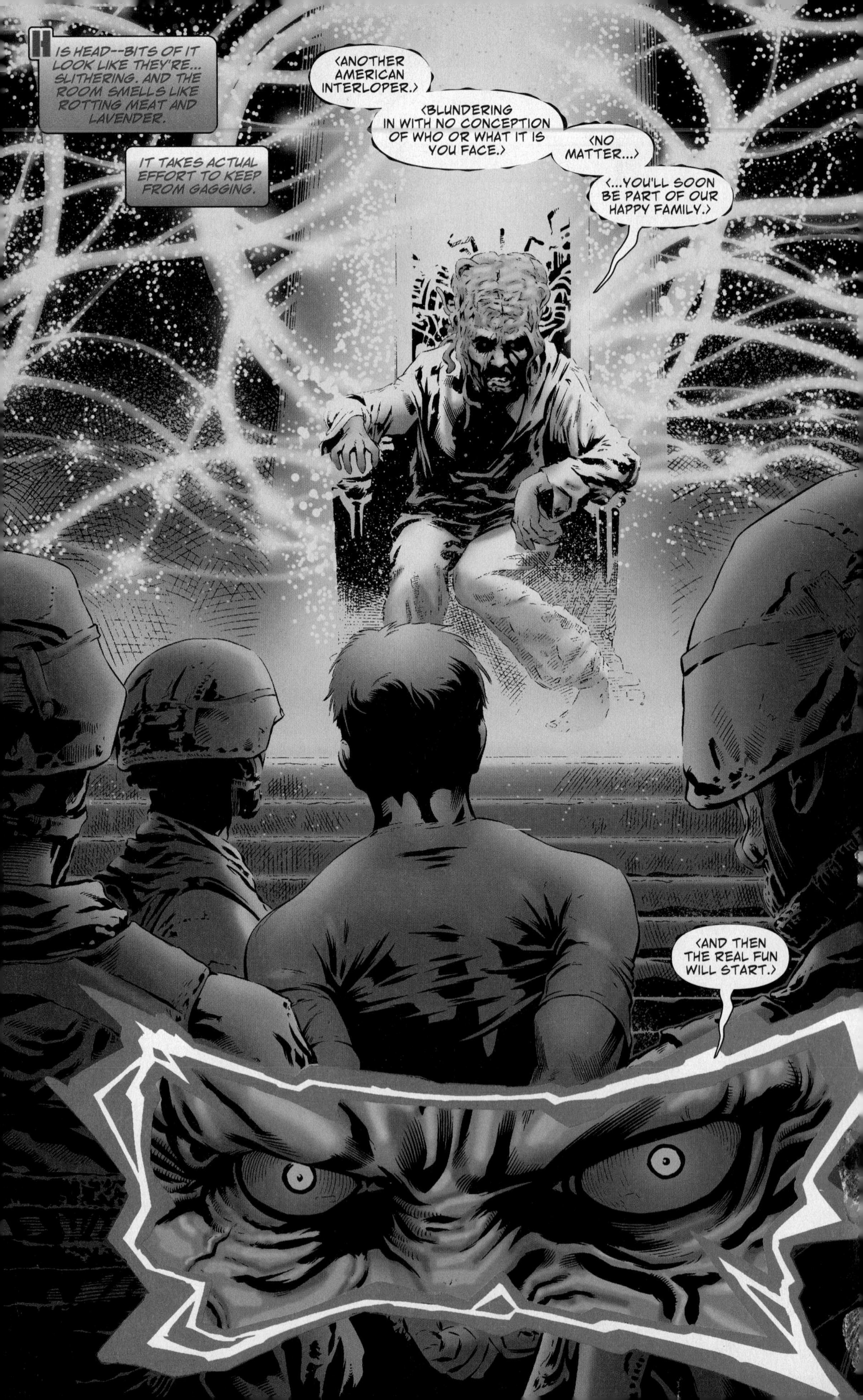
HIS HEAD--BITS OF IT LOOK LIKE THEY'RE... SLITHERING. AND THE ROOM SMELLS LIKE ROTTING MEAT AND LAVENDER.
IT TAKES ACTUAL EFFORT TO KEEP FROM GAGGING.
<ANOTHER AMERICAN INTERLOPER.>
<BLUNDERING IN WITH NO CONCEPTION OF WHO OR WHAT IT IS YOU FACE.>
<NO MATTER...>
<...YOU'LL SOON BE PART OF OUR HAPPY FAMILY.>
<AND THEN THE REAL FUN WILL START.>

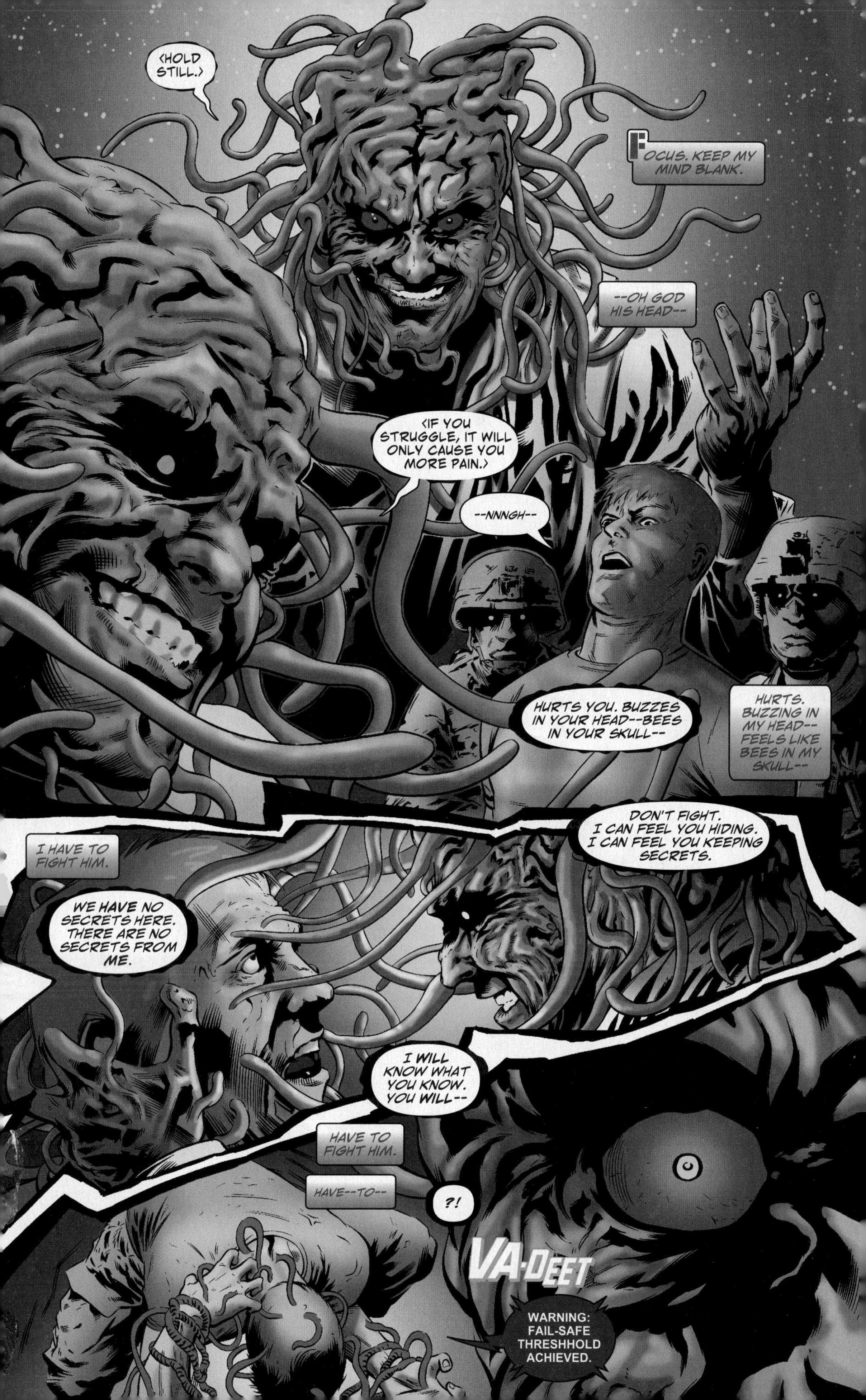
<HOLD STILL.>
FOCUS. KEEP MY MIND BLANK.
--OH GOD HIS HEAD--
<IF YOU STRUGGLE, IT WILL ONLY CAUSE YOU MORE PAIN.>
--NNNGH--
HURTS YOU. BUZZES IN YOUR HEAD--BEES IN YOUR SKULL--
HURTS. BUZZING IN MY HEAD--FEELS LIKE BEES IN MY SKULL--
I HAVE TO FIGHT HIM.
DON'T FIGHT. I CAN FEEL YOU HIDING. I CAN FEEL YOU KEEPING SECRETS.
WE HAVE NO SECRETS HERE. THERE ARE NO SECRETS FROM ME.
I WILL KNOW WHAT YOU KNOW. YOU WILL--
HAVE TO FIGHT HIM.
HAVE--TO--
?!
VA-DEET
WARNING: FAIL-SAFE THRESHHOLD ACHIEVED.

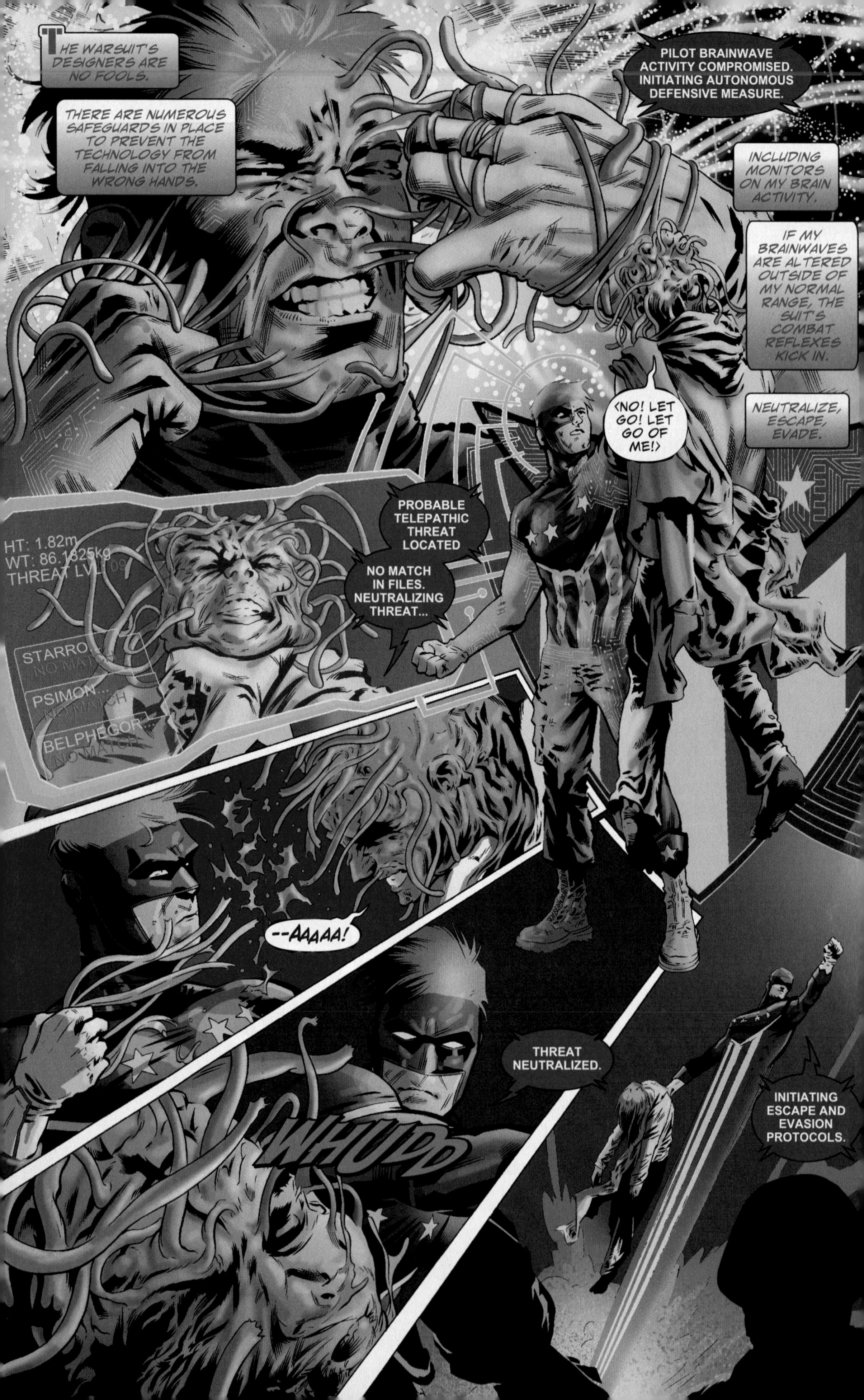
THE WARSUIT'S DESIGNERS ARE NO FOOLS.
THERE ARE NUMEROUS SAFEGUARDS IN PLACE TO PREVENT THE TECHNOLOGY FROM FALLING INTO THE WRONG HANDS.
PILOT BRAINWAVE ACTIVITY COMPROMISED. INITIATING AUTONOMOUS DEFENSIVE MEASURE.
INCLUDING MONITORS ON MY BRAIN ACTIVITY.
IF MY BRAINWAVES ARE ALTERED OUTSIDE OF MY NORMAL RANGE, THE SUIT'S COMBAT REFLEXES KICK IN.
<NO! LET GO! LET GO OF ME!>
NEUTRALIZE, ESCAPE, EVADE.
PROBABLE TELEPATHIC THREAT LOCATED
HT: 1.82m
WT: 86.1825kg
STARRO
PSIMON
BELPHEGOR
NO MATCH IN FILES. NEUTRALIZING THREAT...
--AAAAA!
THREAT NEUTRALIZED.
WHUDD
INITIATING ESCAPE AND EVASION PROTOCOLS.

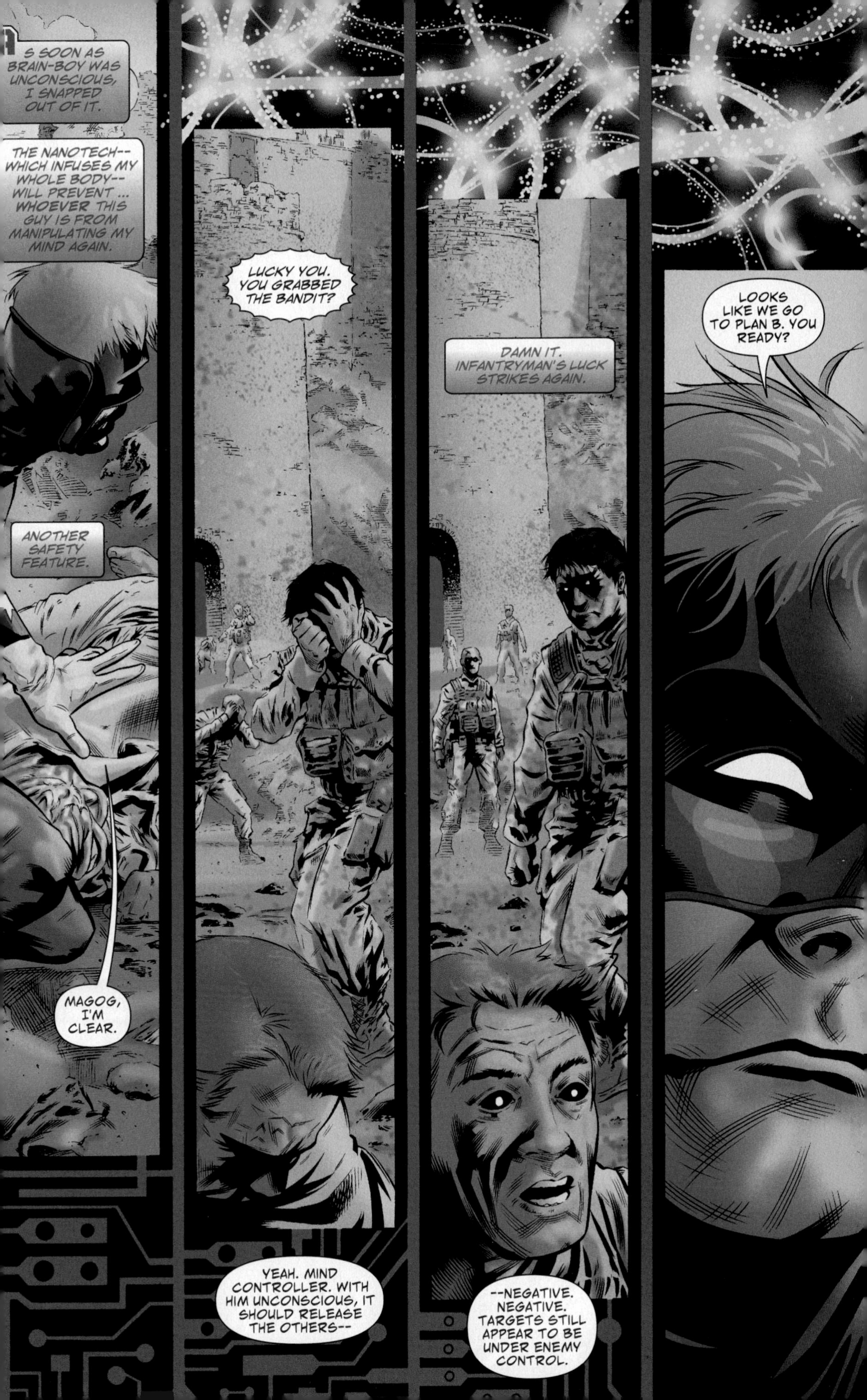
AS SOON AS BRAIN-BOY WAS UNCONSCIOUS, I SNAPPED OUT OF IT.
THE NANOTECH-- WHICH INFUSES MY WHOLE BODY-- WILL PREVENT ... WHOEVER THIS GUY IS FROM MANIPULATING MY MIND AGAIN.
ANOTHER SAFETY FEATURE.
MAGOG, I'M CLEAR.
LUCKY YOU. YOU GRABBED THE BANDIT?
YEAH. MIND CONTROLLER. WITH HIM UNCONSCIOUS, IT SHOULD RELEASE THE OTHERS--
DAMN IT. INFANTRYMAN'S LUCK STRIKES AGAIN.
--NEGATIVE. NEGATIVE. TARGETS STILL APPEAR TO BE UNDER ENEMY CONTROL.
LOOKS LIKE WE GO TO PLAN B. YOU READY?

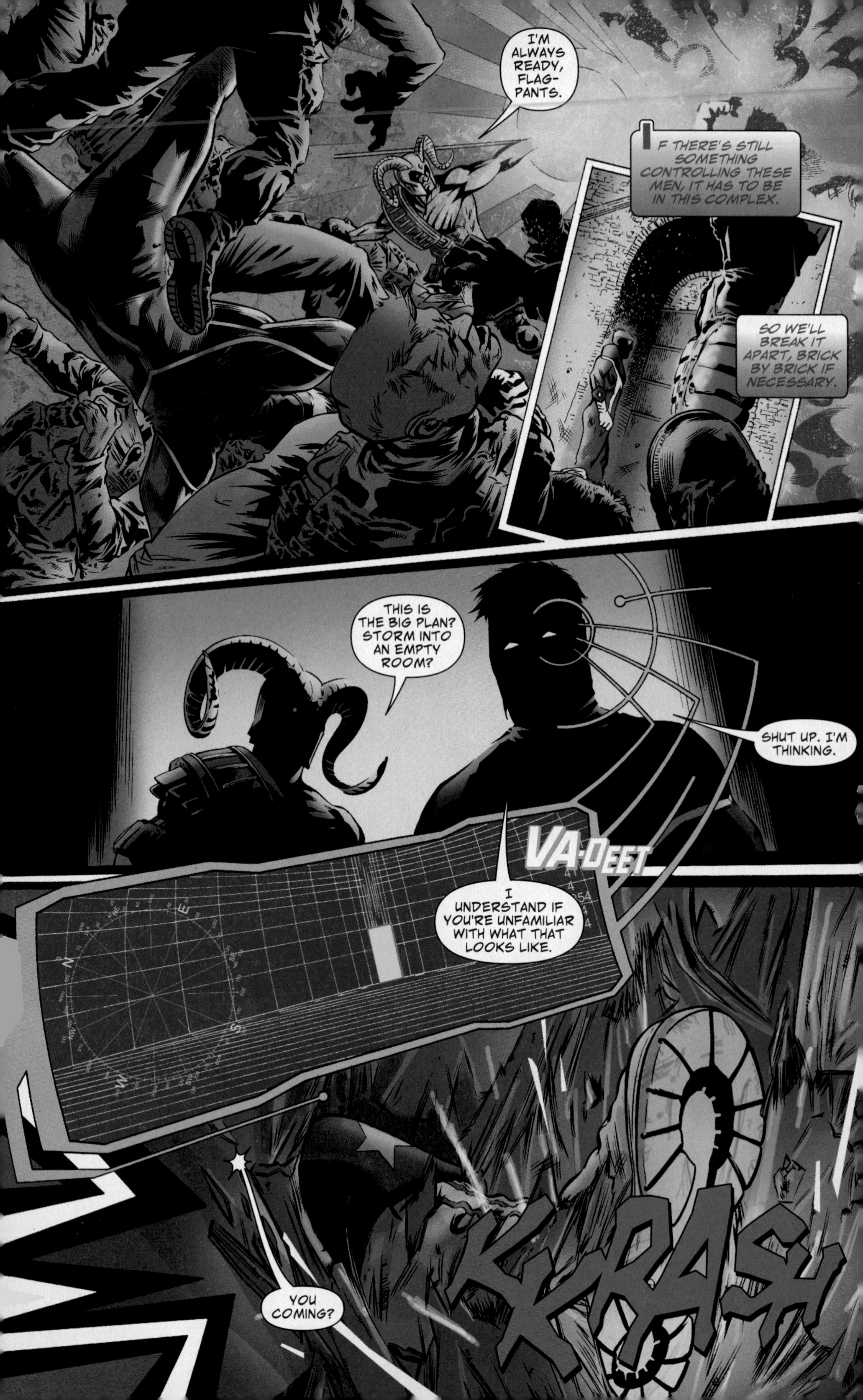
I'M ALWAYS READY, FLAG-PANTS.
IF THERE'S STILL SOMETHING CONTROLLING THESE MEN, IT HAS TO BE IN THIS COMPLEX.
SO WE'LL BREAK IT APART, BRICK BY BRICK IF NECESSARY.
THIS IS THE BIG PLAN? STORM INTO AN EMPTY ROOM?
SHUT UP. I'M THINKING.
VA-DEET
I UNDERSTAND IF YOU'RE UNFAMILIAR WITH WHAT THAT LOOKS LIKE.
YOU COMING?
KRASH

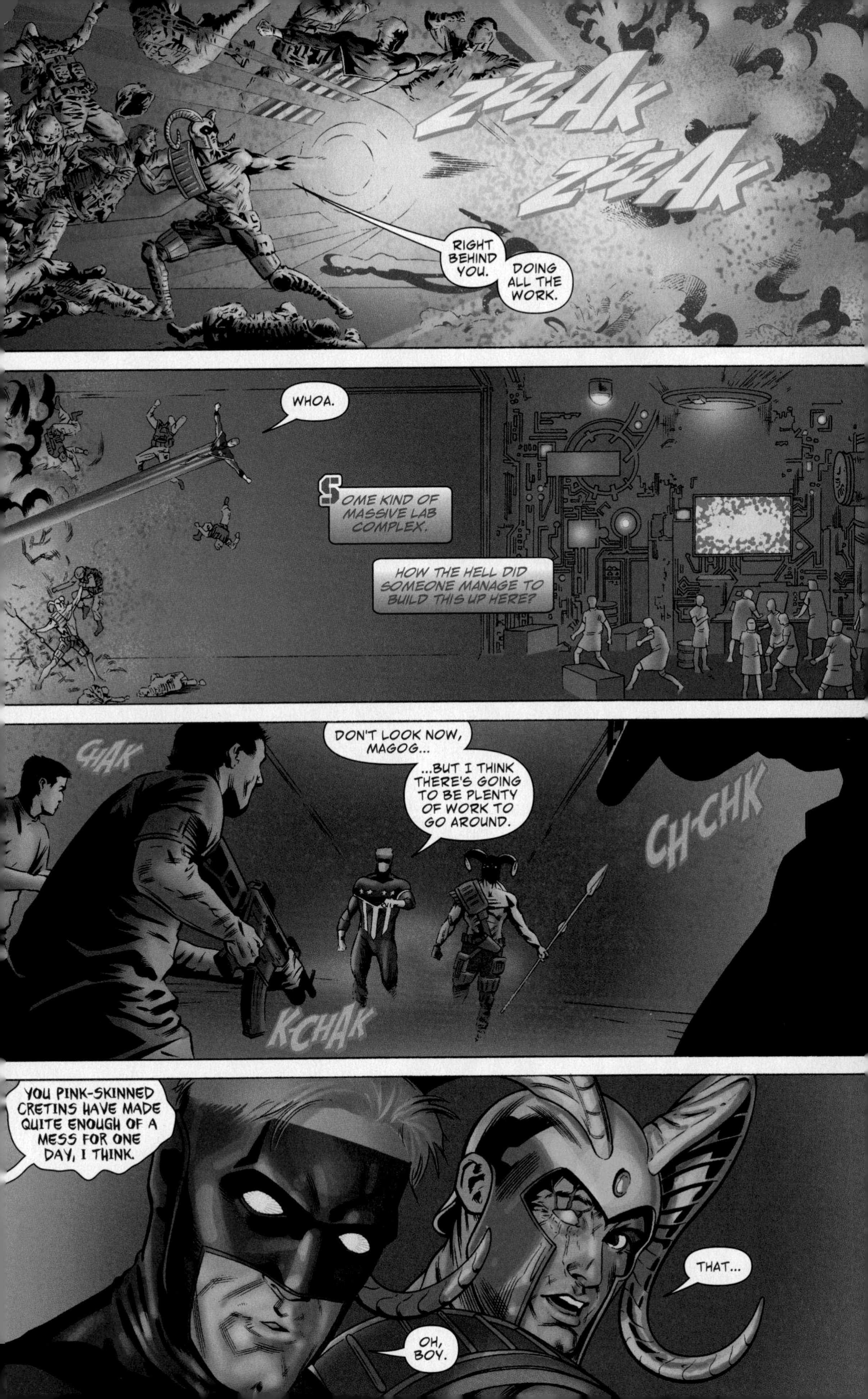
ZZZAK
ZZZAK
RIGHT BEHIND YOU.
DOING ALL THE WORK.
WHOA.
SOME KIND OF MASSIVE LAB COMPLEX.
HOW THE HELL DID SOMEONE MANAGE TO BUILD THIS UP HERE?
CHAK
DON'T LOOK NOW, MAGOG...
...BUT I THINK THERE'S GOING TO BE PLENTY OF WORK TO GO AROUND.
CH-CHK
K-CHAK
YOU PINK-SKINNED CRETINS HAVE MADE QUITE ENOUGH OF A MESS FOR ONE DAY, I THINK.
THAT...
OH, BOY.

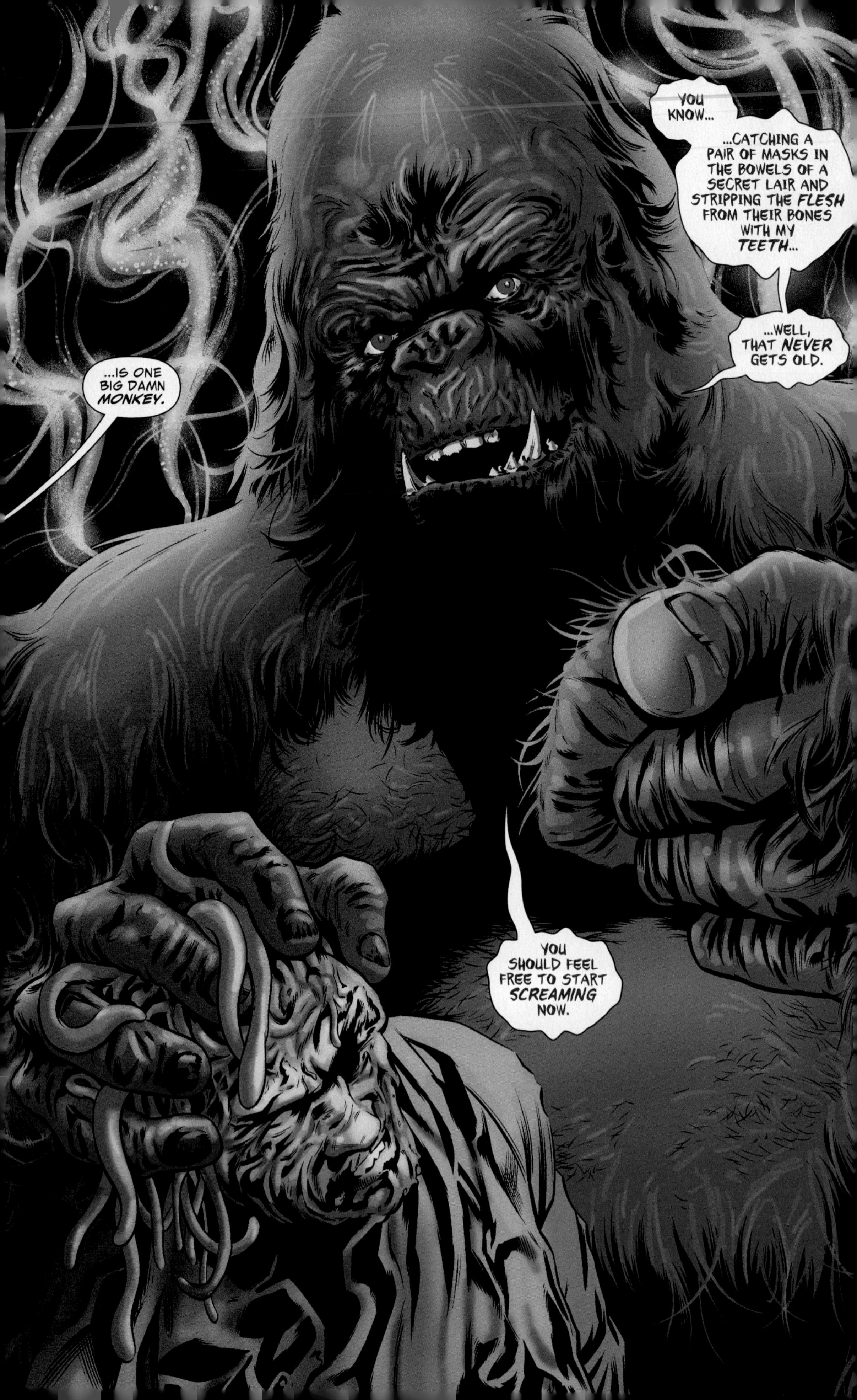
...IS ONE BIG DAMN MONKEY.
YOU KNOW...
...CATCHING A PAIR OF MASKS IN THE BOWELS OF A SECRET LAIR AND STRIPPING THE FLESH FROM THEIR BONES WITH MY TEETH...
...WELL, THAT NEVER GETS OLD.
YOU SHOULD FEEL FREE TO START SCREAMING NOW.

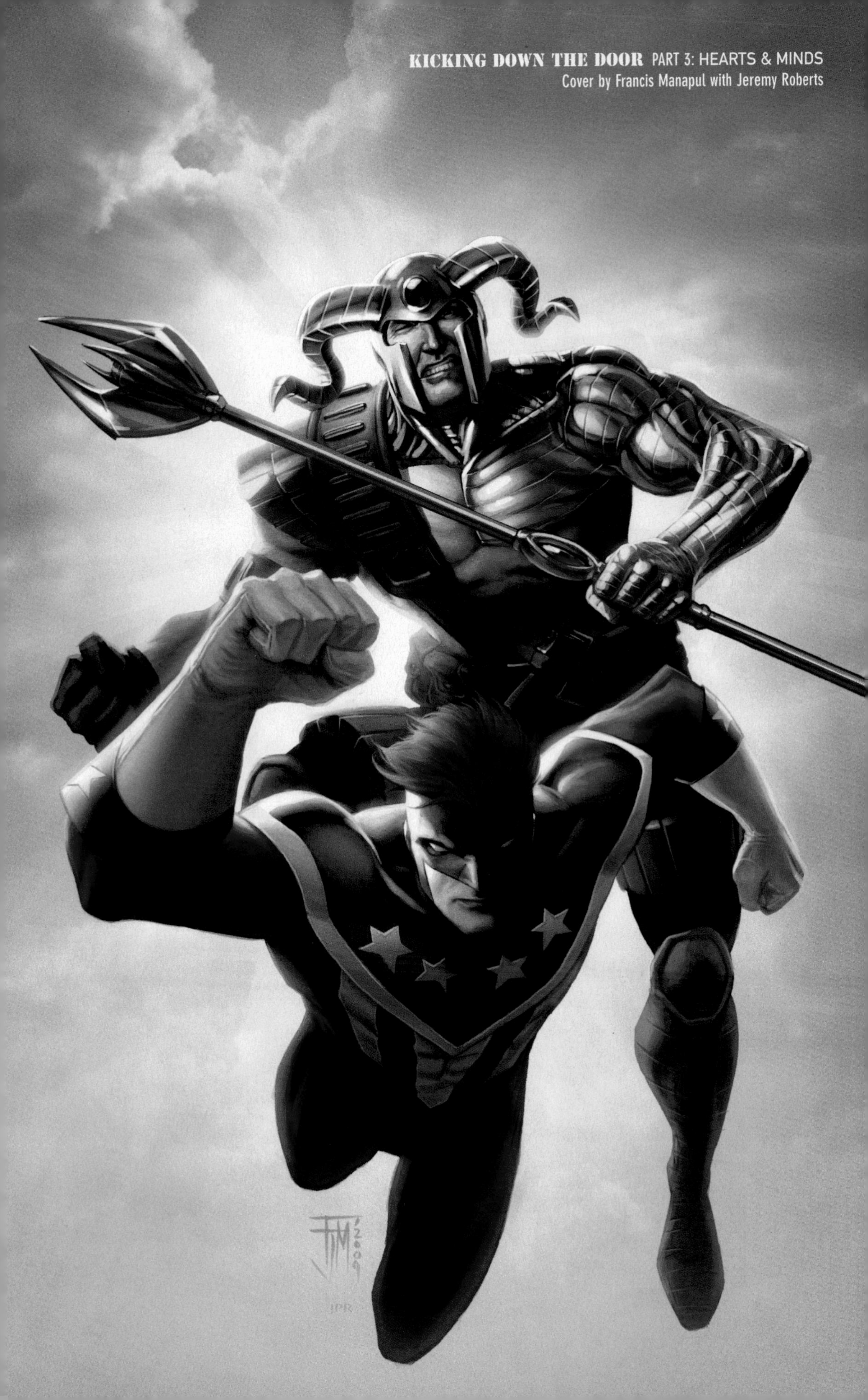

KICKING DOWN THE DOOR PART 3: HEARTS & MINDS
Cover by Francis Manapul with Jeremy Roberts

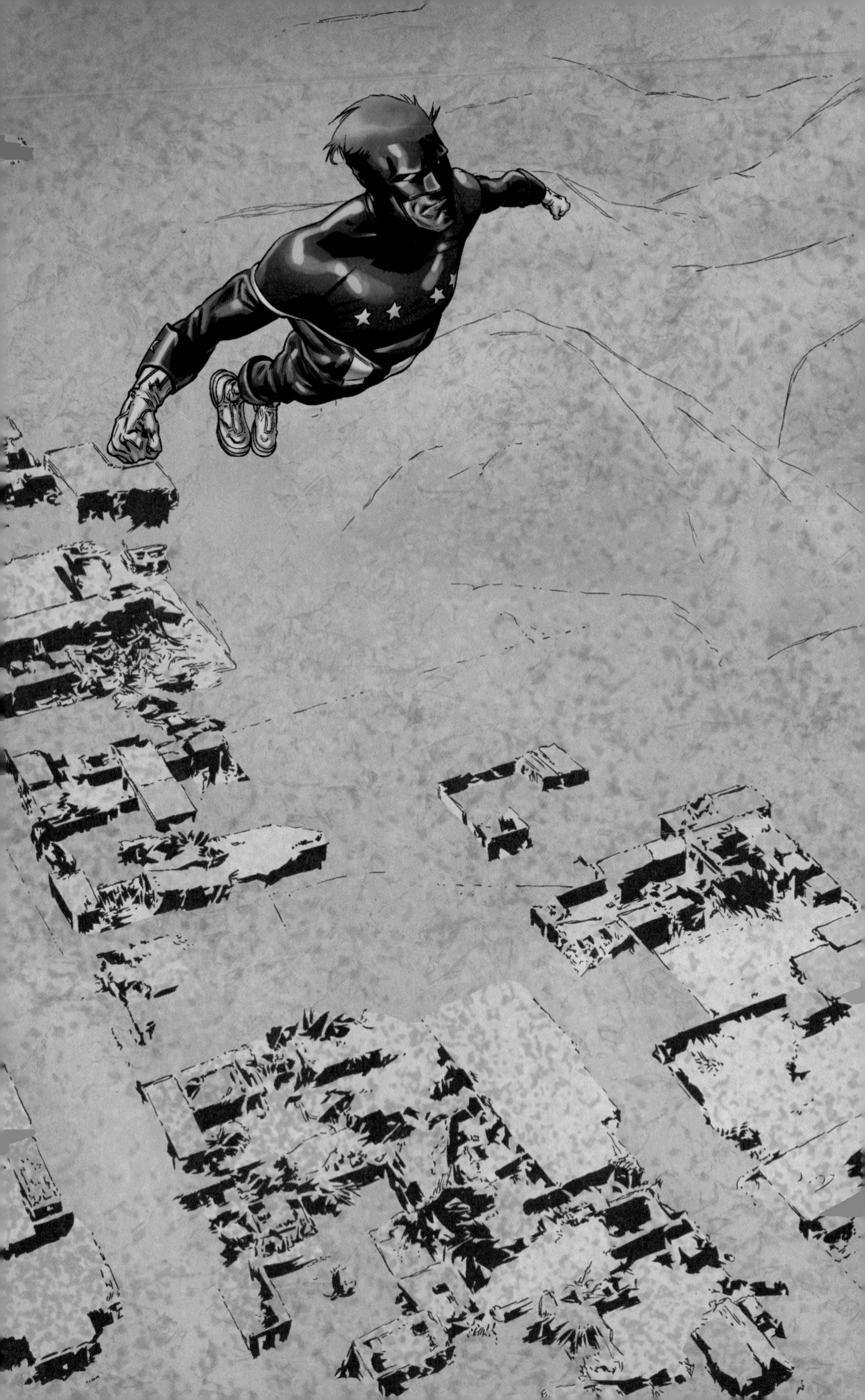

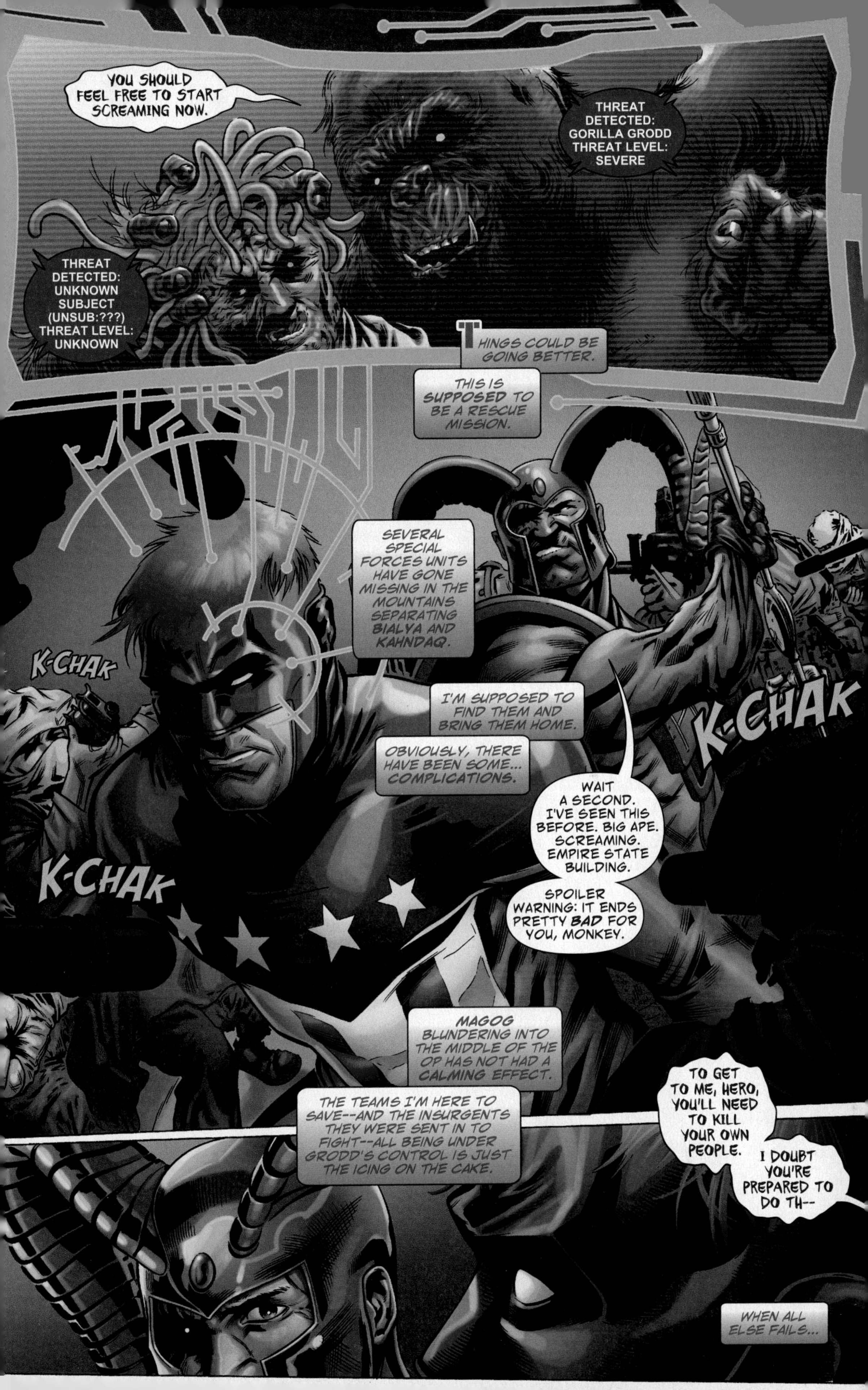
YOU SHOULD FEEL FREE TO START SCREAMING NOW.
THREAT DETECTED: GORILLA GRODD THREAT LEVEL: SEVERE
THREAT DETECTED: UNKNOWN SUBJECT (UNSUB:???) THREAT LEVEL: UNKNOWN
THINGS COULD BE GOING BETTER.
THIS IS SUPPOSED TO BE A RESCUE MISSION.
SEVERAL SPECIAL FORCES UNITS HAVE GONE MISSING IN THE MOUNTAINS SEPARATING BIALYA AND KAHNDAQ.
K-CHAK
I'M SUPPOSED TO FIND THEM AND BRING THEM HOME.
K-CHAK
OBVIOUSLY, THERE HAVE BEEN SOME... COMPLICATIONS.
WAIT A SECOND. I'VE SEEN THIS BEFORE. BIG APE. SCREAMING. EMPIRE STATE BUILDING.
SPOILER WARNING: IT ENDS PRETTY BAD FOR YOU, MONKEY.
K-CHAK
MAGOG BLUNDERING INTO THE MIDDLE OF THE OP HAS NOT HAD A CALMING EFFECT.
THE TEAMS I'M HERE TO SAVE--AND THE INSURGENTS THEY WERE SENT IN TO FIGHT--ALL BEING UNDER GRODD'S CONTROL IS JUST THE ICING ON THE CAKE.
TO GET TO ME, HERO, YOU'LL NEED TO KILL YOUR OWN PEOPLE.
I DOUBT YOU'RE PREPARED TO DO TH--
WHEN ALL ELSE FAILS...

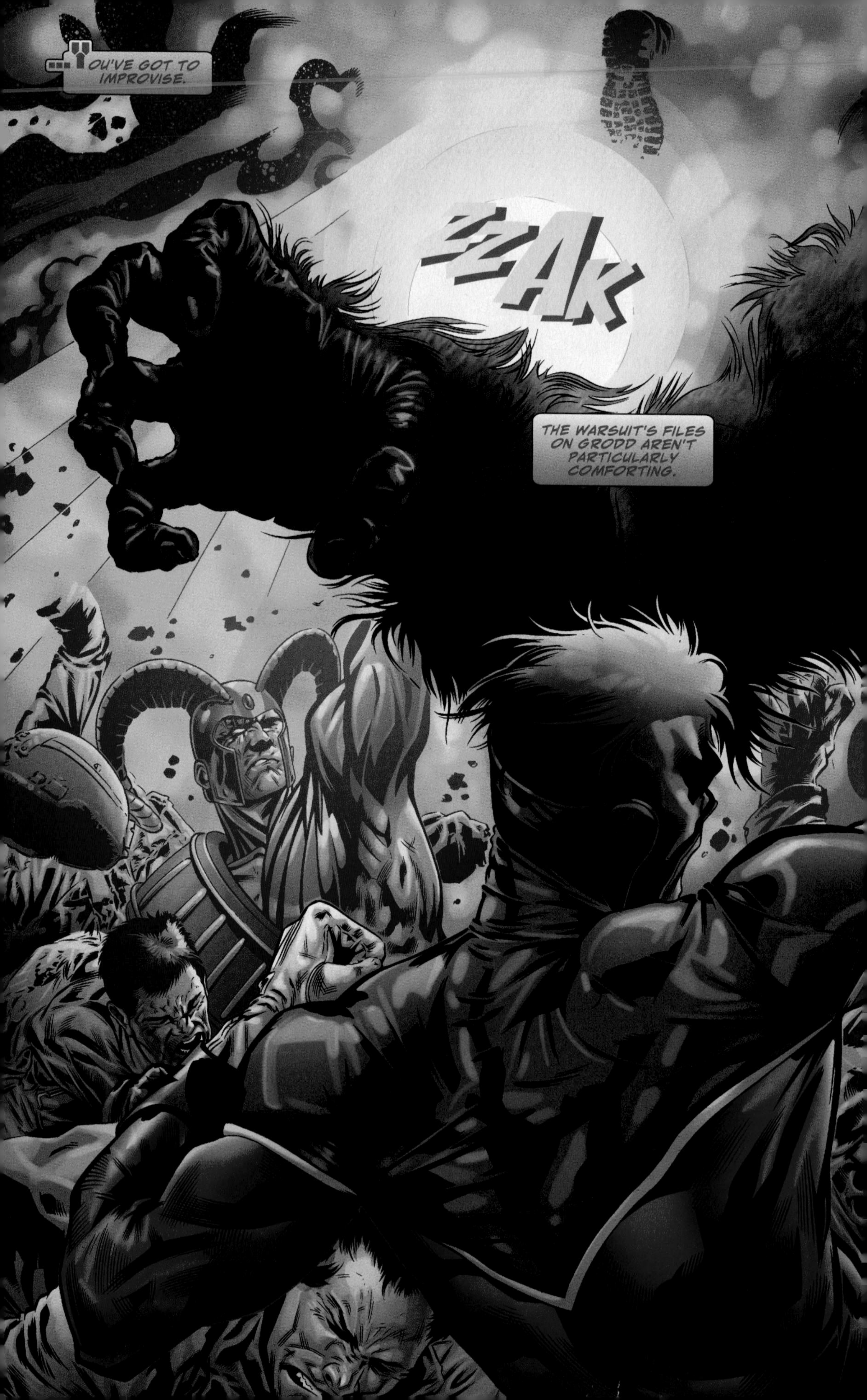
YOU'VE GOT TO
IMPROVISE.
ZZZAK
THE WARSUIT'S FILES
ON GRODD AREN'T
PARTICULARLY
COMFORTING.

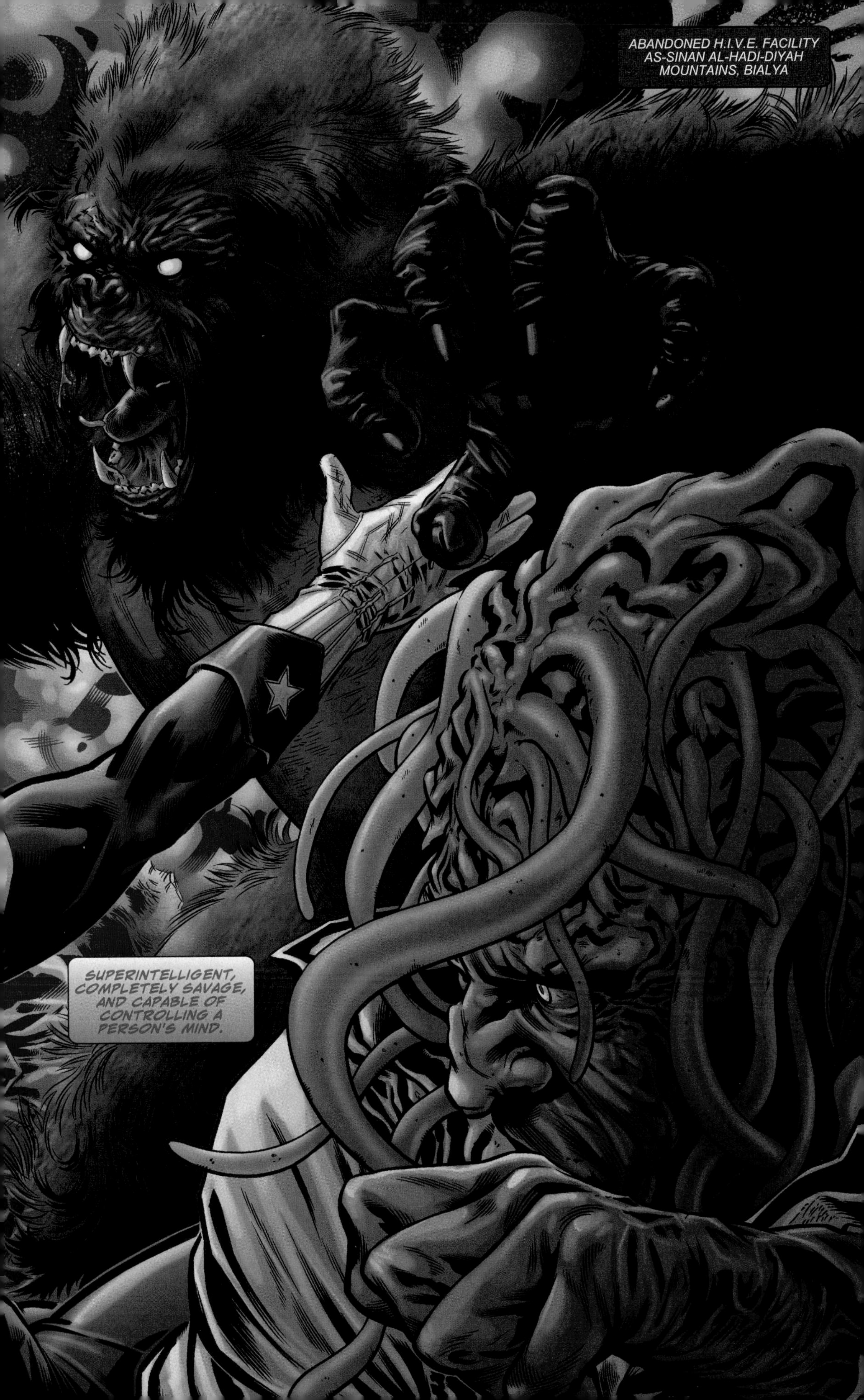
ABANDONED H.I.V.E. FACILITY AS-SINAN AL-HADI-DIYAH MOUNTAINS, BIALYA
SUPERINTELLIGENT, COMPLETELY SAVAGE, AND CAPABLE OF CONTROLLING A PERSON'S MIND.

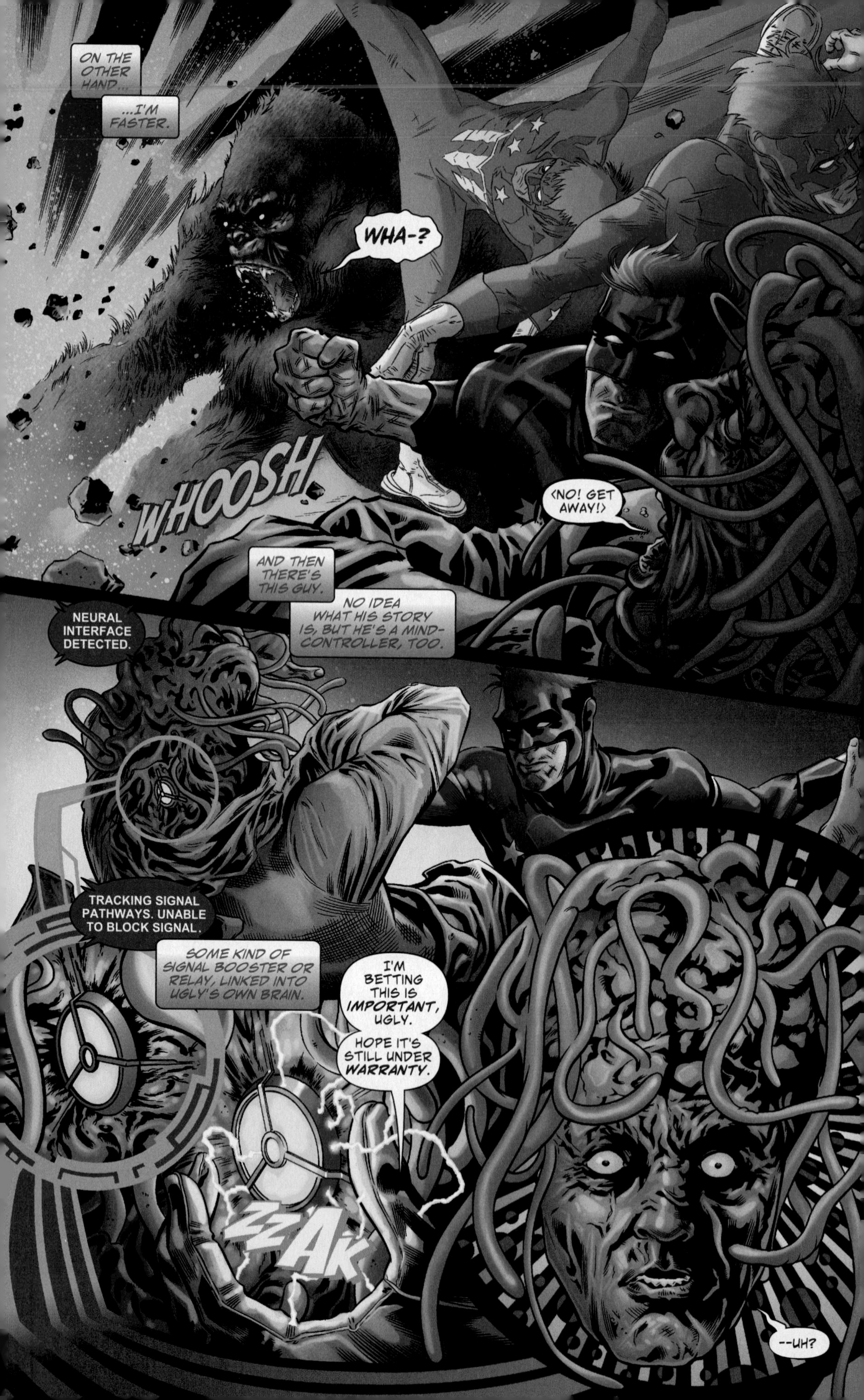
ON THE OTHER HAND...
...I'M FASTER.
WHA-?
WHOOSH
<NO! GET AWAY!>
AND THEN THERE'S THIS GUY.
NO IDEA WHAT HIS STORY IS, BUT HE'S A MIND-CONTROLLER, TOO.
NEURAL INTERFACE DETECTED.
TRACKING SIGNAL PATHWAYS. UNABLE TO BLOCK SIGNAL.
SOME KIND OF SIGNAL BOOSTER OR RELAY, LINKED INTO UGLY'S OWN BRAIN.
I'M BETTING THIS IS IMPORTANT, UGLY.
HOPE IT'S STILL UNDER WARRANTY.
ZZAK
--UH?

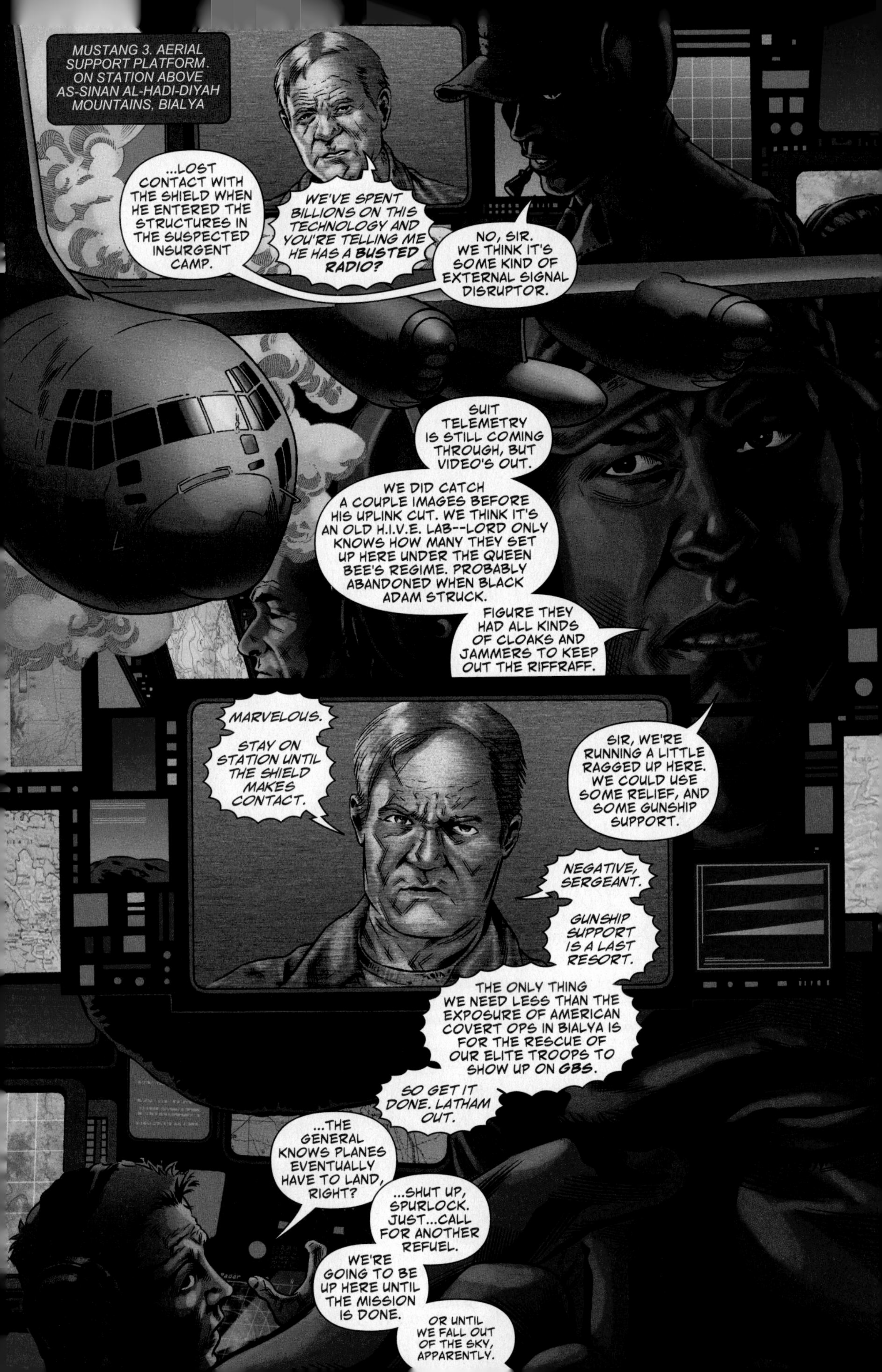
MUSTANG 3. AERIAL SUPPORT PLATFORM. ON STATION ABOVE AS-SINAN AL-HADI-DIYAH MOUNTAINS, BIALYA
...LOST CONTACT WITH THE SHIELD WHEN HE ENTERED THE STRUCTURES IN THE SUSPECTED INSURGENT CAMP.
WE'VE SPENT BILLIONS ON THIS TECHNOLOGY AND YOU'RE TELLING ME HE HAS A BUSTED RADIO?
NO, SIR. WE THINK IT'S SOME KIND OF EXTERNAL SIGNAL DISRUPTOR.
SUIT TELEMETRY IS STILL COMING THROUGH, BUT VIDEO'S OUT.
WE DID CATCH A COUPLE IMAGES BEFORE HIS UPLINK CUT. WE THINK IT'S AN OLD H.I.V.E. LAB--LORD ONLY KNOWS HOW MANY THEY SET UP HERE UNDER THE QUEEN BEE'S REGIME. PROBABLY ABANDONED WHEN BLACK ADAM STRUCK.
FIGURE THEY HAD ALL KINDS OF CLOAKS AND JAMMERS TO KEEP OUT THE RIFFRAFF.
MARVELOUS.
STAY ON STATION UNTIL THE SHIELD MAKES CONTACT.
SIR, WE'RE RUNNING A LITTLE RAGGED UP HERE. WE COULD USE SOME RELIEF, AND SOME GUNSHIP SUPPORT.
NEGATIVE, SERGEANT.
GUNSHIP SUPPORT IS A LAST RESORT.
THE ONLY THING WE NEED LESS THAN THE EXPOSURE OF AMERICAN COVERT OPS IN BIALYA IS FOR THE RESCUE OF OUR ELITE TROOPS TO SHOW UP ON GBS.
SO GET IT DONE. LATHAM OUT.
...THE GENERAL KNOWS PLANES EVENTUALLY HAVE TO LAND, RIGHT?
...SHUT UP, SPURLOCK. JUST...CALL FOR ANOTHER REFUEL.
WE'RE GOING TO BE UP HERE UNTIL THE MISSION IS DONE.
OR UNTIL WE FALL OUT OF THE SKY, APPARENTLY.

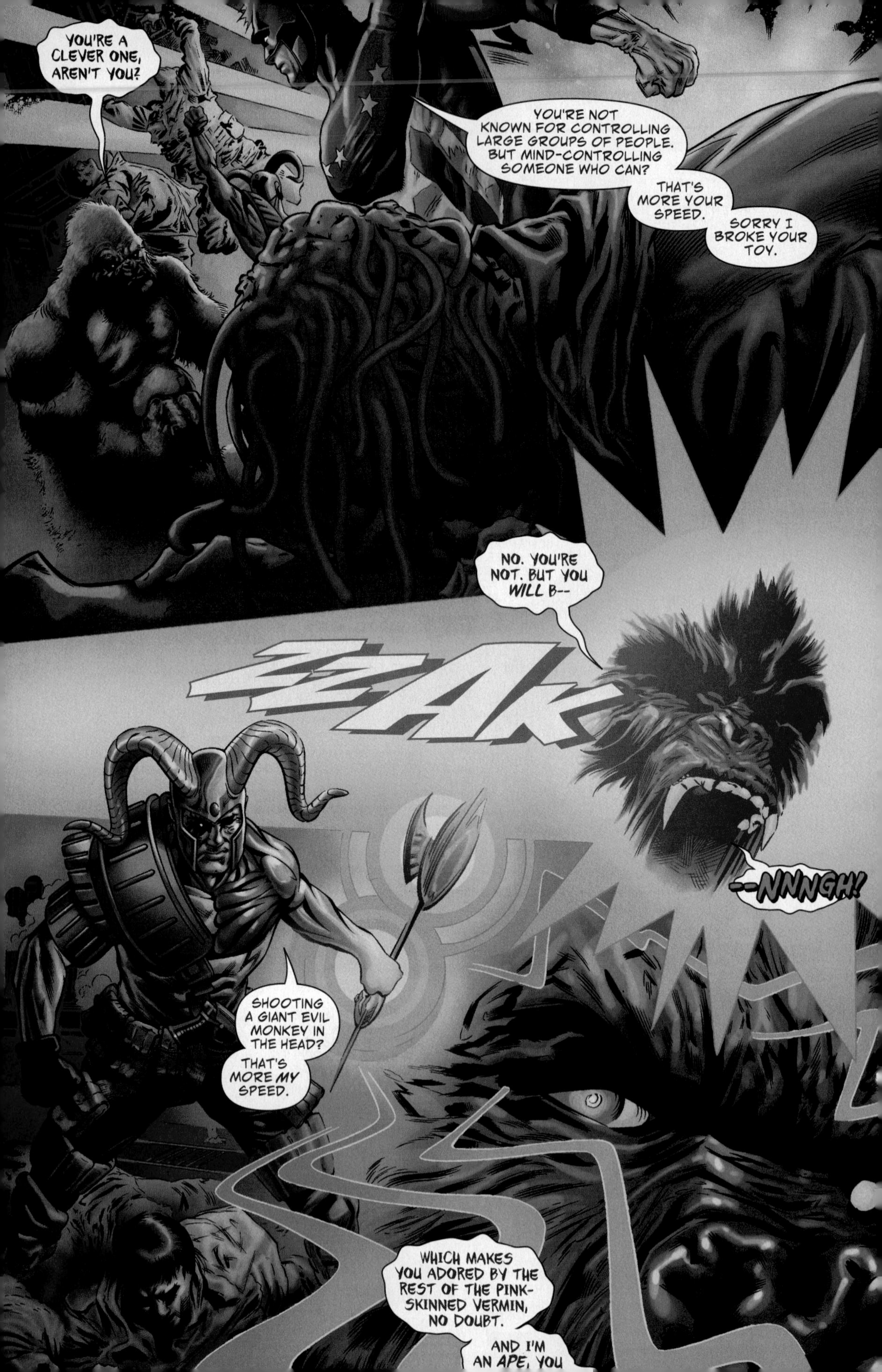
YOU'RE A CLEVER ONE, AREN'T YOU?
YOU'RE NOT KNOWN FOR CONTROLLING LARGE GROUPS OF PEOPLE. BUT MIND-CONTROLLING SOMEONE WHO CAN?
THAT'S MORE YOUR SPEED.
SORRY I BROKE YOUR TOY.
NO. YOU'RE NOT. BUT YOU WILL B--
ZZAK
--NNNGH!
SHOOTING A GIANT EVIL MONKEY IN THE HEAD?
THAT'S MORE MY SPEED.
WHICH MAKES YOU ADORED BY THE REST OF THE PINK-SKINNED VERMIN, NO DOUBT.
AND I'M AN APE, YOU

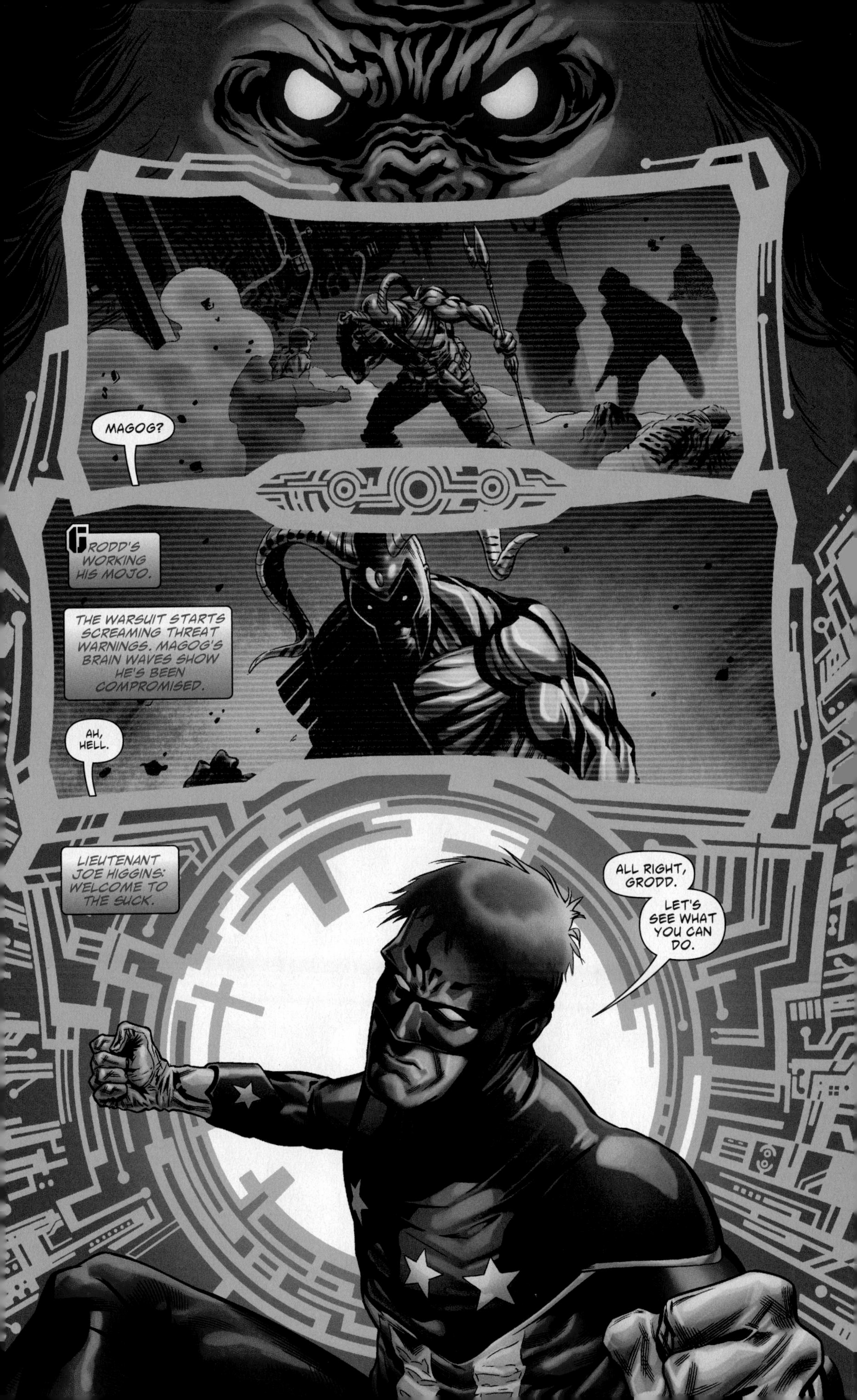
MAGOG?
GRODD'S WORKING HIS MOJO.
THE WARSUIT STARTS SCREAMING THREAT WARNINGS. MAGOG'S BRAIN WAVES SHOW HE'S BEEN COMPROMISED.
AH, HELL.
LIEUTENANT JOE HIGGINS: WELCOME TO THE SUCK.
ALL RIGHT, GRODD.
LET'S SEE WHAT YOU CAN DO.

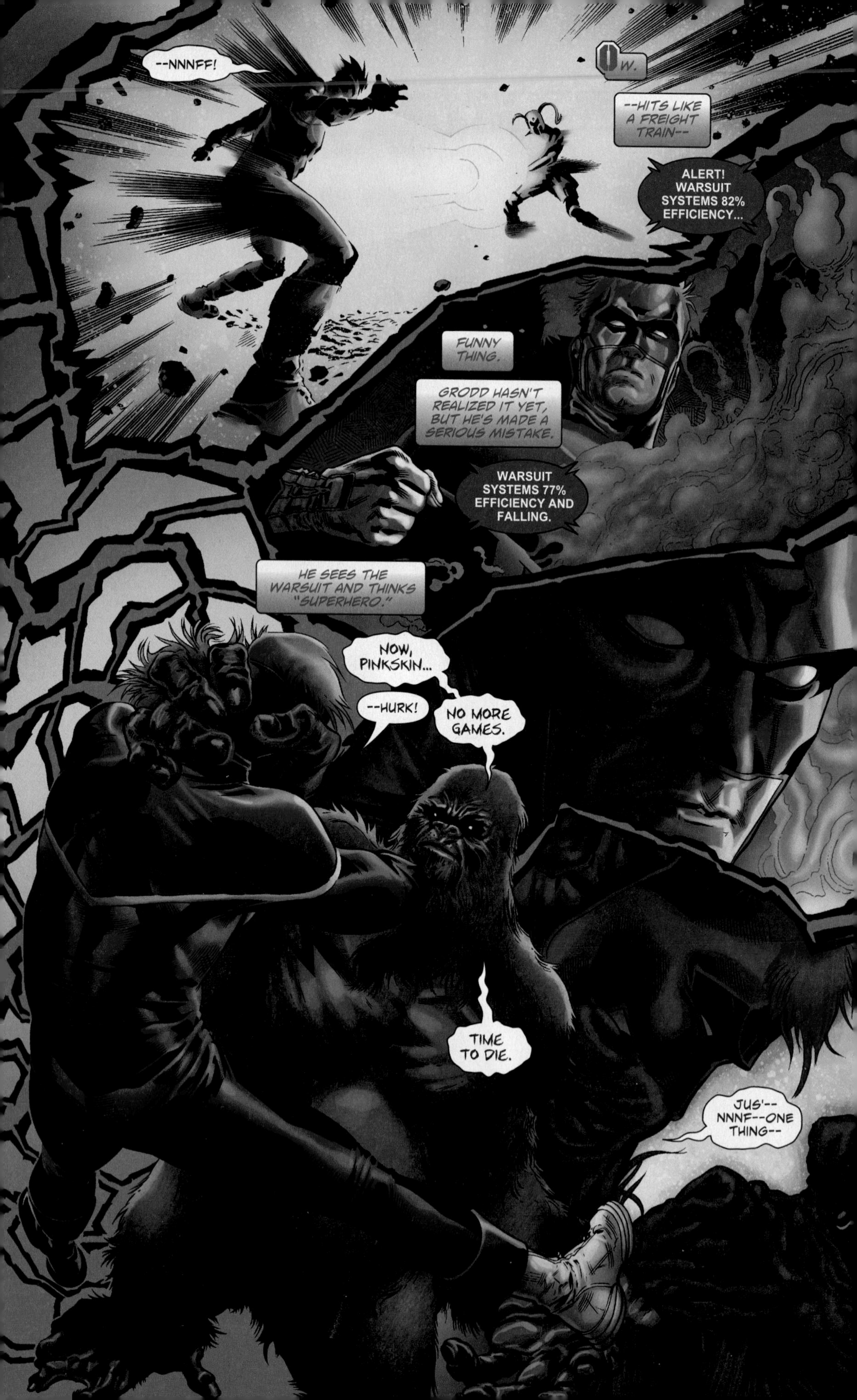
--NNNFF!
Ow.
--HITS LIKE A FREIGHT TRAIN--
ALERT! WARSUIT SYSTEMS 82% EFFICIENCY...
FUNNY THING.
GRODD HASN'T REALIZED IT YET, BUT HE'S MADE A SERIOUS MISTAKE.
WARSUIT SYSTEMS 77% EFFICIENCY AND FALLING.
HE SEES THE WARSUIT AND THINKS "SUPERHERO."
NOW, PINKSKIN...
--HURK!
NO MORE GAMES.
TIME TO DIE.
JUS'--NNNF--ONE THING--

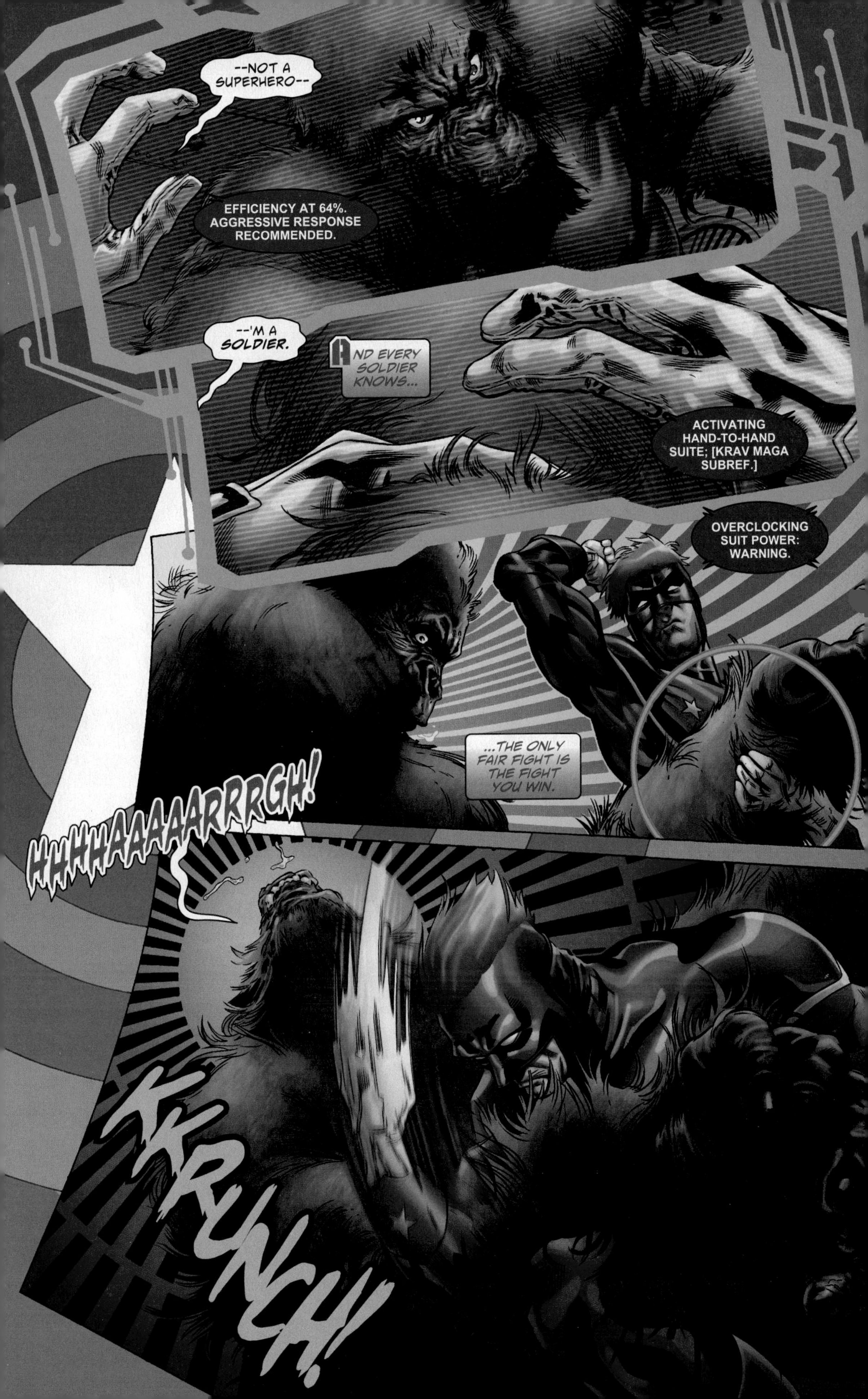
--NOT A SUPERHERO--
EFFICIENCY AT 64%. AGGRESSIVE RESPONSE RECOMMENDED.
--'M A SOLDIER.
AND EVERY SOLDIER KNOWS...
ACTIVATING HAND-TO-HAND SUITE; [KRAV MAGA SUBREF.]
OVERCLOCKING SUIT POWER: WARNING.
...THE ONLY FAIR FIGHT IS THE FIGHT YOU WIN.
HHHHAAAAARRRGH!
KKRUNCH!

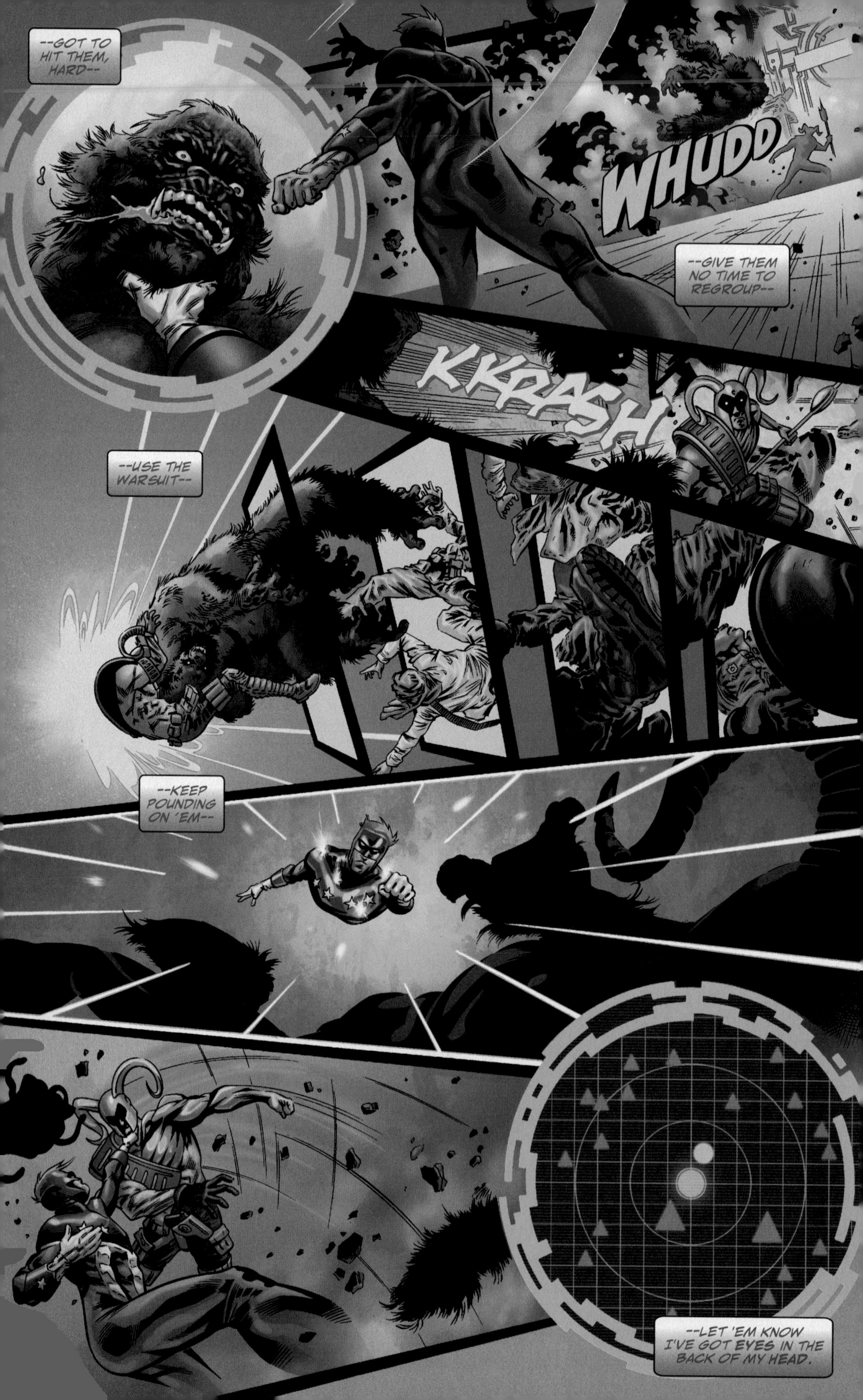
--GOT TO HIT THEM, HARD--
WHUDD
--GIVE THEM NO TIME TO REGROUP--
K KRASH
--USE THE WARSUIT--
--KEEP POUNDING ON 'EM--
--LET 'EM KNOW I'VE GOT EYES IN THE BACK OF MY HEAD.

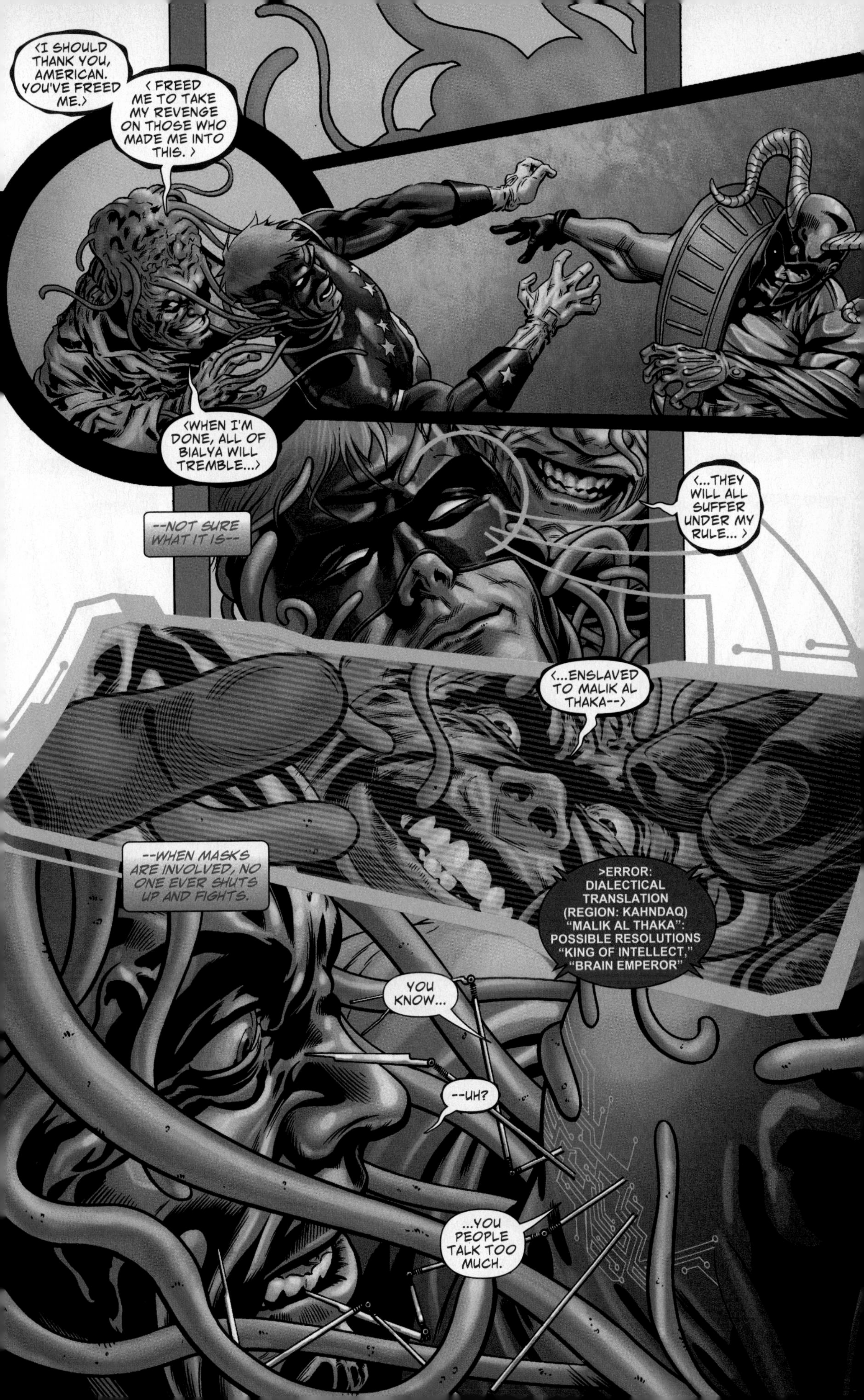

<I SHOULD THANK YOU, AMERICAN. YOU'VE FREED ME.>
< FREED ME TO TAKE MY REVENGE ON THOSE WHO MADE ME INTO THIS. >
<WHEN I'M DONE, ALL OF BIALYA WILL TREMBLE...>
--NOT SURE WHAT IT IS--
<...THEY WILL ALL SUFFER UNDER MY RULE... >
<...ENSLAVED TO MALIK AL THAKA-->
--WHEN MASKS ARE INVOLVED, NO ONE EVER SHUTS UP AND FIGHTS.
>ERROR: DIALECTICAL TRANSLATION (REGION: KAHNDAQ) "MALIK AL THAKA": POSSIBLE RESOLUTIONS "KING OF INTELLECT," "BRAIN EMPEROR"
YOU KNOW...
--UH?
...YOU PEOPLE TALK TOO MUCH.

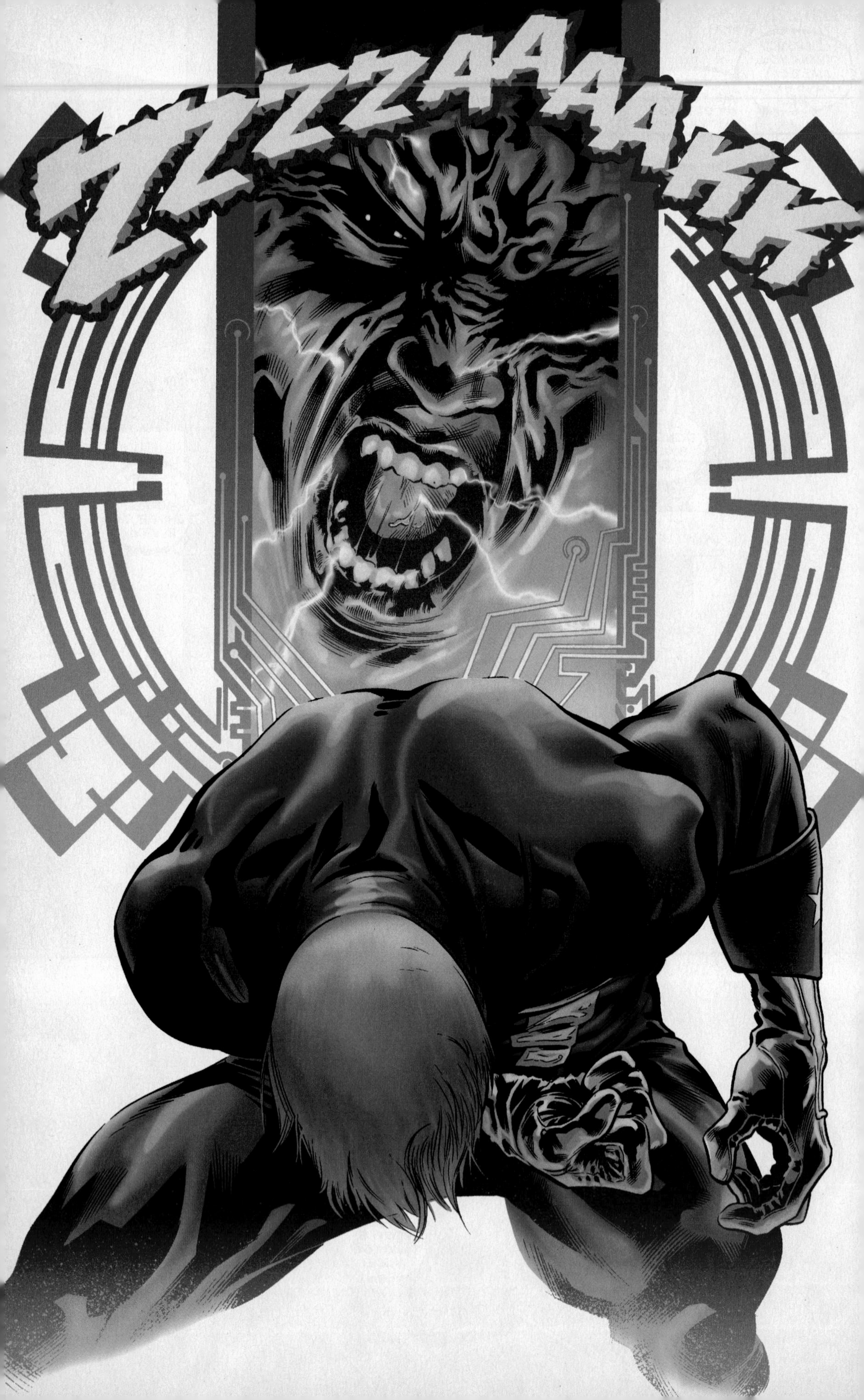
ZZZZAAAAKK

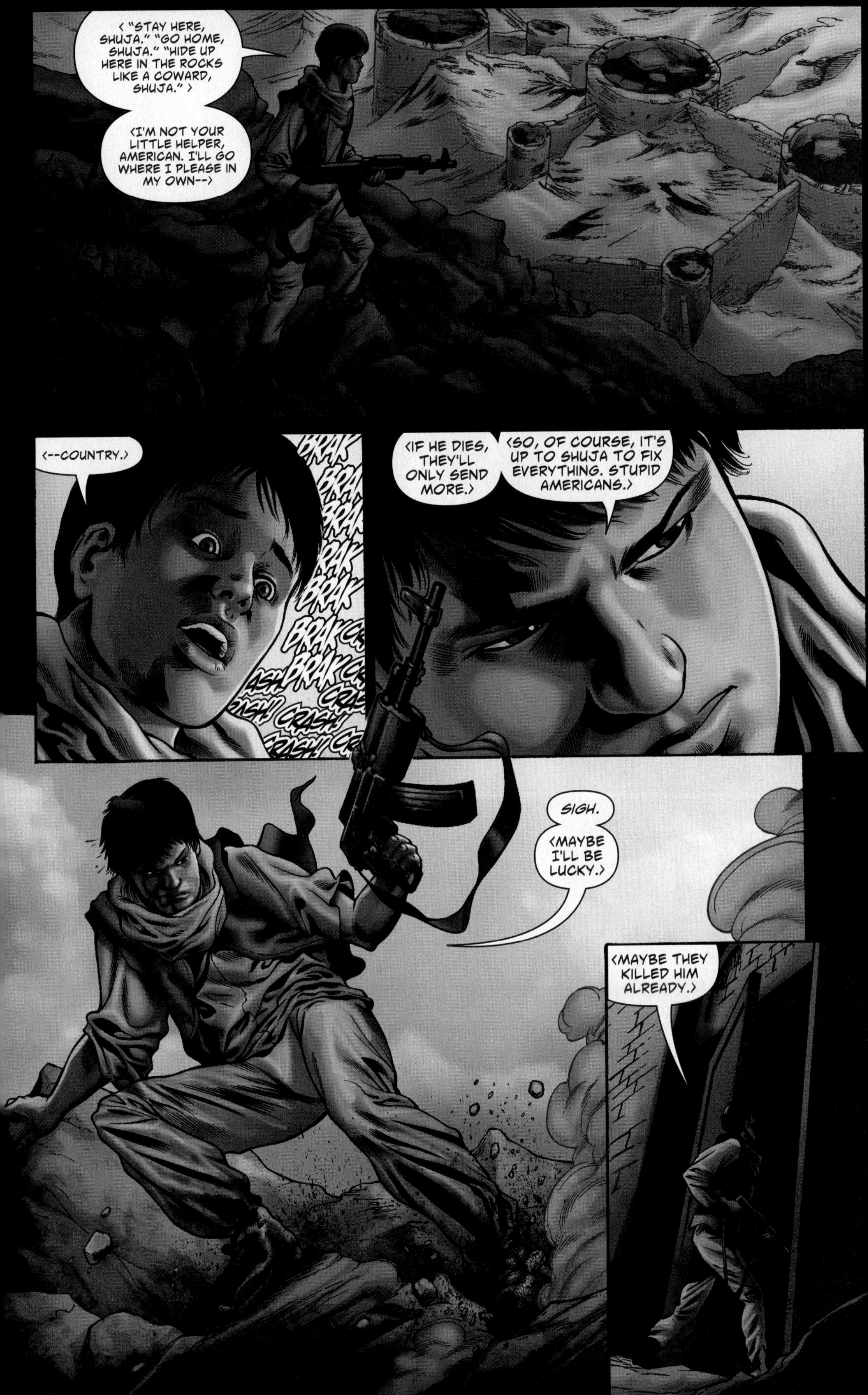

< "STAY HERE, SHUJA." "GO HOME, SHUJA." "HIDE UP HERE IN THE ROCKS LIKE A COWARD, SHUJA." >
<I'M NOT YOUR LITTLE HELPER, AMERICAN. I'LL GO WHERE I PLEASE IN MY OWN-->
<--COUNTRY.>
BRAK BRAK BRAK BRAK BRAK BRAK BRAK BRAK
CRASH! CRASH! CRASH! CRASH!
<IF HE DIES, THEY'LL ONLY SEND MORE.>
<SO, OF COURSE, IT'S UP TO SHUJA TO FIX EVERYTHING. STUPID AMERICANS.>
SIGH.
<MAYBE I'LL BE LUCKY.>
<MAYBE THEY KILLED HIM ALREADY.>

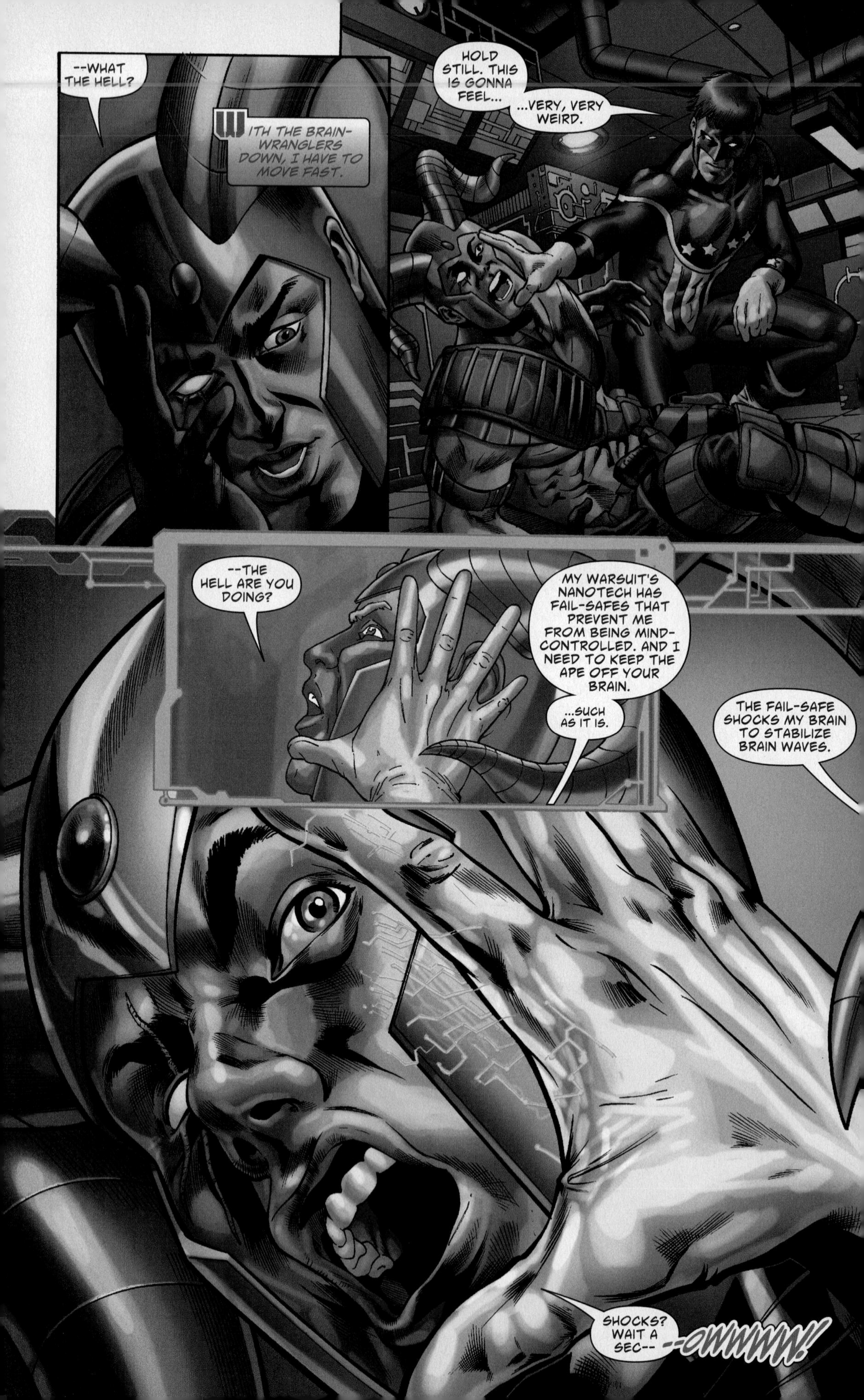
--WHAT THE HELL?
WITH THE BRAIN-WRANGLERS DOWN, I HAVE TO MOVE FAST.
HOLD STILL. THIS IS GONNA FEEL...
...VERY, VERY WEIRD.
--THE HELL ARE YOU DOING?
MY WARSUIT'S NANOTECH HAS FAIL-SAFES THAT PREVENT ME FROM BEING MIND-CONTROLLED. AND I NEED TO KEEP THE APE OFF YOUR BRAIN.
...SUCH AS IT IS.
THE FAIL-SAFE SHOCKS MY BRAIN TO STABILIZE BRAIN WAVES.
SHOCKS? WAIT A SEC--
--OWWWW!

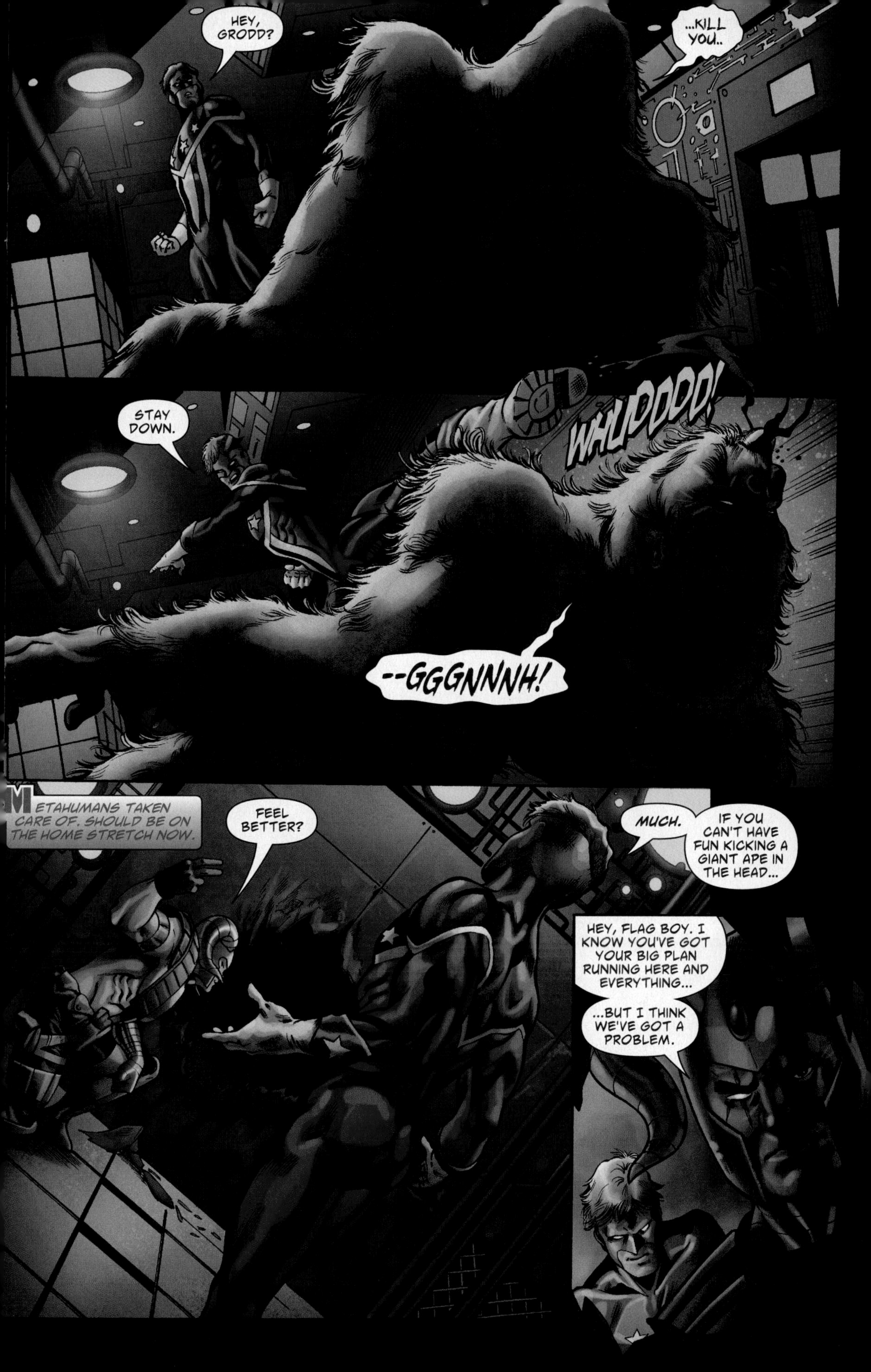
HEY, GRODD?
...KILL YOU..
STAY DOWN.
WHUDDDD!
--GGGNNNH!
METAHUMANS TAKEN CARE OF. SHOULD BE ON THE HOME STRETCH NOW.
FEEL BETTER?
MUCH.
IF YOU CAN'T HAVE FUN KICKING A GIANT APE IN THE HEAD...
HEY, FLAG BOY. I KNOW YOU'VE GOT YOUR BIG PLAN RUNNING HERE AND EVERYTHING...
...BUT I THINK WE'VE GOT A PROBLEM.

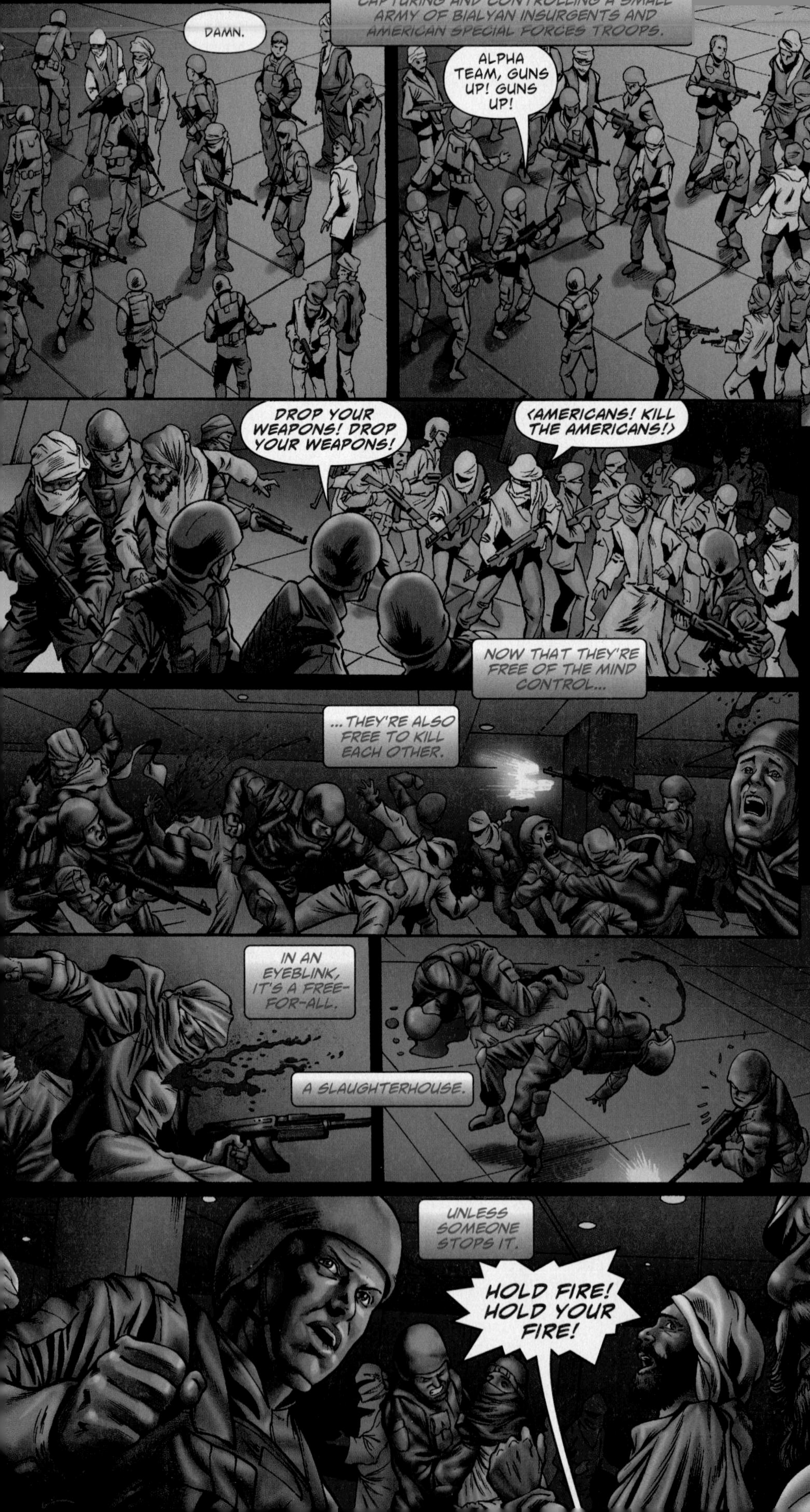
CAPTURING AND CONTROLLING A SMALL ARMY OF BIALYAN INSURGENTS AND AMERICAN SPECIAL FORCES TROOPS.
DAMN.
ALPHA TEAM, GUNS UP! GUNS UP!
DROP YOUR WEAPONS! DROP YOUR WEAPONS!
<AMERICANS! KILL THE AMERICANS!>
NOW THAT THEY'RE FREE OF THE MIND CONTROL...
...THEY'RE ALSO FREE TO KILL EACH OTHER.
IN AN EYEBLINK, IT'S A FREE-FOR-ALL.
A SLAUGHTERHOUSE.
UNLESS SOMEONE STOPS IT.
HOLD FIRE! HOLD YOUR FIRE!

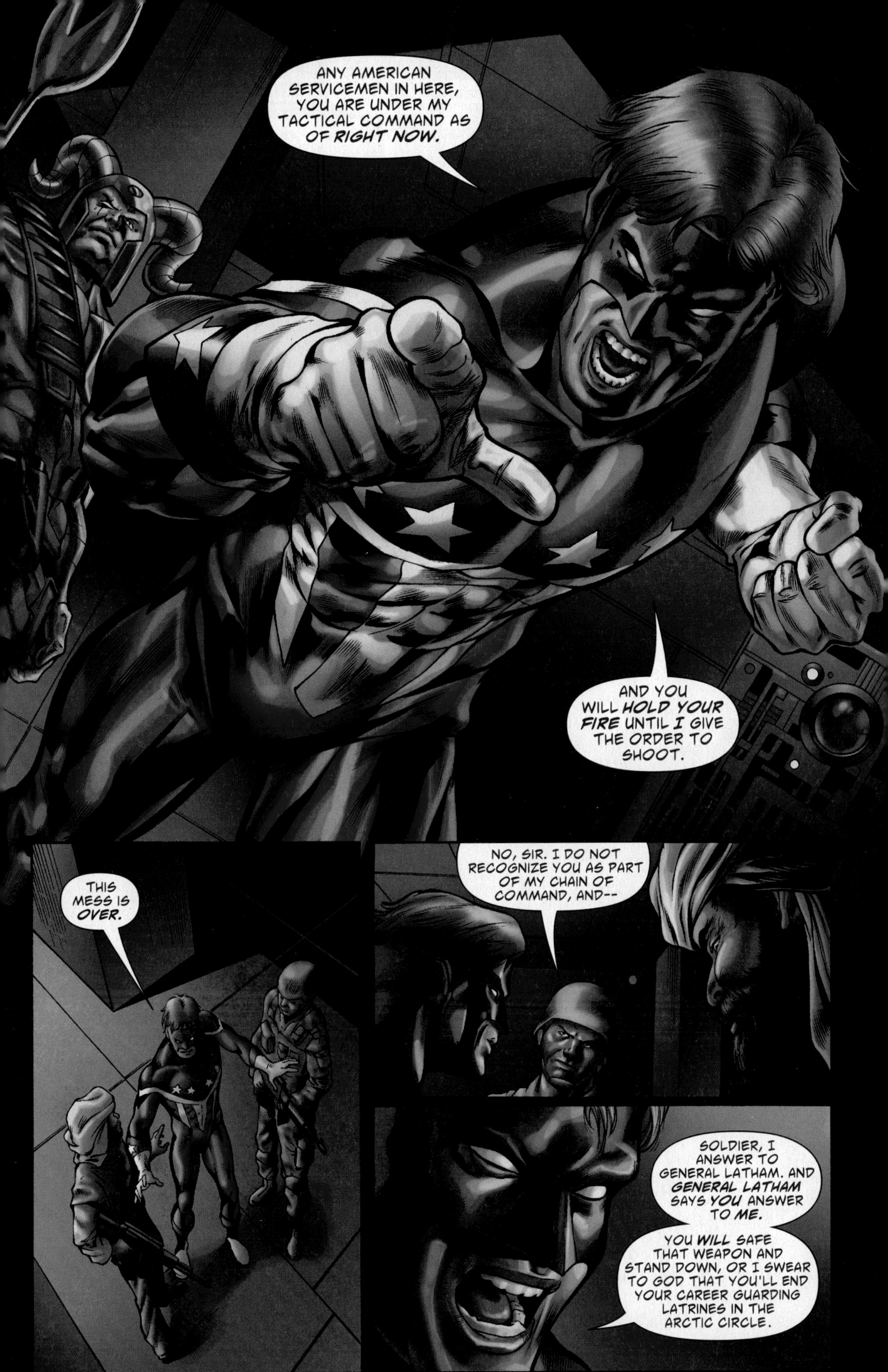
ANY AMERICAN SERVICEMEN IN HERE, YOU ARE UNDER MY TACTICAL COMMAND AS OF RIGHT NOW.
AND YOU WILL HOLD YOUR FIRE UNTIL I GIVE THE ORDER TO SHOOT.
THIS MESS IS OVER.
NO, SIR. I DO NOT RECOGNIZE YOU AS PART OF MY CHAIN OF COMMAND, AND--
SOLDIER, I ANSWER TO GENERAL LATHAM. AND GENERAL LATHAM SAYS YOU ANSWER TO ME.
YOU WILL SAFE THAT WEAPON AND STAND DOWN, OR I SWEAR TO GOD THAT YOU'LL END YOUR CAREER GUARDING LATRINES IN THE ARCTIC CIRCLE.

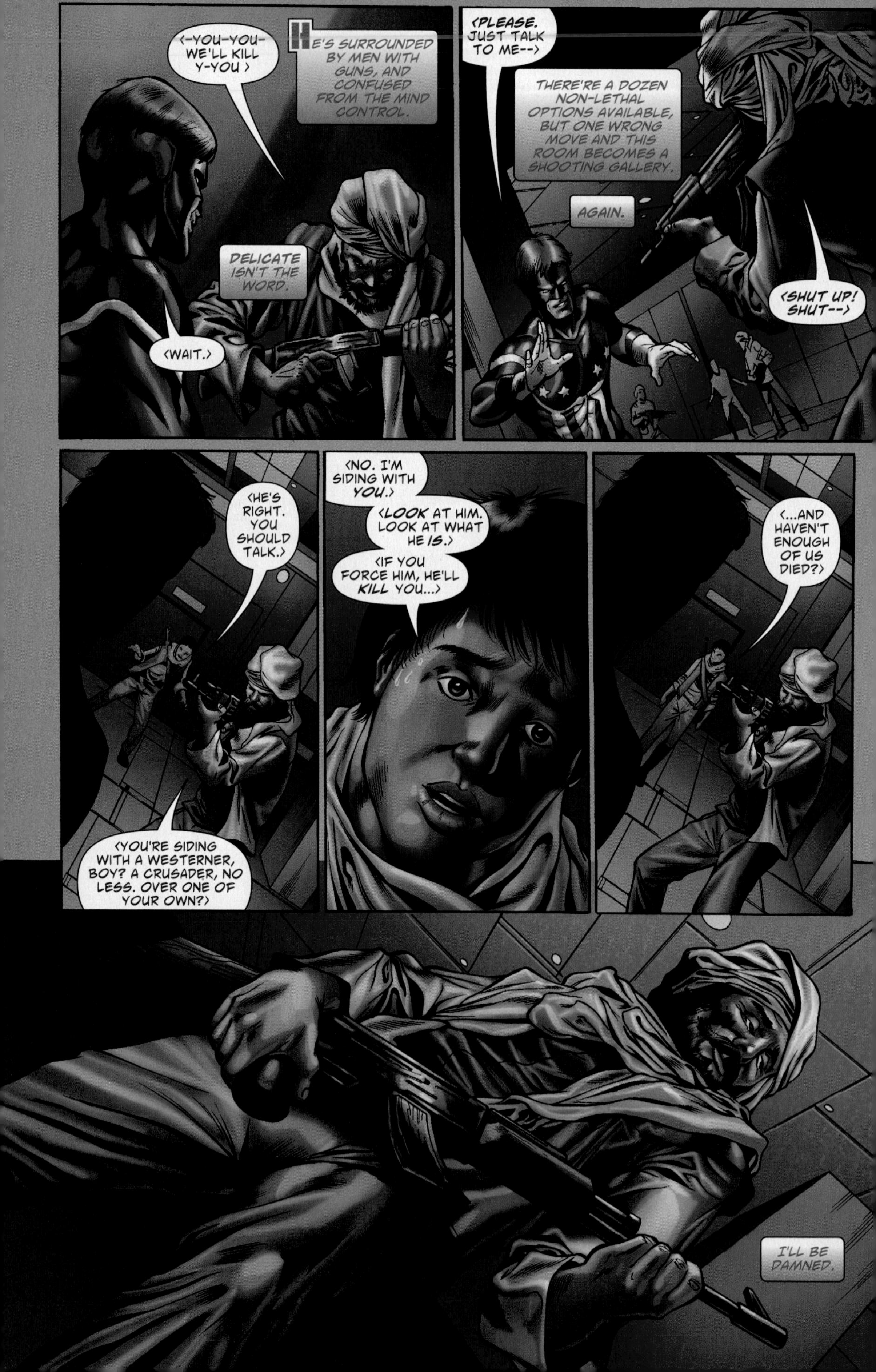

HE'S SURROUNDED BY MEN WITH GUNS, AND CONFUSED FROM THE MIND CONTROL.
<-YOU-YOU- WE'LL KILL Y-YOU >
DELICATE ISN'T THE WORD.
<WAIT.>
<PLEASE. JUST TALK TO ME-->
THERE'RE A DOZEN NON-LETHAL OPTIONS AVAILABLE, BUT ONE WRONG MOVE AND THIS ROOM BECOMES A SHOOTING GALLERY.
AGAIN.
<SHUT UP! SHUT-->
<HE'S RIGHT. YOU SHOULD TALK.>
<YOU'RE SIDING WITH A WESTERNER, BOY? A CRUSADER, NO LESS. OVER ONE OF YOUR OWN?>
<NO. I'M SIDING WITH YOU.>
<LOOK AT HIM. LOOK AT WHAT HE IS.>
<IF YOU FORCE HIM, HE'LL KILL YOU...>
<...AND HAVEN'T ENOUGH OF US DIED?>
I'LL BE DAMNED.

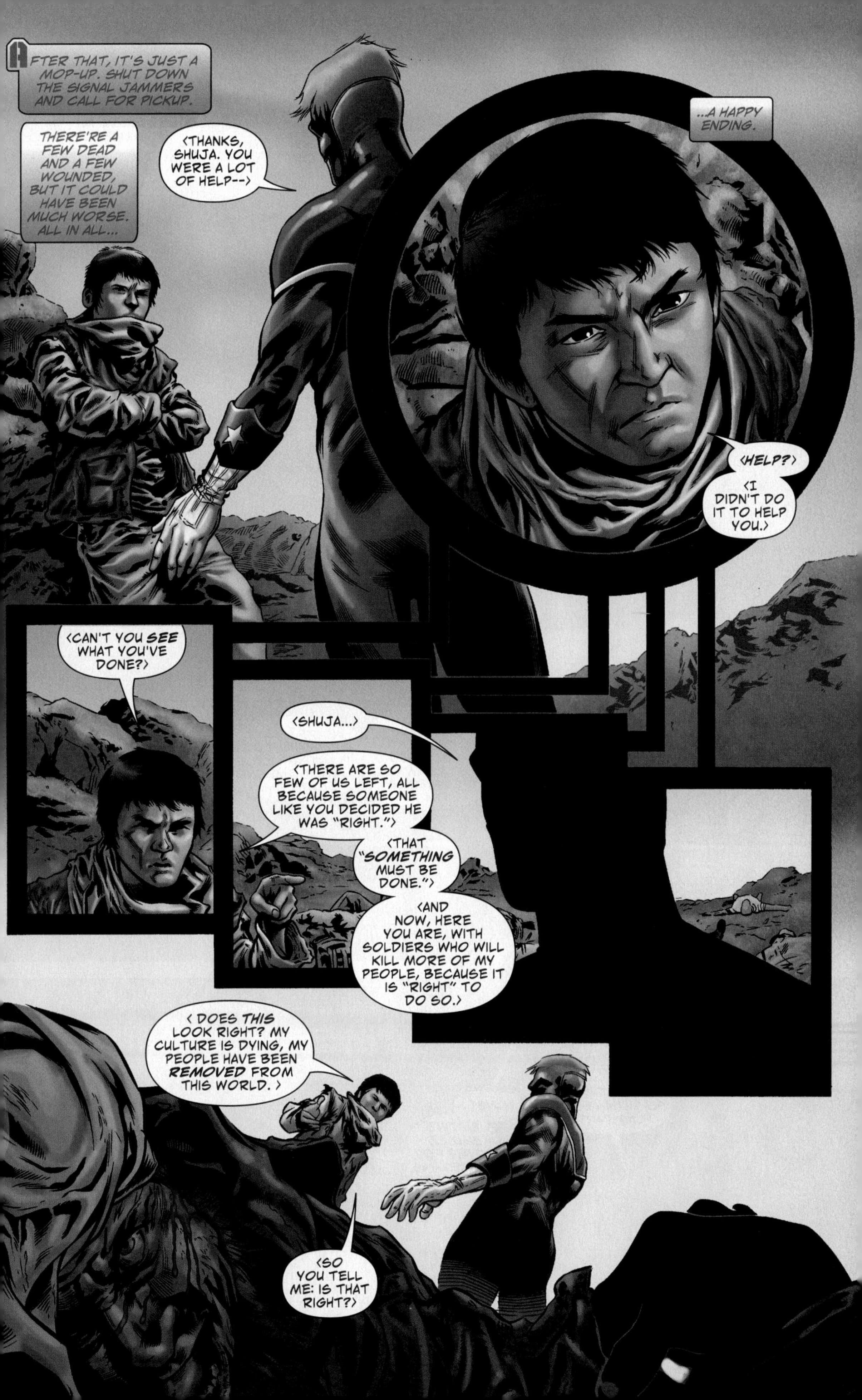
AFTER THAT, IT'S JUST A MOP-UP. SHUT DOWN THE SIGNAL JAMMERS AND CALL FOR PICKUP.
THERE'RE A FEW DEAD AND A FEW WOUNDED, BUT IT COULD HAVE BEEN MUCH WORSE. ALL IN ALL...
‹THANKS, SHUJA. YOU WERE A LOT OF HELP--›
...A HAPPY ENDING.
‹HELP?›
‹I DIDN'T DO IT TO HELP YOU.›
‹CAN'T YOU SEE WHAT YOU'VE DONE?›
‹SHUJA...›
‹THERE ARE SO FEW OF US LEFT, ALL BECAUSE SOMEONE LIKE YOU DECIDED HE WAS "RIGHT."›
‹THAT "SOMETHING MUST BE DONE."›
‹AND NOW, HERE YOU ARE, WITH SOLDIERS WHO WILL KILL MORE OF MY PEOPLE, BECAUSE IT IS "RIGHT" TO DO SO.›
‹ DOES THIS LOOK RIGHT? MY CULTURE IS DYING, MY PEOPLE HAVE BEEN REMOVED FROM THIS WORLD. ›
‹SO YOU TELL ME: IS THAT RIGHT?›

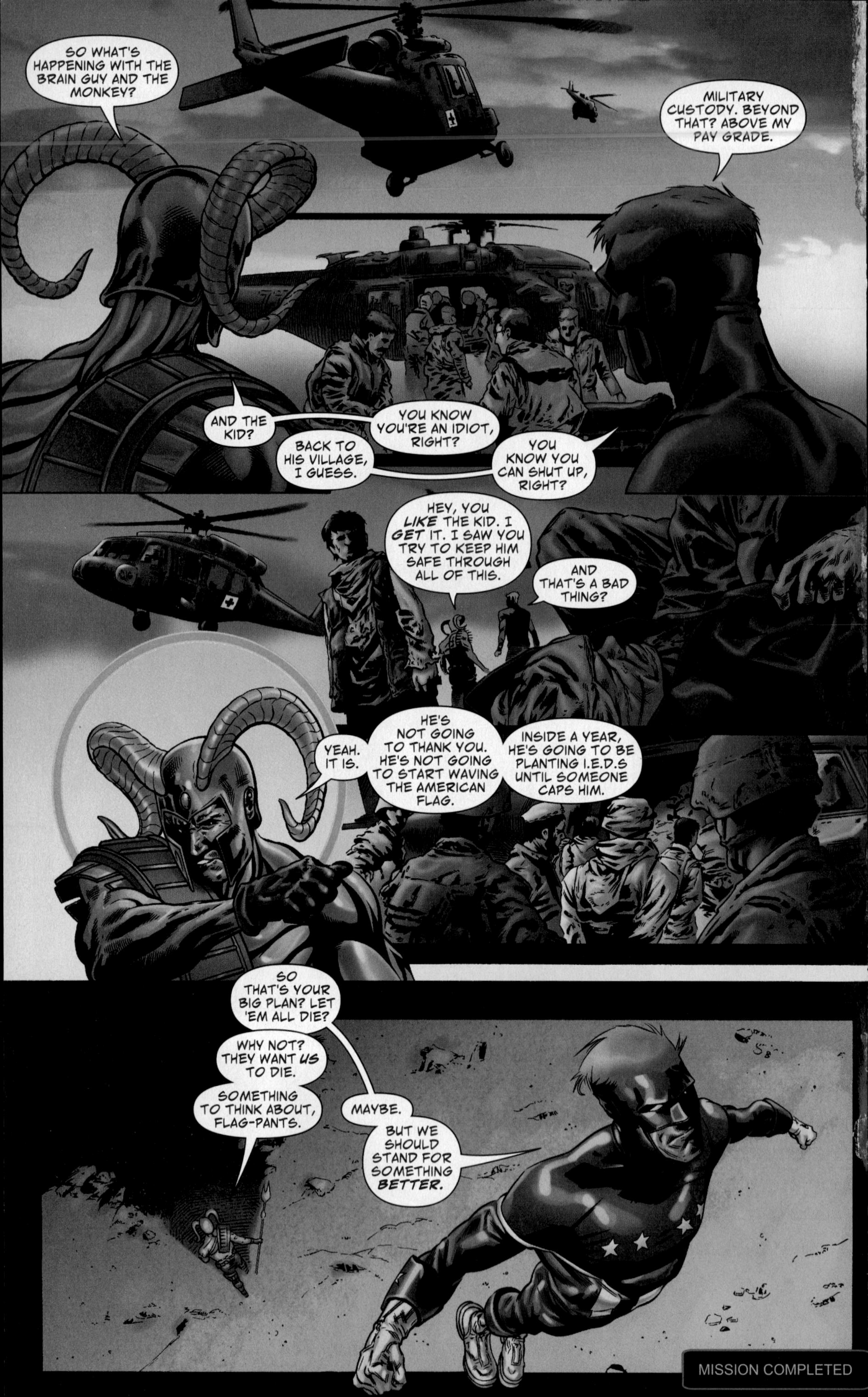
SO WHAT'S HAPPENING WITH THE BRAIN GUY AND THE MONKEY?
MILITARY CUSTODY. BEYOND THAT? ABOVE MY PAY GRADE.
AND THE KID?
BACK TO HIS VILLAGE, I GUESS.
YOU KNOW YOU'RE AN IDIOT, RIGHT?
YOU KNOW YOU CAN SHUT UP, RIGHT?
HEY, YOU LIKE THE KID. I GET IT. I SAW YOU TRY TO KEEP HIM SAFE THROUGH ALL OF THIS.
AND THAT'S A BAD THING?
YEAH. IT IS.
HE'S NOT GOING TO THANK YOU. HE'S NOT GOING TO START WAVING THE AMERICAN FLAG.
INSIDE A YEAR, HE'S GOING TO BE PLANTING I.E.D.S UNTIL SOMEONE CAPS HIM.
SO THAT'S YOUR BIG PLAN? LET 'EM ALL DIE?
WHY NOT? THEY WANT US TO DIE.
SOMETHING TO THINK ABOUT, FLAG-PANTS.
MAYBE.
BUT WE SHOULD STAND FOR SOMETHING BETTER.
MISSION COMPLETED

GHOSTS PART 1: MORGAN DIE WELT

Cover by Sami Basri

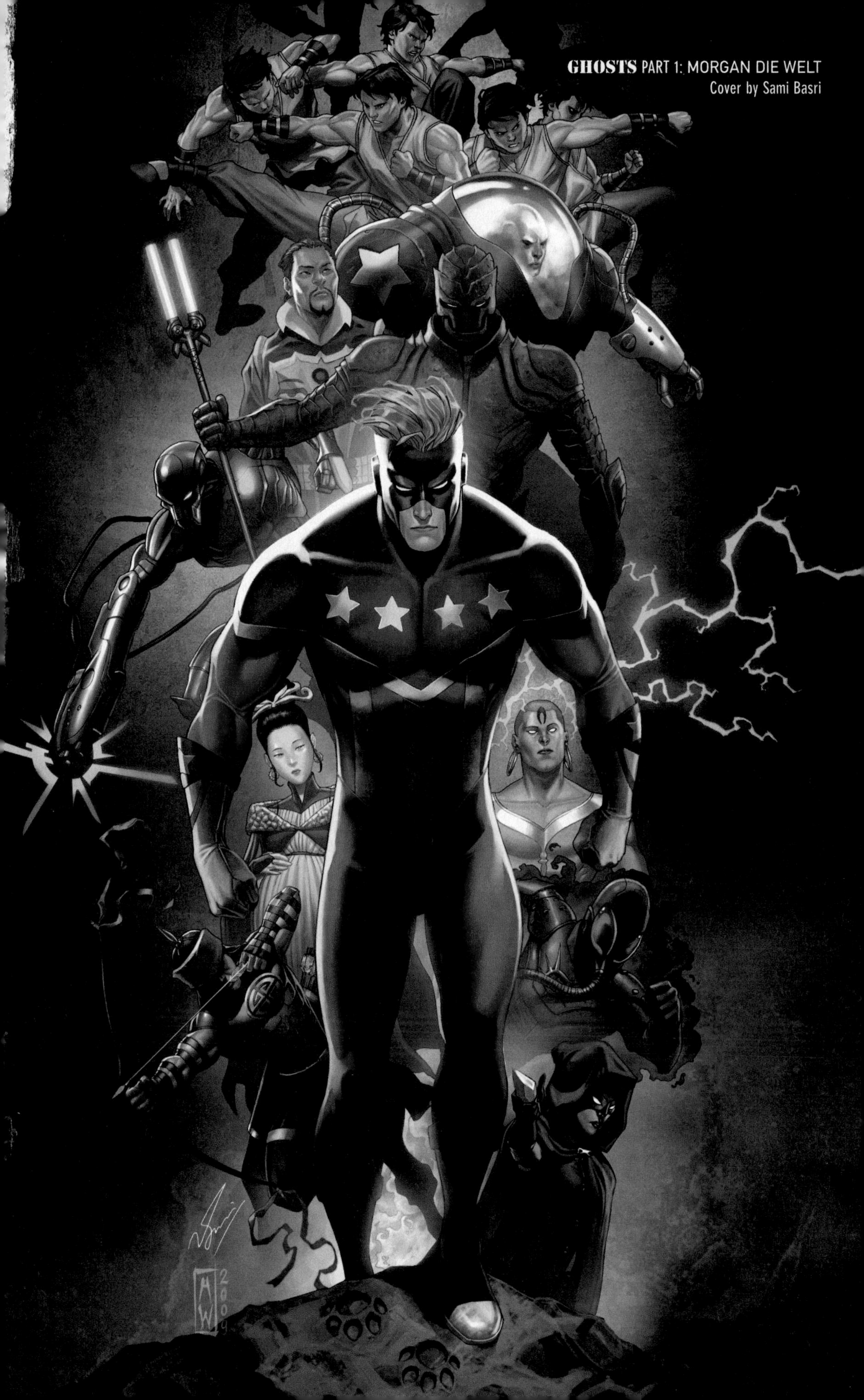

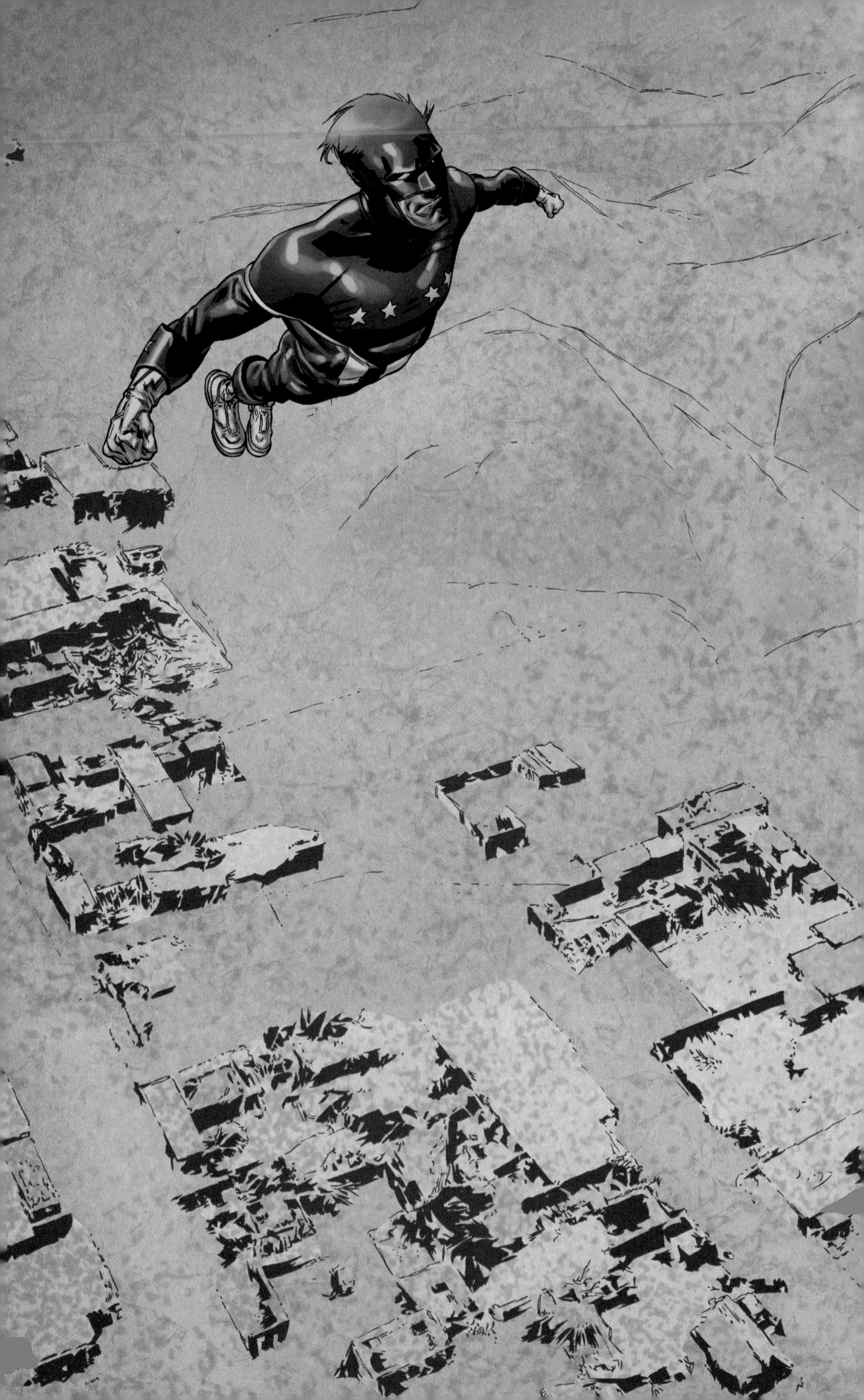

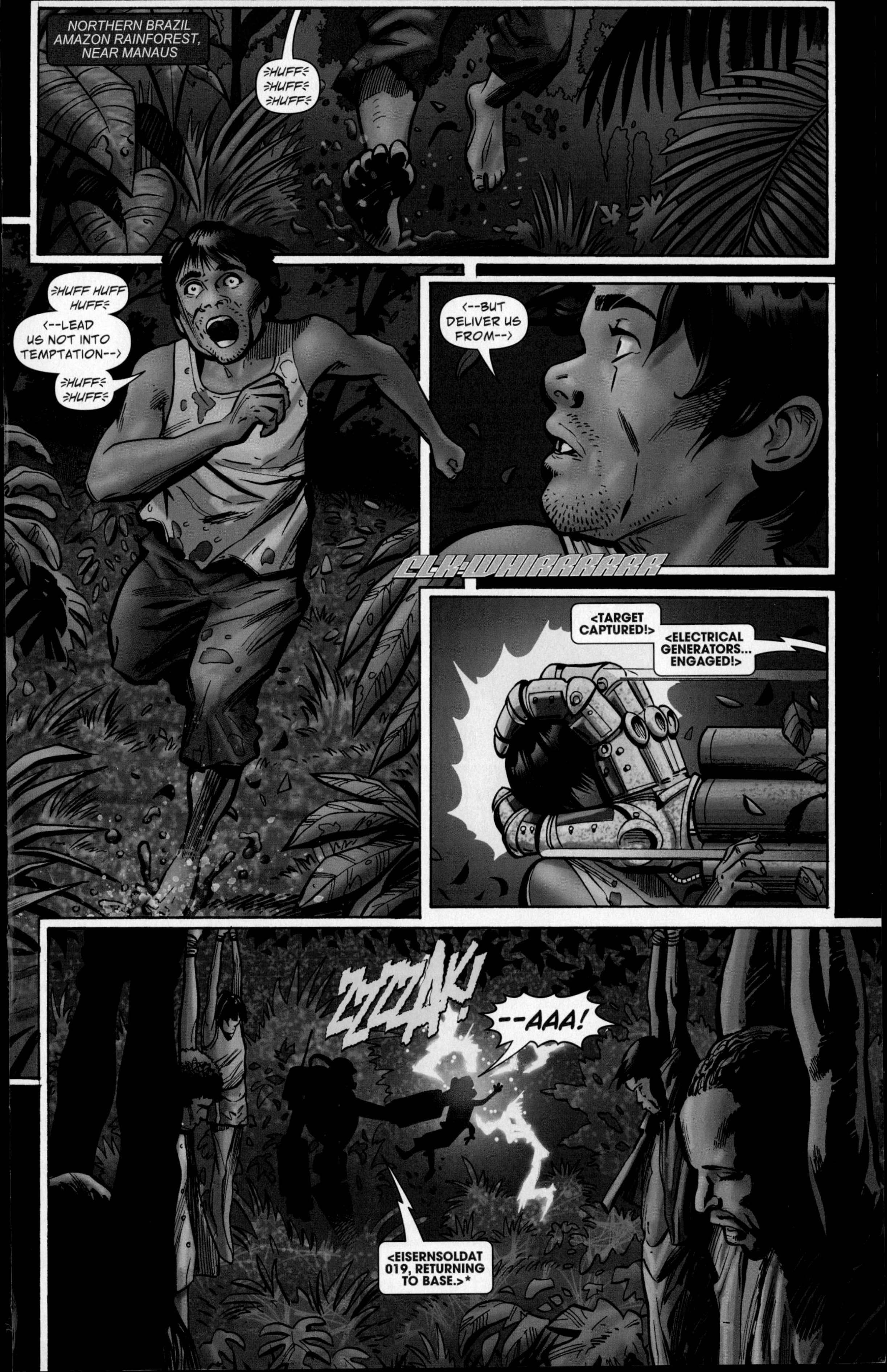
NORTHERN BRAZIL AMAZON RAINFOREST, NEAR MANAUS
HUFF HUFF HUFF
HUFF HUFF HUFF
<--LEAD US NOT INTO TEMPTATION-->
HUFF HUFF
<--BUT DELIVER US FROM-->
CLK-WHIRRRRRR
<TARGET CAPTURED!>
<ELECTRICAL GENERATORS... ENGAGED!>
ZZZZAK!
--AAA!
<EISERNSOLDAT 019, RETURNING TO BASE.>*

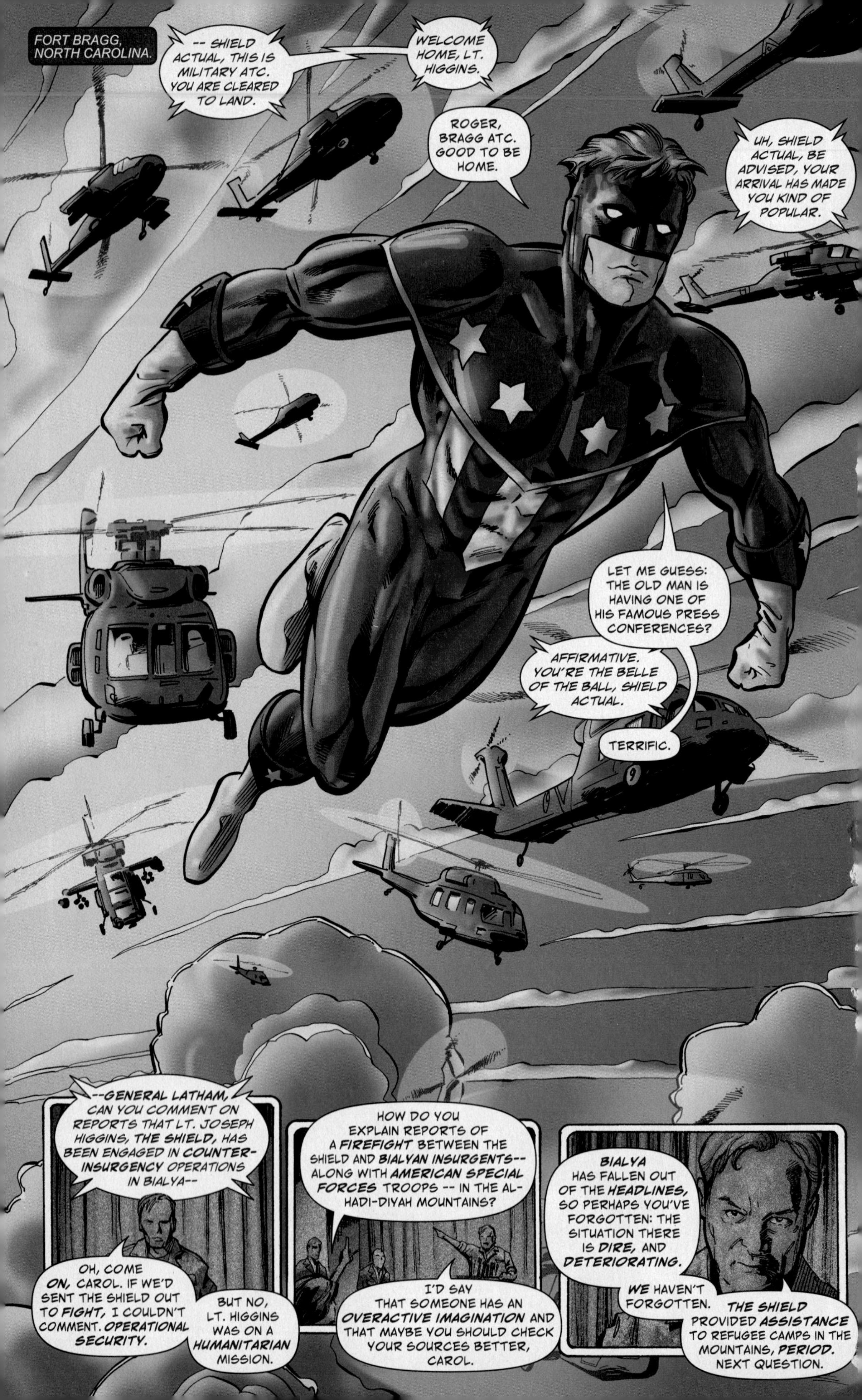
FORT BRAGG, NORTH CAROLINA.
-- SHIELD ACTUAL, THIS IS MILITARY ATC. YOU ARE CLEARED TO LAND.
WELCOME HOME, LT. HIGGINS.
ROGER, BRAGG ATC. GOOD TO BE HOME.
UH, SHIELD ACTUAL, BE ADVISED, YOUR ARRIVAL HAS MADE YOU KIND OF POPULAR.
LET ME GUESS: THE OLD MAN IS HAVING ONE OF HIS FAMOUS PRESS CONFERENCES?
AFFIRMATIVE. YOU'RE THE BELLE OF THE BALL, SHIELD ACTUAL.
TERRIFIC.
--GENERAL LATHAM, CAN YOU COMMENT ON REPORTS THAT LT. JOSEPH HIGGINS, THE SHIELD, HAS BEEN ENGAGED IN COUNTER-INSURGENCY OPERATIONS IN BIALYA--
OH, COME ON, CAROL. IF WE'D SENT THE SHIELD OUT TO FIGHT, I COULDN'T COMMENT. OPERATIONAL SECURITY.
BUT NO, LT. HIGGINS WAS ON A HUMANITARIAN MISSION.
HOW DO YOU EXPLAIN REPORTS OF A FIREFIGHT BETWEEN THE SHIELD AND BIALYAN INSURGENTS--ALONG WITH AMERICAN SPECIAL FORCES TROOPS -- IN THE AL-HADI-DIYAH MOUNTAINS?
I'D SAY THAT SOMEONE HAS AN OVERACTIVE IMAGINATION AND THAT MAYBE YOU SHOULD CHECK YOUR SOURCES BETTER, CAROL.
BIALYA HAS FALLEN OUT OF THE HEADLINES, SO PERHAPS YOU'VE FORGOTTEN: THE SITUATION THERE IS DIRE, AND DETERIORATING.
WE HAVEN'T FORGOTTEN.
THE SHIELD PROVIDED ASSISTANCE TO REFUGEE CAMPS IN THE MOUNTAINS, PERIOD. NEXT QUESTION.

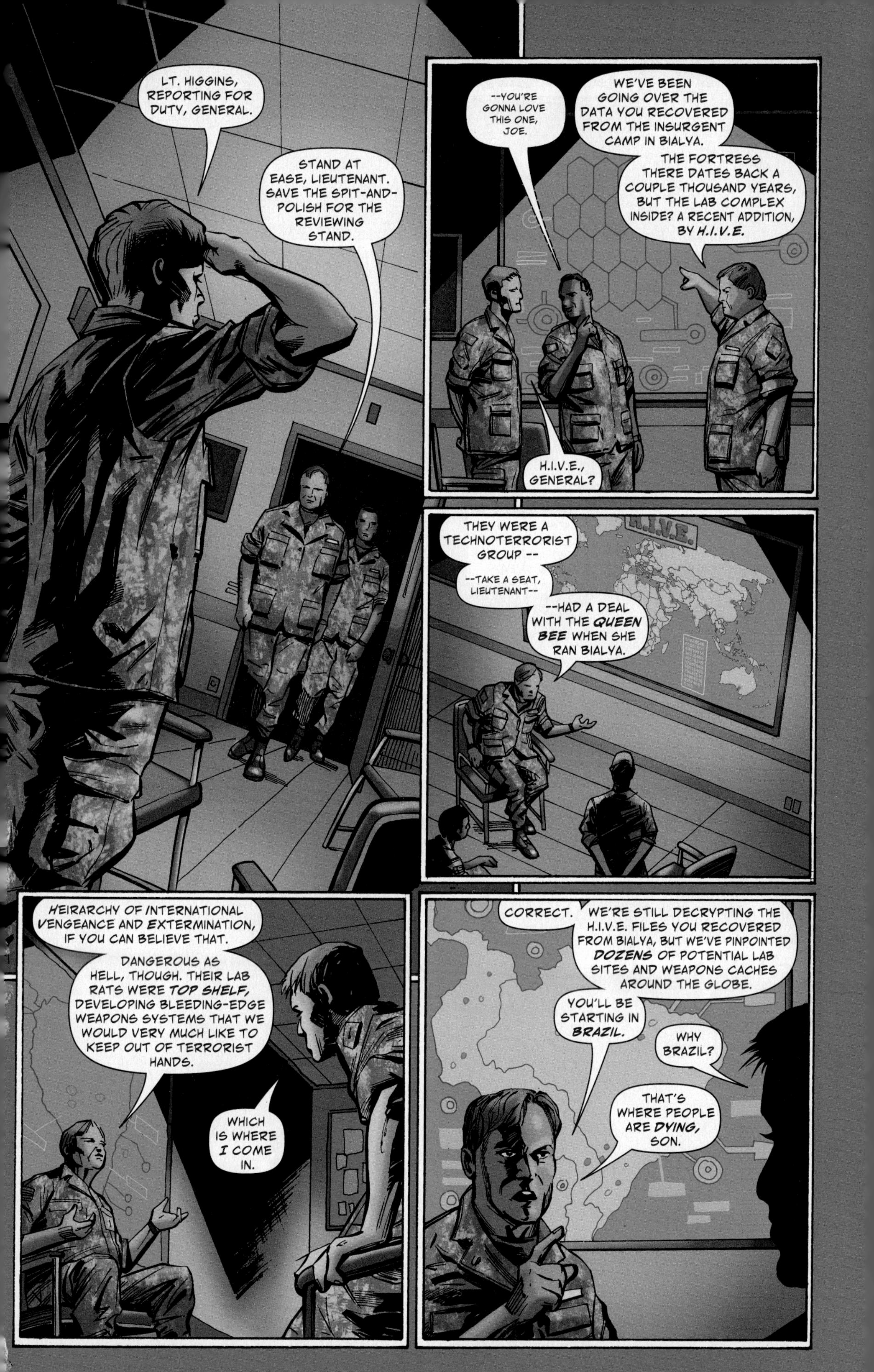
LT. HIGGINS, REPORTING FOR DUTY, GENERAL.
STAND AT EASE, LIEUTENANT. SAVE THE SPIT-AND-POLISH FOR THE REVIEWING STAND.
WE'VE BEEN GOING OVER THE DATA YOU RECOVERED FROM THE INSURGENT CAMP IN BIALYA.
--YOU'RE GONNA LOVE THIS ONE, JOE.
THE FORTRESS THERE DATES BACK A COUPLE THOUSAND YEARS, BUT THE LAB COMPLEX INSIDE? A RECENT ADDITION, BY H.I.V.E.
H.I.V.E., GENERAL?
THEY WERE A TECHNOTERRORIST GROUP --
--TAKE A SEAT, LIEUTENANT--
--HAD A DEAL WITH THE QUEEN BEE WHEN SHE RAN BIALYA.
H.I.V.E.
HEIRARCHY OF INTERNATIONAL VENGEANCE AND EXTERMINATION, IF YOU CAN BELIEVE THAT.
DANGEROUS AS HELL, THOUGH. THEIR LAB RATS WERE TOP SHELF, DEVELOPING BLEEDING-EDGE WEAPONS SYSTEMS THAT WE WOULD VERY MUCH LIKE TO KEEP OUT OF TERRORIST HANDS.
WHICH IS WHERE I COME IN.
CORRECT.
WE'RE STILL DECRYPTING THE H.I.V.E. FILES YOU RECOVERED FROM BIALYA, BUT WE'VE PINPOINTED DOZENS OF POTENTIAL LAB SITES AND WEAPONS CACHES AROUND THE GLOBE.
YOU'LL BE STARTING IN BRAZIL.
WHY BRAZIL?
THAT'S WHERE PEOPLE ARE DYING, SON.

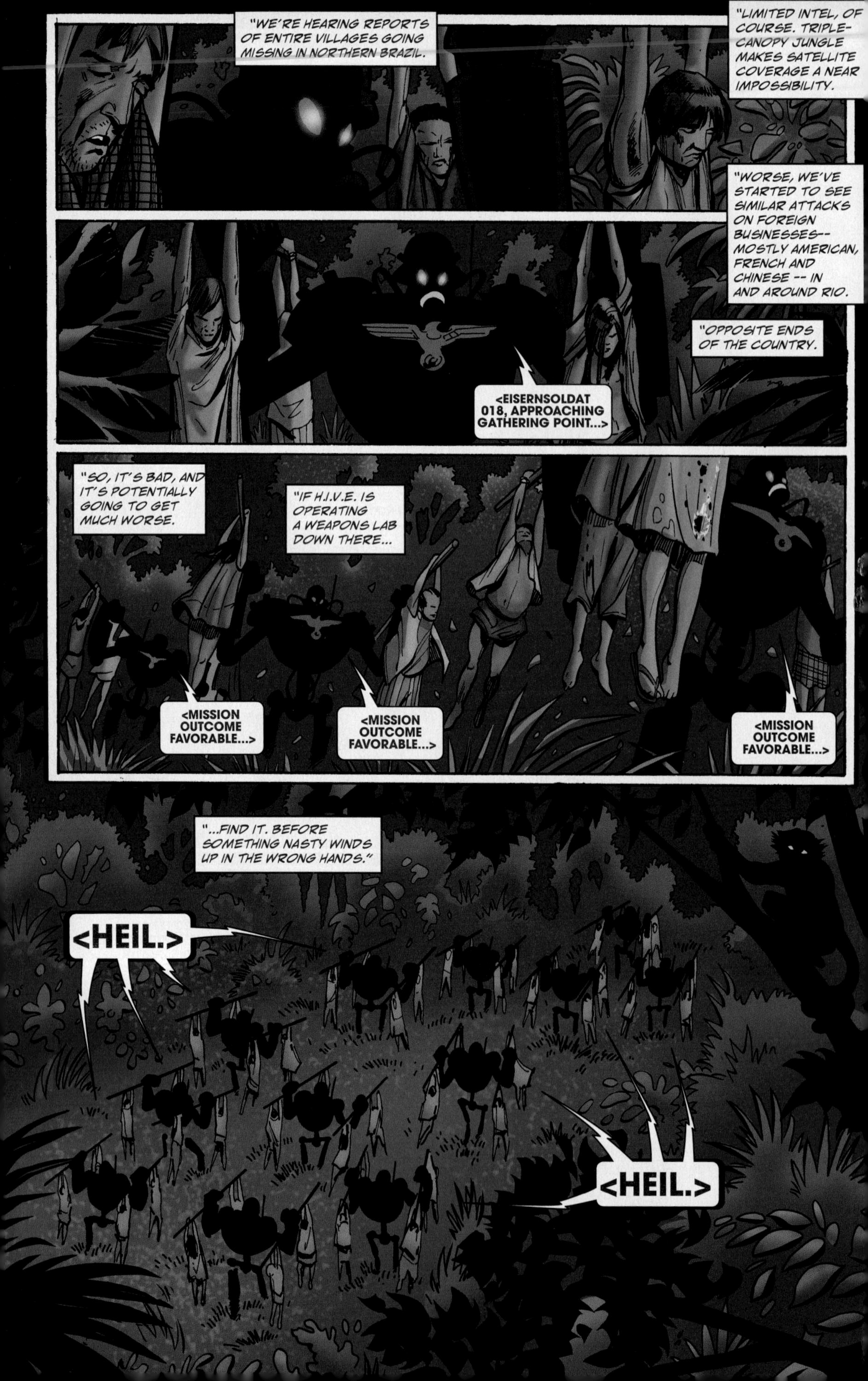
"WE'RE HEARING REPORTS OF ENTIRE VILLAGES GOING MISSING IN NORTHERN BRAZIL.
"LIMITED INTEL, OF COURSE. TRIPLE-CANOPY JUNGLE MAKES SATELLITE COVERAGE A NEAR IMPOSSIBILITY.
"WORSE, WE'VE STARTED TO SEE SIMILAR ATTACKS ON FOREIGN BUSINESSES-- MOSTLY AMERICAN, FRENCH AND CHINESE -- IN AND AROUND RIO.
"OPPOSITE ENDS OF THE COUNTRY.
<EISERNSOLDAT 018, APPROACHING GATHERING POINT...>
"SO, IT'S BAD, AND IT'S POTENTIALLY GOING TO GET MUCH WORSE.
"IF H.I.V.E. IS OPERATING A WEAPONS LAB DOWN THERE...
<MISSION OUTCOME FAVORABLE...>
<MISSION OUTCOME FAVORABLE...>
<MISSION OUTCOME FAVORABLE...>
"...FIND IT. BEFORE SOMETHING NASTY WINDS UP IN THE WRONG HANDS."
<HEIL.>
<HEIL.>

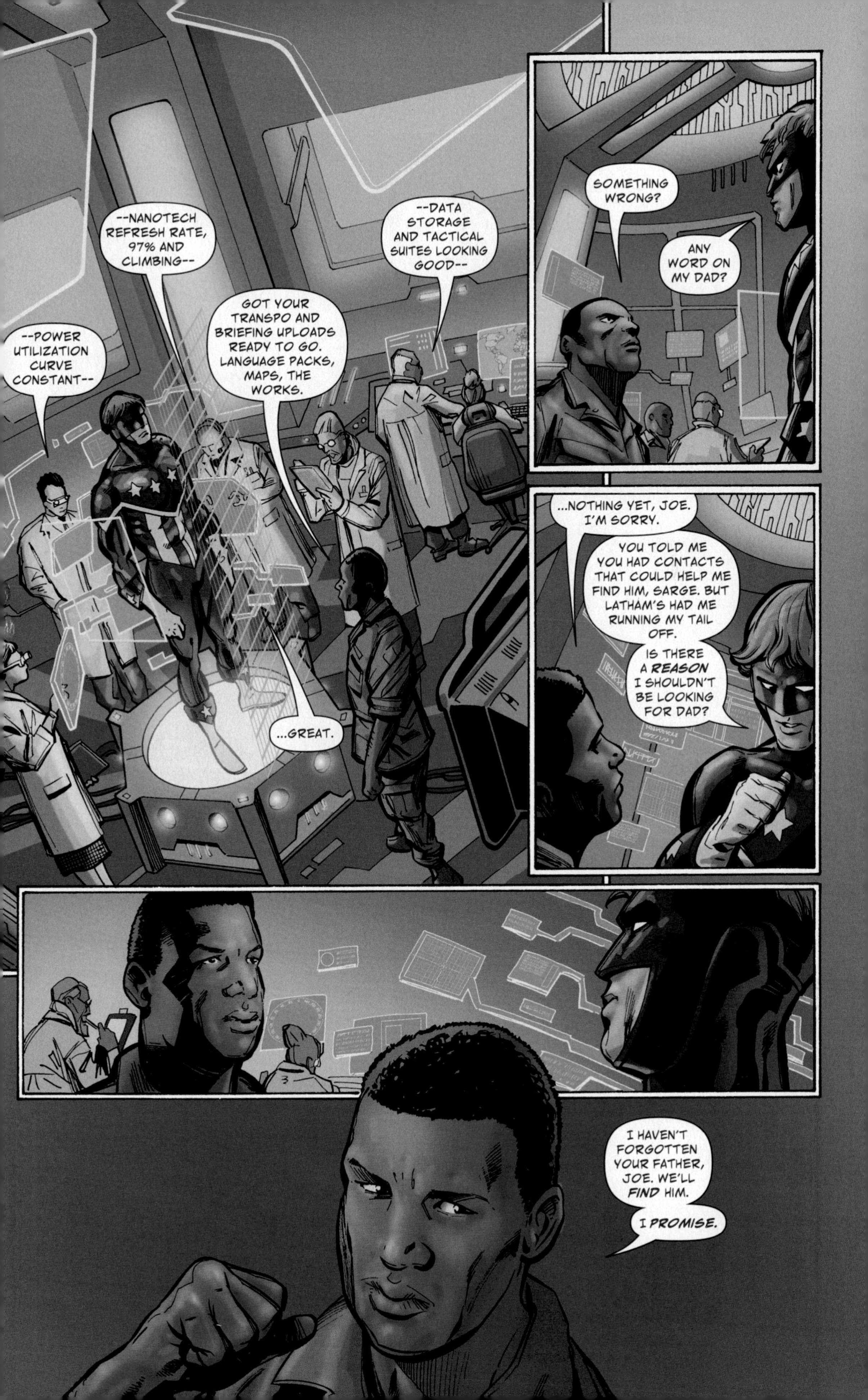
--POWER UTILIZATION CURVE CONSTANT--
--NANOTECH REFRESH RATE, 97% AND CLIMBING--
GOT YOUR TRANSPO AND BRIEFING UPLOADS READY TO GO. LANGUAGE PACKS, MAPS, THE WORKS.
--DATA STORAGE AND TACTICAL SUITES LOOKING GOOD--
...GREAT.
SOMETHING WRONG?
ANY WORD ON MY DAD?
...NOTHING YET, JOE. I'M SORRY.
YOU TOLD ME YOU HAD CONTACTS THAT COULD HELP ME FIND HIM, SARGE. BUT LATHAM'S HAD ME RUNNING MY TAIL OFF.
IS THERE A *REASON* I SHOULDN'T BE LOOKING FOR DAD?
I HAVEN'T FORGOTTEN YOUR FATHER, JOE. WE'LL *FIND* HIM.
I *PROMISE*.

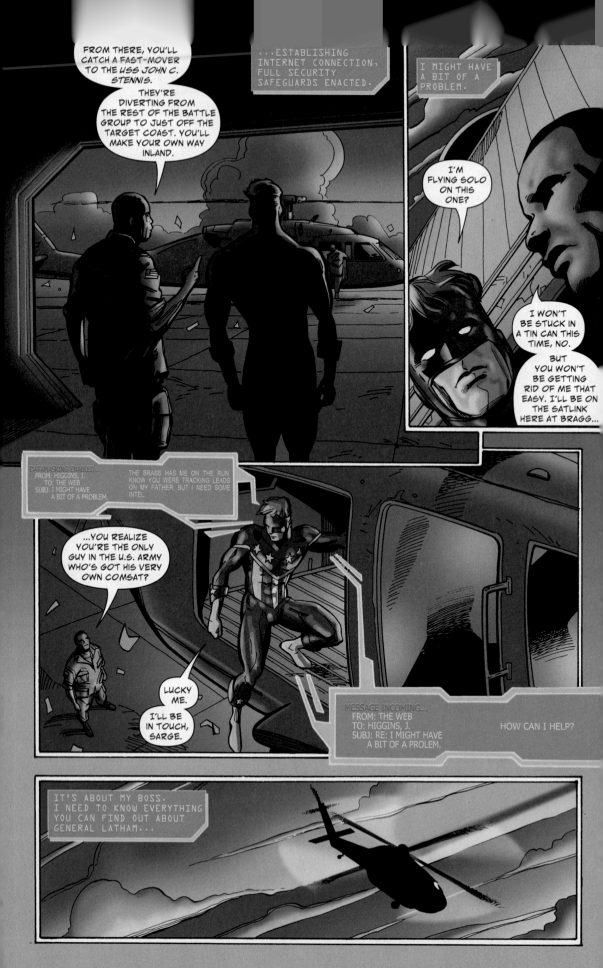

FROM THERE, YOU'LL CATCH A FAST-MOVER TO THE *USS JOHN C. STENNIS*.

THEY'RE DIVERTING FROM THE REST OF THE BATTLE GROUP TO JUST OFF THE TARGET COAST. YOU'LL MAKE YOUR OWN WAY INLAND.

...ESTABLISHING INTERNET CONNECTION, FULL SECURITY SAFEGUARDS ENACTED.

I MIGHT HAVE A BIT OF A PROBLEM.

I'M FLYING SOLO ON THIS ONE?

I WON'T BE STUCK IN A TIN CAN THIS TIME, NO.

BUT YOU WON'T BE GETTING RID OF ME THAT EASY. I'LL BE ON THE SATLINK HERE AT BRAGG...

DATAMASKING ENABLED...
FROM: HIGGINS, J.
TO: THE WEB
SUBJ: I MIGHT HAVE A BIT OF A PROBLEM.
THE BRASS HAS ME ON THE RUN. KNOW YOU WERE TRACKING LEADS ON MY FATHER, BUT I NEED SOME INTEL.

...YOU REALIZE YOU'RE THE ONLY GUY IN THE U.S. ARMY WHO'S GOT HIS VERY OWN COMSAT?

LUCKY ME.

I'LL BE IN TOUCH, SARGE.

MESSAGE INCOMING...
FROM: THE WEB
TO: HIGGINS, J.
SUBJ: RE: I MIGHT HAVE A BIT OF A PROLEM.
HOW CAN I HELP?

IT'S ABOUT MY BOSS. I NEED TO KNOW EVERYTHING YOU CAN FIND OUT ABOUT GENERAL LATHAM...

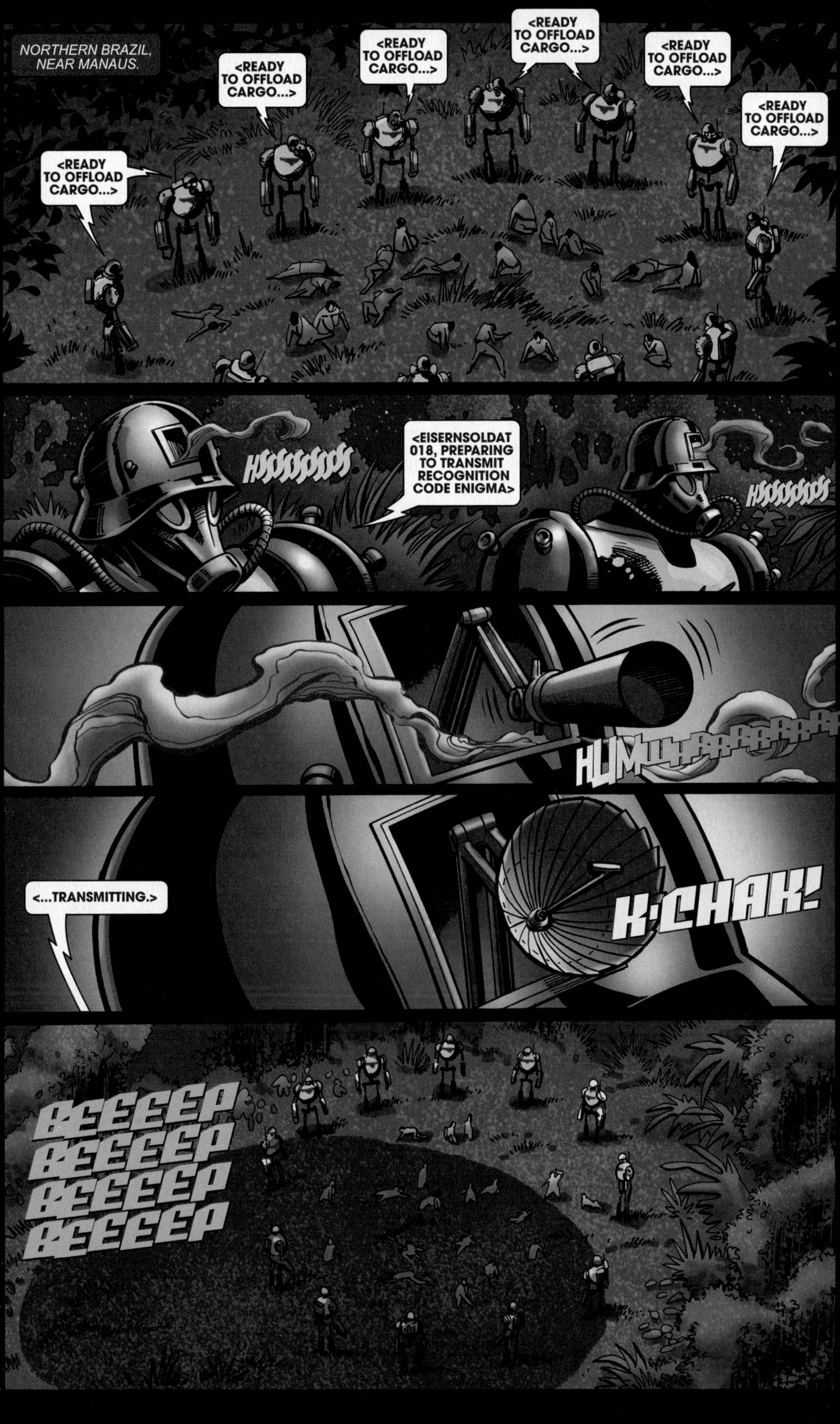
NORTHERN BRAZIL, NEAR MANAUS.
<READY TO OFFLOAD CARGO...>
<READY TO OFFLOAD CARGO...>
<READY TO OFFLOAD CARGO...>
<READY TO OFFLOAD CARGO...>
<READY TO OFFLOAD CARGO...>
<READY TO OFFLOAD CARGO...>
<EISERNSOLDAT 018, PREPARING TO TRANSMIT RECOGNITION CODE ENIGMA>
<...TRANSMITTING.>
K-CHAK!
BEEEEP
BEEEEP
BEEEEP
BEEEEP

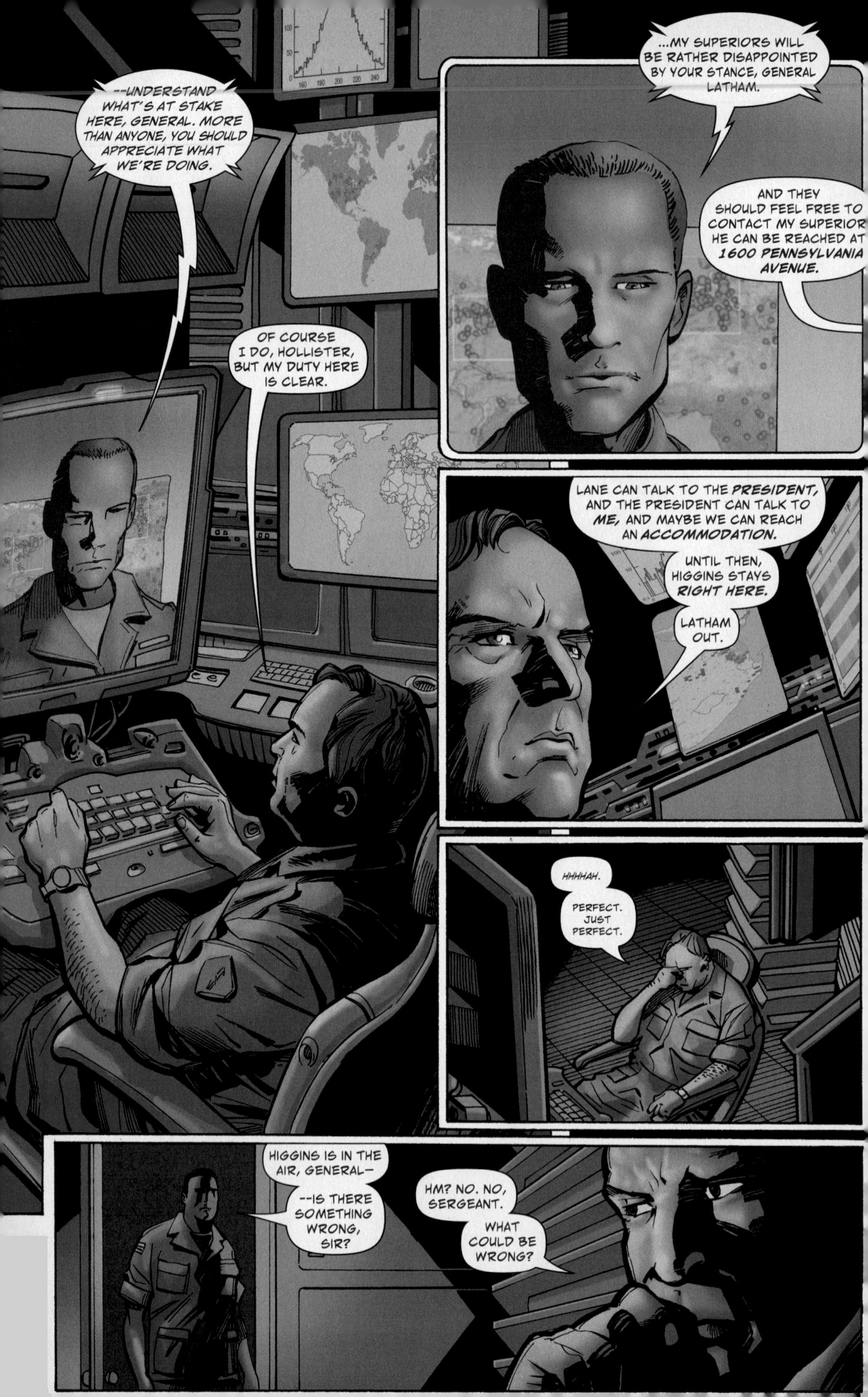
--UNDERSTAND WHAT'S AT STAKE HERE, GENERAL. MORE THAN ANYONE, YOU SHOULD APPRECIATE WHAT WE'RE DOING.
OF COURSE I DO, HOLLISTER, BUT MY DUTY HERE IS CLEAR.
...MY SUPERIORS WILL BE RATHER DISAPPOINTED BY YOUR STANCE, GENERAL LATHAM.
AND THEY SHOULD FEEL FREE TO CONTACT MY SUPERIOR. HE CAN BE REACHED AT 1600 PENNSYLVANIA AVENUE.
LANE CAN TALK TO THE PRESIDENT, AND THE PRESIDENT CAN TALK TO ME, AND MAYBE WE CAN REACH AN ACCOMMODATION.
UNTIL THEN, HIGGINS STAYS RIGHT HERE.
LATHAM OUT.
HHHHAH.
PERFECT. JUST PERFECT.
HIGGINS IS IN THE AIR, GENERAL—
--IS THERE SOMETHING WRONG, SIR?
HM? NO. NO, SERGEANT.
WHAT COULD BE WRONG?

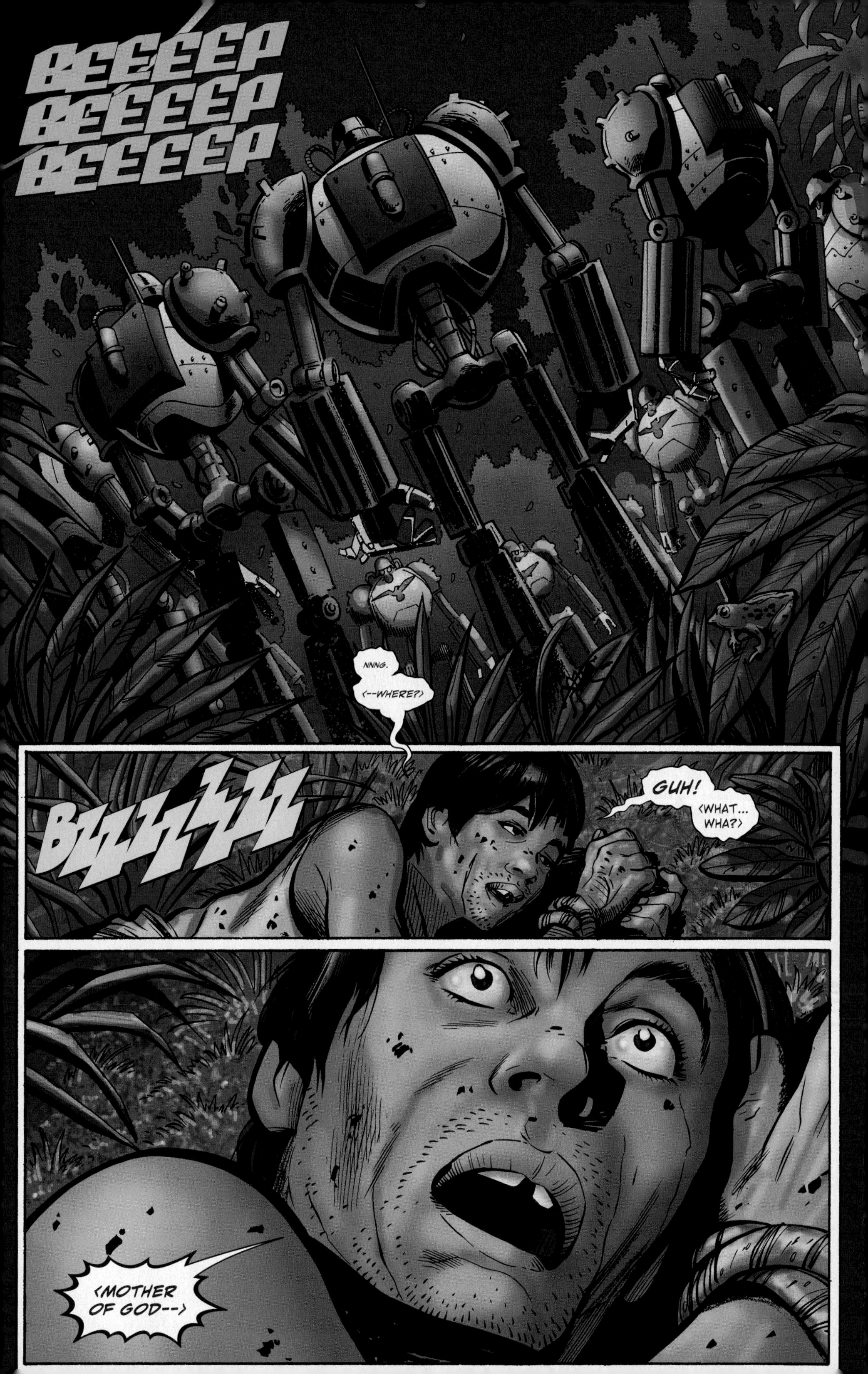
BEEEEP
BEEEEP
BEEEEP
NNNG.
<--WHERE?>
BZZZZZ
GUH!
<WHAT... WHA?>
<MOTHER OF GOD-->

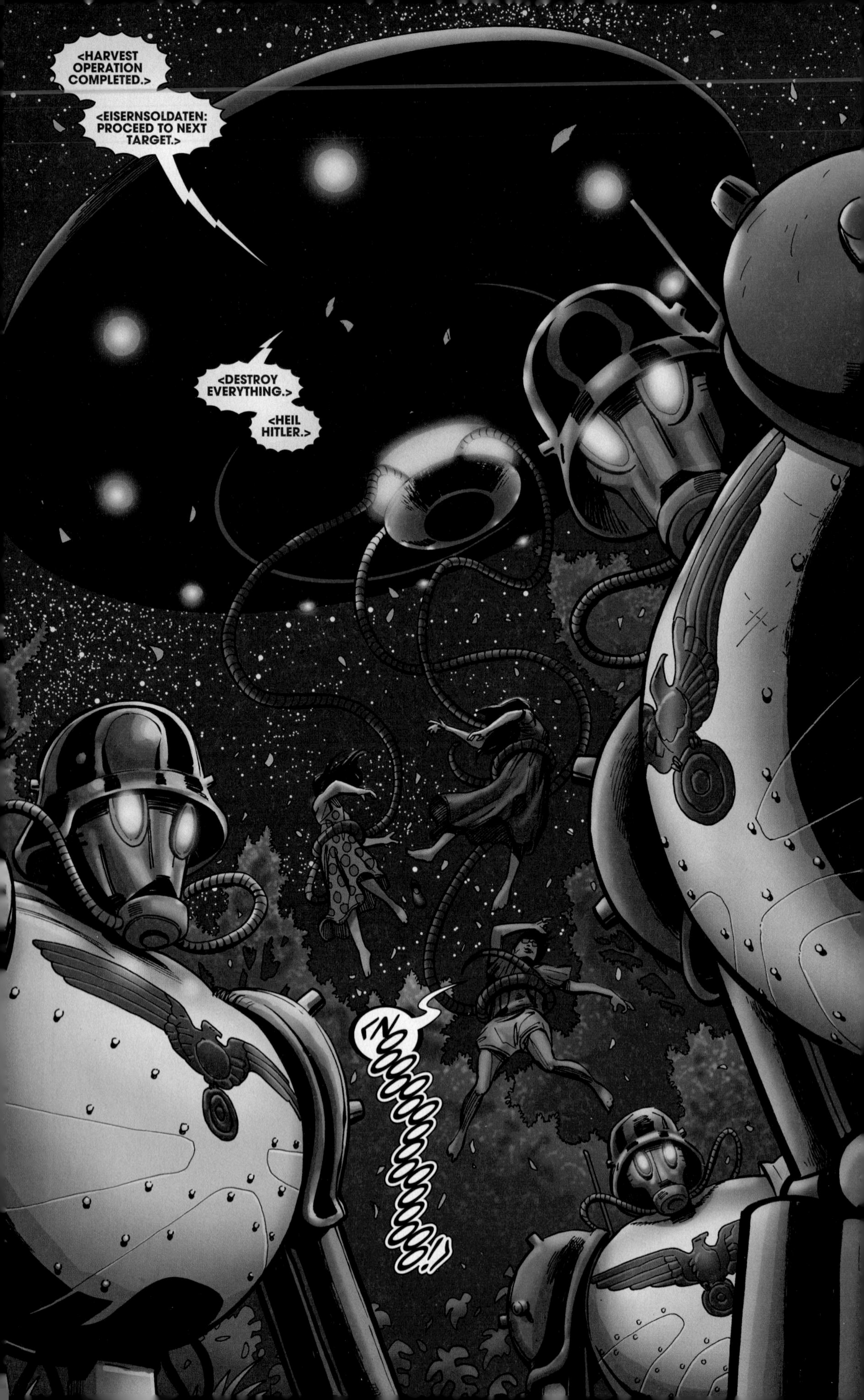
<HARVEST OPERATION COMPLETED.>
<EISERNSOLDATEN: PROCEED TO NEXT TARGET.>
<DESTROY EVERYTHING.>
<HEIL HITLER.>
NOOOOOOOOOOOOO!!

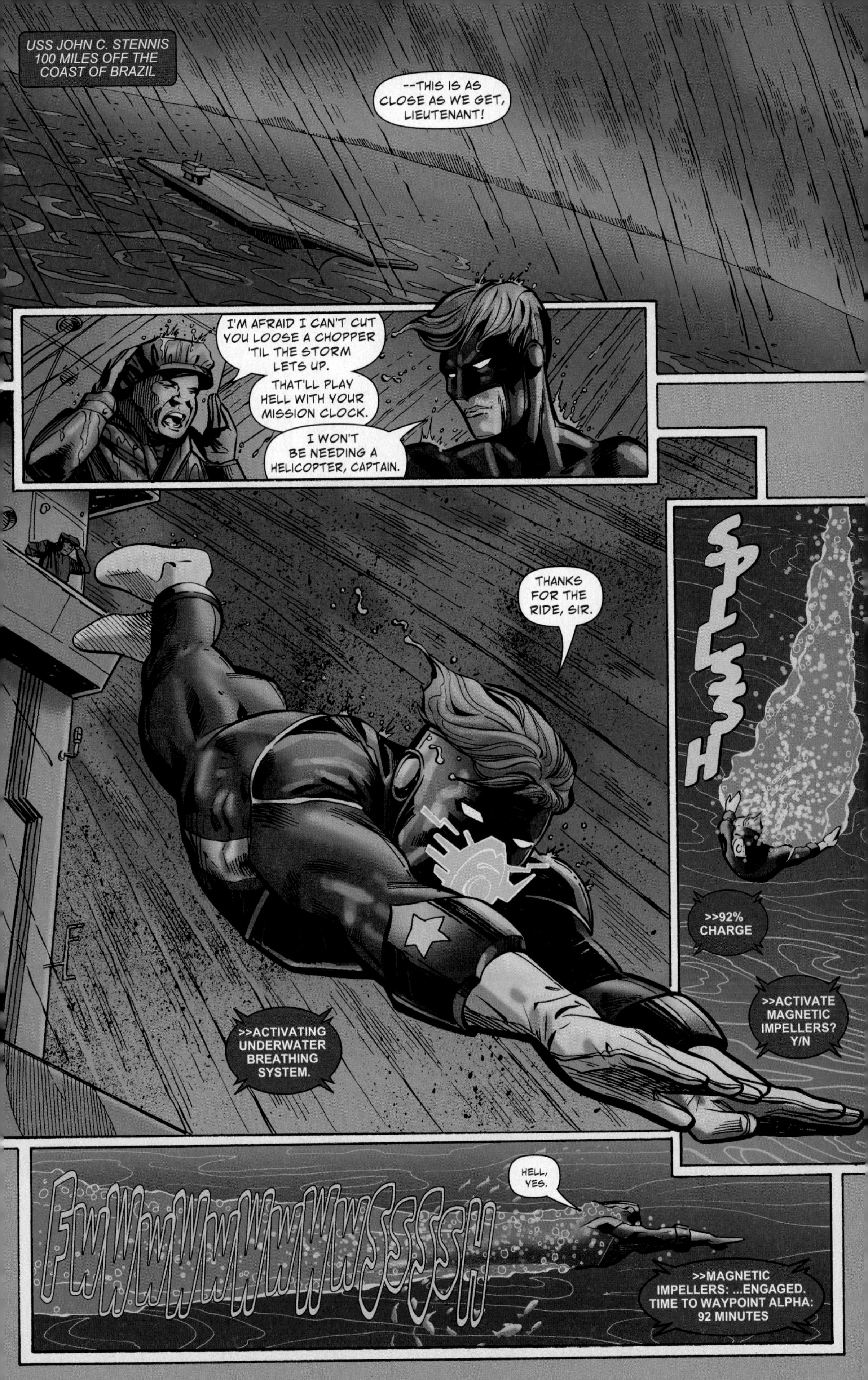
USS JOHN C. STENNIS 100 MILES OFF THE COAST OF BRAZIL
--THIS IS AS CLOSE AS WE GET, LIEUTENANT!
I'M AFRAID I CAN'T CUT YOU LOOSE A CHOPPER 'TIL THE STORM LETS UP.
THAT'LL PLAY HELL WITH YOUR MISSION CLOCK.
I WON'T BE NEEDING A HELICOPTER, CAPTAIN.
THANKS FOR THE RIDE, SIR.
>>ACTIVATING UNDERWATER BREATHING SYSTEM.
SPLSSH
>>92% CHARGE
>>ACTIVATE MAGNETIC IMPELLERS? Y/N
FWWWWWWWWWWWWSSSSSH
HELL, YES.
>>MAGNETIC IMPELLERS: ...ENGAGED. TIME TO WAYPOINT ALPHA: 92 MINUTES

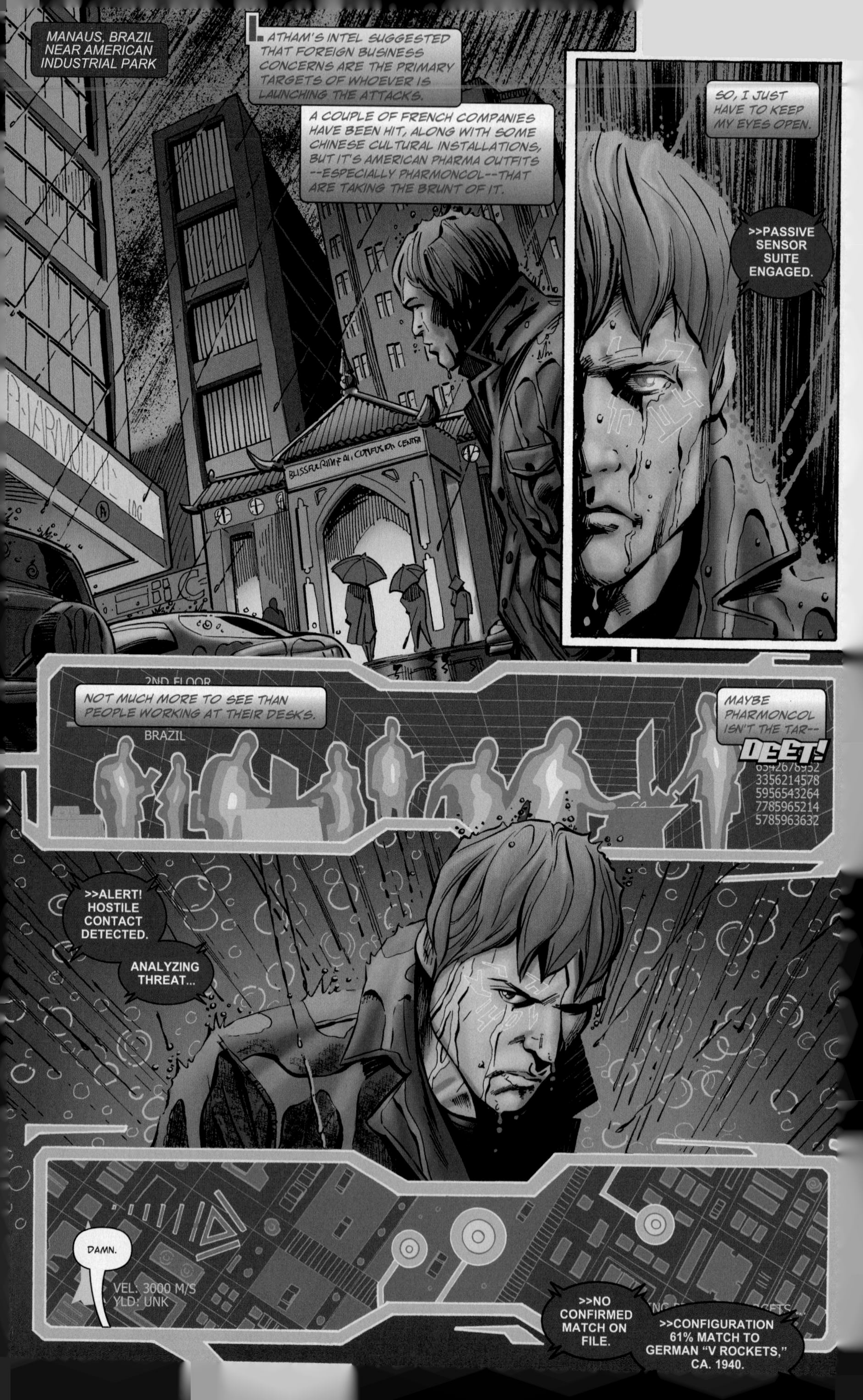
MANAUS, BRAZIL
NEAR AMERICAN
INDUSTRIAL PARK
LATHAM'S INTEL SUGGESTED THAT FOREIGN BUSINESS CONCERNS ARE THE PRIMARY TARGETS OF WHOEVER IS LAUNCHING THE ATTACKS.
A COUPLE OF FRENCH COMPANIES HAVE BEEN HIT, ALONG WITH SOME CHINESE CULTURAL INSTALLATIONS, BUT IT'S AMERICAN PHARMA OUTFITS --ESPECIALLY PHARMONCOL--THAT ARE TAKING THE BRUNT OF IT.
SO, I JUST HAVE TO KEEP MY EYES OPEN.
>>PASSIVE SENSOR SUITE ENGAGED.
2ND FLOOR
BRAZIL
NOT MUCH MORE TO SEE THAN PEOPLE WORKING AT THEIR DESKS.
MAYBE PHARMONCOL ISN'T THE TAR--
DEET!
3356214578
5956543264
7785965214
5785963632
>>ALERT! HOSTILE CONTACT DETECTED.
ANALYZING THREAT...
DAMN.
VEL: 3000 M/S
YLD: UNK
>>NO CONFIRMED MATCH ON FILE.
>>CONFIGURATION 61% MATCH TO GERMAN "V ROCKETS," CA. 1940.

SHIELD ACTUAL TO MUSTANG BASE...

...MUSTANG BASE, RESPOND.

SGT. CAYCE, RESPOND PLEASE.

>>SATLINK SEVERED. UNKNOWN INTERFERENCE TYPE. ATTEMPTING CONNECTION...

LOOKS LIKE I'M ON MY OWN, THEN.

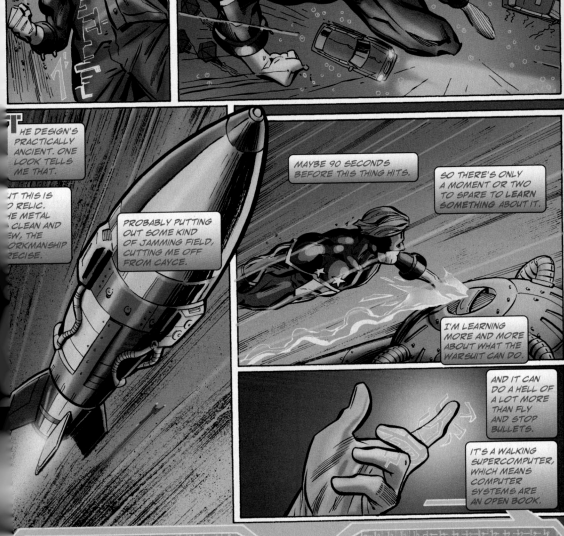

THE DESIGN'S PRACTICALLY ANCIENT. ONE LOOK TELLS ME THAT.

BUT THIS IS NO RELIC. THE METAL IS CLEAN AND NEW, THE WORKMANSHIP PRECISE.

PROBABLY PUTTING OUT SOME KIND OF JAMMING FIELD, CUTTING ME OFF FROM CAYCE.

MAYBE 90 SECONDS BEFORE THIS THING HITS.

SO THERE'S ONLY A MOMENT OR TWO TO SPARE TO LEARN SOMETHING ABOUT IT.

I'M LEARNING MORE AND MORE ABOUT WHAT THE WARSUIT CAN DO.

AND IT CAN DO A HELL OF A LOT MORE THAN FLY AND STOP BULLETS.

IT'S A WALKING SUPERCOMPUTER, WHICH MEANS COMPUTER SYSTEMS ARE AN OPEN BOOK.

IF I START TEARING AT THE WEAPON, IT MIGHT DETONATE. BUT MAYBE I CAN DEFUSE IT, INSTEAD.

OKAY.

LET'S JUST SEE WHAT MAKES YOU TICK.

CODE...

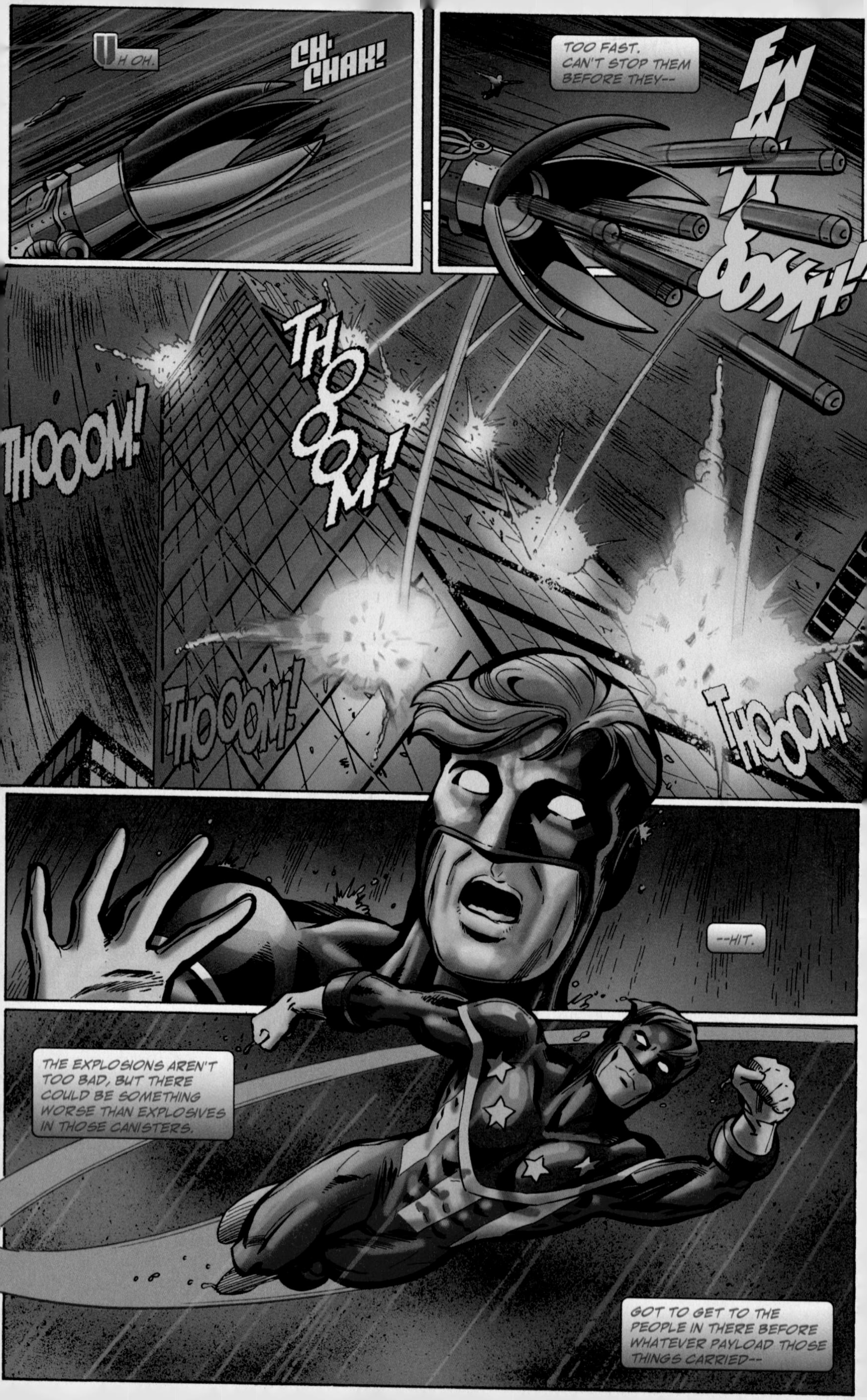
UH OH.
CH-CHAK!
TOO FAST. CAN'T STOP THEM BEFORE THEY--
FWOOSH!
THOOOM!
THOOOOM!
THOOOM!
THOOOM!
--HIT.
THE EXPLOSIONS AREN'T TOO BAD, BUT THERE COULD BE SOMETHING WORSE THAN EXPLOSIVES IN THOSE CANISTERS.
GOT TO GET TO THE PEOPLE IN THERE BEFORE WHATEVER PAYLOAD THOSE THINGS CARRIED--

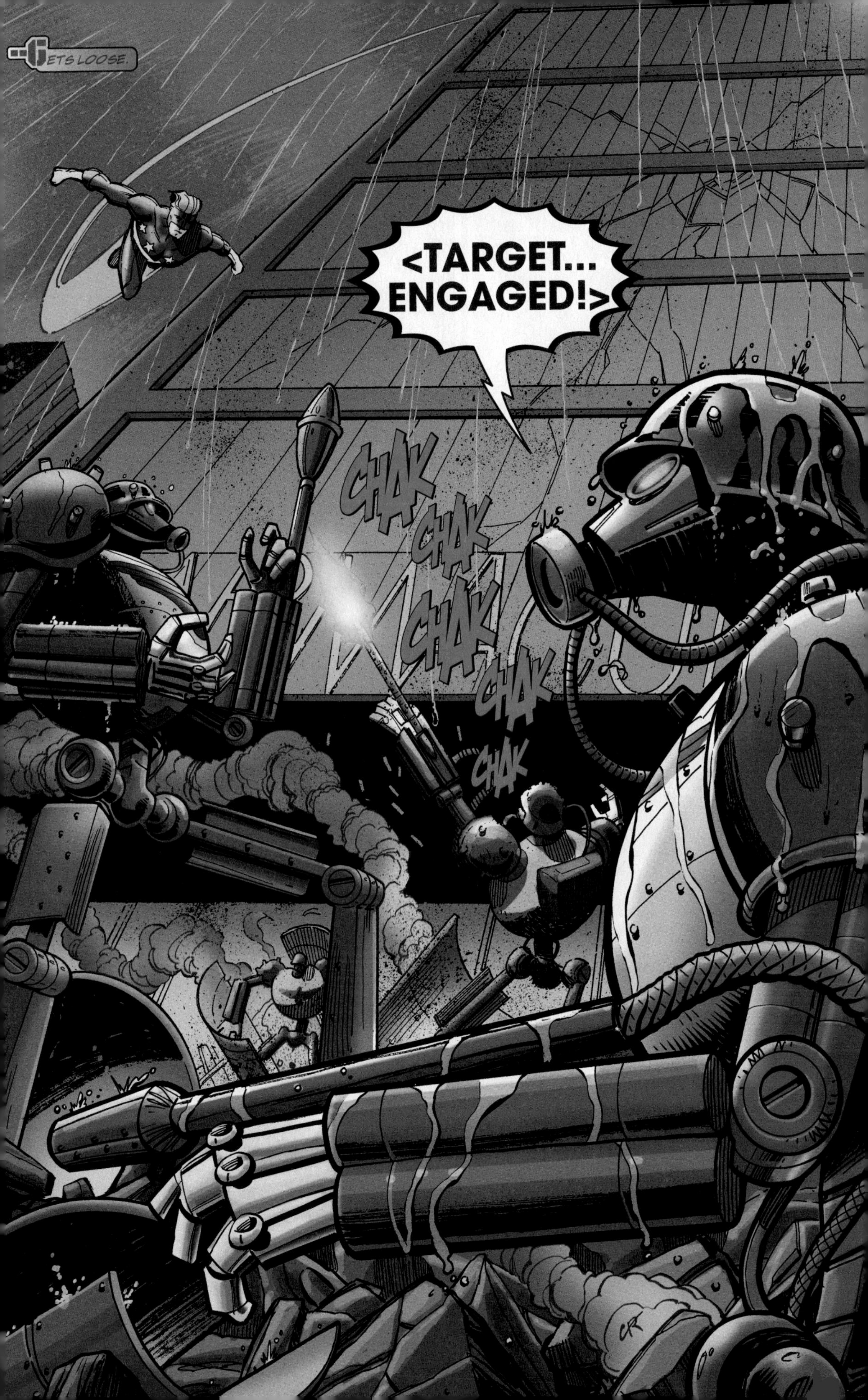
GETS LOOSE.
<TARGET... ENGAGED!>
CHAK
CHAK
CHAK
CHAK
CHAK

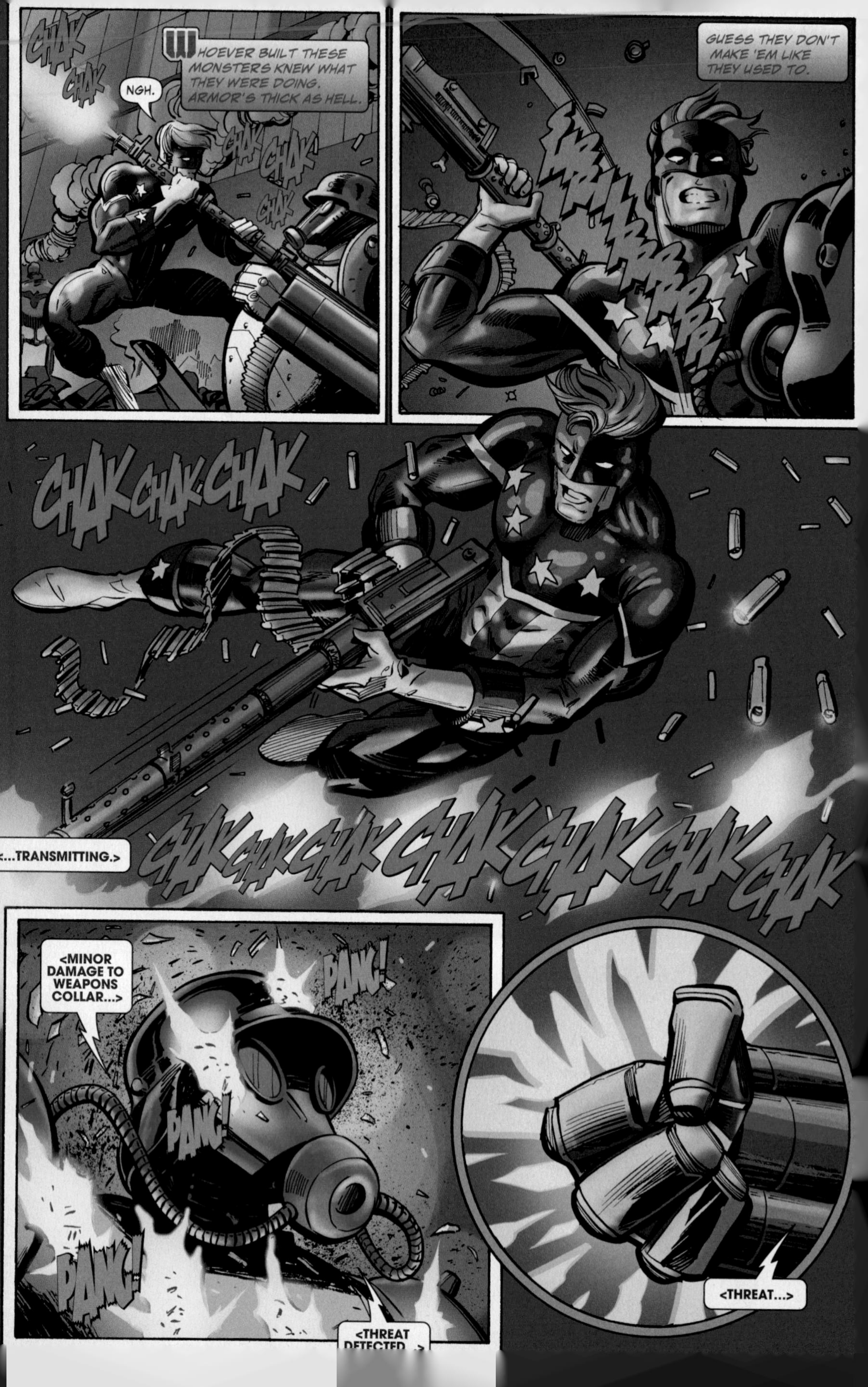
CHAK
CHAK
WHOEVER BUILT THESE MONSTERS KNEW WHAT THEY WERE DOING. ARMOR'S THICK AS HELL.
NGH.
CHAK
CHAK
CHAK
GUESS THEY DON'T MAKE 'EM LIKE THEY USED TO.
CHAK CHAK CHAK
<...TRANSMITTING.>
CHAK CHAK CHAK CHAK CHAK CHAK CHAK
<MINOR DAMAGE TO WEAPONS COLLAR...>
PANG!
PANG!
PANG!
<THREAT DETECTED...>
<THREAT...>

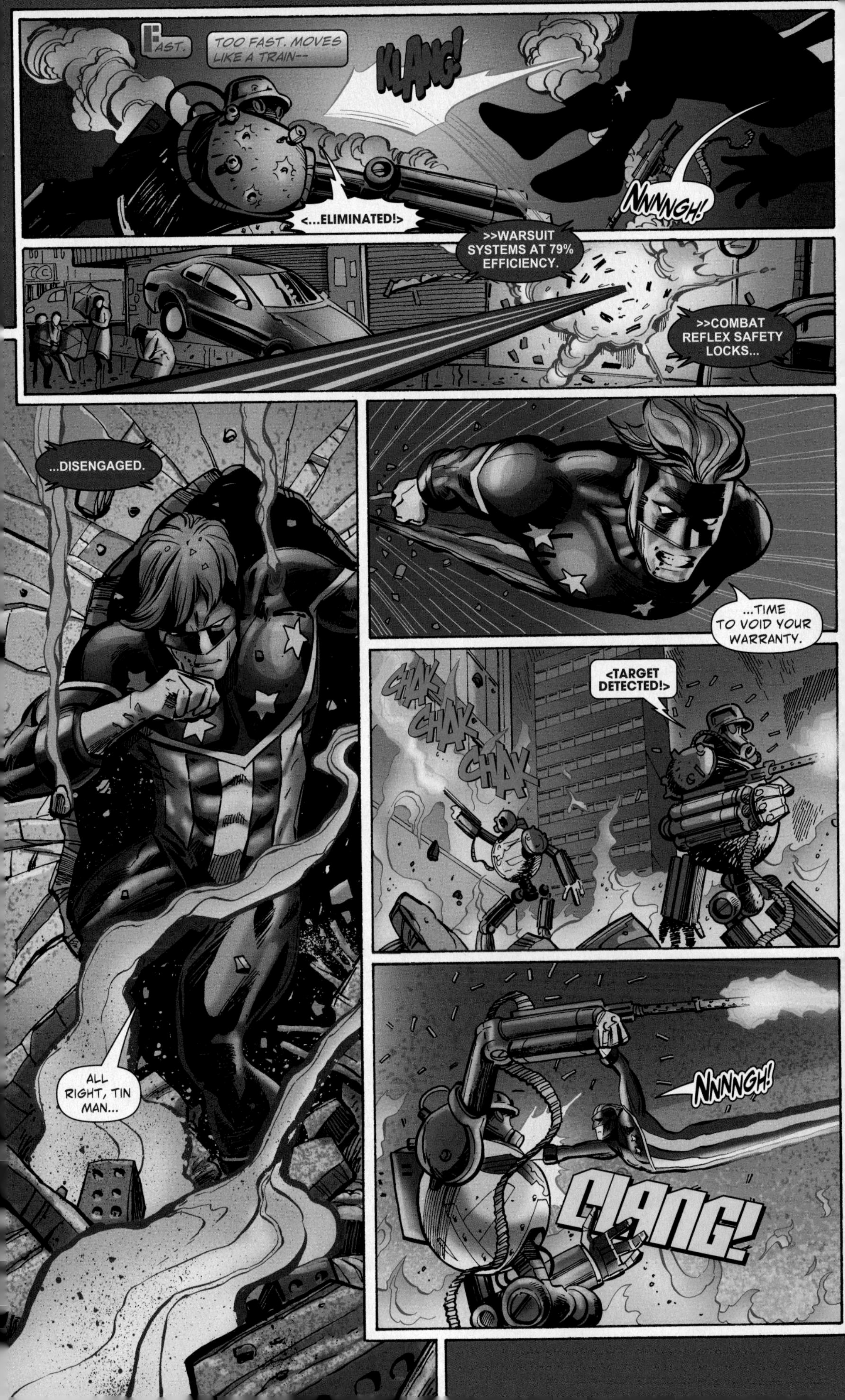
FAST.
TOO FAST. MOVES LIKE A TRAIN--
KLANG!
NNNNGH!
<...ELIMINATED!>
>>WARSUIT SYSTEMS AT 79% EFFICIENCY.
>>COMBAT REFLEX SAFETY LOCKS...
...DISENGAGED.
ALL RIGHT, TIN MAN...
...TIME TO VOID YOUR WARRANTY.
<TARGET DETECTED!>
CHAK CHAK CHAK
NNNNGH!
CLANG!

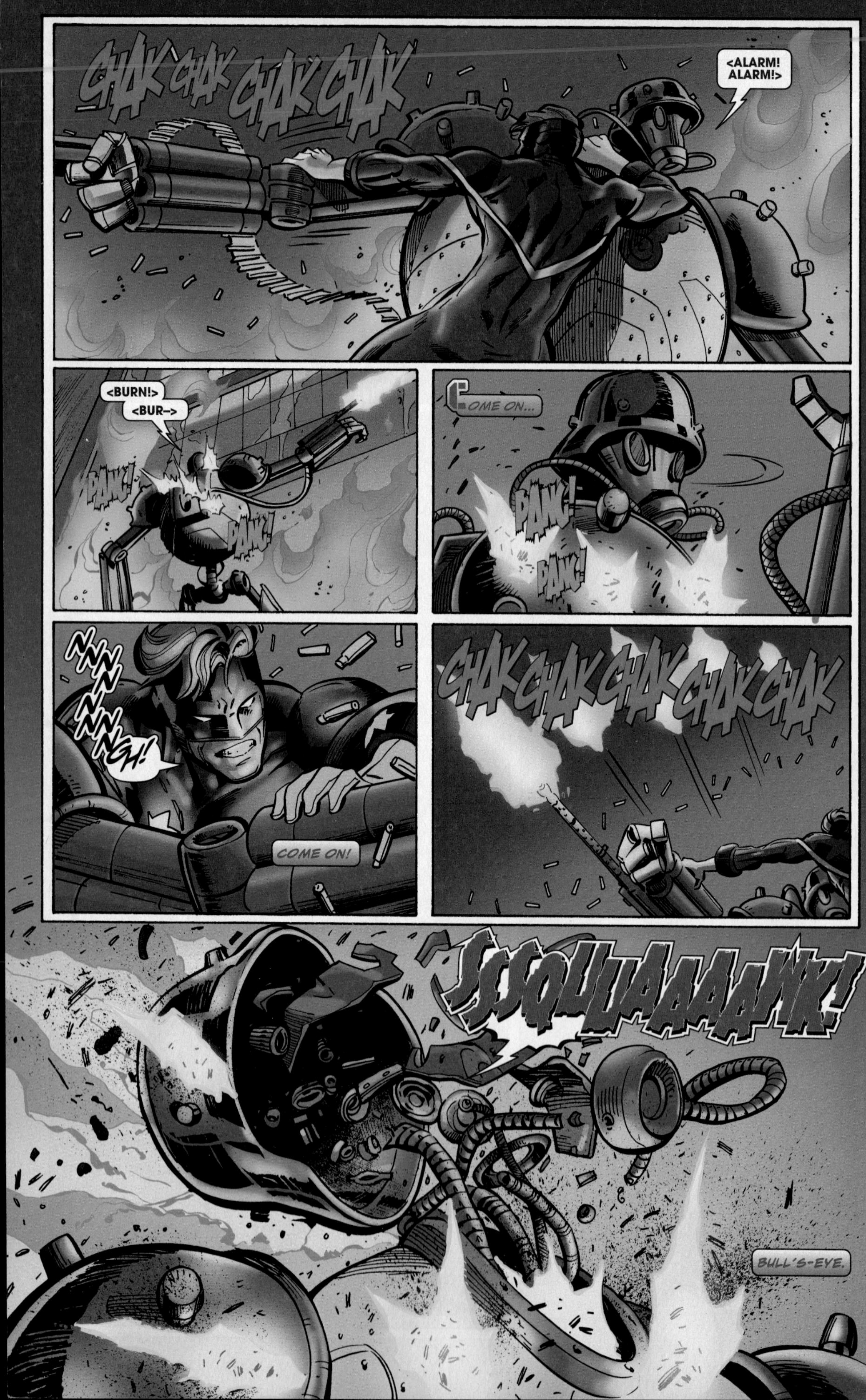
CHAK CHAK CHAK CHAK
<ALARM! ALARM!>
<BURN!>
<BUR-->
PANG!
PANG!
COME ON...
PANG!
PANG!
NNNNNNNGH!
COME ON!
CHAK CHAK CHAK CHAK CHAK
SSQUUAAAAWK!
BULL'S-EYE.

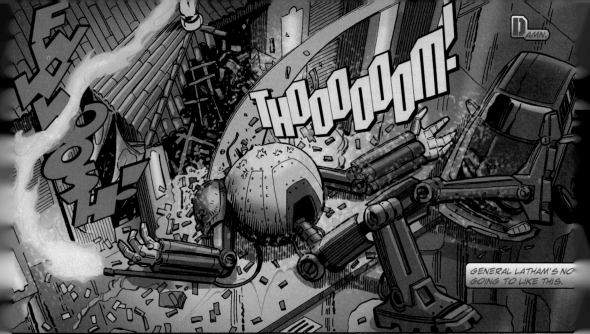

THOOOOOOM!

D*amn.*

GENERAL LATHAM'S NO GOING TO LIKE THIS.

MOVE! GET CLEAR!

LOTS OF CIVILIANS IN THE RUBBLE. NO TELLING HOW MANY ARE DEAD OR WOUNDED.

GOT TO FIND A WAY TO LEAD THESE THINGS OFF, OR IT'LL BE A MASSACRE--

DEET DEET

<MISSION CLOCK EXPIRED. EISERNSOLDAT 018 TO ALL UNITS, RETURN TO BASE.>

MAGLEV DRIVES DETECTED.

SIGNAL INTERFERENCE RECEDING. ESTABLISHING SATLINK...

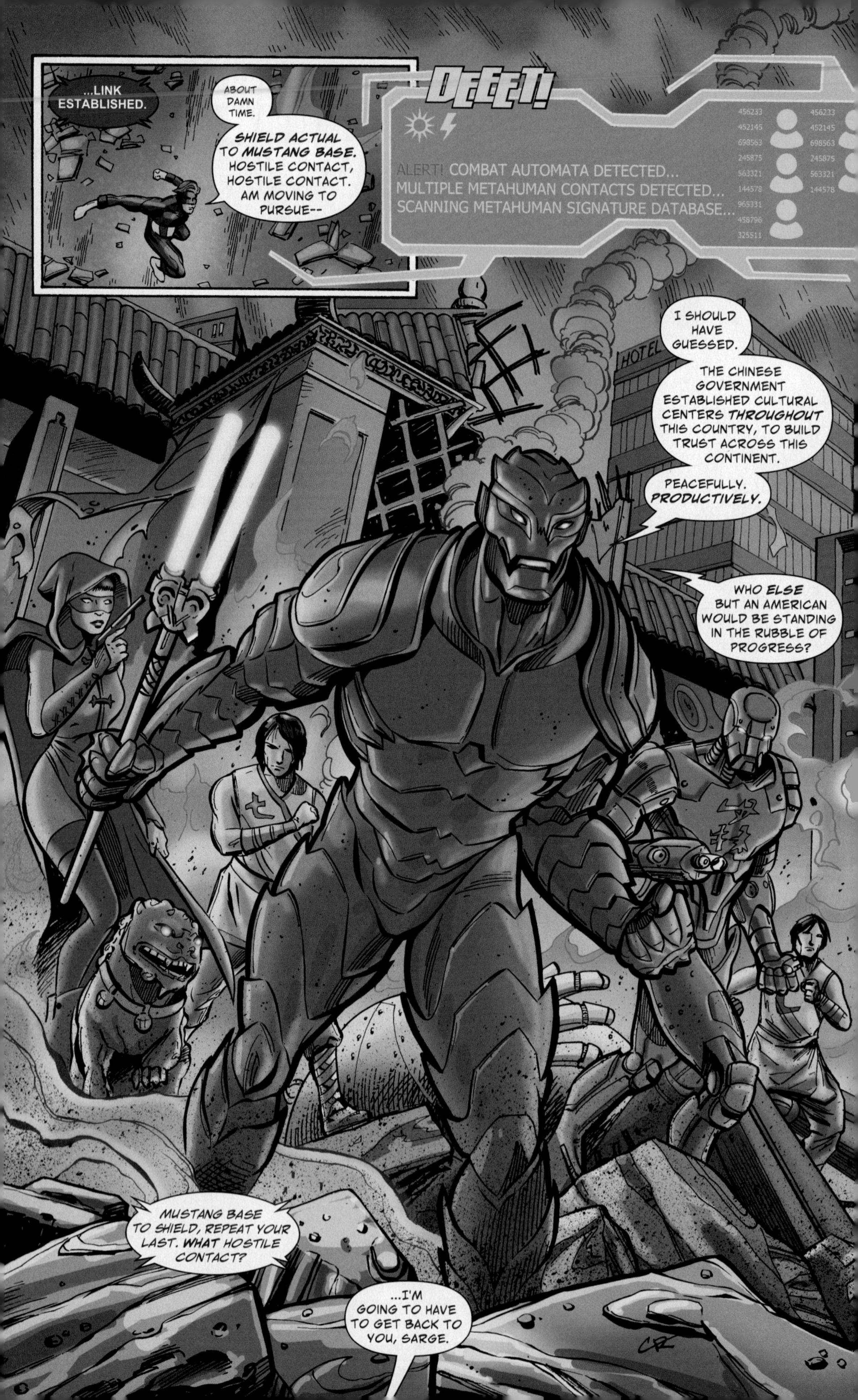

...LINK ESTABLISHED.
ABOUT DAMN TIME.
SHIELD ACTUAL TO MUSTANG BASE. HOSTILE CONTACT, HOSTILE CONTACT. AM MOVING TO PURSUE--
DEEEET!
ALERT! COMBAT AUTOMATA DETECTED...
MULTIPLE METAHUMAN CONTACTS DETECTED...
SCANNING METAHUMAN SIGNATURE DATABASE...
456233 452145 698563 245875 563321 144578 965331 458796 325511
456233 452145 698563 245875 563321 144578
HOTEL
I SHOULD HAVE GUESSED.
THE CHINESE GOVERNMENT ESTABLISHED CULTURAL CENTERS THROUGHOUT THIS COUNTRY, TO BUILD TRUST ACROSS THIS CONTINENT.
PEACEFULLY. PRODUCTIVELY.
WHO ELSE BUT AN AMERICAN WOULD BE STANDING IN THE RUBBLE OF PROGRESS?
MUSTANG BASE TO SHIELD, REPEAT YOUR LAST. WHAT HOSTILE CONTACT?
...I'M GOING TO HAVE TO GET BACK TO YOU, SARGE.

GHOSTS PART 2: JUNGLE WARFARE

Cover by Sami Basri

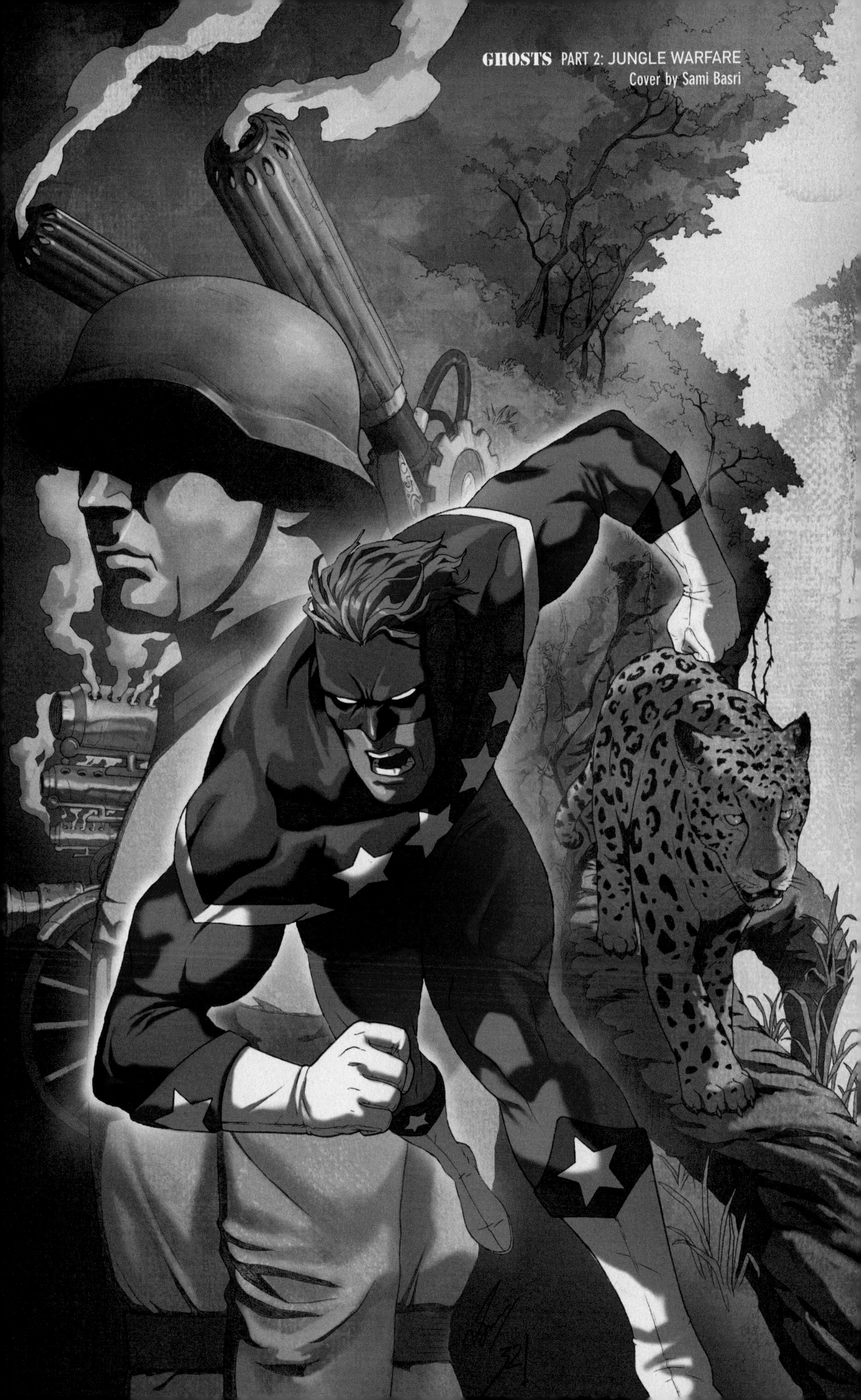

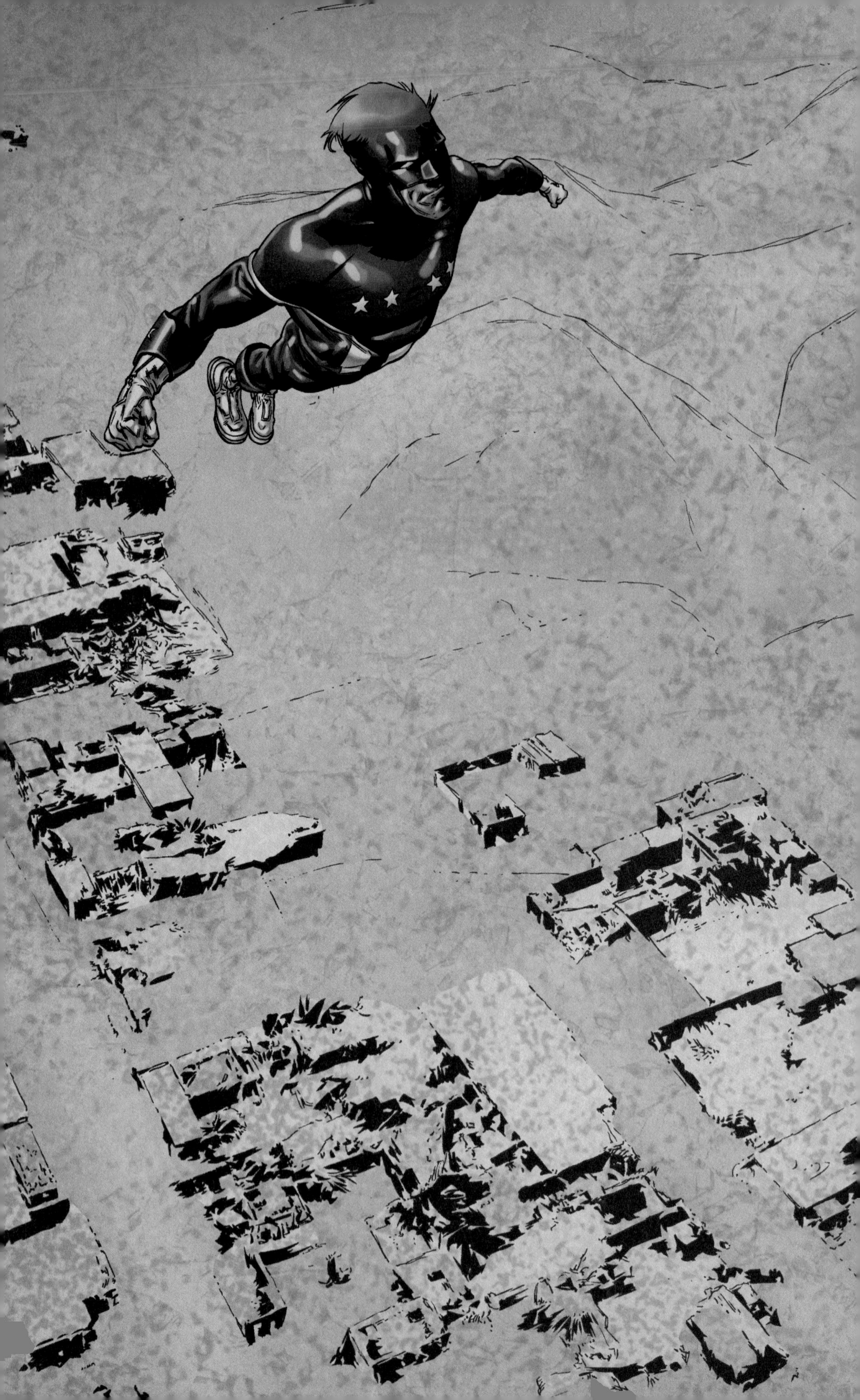

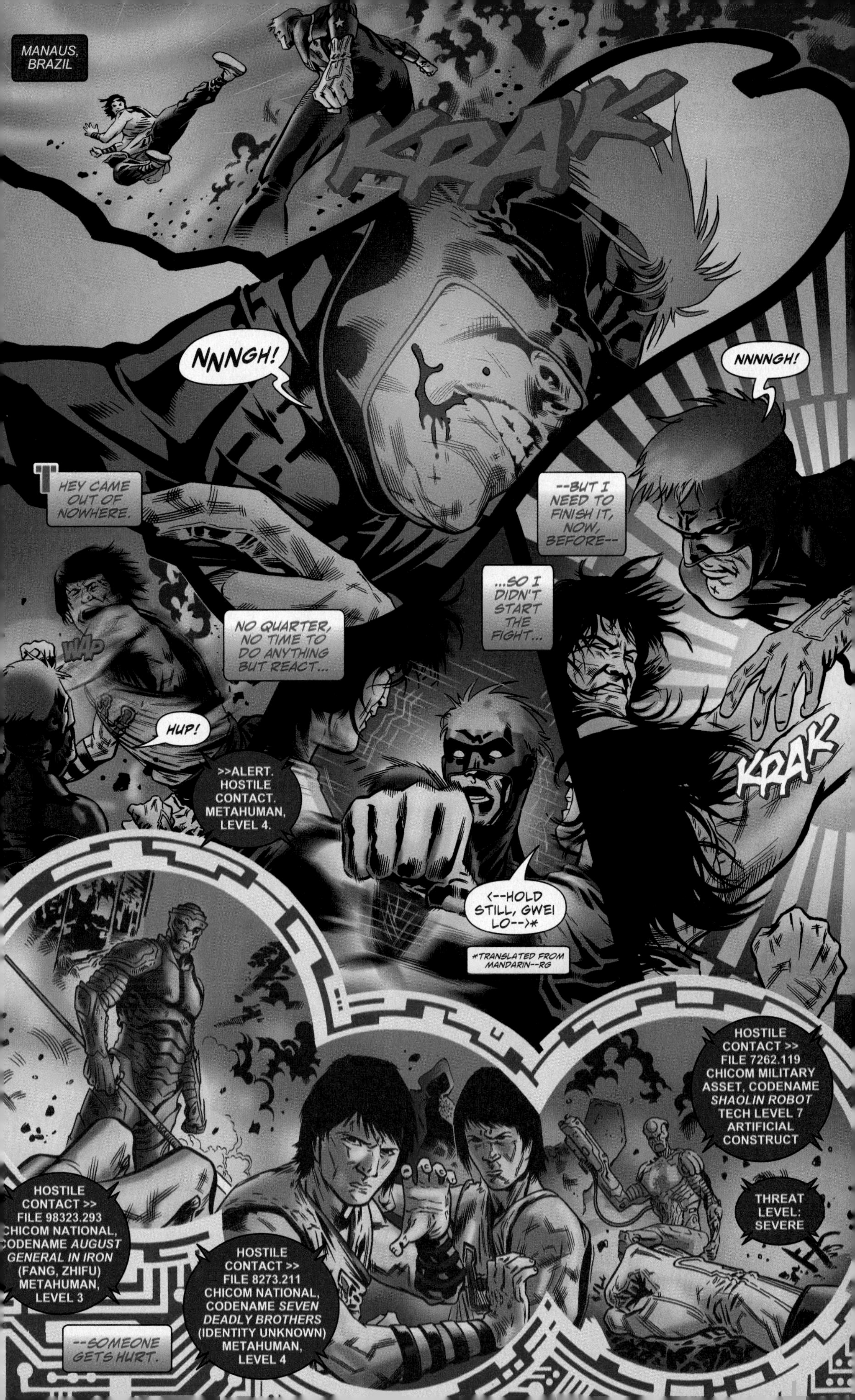
MANAUS, BRAZIL
KRAK
NNNGH!
THEY CAME OUT OF NOWHERE.
NNNNGH!
--BUT I NEED TO FINISH IT, NOW, BEFORE--
...SO I DIDN'T START THE FIGHT...
NO QUARTER, NO TIME TO DO ANYTHING BUT REACT...
WAP
HUP!
>>ALERT. HOSTILE CONTACT. METAHUMAN, LEVEL 4.
KRAK
<--HOLD STILL, GWEI LO-->*
*TRANSLATED FROM MANDARIN--RG
HOSTILE CONTACT >> FILE 7262.119 CHICOM MILITARY ASSET, CODENAME *SHAOLIN ROBOT* TECH LEVEL 7 ARTIFICIAL CONSTRUCT
THREAT LEVEL: SEVERE
HOSTILE CONTACT >> FILE 98323.293 CHICOM NATIONAL, CODENAME *AUGUST GENERAL IN IRON* (FANG, ZHIFU) METAHUMAN, LEVEL 3
HOSTILE CONTACT >> FILE 8273.211 CHICOM NATIONAL, CODENAME *SEVEN DEADLY BROTHERS* (IDENTITY UNKNOWN) METAHUMAN, LEVEL 4
--SOMEONE GETS HURT.

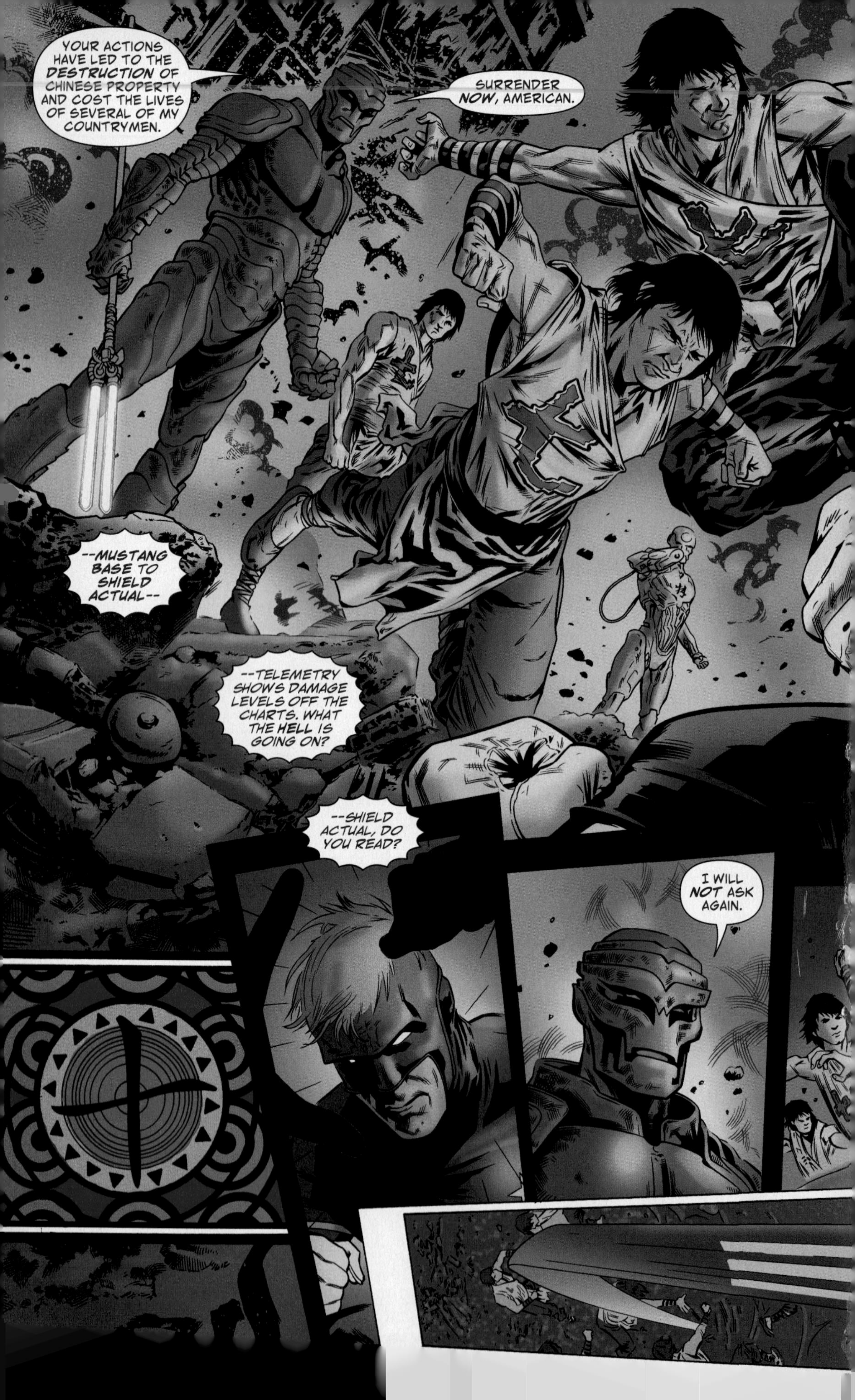
YOUR ACTIONS HAVE LED TO THE DESTRUCTION OF CHINESE PROPERTY AND COST THE LIVES OF SEVERAL OF MY COUNTRYMEN.
SURRENDER NOW, AMERICAN.
--MUSTANG BASE TO SHIELD ACTUAL--
--TELEMETRY SHOWS DAMAGE LEVELS OFF THE CHARTS. WHAT THE HELL IS GOING ON?
--SHIELD ACTUAL, DO YOU READ?
I WILL NOT ASK AGAIN.

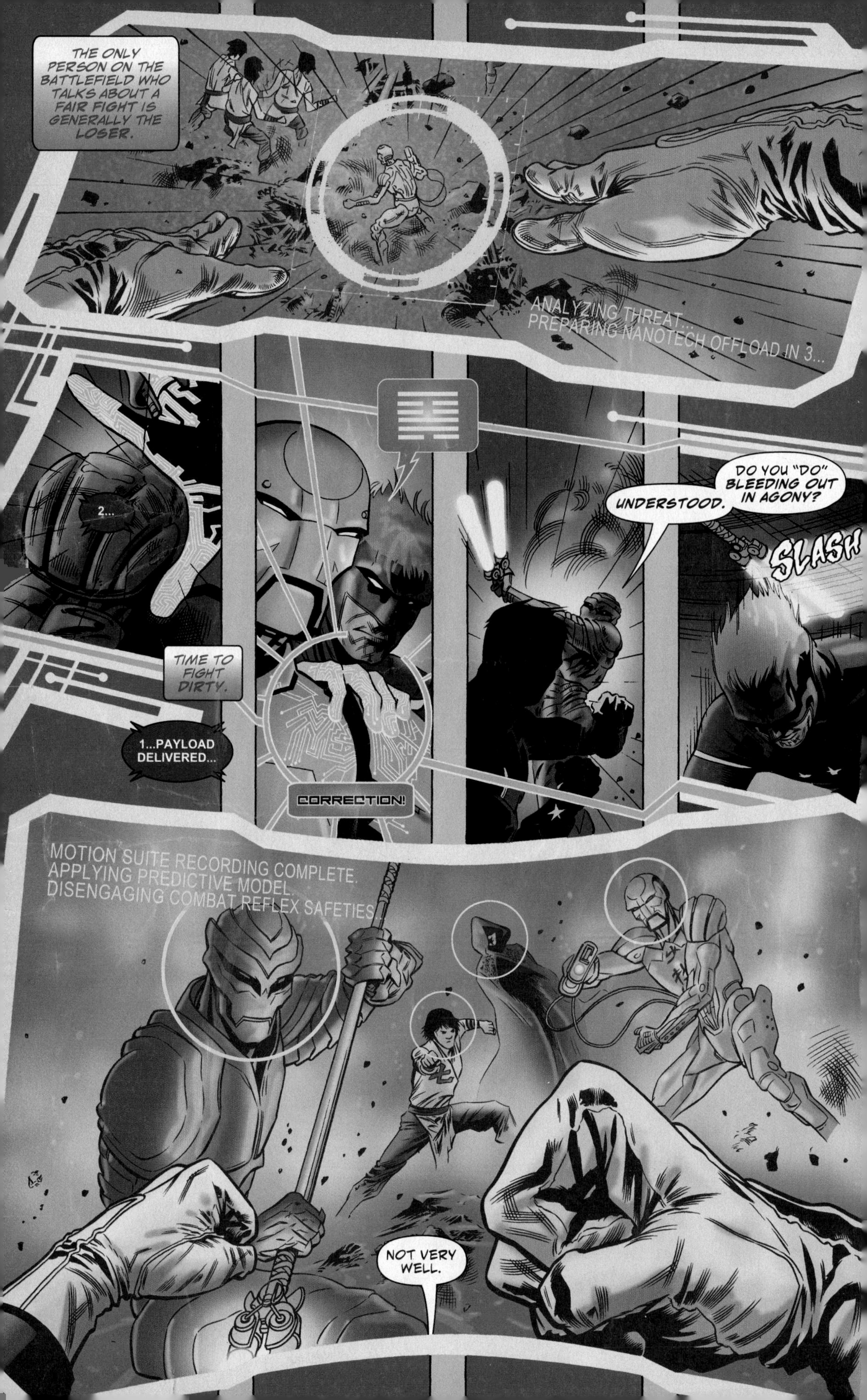

THE ONLY PERSON ON THE BATTLEFIELD WHO TALKS ABOUT A FAIR FIGHT IS GENERALLY THE LOSER.
ANALYZING THREAT...
PREPARING NANOTECH OFFLOAD IN 3...
2...
TIME TO FIGHT DIRTY.
1...PAYLOAD DELIVERED...
CORRECTION!
UNDERSTOOD.
DO YOU "DO" BLEEDING OUT IN AGONY?
SLASH
MOTION SUITE RECORDING COMPLETE.
APPLYING PREDICTIVE MODEL.
DISENGAGING COMBAT REFLEX SAFETIES.
NOT VERY WELL.

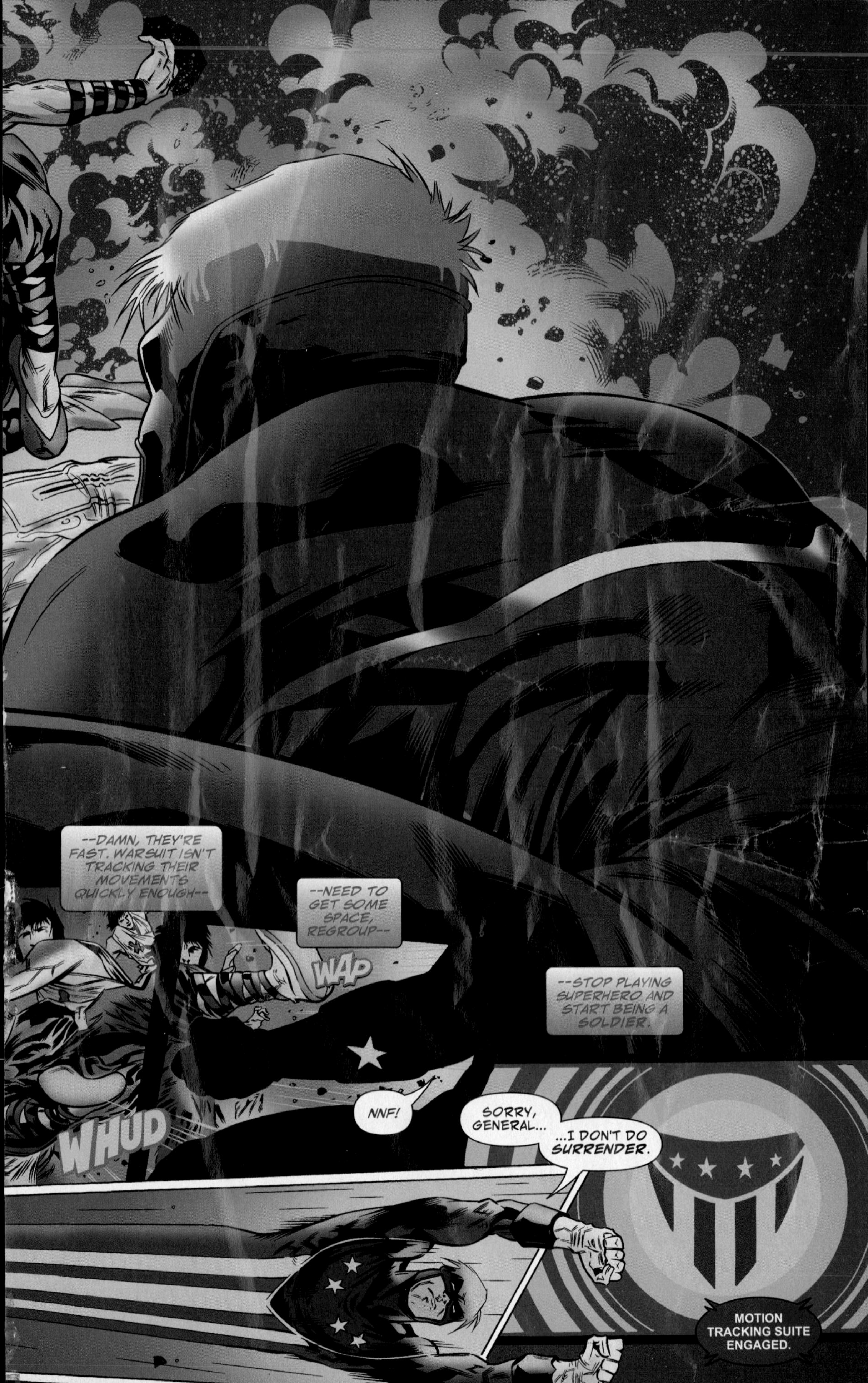

--DAMN, THEY'RE FAST. WARSUIT ISN'T TRACKING THEIR MOVEMENTS QUICKLY ENOUGH--
--NEED TO GET SOME SPACE, REGROUP--
WAP
--STOP PLAYING SUPERHERO AND START BEING A SOLDIER.
WHUD
NNF!
SORRY, GENERAL...
...I DON'T DO SURRENDER.
MOTION TRACKING SUITE ENGAGED.

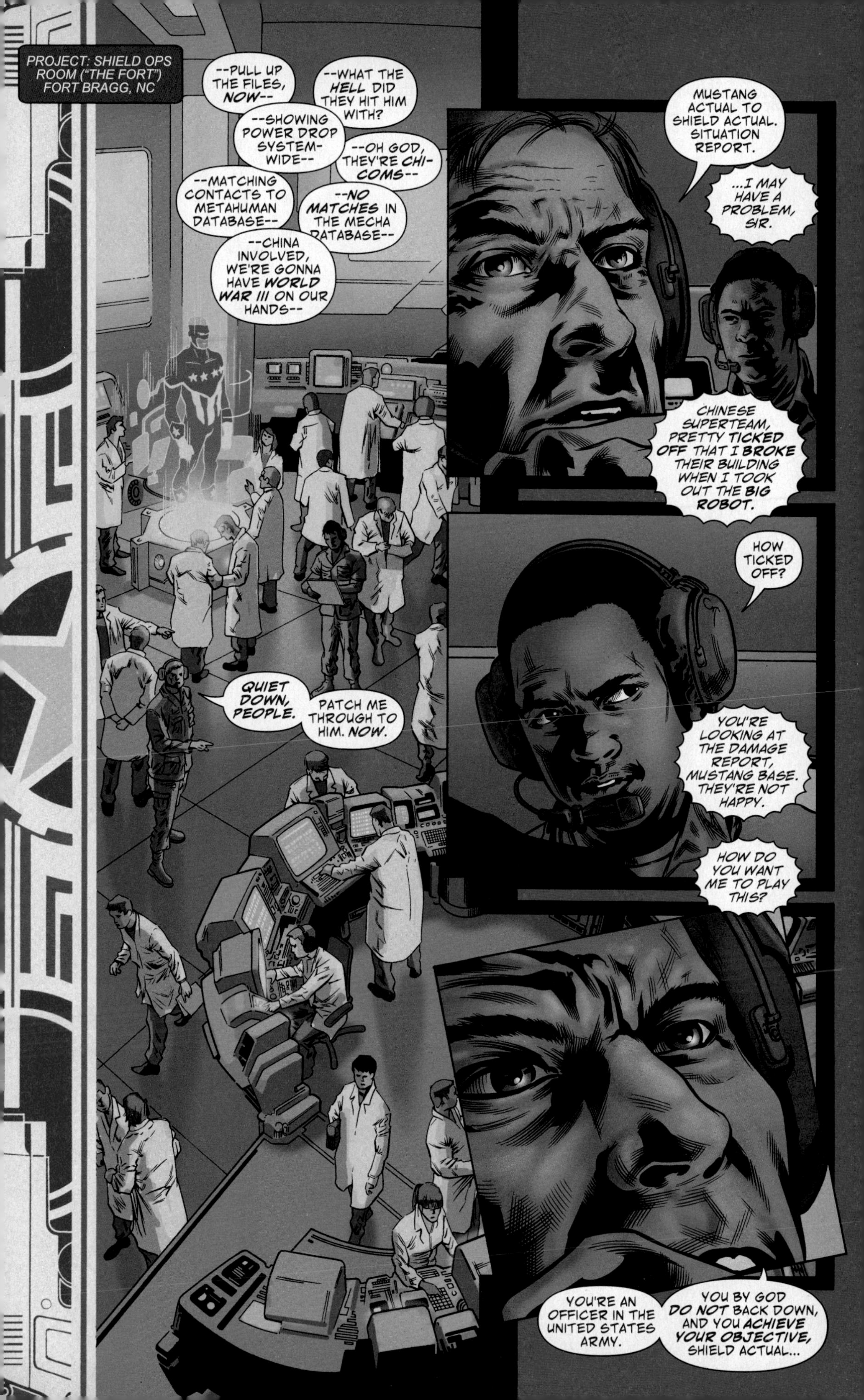
PROJECT: SHIELD OPS ROOM ("THE FORT") FORT BRAGG, NC
--PULL UP THE FILES, NOW--
--WHAT THE HELL DID THEY HIT HIM WITH?
--SHOWING POWER DROP SYSTEM-WIDE--
--OH GOD, THEY'RE CHI-COMS--
--MATCHING CONTACTS TO METAHUMAN DATABASE--
--NO MATCHES IN THE MECHA DATABASE--
--CHINA INVOLVED, WE'RE GONNA HAVE WORLD WAR III ON OUR HANDS--
QUIET DOWN, PEOPLE.
PATCH ME THROUGH TO HIM. NOW.
MUSTANG ACTUAL TO SHIELD ACTUAL. SITUATION REPORT.
...I MAY HAVE A PROBLEM, SIR.
CHINESE SUPERTEAM, PRETTY TICKED OFF THAT I BROKE THEIR BUILDING WHEN I TOOK OUT THE BIG ROBOT.
HOW TICKED OFF?
YOU'RE LOOKING AT THE DAMAGE REPORT, MUSTANG BASE. THEY'RE NOT HAPPY.
HOW DO YOU WANT ME TO PLAY THIS?
YOU'RE AN OFFICER IN THE UNITED STATES ARMY.
YOU BY GOD DO NOT BACK DOWN, AND YOU ACHIEVE YOUR OBJECTIVE, SHIELD ACTUAL...

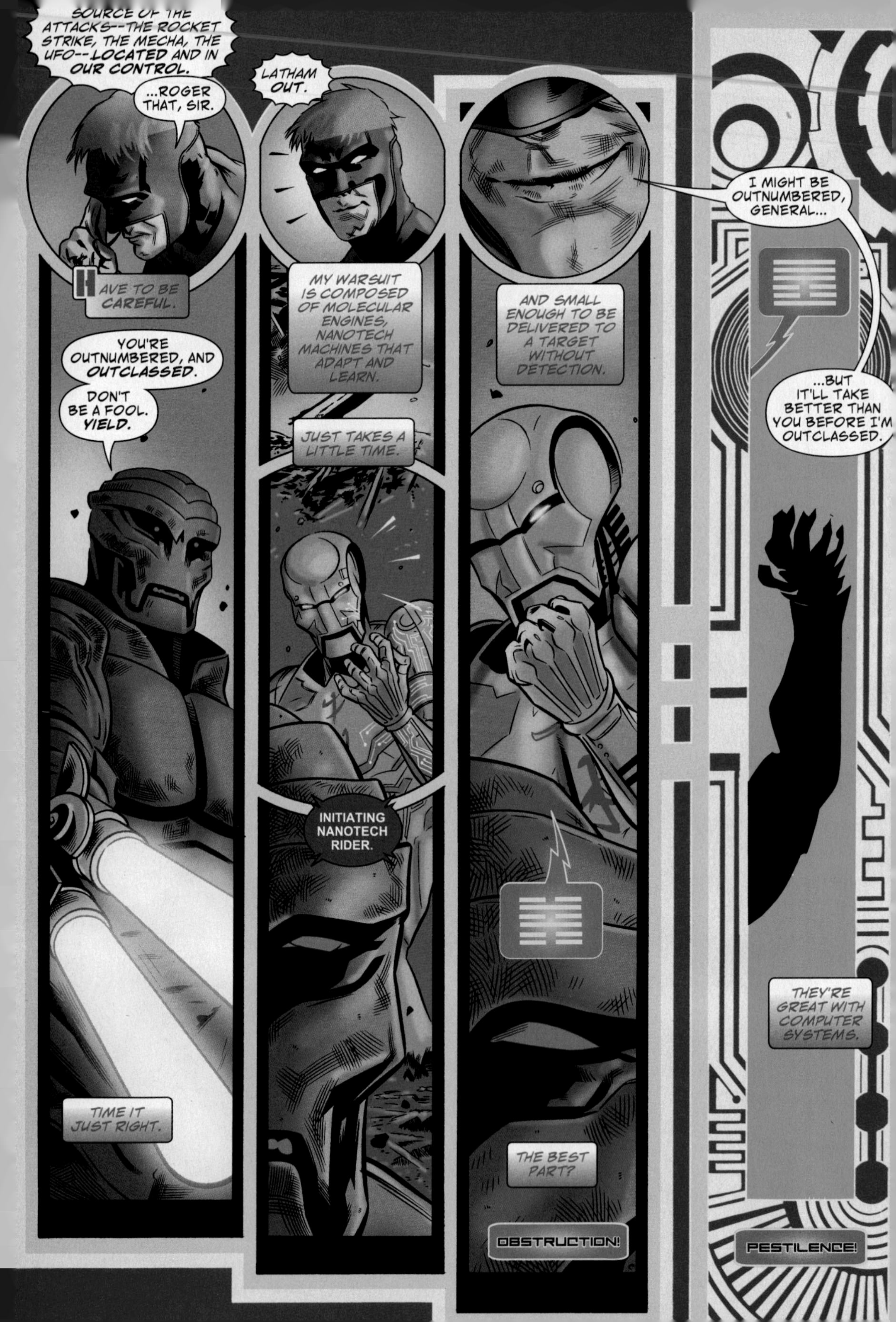
SOURCE OF THE ATTACKS--THE ROCKET STRIKE, THE MECHA, THE UFO--LOCATED AND IN OUR CONTROL.
...ROGER THAT, SIR.
LATHAM OUT.
HAVE TO BE CAREFUL.
YOU'RE OUTNUMBERED, AND OUTCLASSED.
DON'T BE A FOOL. YIELD.
TIME IT JUST RIGHT.
MY WARSUIT IS COMPOSED OF MOLECULAR ENGINES, NANOTECH MACHINES THAT ADAPT AND LEARN.
JUST TAKES A LITTLE TIME.
INITIATING NANOTECH RIDER.
AND SMALL ENOUGH TO BE DELIVERED TO A TARGET WITHOUT DETECTION.
THE BEST PART?
OBSTRUCTION!
I MIGHT BE OUTNUMBERED, GENERAL...
...BUT IT'LL TAKE BETTER THAN YOU BEFORE I'M OUTCLASSED.
THEY'RE GREAT WITH COMPUTER SYSTEMS.
PESTILENCE!

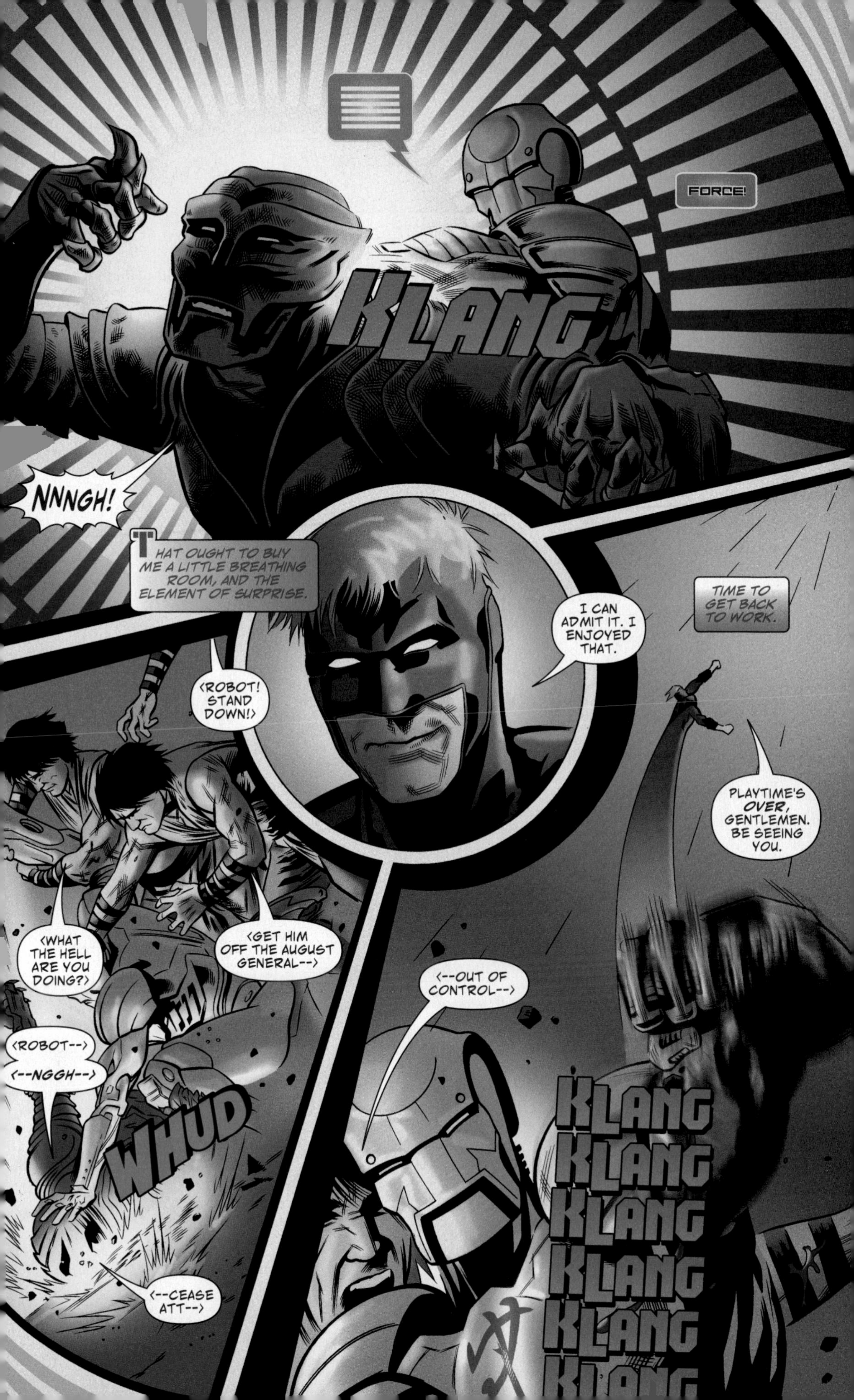
FORCE!
KLANG
NNNGH!
THAT OUGHT TO BUY ME A LITTLE BREATHING ROOM, AND THE ELEMENT OF SURPRISE.
I CAN ADMIT IT. I ENJOYED THAT.
TIME TO GET BACK TO WORK.
<ROBOT! STAND DOWN!>
PLAYTIME'S *OVER*, GENTLEMEN. BE SEEING YOU.
<WHAT THE HELL ARE YOU DOING?>
<GET HIM OFF THE AUGUST GENERAL-->
<--OUT OF CONTROL-->
<ROBOT-->
<--NGGH-->
WHUD
KLANG
KLANG
KLANG
KLANG
KLANG
<--CEASE ATT-->

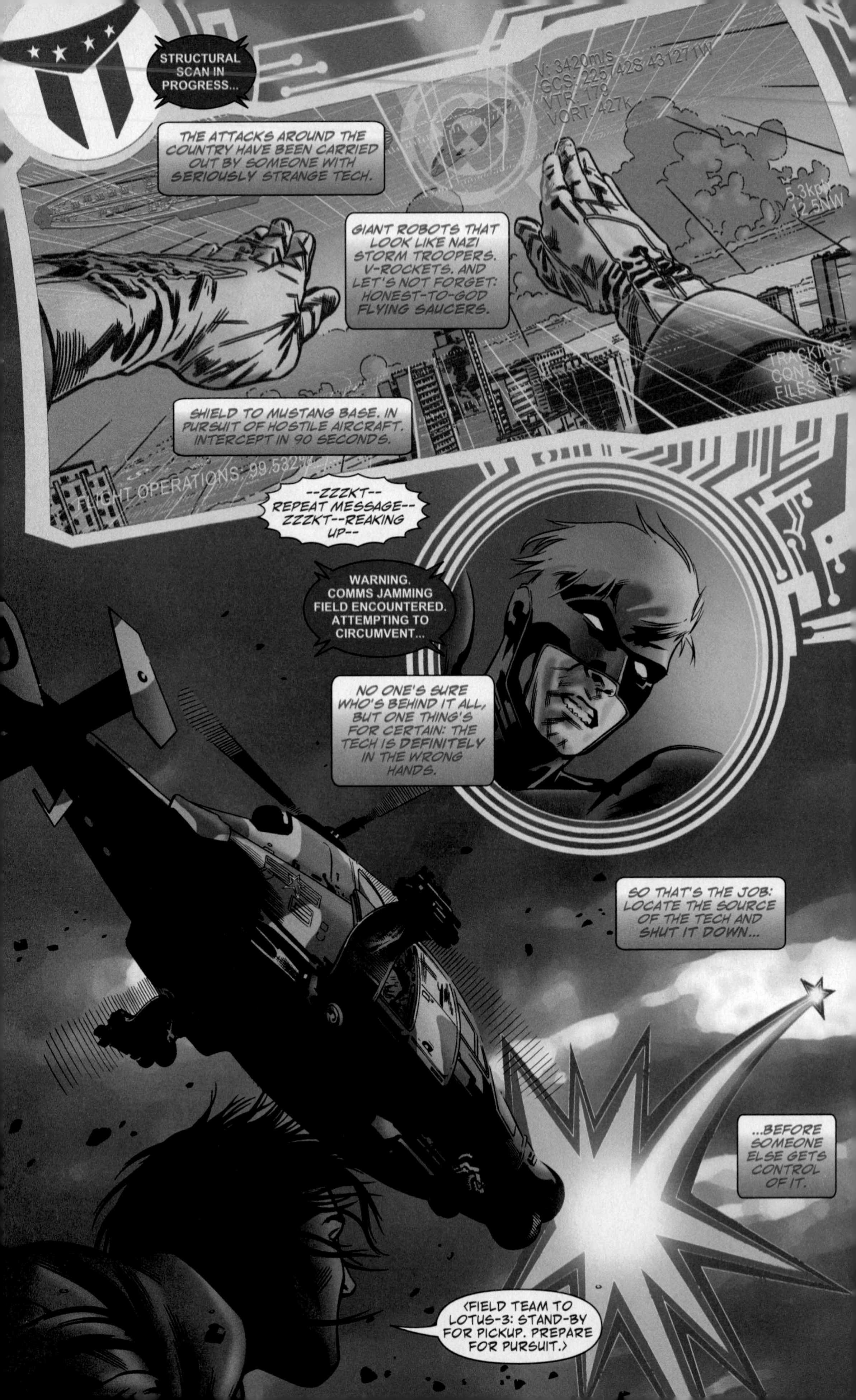
STRUCTURAL SCAN IN PROGRESS...
V: 3420m/s
GCS: 225742S 431271W
VTR: 178
VORT: 427k
THE ATTACKS AROUND THE COUNTRY HAVE BEEN CARRIED OUT BY SOMEONE WITH SERIOUSLY STRANGE TECH.
5.3kph
12.5NW
GIANT ROBOTS THAT LOOK LIKE NAZI STORM TROOPERS. V-ROCKETS. AND LET'S NOT FORGET: HONEST-TO-GOD FLYING SAUCERS.
TRACKING CONTACT FILES 17
SHIELD TO MUSTANG BASE. IN PURSUIT OF HOSTILE AIRCRAFT. INTERCEPT IN 90 SECONDS.
FLIGHT OPERATIONS: 99.532%
--ZZZKT-- REPEAT MESSAGE-- ZZZKT--REAKING UP--
WARNING. COMMS JAMMING FIELD ENCOUNTERED. ATTEMPTING TO CIRCUMVENT...
NO ONE'S SURE WHO'S BEHIND IT ALL, BUT ONE THING'S FOR CERTAIN: THE TECH IS DEFINITELY IN THE WRONG HANDS.
SO THAT'S THE JOB: LOCATE THE SOURCE OF THE TECH AND SHUT IT DOWN...
...BEFORE SOMEONE ELSE GETS CONTROL OF IT.
⟨FIELD TEAM TO LOTUS-3: STAND-BY FOR PICKUP. PREPARE FOR PURSUIT.⟩

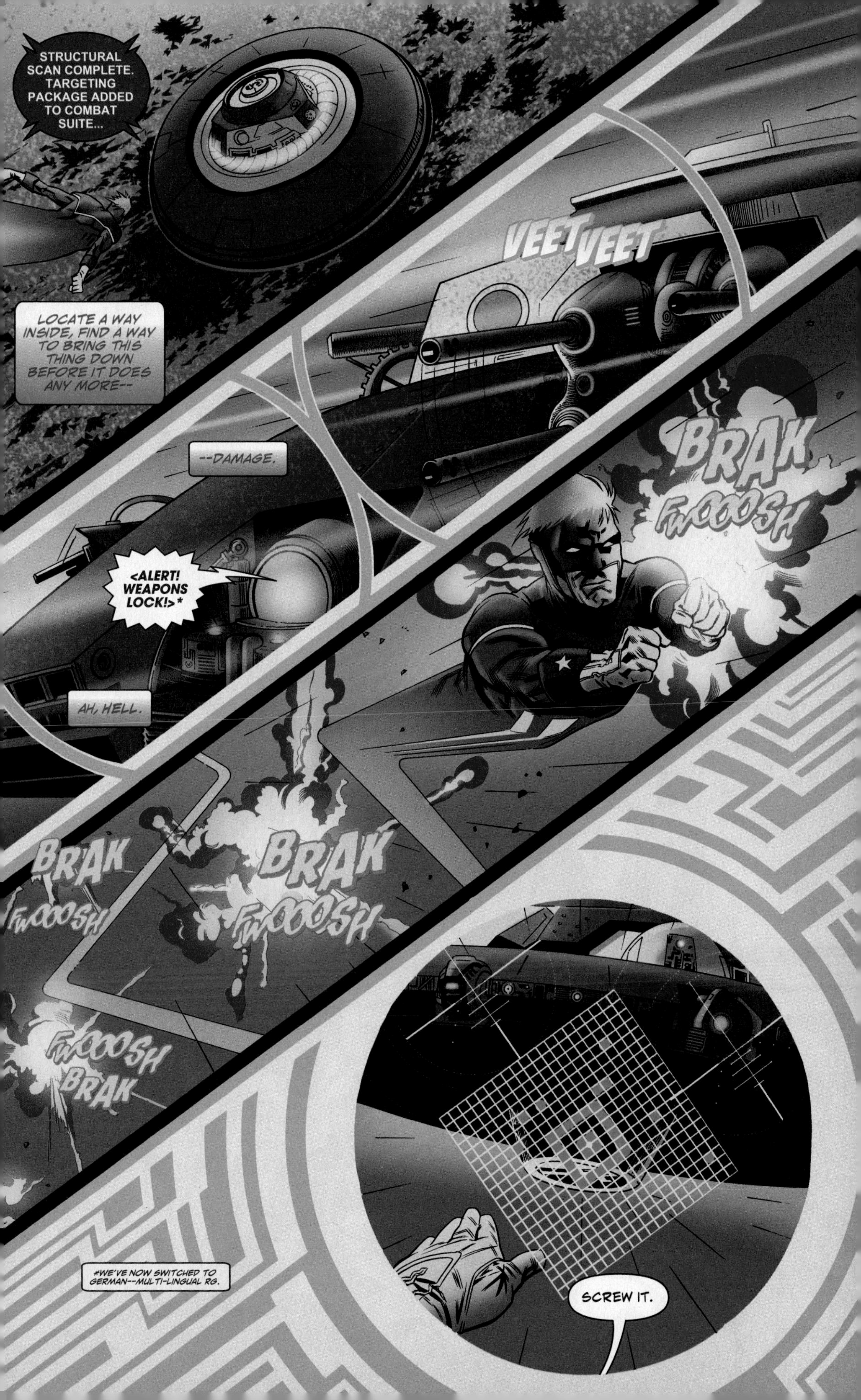
STRUCTURAL SCAN COMPLETE. TARGETING PACKAGE ADDED TO COMBAT SUITE...
LOCATE A WAY INSIDE, FIND A WAY TO BRING THIS THING DOWN BEFORE IT DOES ANY MORE--
VEET VEET
--DAMAGE.
<ALERT! WEAPONS LOCK!>*
AH, HELL.
BRAK
FWOOOSH
BRAK
FWOOOSH
BRAK
FWOOOSH
FWOOOSH
BRAK
*WE'VE NOW SWITCHED TO GERMAN--MULTI-LINGUAL RG.
SCREW IT.

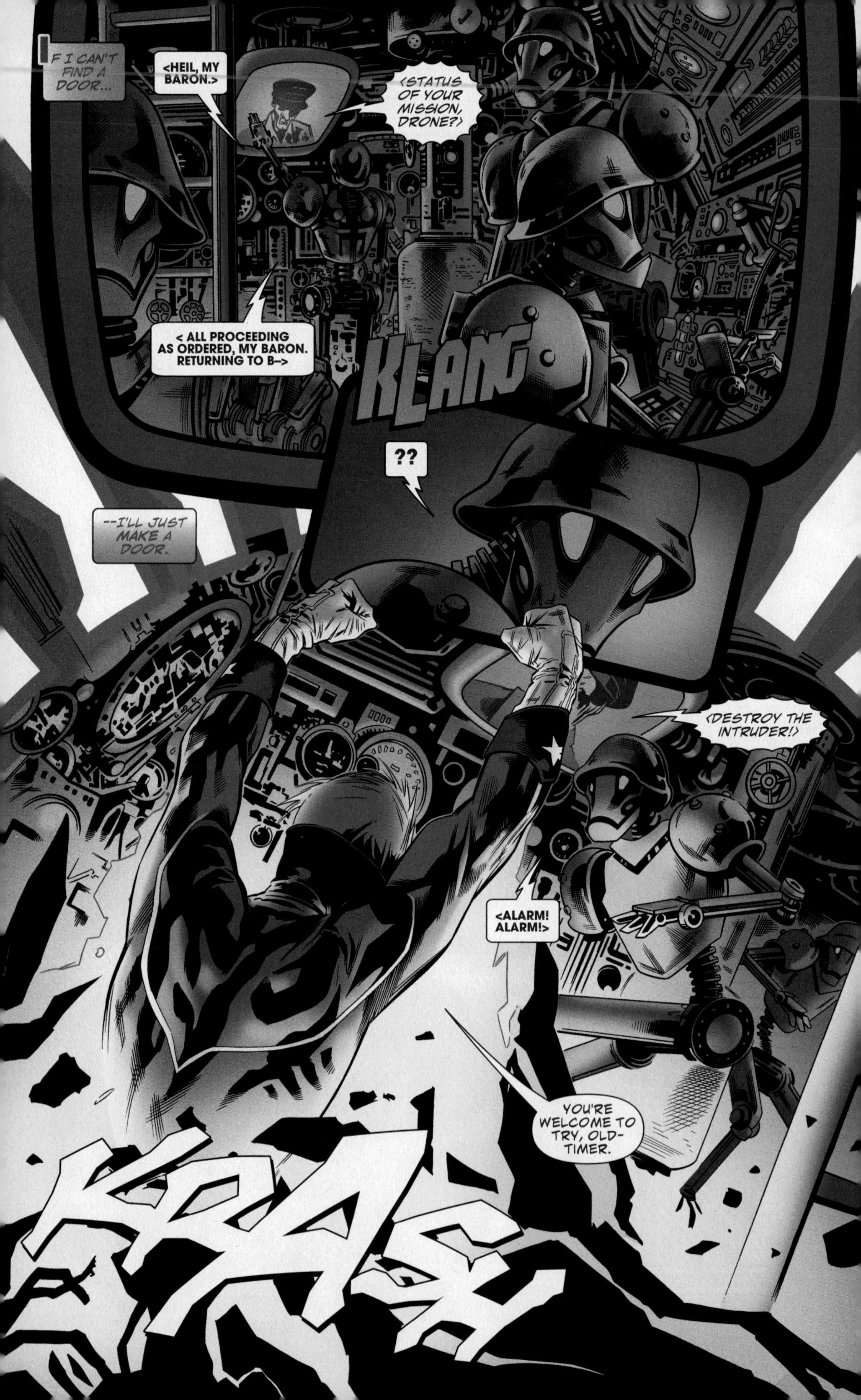
F I CAN'T FIND A DOOR...
<HEIL, MY BARON.>
<STATUS OF YOUR MISSION, DRONE?>
< ALL PROCEEDING AS ORDERED, MY BARON. RETURNING TO B-->
KLANG
??
--I'LL JUST MAKE A DOOR.
<DESTROY THE INTRUDER!>
<ALARM! ALARM!>
YOU'RE WELCOME TO TRY, OLD-TIMER.
KRAS

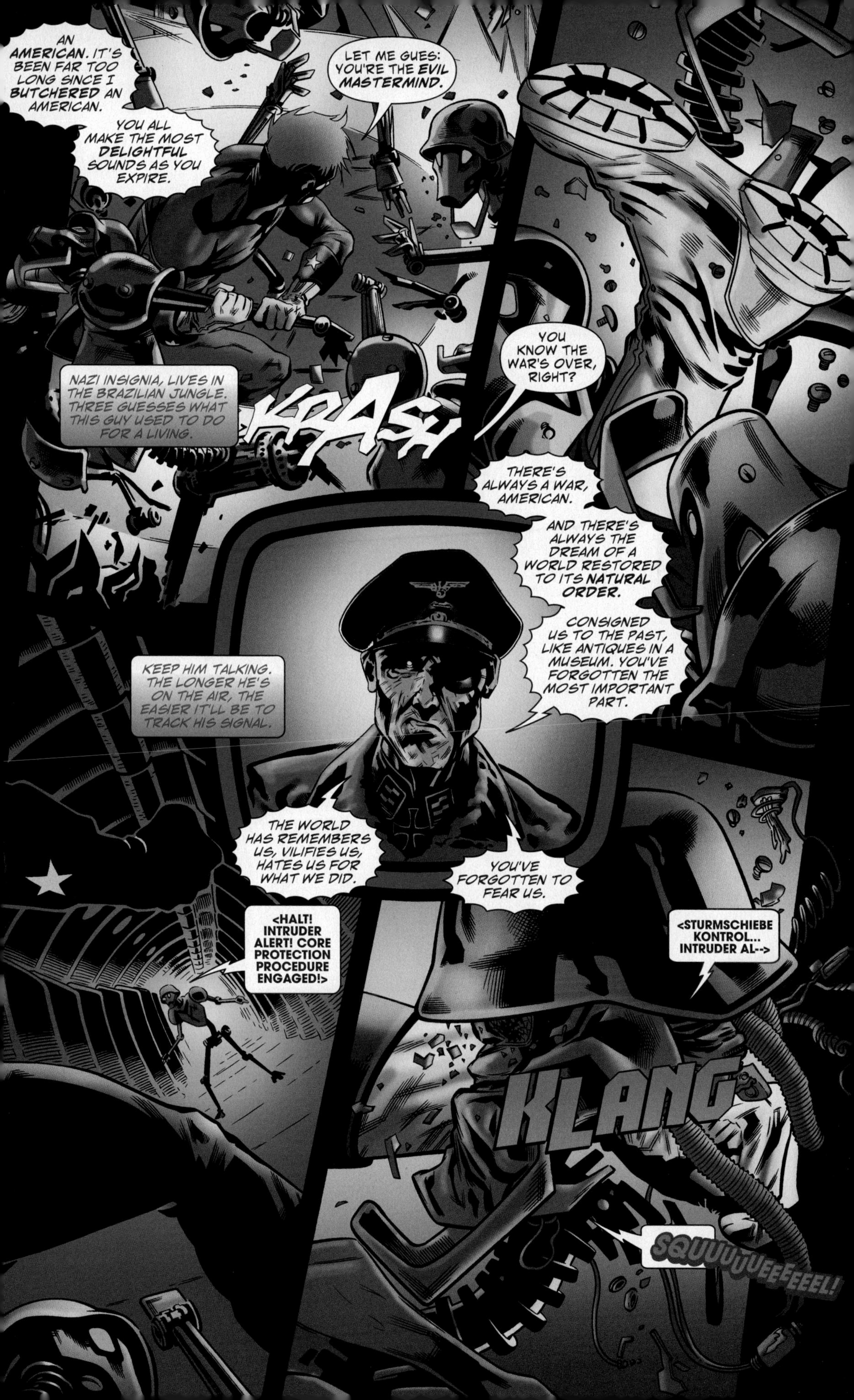
AN AMERICAN. IT'S BEEN FAR TOO LONG SINCE I BUTCHERED AN AMERICAN.
YOU ALL MAKE THE MOST DELIGHTFUL SOUNDS AS YOU EXPIRE.
LET ME GUES: YOU'RE THE EVIL MASTERMIND.
NAZI INSIGNIA, LIVES IN THE BRAZILIAN JUNGLE. THREE GUESSES WHAT THIS GUY USED TO DO FOR A LIVING.
KRASH
YOU KNOW THE WAR'S OVER, RIGHT?
THERE'S ALWAYS A WAR, AMERICAN.
AND THERE'S ALWAYS THE DREAM OF A WORLD RESTORED TO ITS NATURAL ORDER.
CONSIGNED US TO THE PAST, LIKE ANTIQUES IN A MUSEUM. YOU'VE FORGOTTEN THE MOST IMPORTANT PART.
KEEP HIM TALKING. THE LONGER HE'S ON THE AIR, THE EASIER IT'LL BE TO TRACK HIS SIGNAL.
THE WORLD HAS REMEMBERS US, VILIFIES US, HATES US FOR WHAT WE DID.
YOU'VE FORGOTTEN TO FEAR US.
<HALT! INTRUDER ALERT! CORE PROTECTION PROCEDURE ENGAGED!>
<STURMSCHIEBE KONTROL... INTRUDER AL-->
KLANG
SQUUUUTUEEEEEEL!

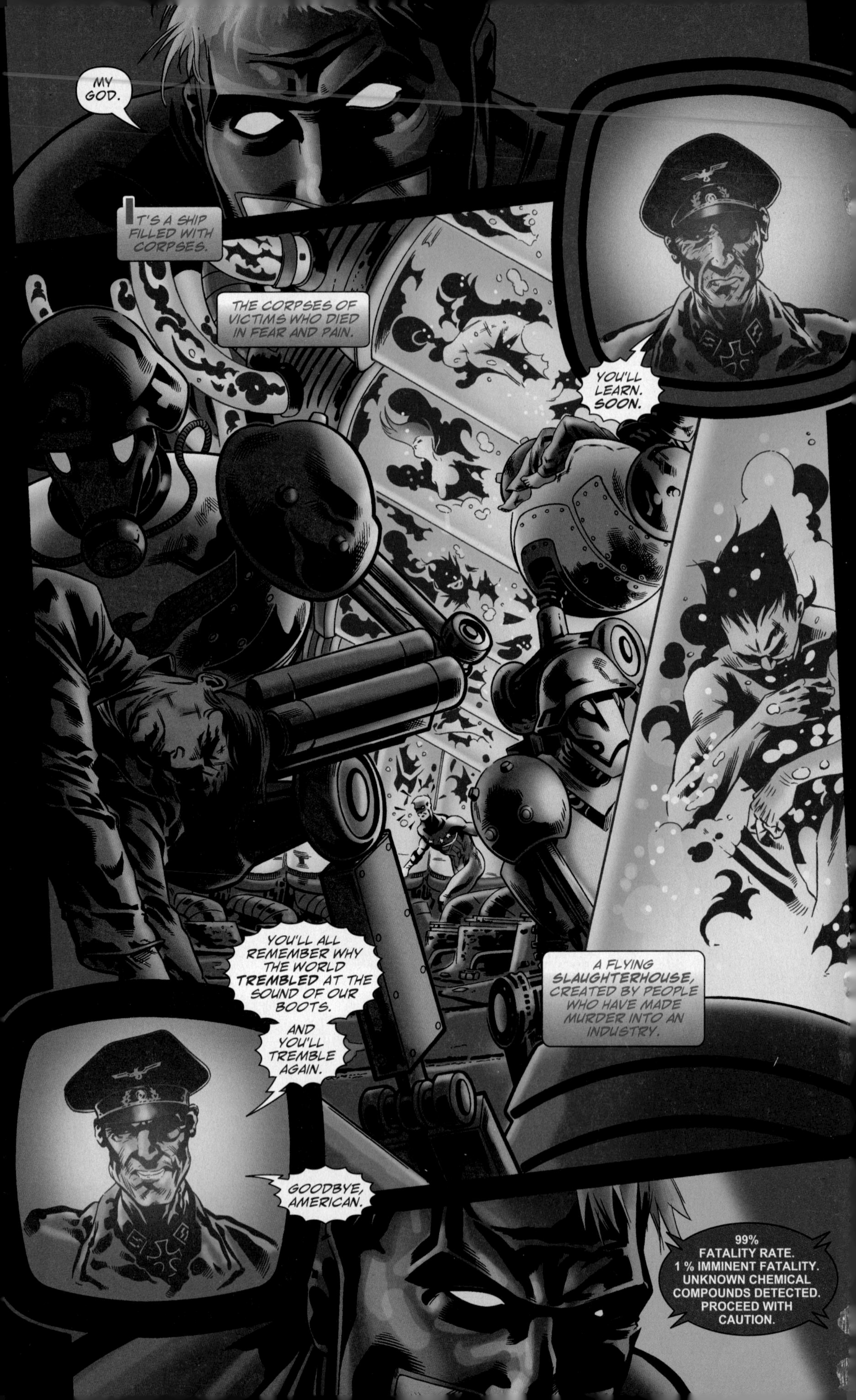
MY GOD.
IT'S A SHIP FILLED WITH CORPSES.
THE CORPSES OF VICTIMS WHO DIED IN FEAR AND PAIN.
YOU'LL LEARN. SOON.
YOU'LL ALL REMEMBER WHY THE WORLD TREMBLED AT THE SOUND OF OUR BOOTS.
AND YOU'LL TREMBLE AGAIN.
A FLYING SLAUGHTERHOUSE, CREATED BY PEOPLE WHO HAVE MADE MURDER INTO AN INDUSTRY.
GOODBYE, AMERICAN.
99% FATALITY RATE. 1 % IMMINENT FATALITY. UNKNOWN CHEMICAL COMPOUNDS DETECTED. PROCEED WITH CAUTION.

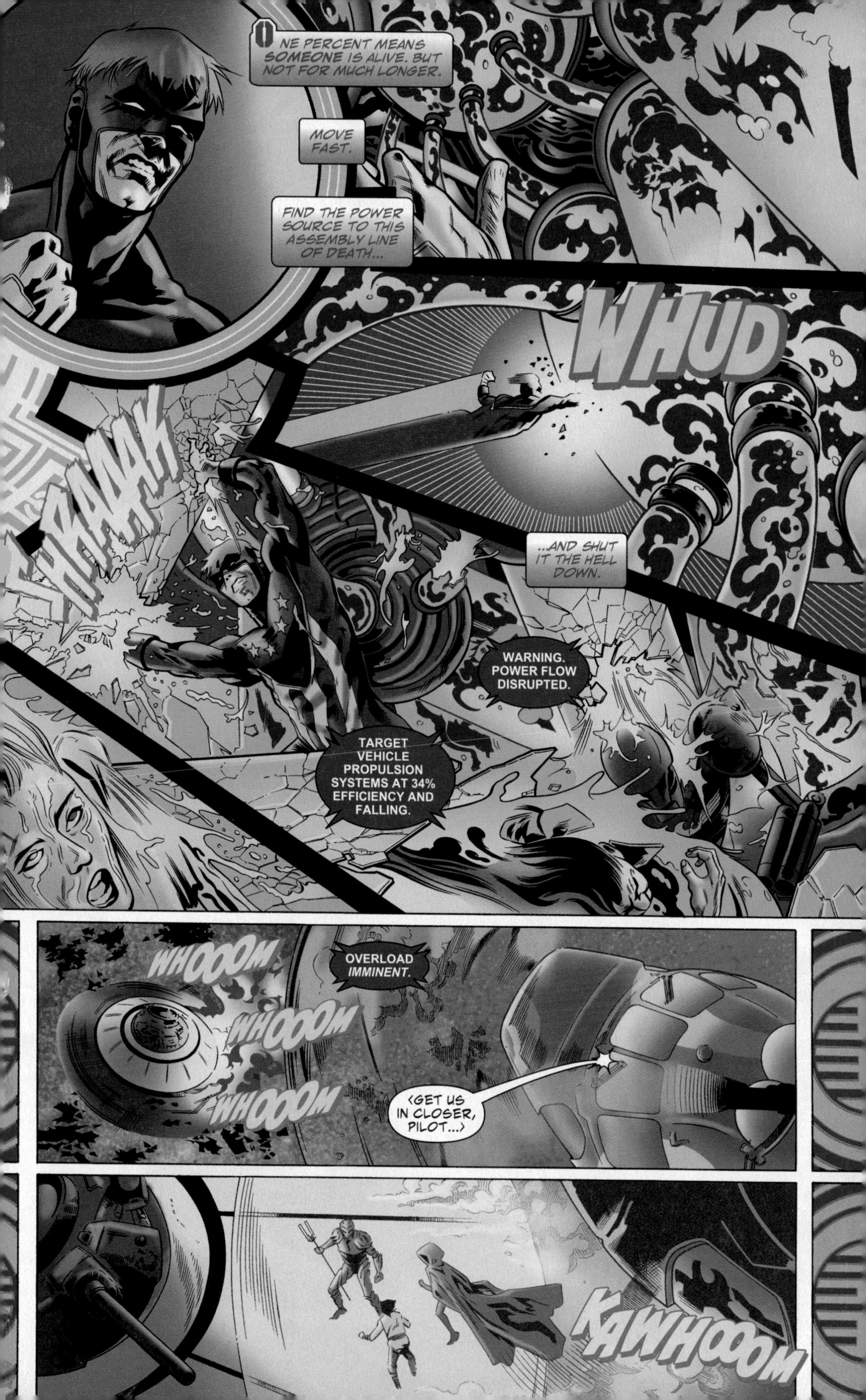
ONE PERCENT MEANS SOMEONE IS ALIVE. BUT NOT FOR MUCH LONGER.
MOVE FAST.
FIND THE POWER SOURCE TO THIS ASSEMBLY LINE OF DEATH...
WHUD
...AND SHUT IT THE HELL DOWN.
WARNING. POWER FLOW DISRUPTED.
TARGET VEHICLE PROPULSION SYSTEMS AT 34% EFFICIENCY AND FALLING.
WHOOOM
OVERLOAD IMMINENT.
WHOOOM
WHOOOM
<GET US IN CLOSER, PILOT...>
KAWHOOOM

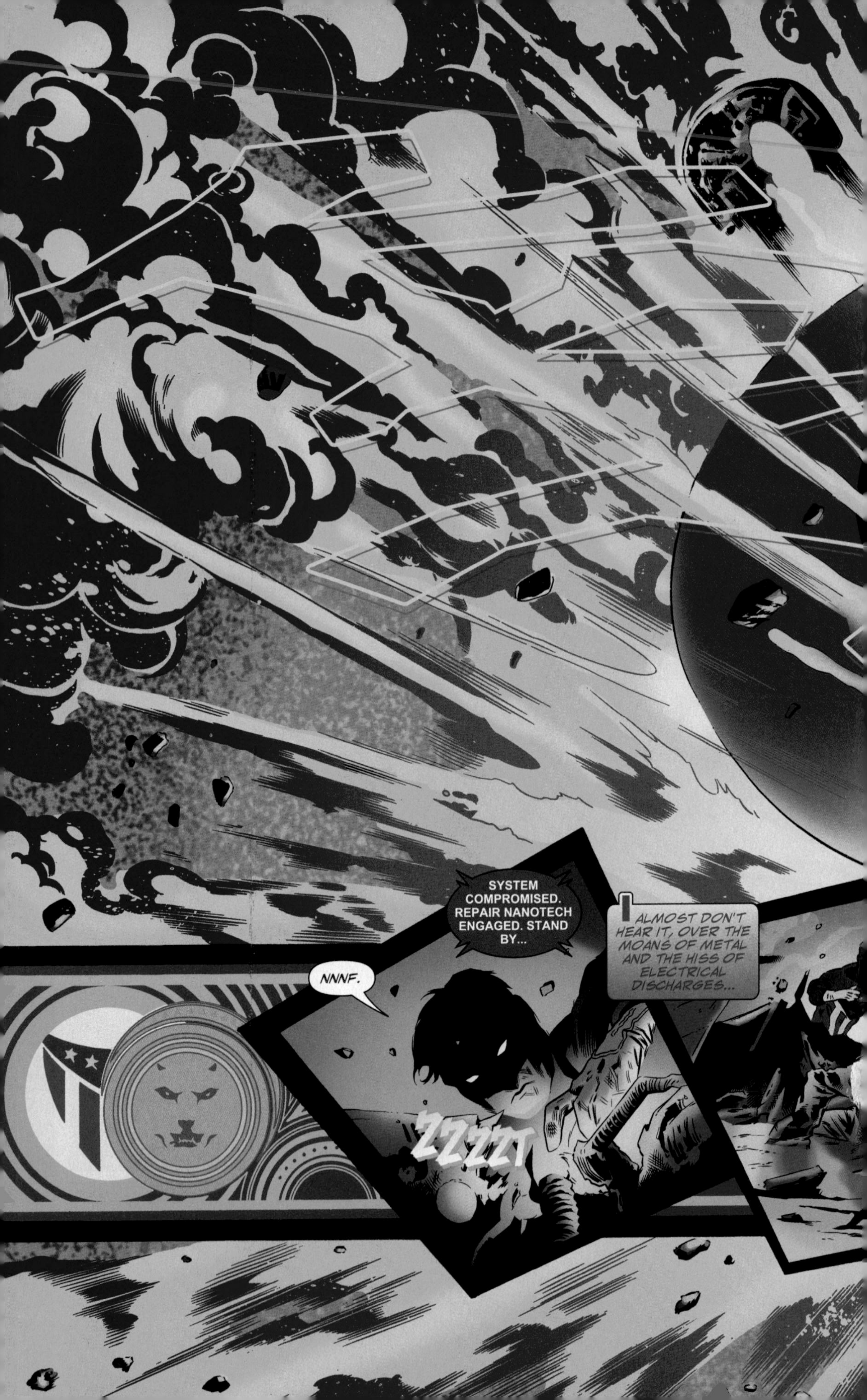
SYSTEM COMPROMISED. REPAIR NANOTECH ENGAGED. STAND BY...
I ALMOST DON'T HEAR IT, OVER THE MOANS OF METAL AND THE HISS OF ELECTRICAL DISCHARGES...
NNNF.
ZZZZT

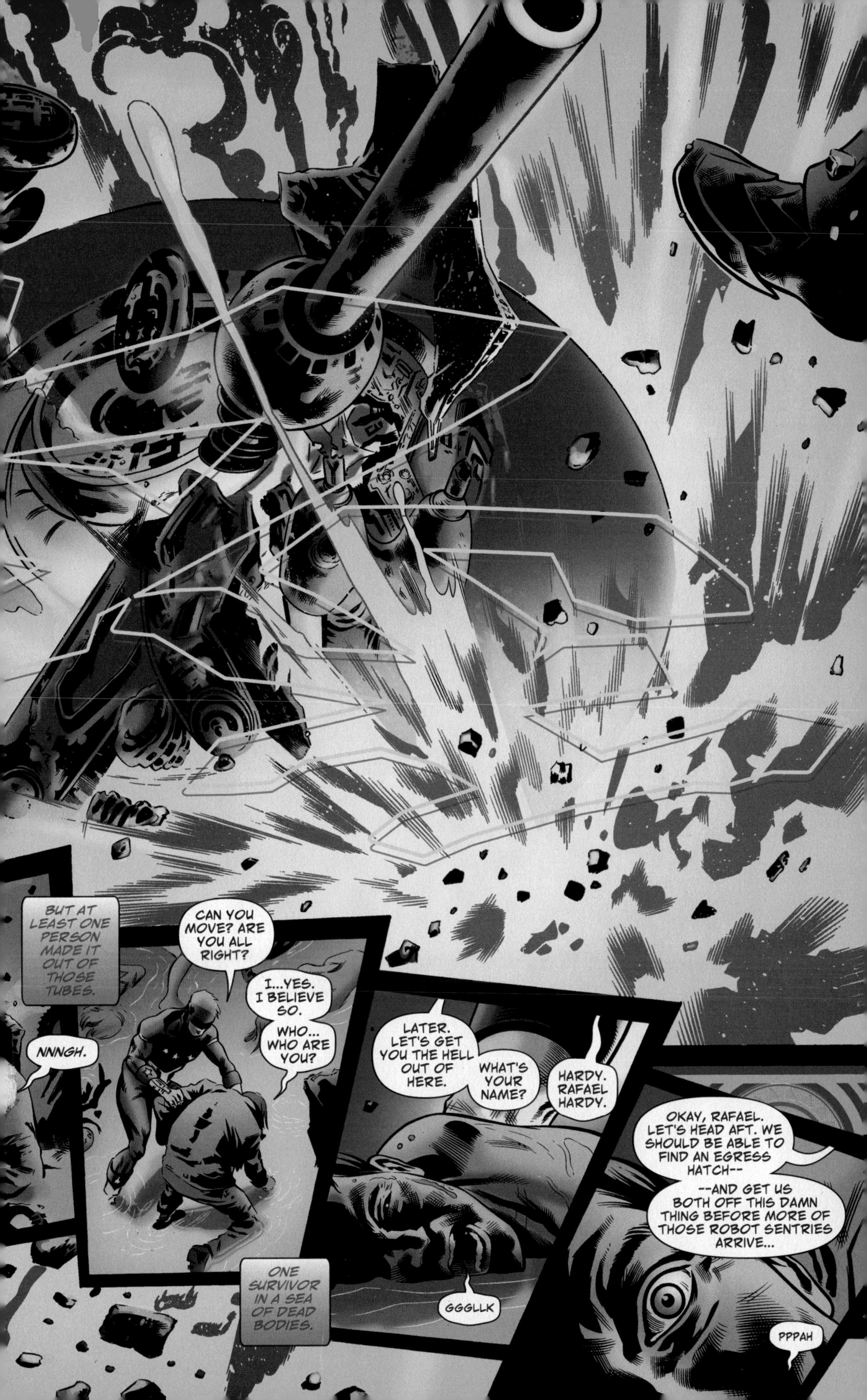
BUT AT LEAST ONE PERSON MADE IT OUT OF THOSE TUBES.
NNNGH.
CAN YOU MOVE? ARE YOU ALL RIGHT?
I...YES. I BELIEVE SO.
WHO... WHO ARE YOU?
ONE SURVIVOR IN A SEA OF DEAD BODIES.
LATER. LET'S GET YOU THE HELL OUT OF HERE.
WHAT'S YOUR NAME?
HARDY. RAFAEL HARDY.
GGGLLK
OKAY, RAFAEL. LET'S HEAD AFT. WE SHOULD BE ABLE TO FIND AN EGRESS HATCH--
--AND GET US BOTH OFF THIS DAMN THING BEFORE MORE OF THOSE ROBOT SENTRIES ARRIVE...
PPPAH

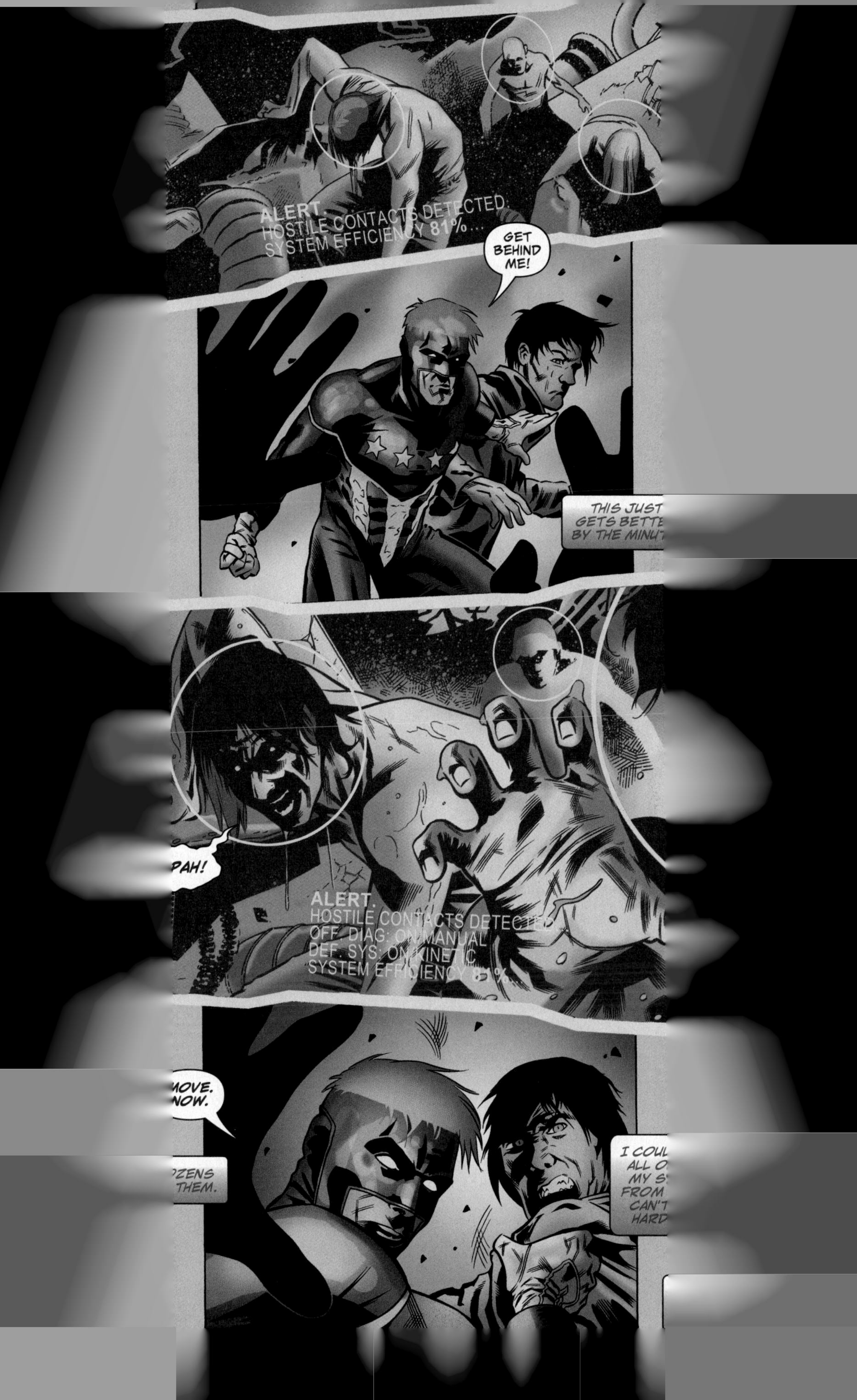
ALERT.
HOSTILE CONTACTS DETECTED.
SYSTEM EFFICIENCY 81%...
GET BEHIND ME!
THIS JUST GETS BETTE BY THE MINUT
PAH!
ALERT.
HOSTILE CONTACTS DETECTED.
OFF. DIAG: ON/MANUAL
DEF. SYS: ON/KINETIC
SYSTEM EFFICIENCY 81%.
MOVE. NOW.
ZENS THEM.
I COUL ALL O MY S FROM CAN'T HARD

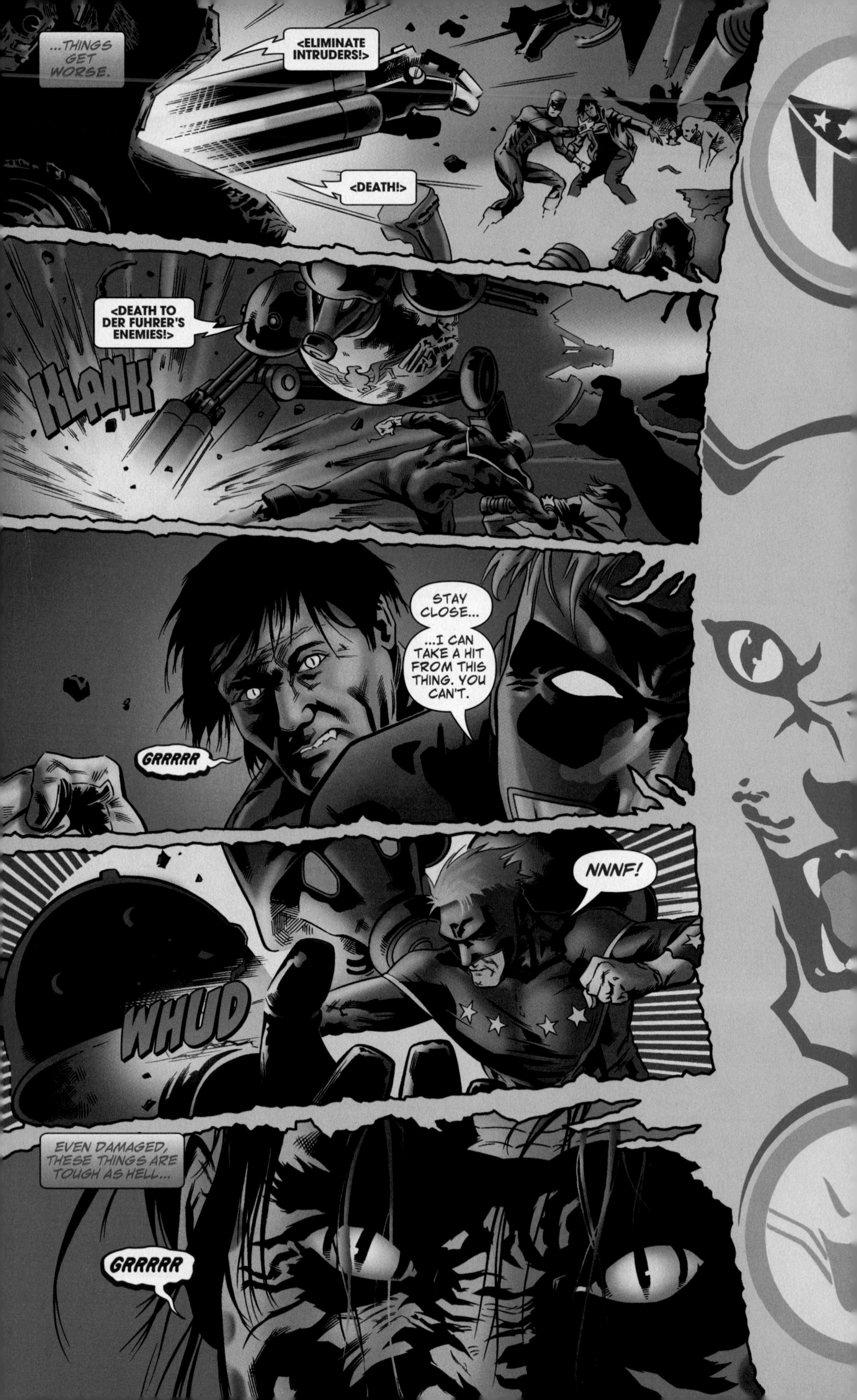
...THINGS GET WORSE.
<ELIMINATE INTRUDERS!>
<DEATH!>
<DEATH TO DER FUHRER'S ENEMIES!>
KLANK
STAY CLOSE...
...I CAN TAKE A HIT FROM THIS THING. YOU CAN'T.
GRRRRR
NNNF!
WHUD
EVEN DAMAGED, THESE THINGS ARE TOUGH AS HELL...
GRRRRR

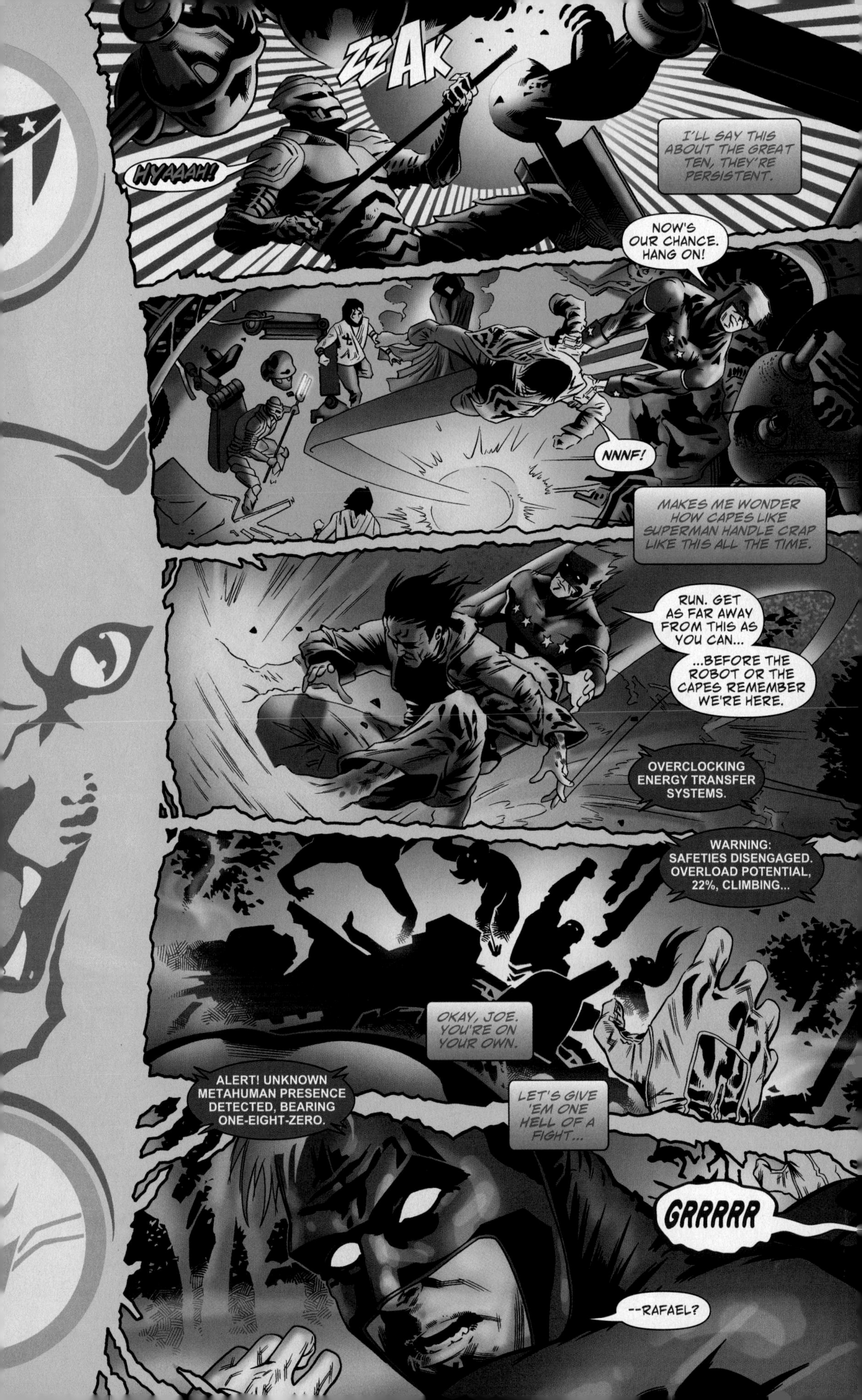
ZZAK
HYAAAH!
I'LL SAY THIS ABOUT THE GREAT TEN, THEY'RE PERSISTENT.
NOW'S OUR CHANCE. HANG ON!
NNNF!
MAKES ME WONDER HOW CAPES LIKE SUPERMAN HANDLE CRAP LIKE THIS ALL THE TIME.
RUN. GET AS FAR AWAY FROM THIS AS YOU CAN...
...BEFORE THE ROBOT OR THE CAPES REMEMBER WE'RE HERE.
OVERCLOCKING ENERGY TRANSFER SYSTEMS.
WARNING: SAFETIES DISENGAGED. OVERLOAD POTENTIAL, 22%, CLIMBING...
OKAY, JOE. YOU'RE ON YOUR OWN.
ALERT! UNKNOWN METAHUMAN PRESENCE DETECTED, BEARING ONE-EIGHT-ZERO.
LET'S GIVE 'EM ONE HELL OF A FIGHT...
GRRRRR
--RAFAEL?

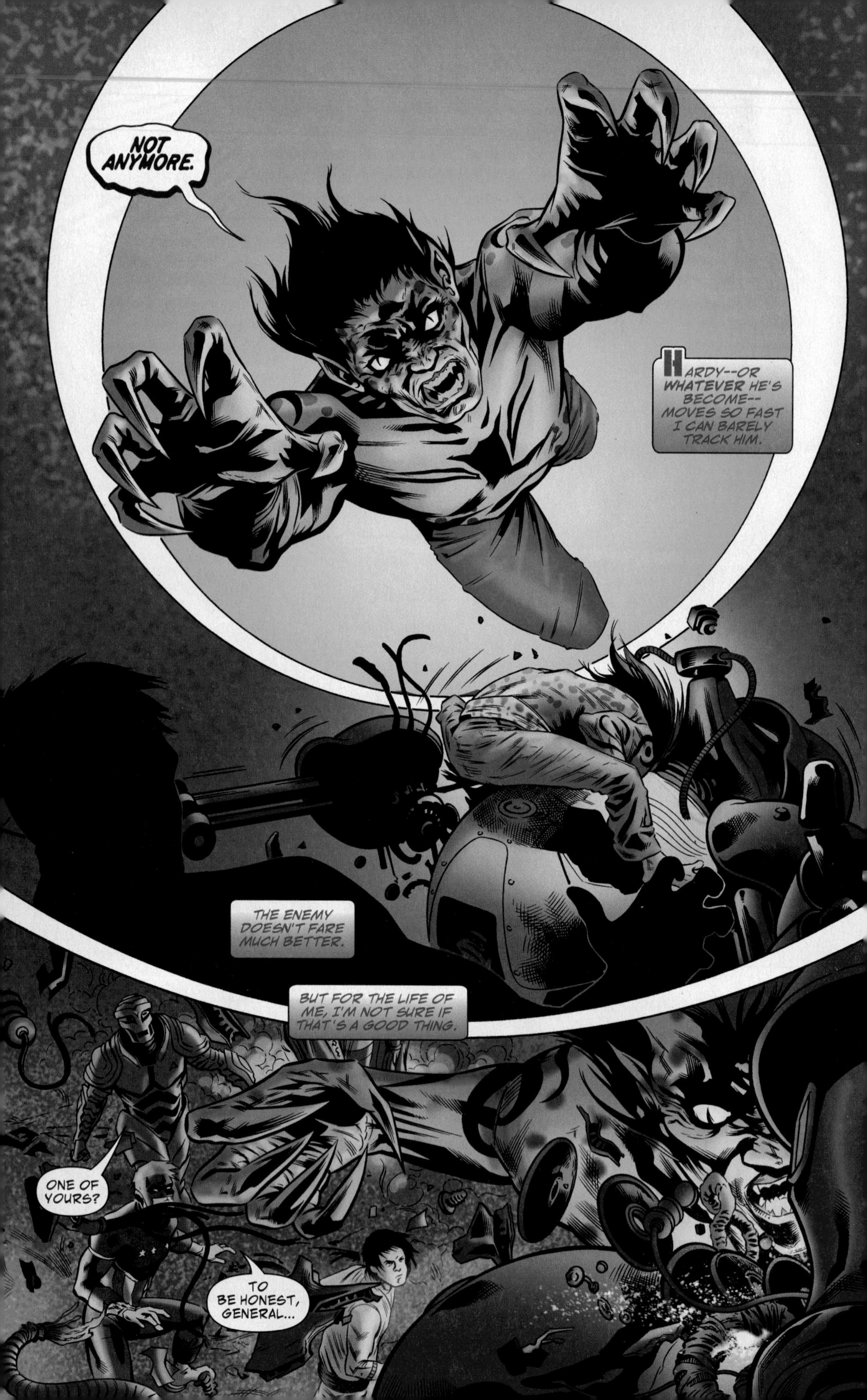
NOT ANYMORE.
HARDY--OR WHATEVER HE'S BECOME--MOVES SO FAST I CAN BARELY TRACK HIM.
THE ENEMY DOESN'T FARE MUCH BETTER.
BUT FOR THE LIFE OF ME, I'M NOT SURE IF THAT'S A GOOD THING.
ONE OF YOURS?
TO BE HONEST, GENERAL...

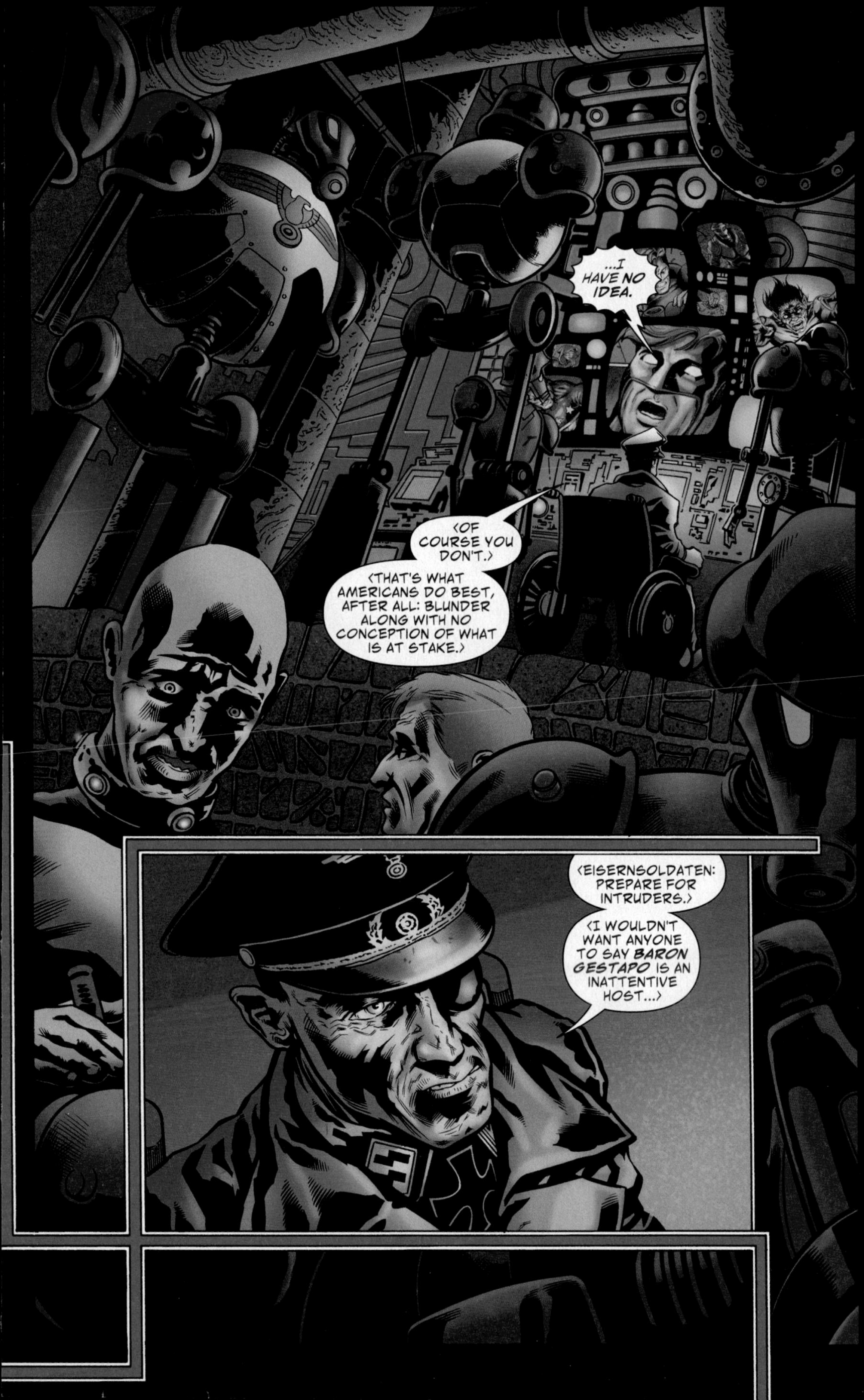
...I HAVE NO IDEA.
<OF COURSE YOU DON'T.>
<THAT'S WHAT AMERICANS DO BEST, AFTER ALL: BLUNDER ALONG WITH NO CONCEPTION OF WHAT IS AT STAKE.>
<EISERNSOLDATEN: PREPARE FOR INTRUDERS.>
<I WOULDN'T WANT ANYONE TO SAY BARON GESTAPO IS AN INATTENTIVE HOST...>

GHOSTS PART 5: ROCKETS' RED GLARE

Cover by Sami Basri

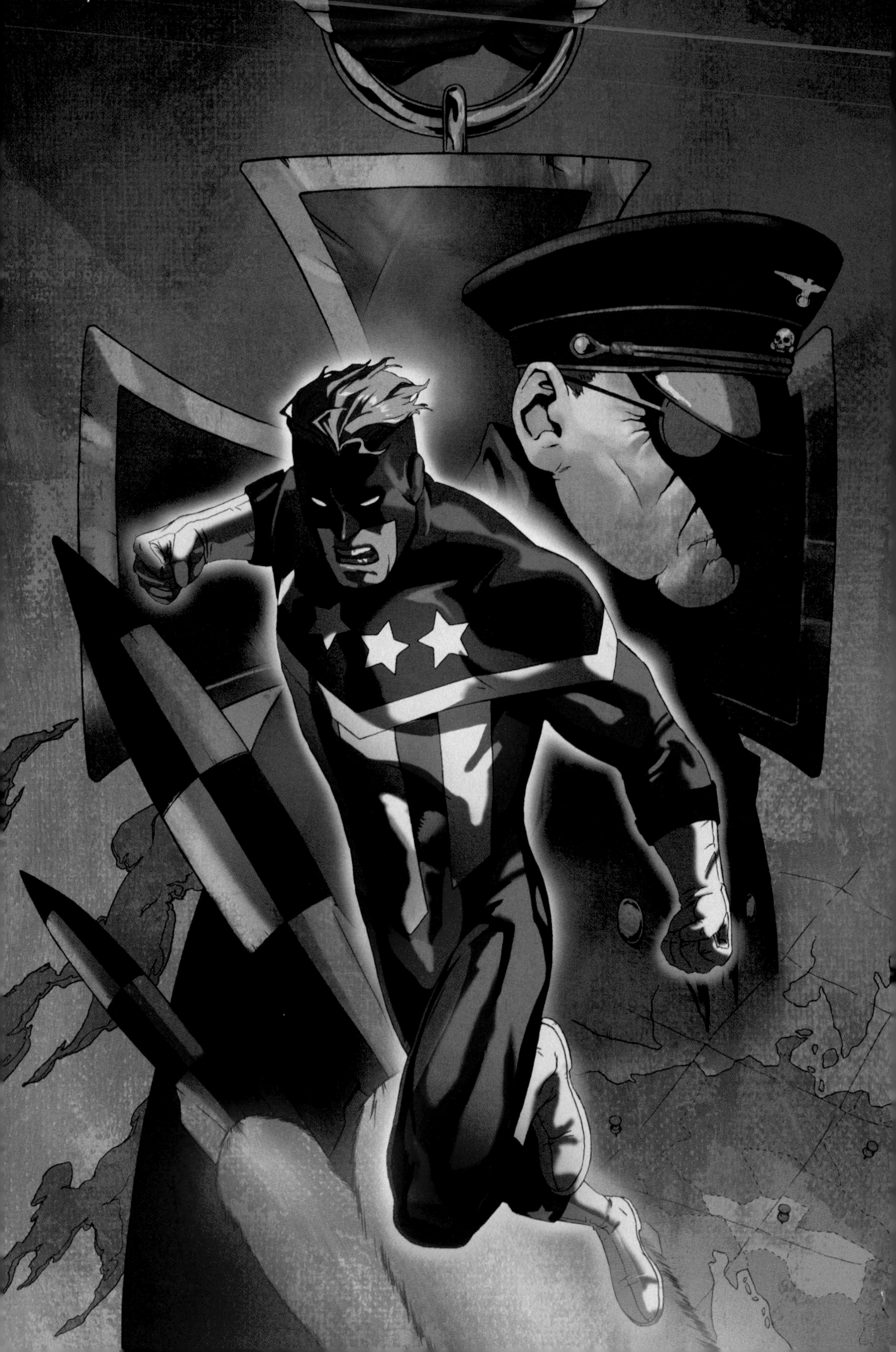

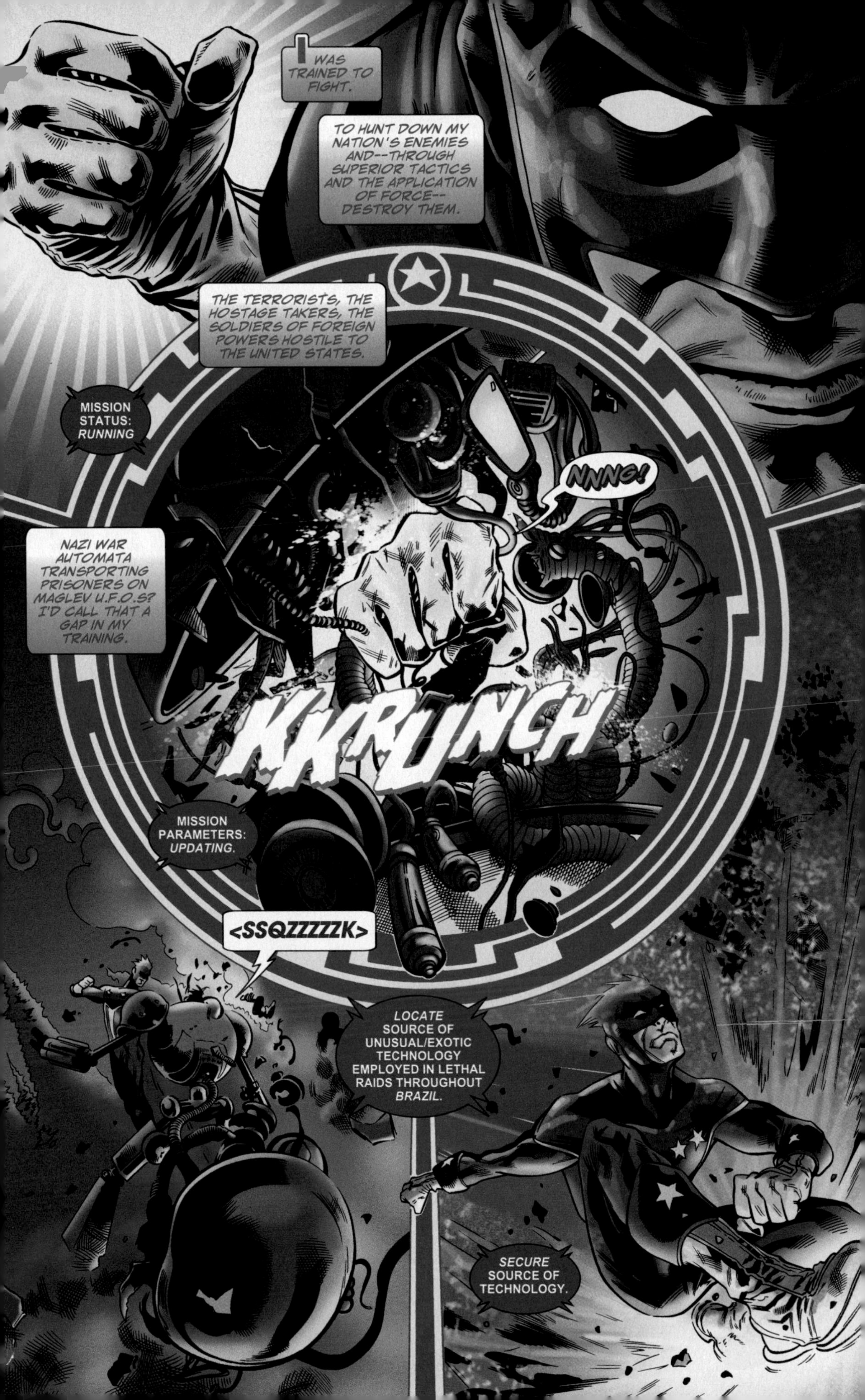
I WAS TRAINED TO FIGHT.
TO HUNT DOWN MY NATION'S ENEMIES AND--THROUGH SUPERIOR TACTICS AND THE APPLICATION OF FORCE--DESTROY THEM.
THE TERRORISTS, THE HOSTAGE TAKERS, THE SOLDIERS OF FOREIGN POWERS HOSTILE TO THE UNITED STATES.
MISSION STATUS: *RUNNING*
NNNG!
NAZI WAR AUTOMATA TRANSPORTING PRISONERS ON MAGLEV U.F.O.S? I'D CALL THAT A GAP IN MY TRAINING.
KKRUNCH
MISSION PARAMETERS: *UPDATING.*
<SSQZZZZZK>
LOCATE SOURCE OF UNUSUAL/EXOTIC TECHNOLOGY EMPLOYED IN LETHAL RAIDS THROUGHOUT *BRAZIL.*
SECURE SOURCE OF TECHNOLOGY.

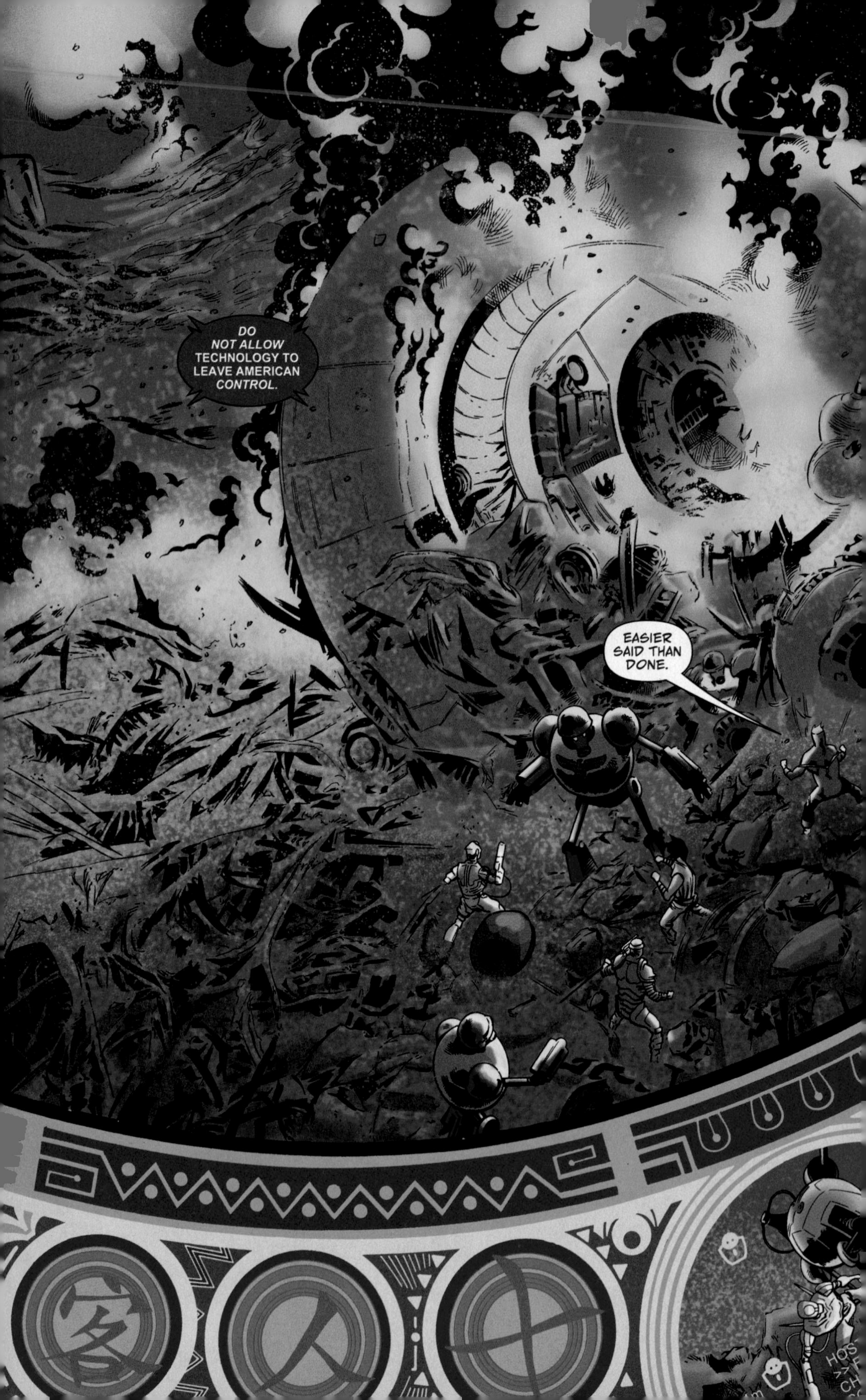
DO NOT ALLOW TECHNOLOGY TO LEAVE AMERICAN CONTROL.
EASIER SAID THAN DONE.

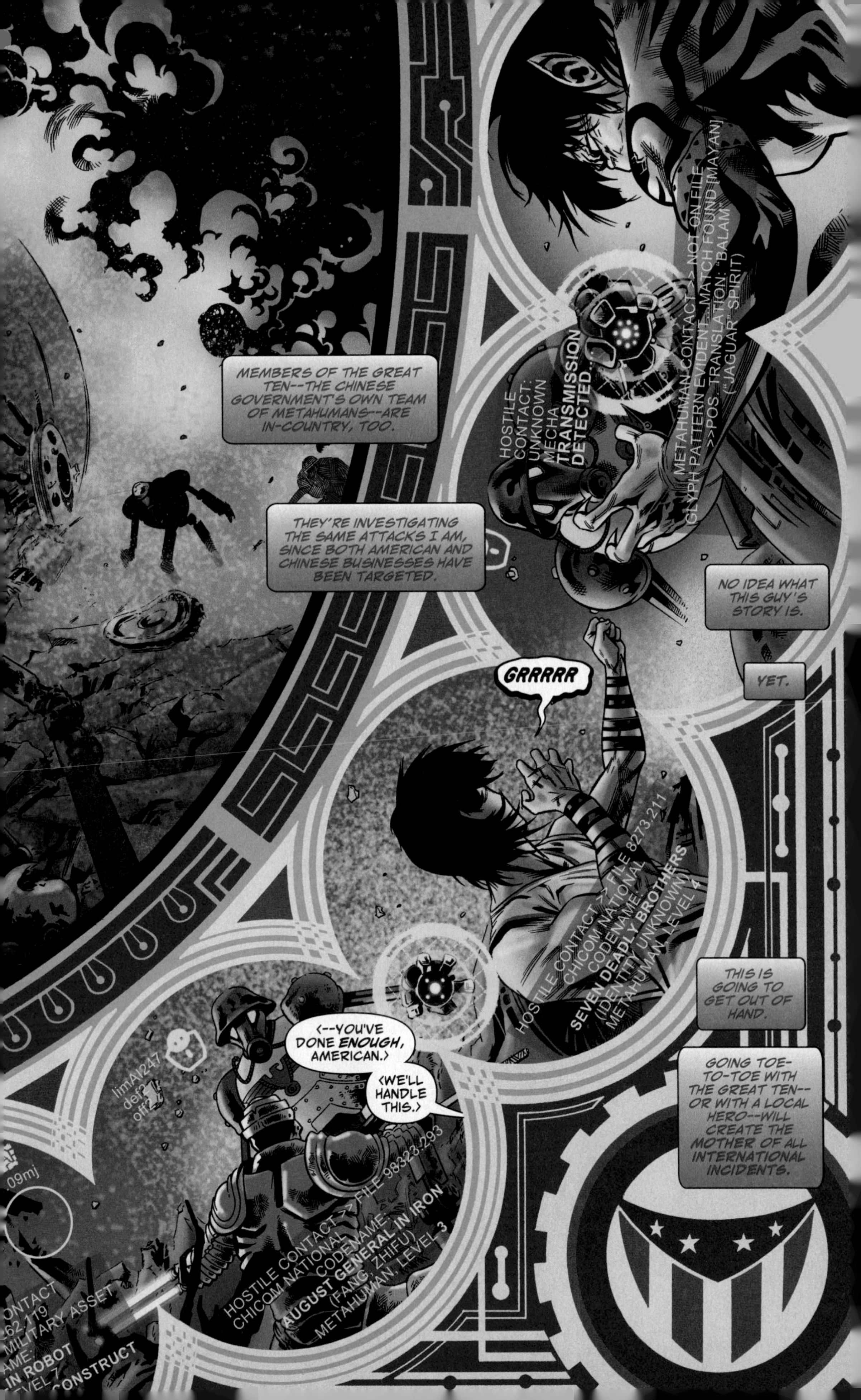

MEMBERS OF THE GREAT TEN--THE CHINESE GOVERNMENT'S OWN TEAM OF METAHUMANS--ARE IN-COUNTRY, TOO.
HOSTILE CONTACT: UNKNOWN MECHA TRANSMISSION DETECTED...
METAHUMAN CONTACT >> NOT ON FILE GLYPH PATTERN EVIDENT...MATCH FOUND [MAYAN] >>POS. TRANSLATION: "BALAM" ("JAGUAR" SPIRIT)
THEY'RE INVESTIGATING THE SAME ATTACKS I AM, SINCE BOTH AMERICAN AND CHINESE BUSINESSES HAVE BEEN TARGETED.
NO IDEA WHAT THIS GUY'S STORY IS.
YET.
GRRRRR
HOSTILE CONTACT >> FILE 8273.211 CHICOM NATIONAL CODENAME: SEVEN DEADLY BROTHERS (IDENTITY UNKNOWN) METAHUMAN, LEVEL 4
THIS IS GOING TO GET OUT OF HAND.
<--YOU'VE DONE ENOUGH, AMERICAN.>
<WE'LL HANDLE THIS.>
HOSTILE CONTACT >> FILE 98323.293 CHICOM NATIONAL CODENAME: AUGUST GENERAL IN IRON (FANG, ZHIFU) METAHUMAN, LEVEL 3
GOING TOE-TO-TOE WITH THE GREAT TEN--OR WITH A LOCAL HERO--WILL CREATE THE MOTHER OF ALL INTERNATIONAL INCIDENTS.

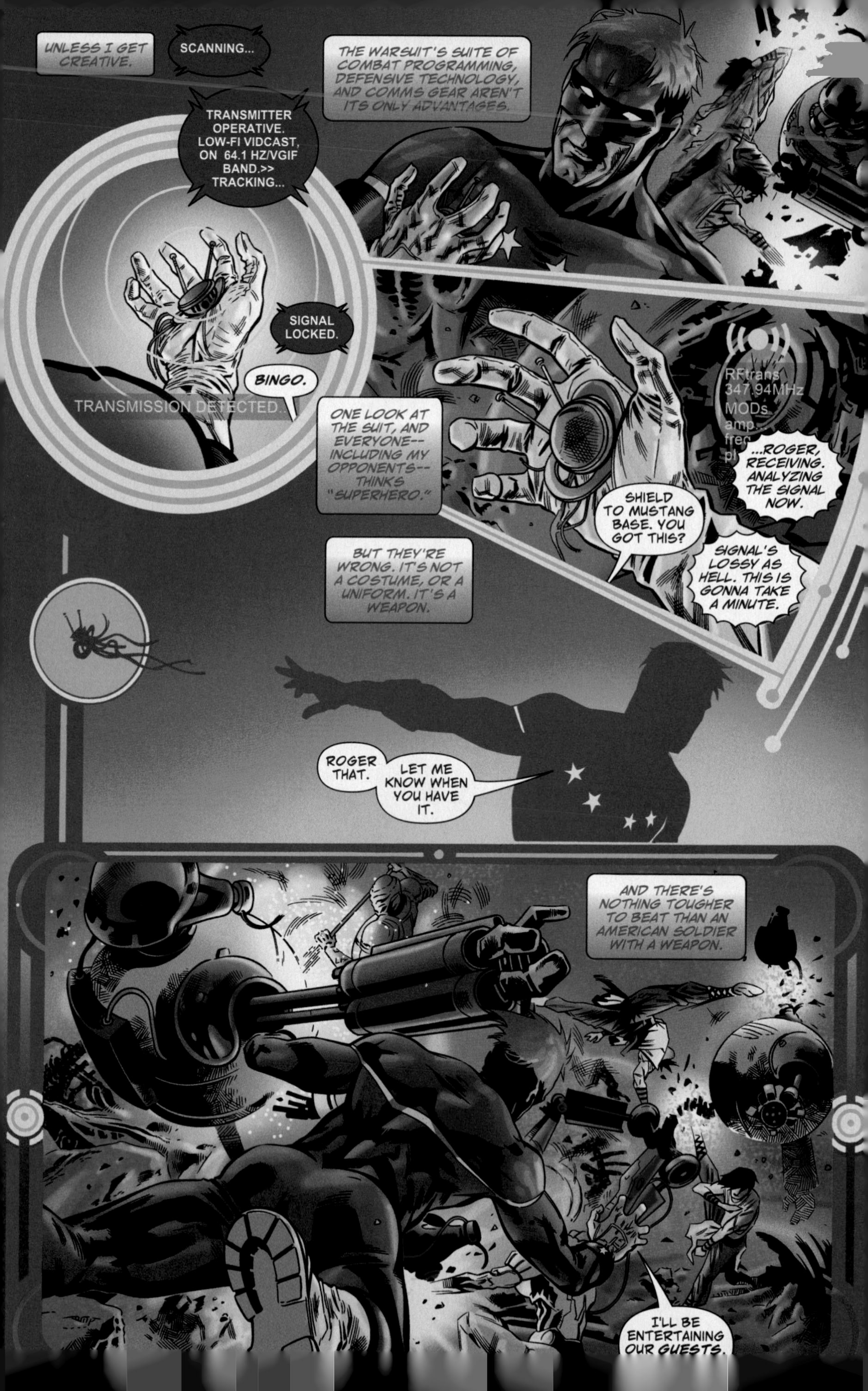
UNLESS I GET CREATIVE.
SCANNING...
THE WARSUIT'S SUITE OF COMBAT PROGRAMMING, DEFENSIVE TECHNOLOGY, AND COMMS GEAR AREN'T ITS ONLY ADVANTAGES.
TRANSMITTER OPERATIVE. LOW-FI VIDCAST, ON 64.1 HZ/VGIF BAND.>> TRACKING...
SIGNAL LOCKED.
BINGO.
TRANSMISSION DETECTED...
ONE LOOK AT THE SUIT, AND EVERYONE-- INCLUDING MY OPPONENTS-- THINKS "SUPERHERO."
RFtrans 347.94MHz
MODs
SHIELD TO MUSTANG BASE. YOU GOT THIS?
...ROGER, RECEIVING. ANALYZING THE SIGNAL NOW.
BUT THEY'RE WRONG. IT'S NOT A COSTUME, OR A UNIFORM. IT'S A WEAPON.
SIGNAL'S LOSSY AS HELL. THIS IS GONNA TAKE A MINUTE.
ROGER THAT.
LET ME KNOW WHEN YOU HAVE IT.
AND THERE'S NOTHING TOUGHER TO BEAT THAN AN AMERICAN SOLDIER WITH A WEAPON.
I'LL BE ENTERTAINING OUR GUESTS.

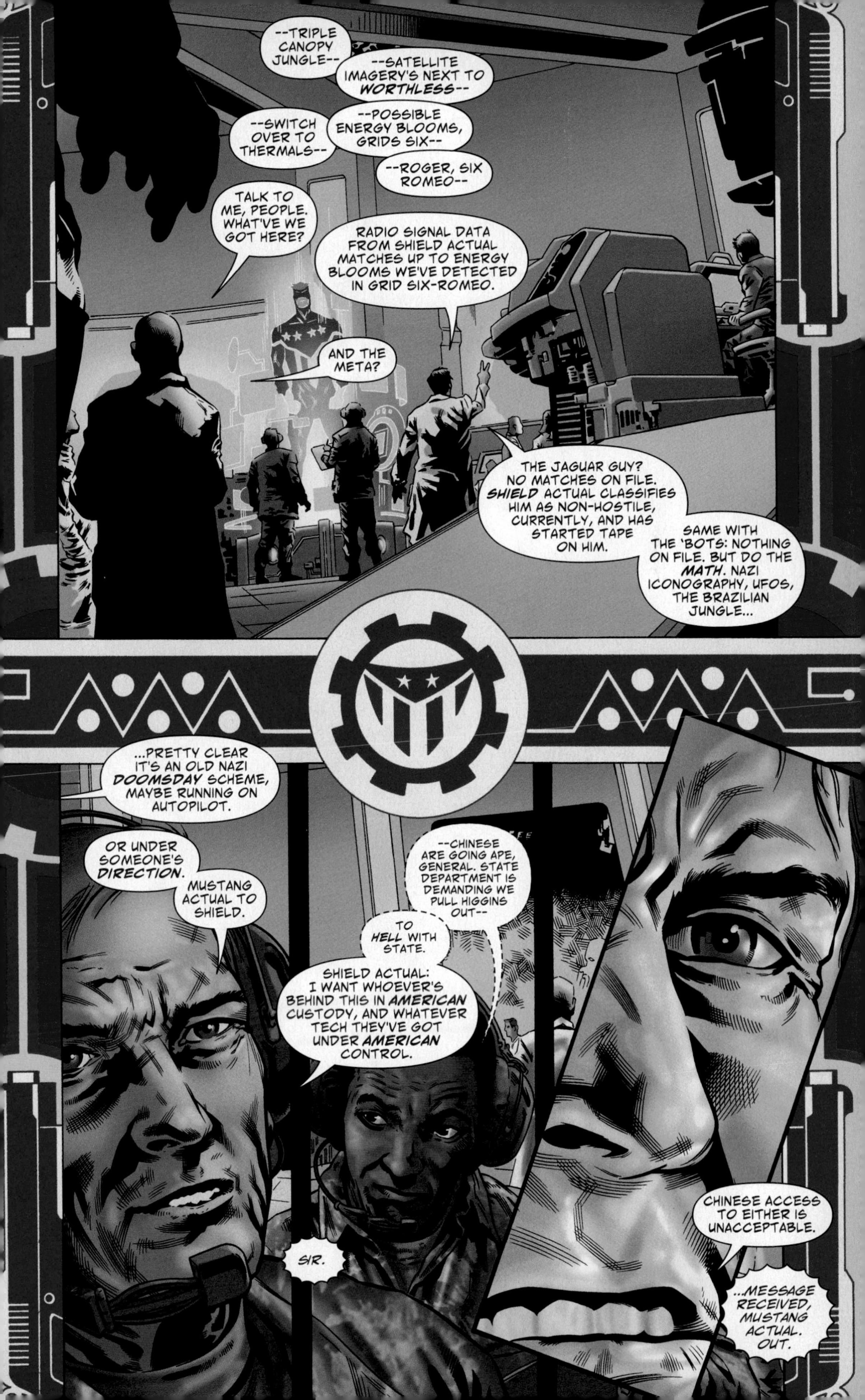
--TRIPLE CANOPY JUNGLE--
--SATELLITE IMAGERY'S NEXT TO WORTHLESS--
--SWITCH OVER TO THERMALS--
--POSSIBLE ENERGY BLOOMS, GRIDS SIX--
--ROGER, SIX ROMEO--
TALK TO ME, PEOPLE. WHAT'VE WE GOT HERE?
RADIO SIGNAL DATA FROM SHIELD ACTUAL MATCHES UP TO ENERGY BLOOMS WE'VE DETECTED IN GRID SIX-ROMEO.
AND THE META?
THE JAGUAR GUY? NO MATCHES ON FILE. SHIELD ACTUAL CLASSIFIES HIM AS NON-HOSTILE, CURRENTLY, AND HAS STARTED TAPE ON HIM.
SAME WITH THE 'BOTS: NOTHING ON FILE. BUT DO THE MATH. NAZI ICONOGRAPHY, UFOS, THE BRAZILIAN JUNGLE...
...PRETTY CLEAR IT'S AN OLD NAZI DOOMSDAY SCHEME, MAYBE RUNNING ON AUTOPILOT.
OR UNDER SOMEONE'S DIRECTION.
MUSTANG ACTUAL TO SHIELD.
--CHINESE ARE GOING APE, GENERAL. STATE DEPARTMENT IS DEMANDING WE PULL HIGGINS OUT--
TO HELL WITH STATE.
SHIELD ACTUAL: I WANT WHOEVER'S BEHIND THIS IN AMERICAN CUSTODY, AND WHATEVER TECH THEY'VE GOT UNDER AMERICAN CONTROL.
SIR.
CHINESE ACCESS TO EITHER IS UNACCEPTABLE.
...MESSAGE RECEIVED, MUSTANG ACTUAL. OUT.

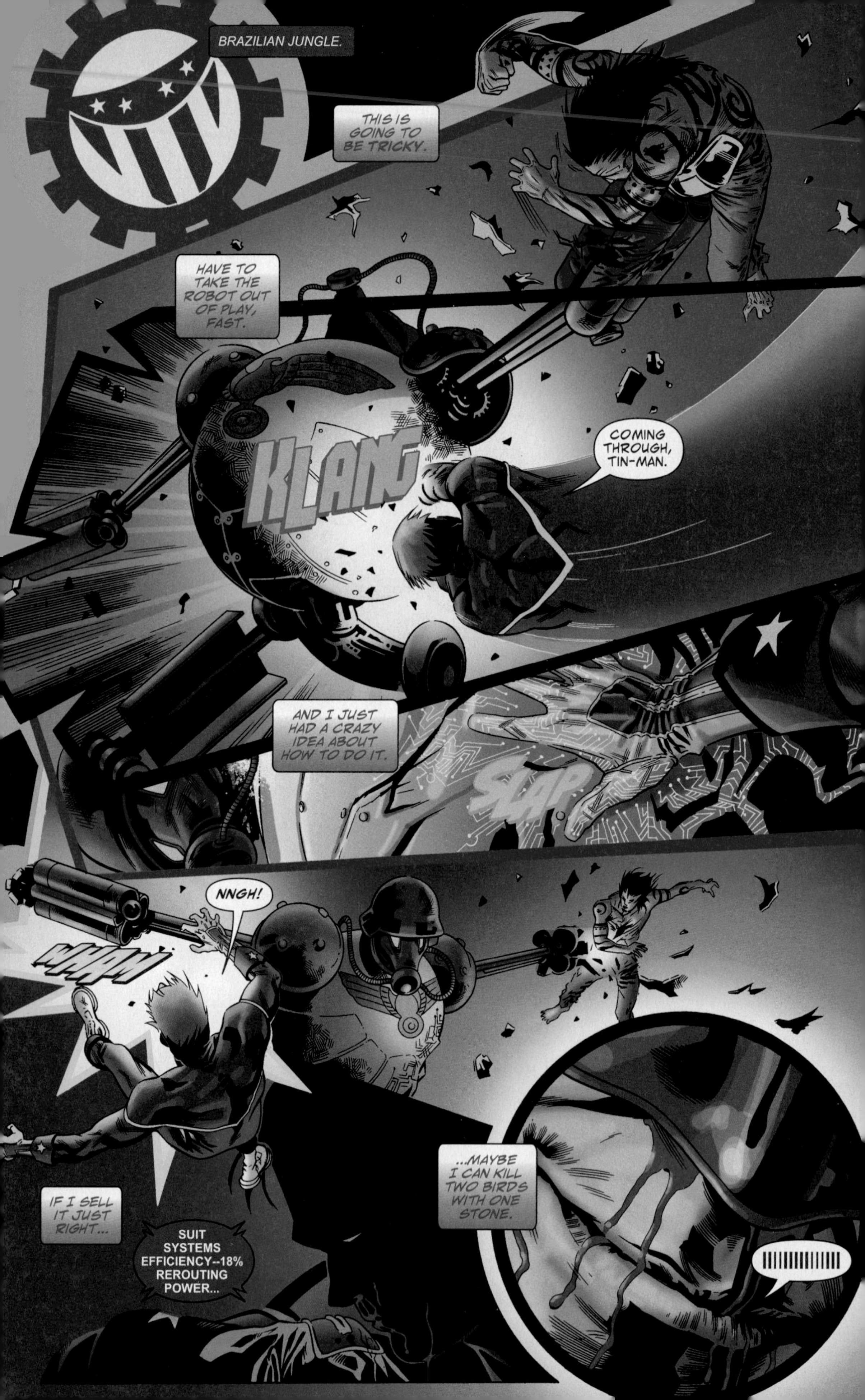
BRAZILIAN JUNGLE.
THIS IS GOING TO BE TRICKY.
HAVE TO TAKE THE ROBOT OUT OF PLAY, FAST.
KLANG
COMING THROUGH, TIN-MAN.
AND I JUST HAD A CRAZY IDEA ABOUT HOW TO DO IT.
SLAP
NNGH!
WHAM
IF I SELL IT JUST RIGHT...
SUIT SYSTEMS EFFICIENCY--18% REROUTING POWER...
...MAYBE I CAN KILL TWO BIRDS WITH ONE STONE.

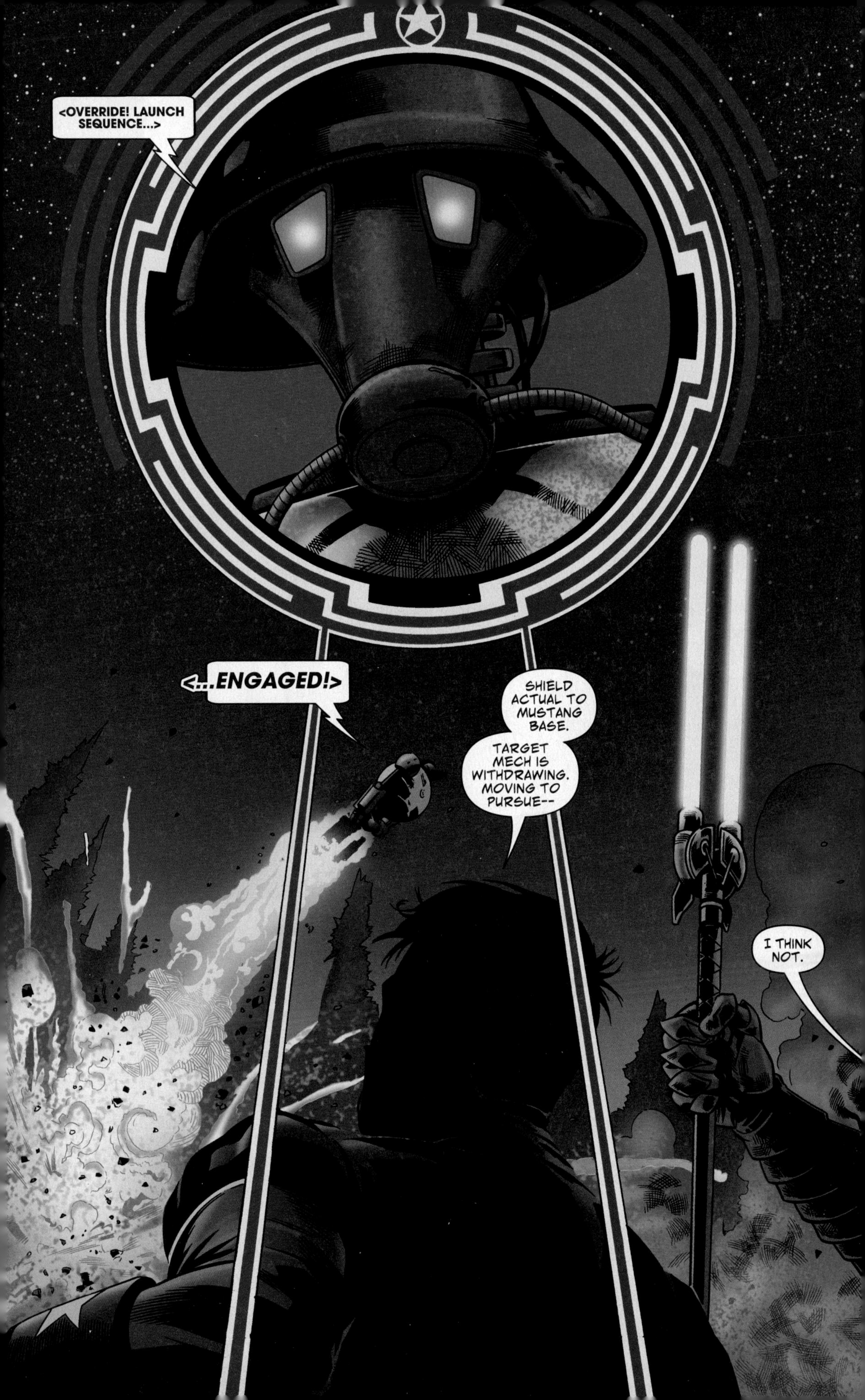

<OVERRIDE! LAUNCH SEQUENCE...>
<...ENGAGED!>
SHIELD ACTUAL TO MUSTANG BASE.
TARGET MECH IS WITHDRAWING. MOVING TO PURSUE--
I THINK NOT.

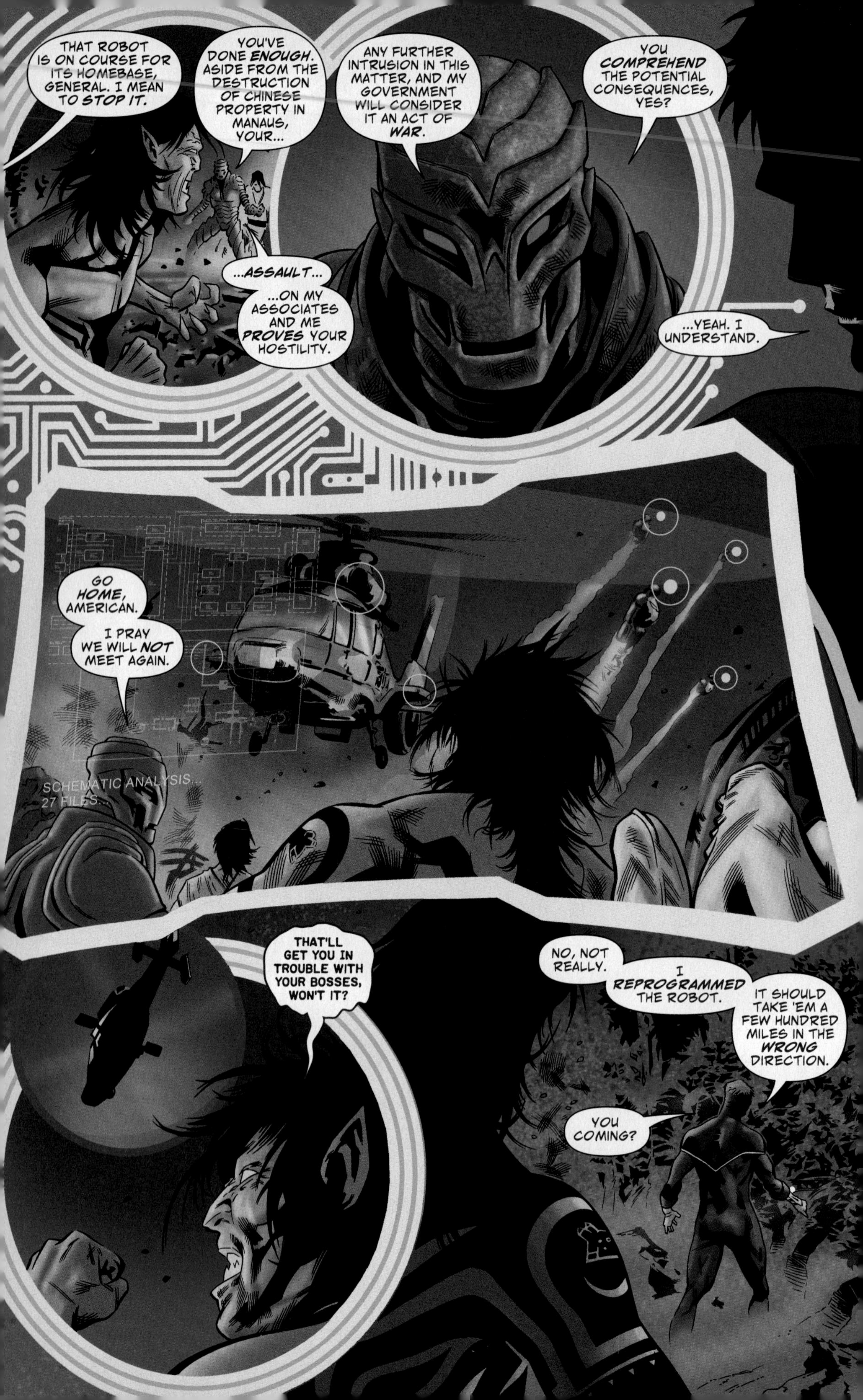
THAT ROBOT IS ON COURSE FOR ITS HOMEBASE, GENERAL. I MEAN TO STOP IT.
YOU'VE DONE ENOUGH. ASIDE FROM THE DESTRUCTION OF CHINESE PROPERTY IN MANAUS, YOUR...
...ASSAULT...
...ON MY ASSOCIATES AND ME PROVES YOUR HOSTILITY.
ANY FURTHER INTRUSION IN THIS MATTER, AND MY GOVERNMENT WILL CONSIDER IT AN ACT OF WAR.
YOU COMPREHEND THE POTENTIAL CONSEQUENCES, YES?
...YEAH. I UNDERSTAND.
GO HOME, AMERICAN.
I PRAY WE WILL NOT MEET AGAIN.
SCHEMATIC ANALYSIS... 27 FILES...
THAT'LL GET YOU IN TROUBLE WITH YOUR BOSSES, WON'T IT?
NO, NOT REALLY.
I REPROGRAMMED THE ROBOT.
IT SHOULD TAKE 'EM A FEW HUNDRED MILES IN THE WRONG DIRECTION.
YOU COMING?

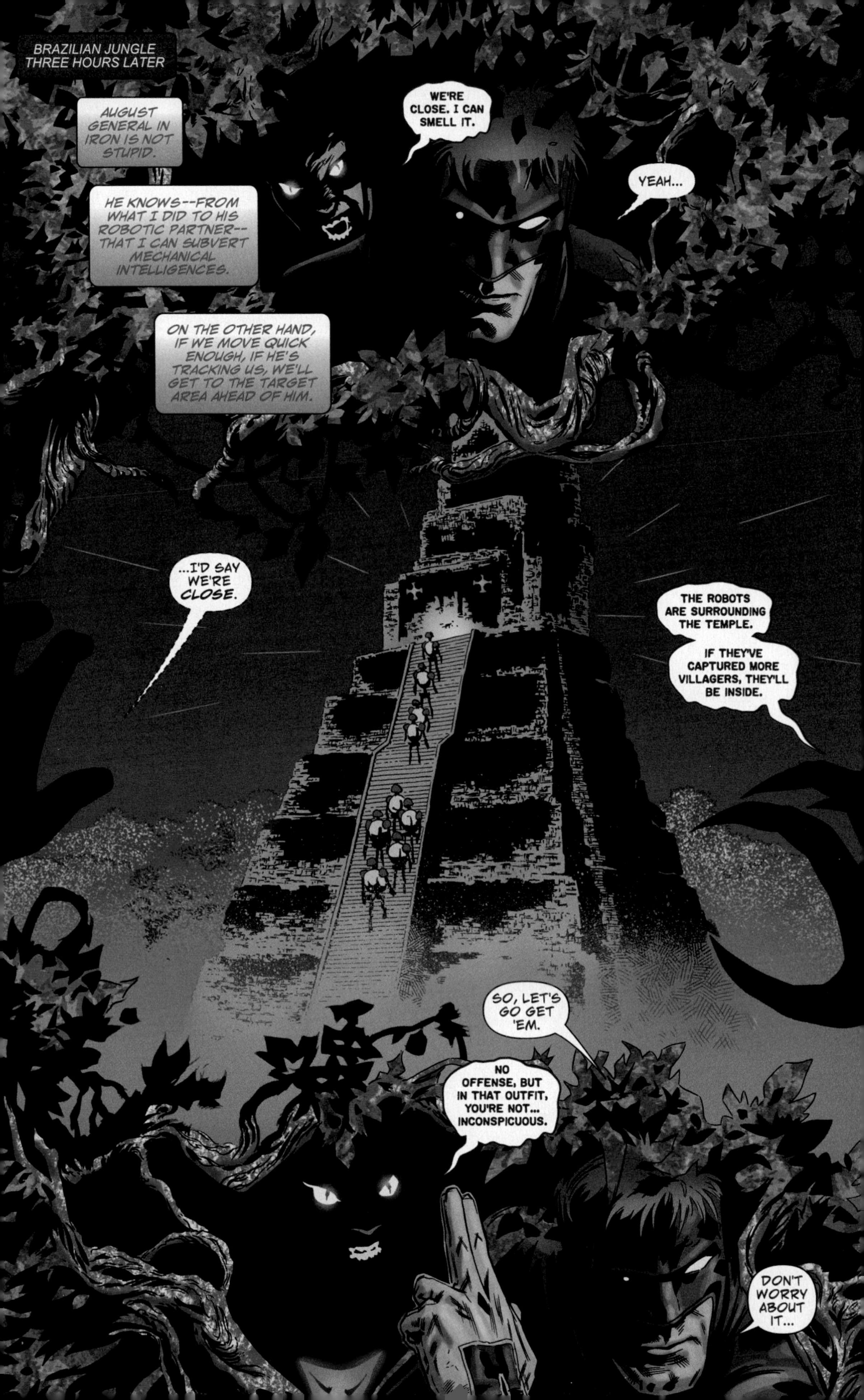
BRAZILIAN JUNGLE
THREE HOURS LATER
AUGUST GENERAL IN IRON IS NOT STUPID.
WE'RE CLOSE. I CAN SMELL IT.
YEAH...
HE KNOWS--FROM WHAT I DID TO HIS ROBOTIC PARTNER--THAT I CAN SUBVERT MECHANICAL INTELLIGENCES.
ON THE OTHER HAND, IF WE MOVE QUICK ENOUGH, IF HE'S TRACKING US, WE'LL GET TO THE TARGET AREA AHEAD OF HIM.
...I'D SAY WE'RE CLOSE.
THE ROBOTS ARE SURROUNDING THE TEMPLE.
IF THEY'VE CAPTURED MORE VILLAGERS, THEY'LL BE INSIDE.
SO, LET'S GO GET 'EM.
NO OFFENSE, BUT IN THAT OUTFIT, YOU'RE NOT... INCONSPICUOUS.
DON'T WORRY ABOUT IT...

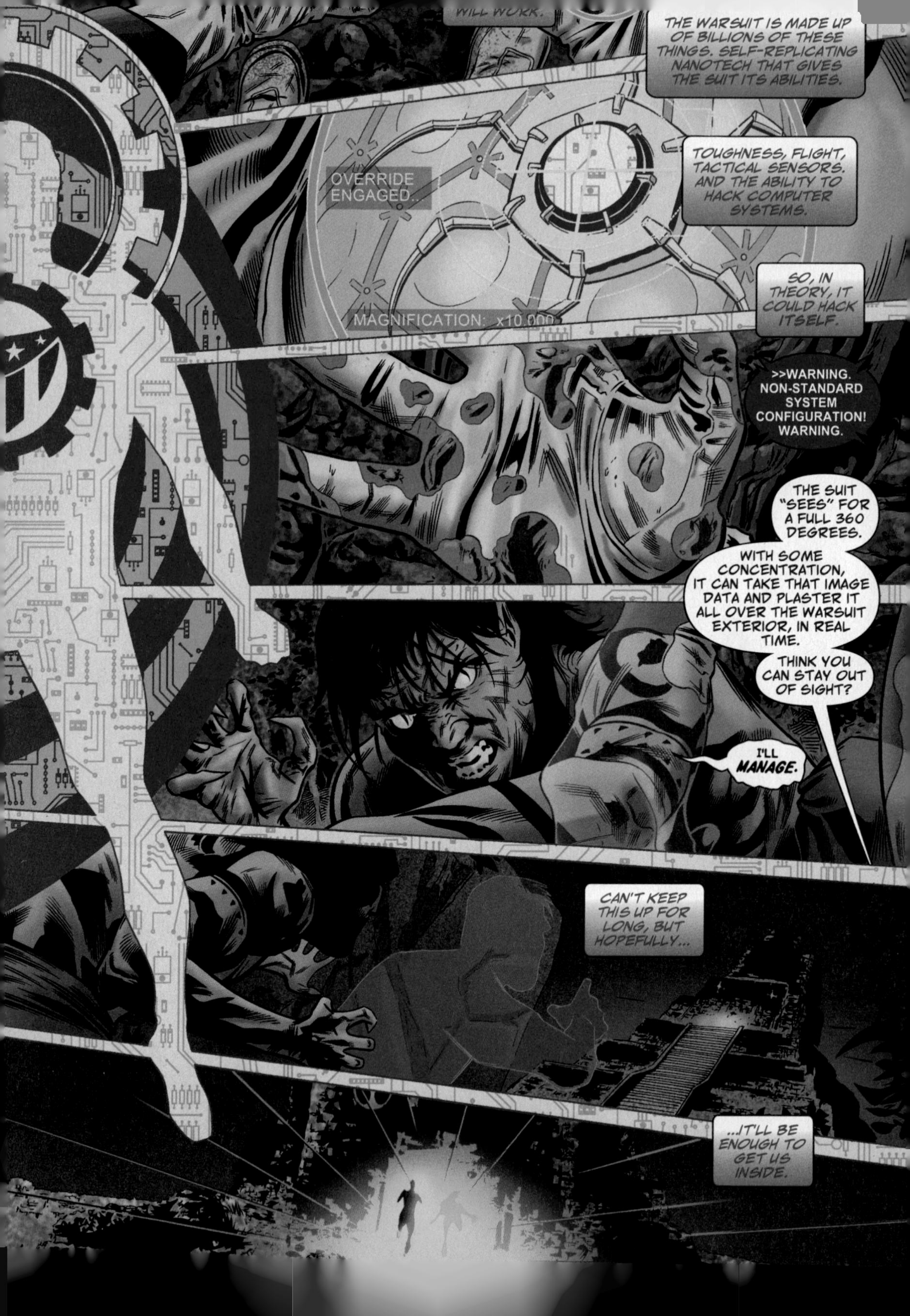

WILL WORK.
THE WARSUIT IS MADE UP OF BILLIONS OF THESE THINGS. SELF-REPLICATING NANOTECH THAT GIVES THE SUIT ITS ABILITIES.
OVERRIDE ENGAGED...
TOUGHNESS, FLIGHT, TACTICAL SENSORS. AND THE ABILITY TO HACK COMPUTER SYSTEMS.
SO, IN THEORY, IT COULD HACK ITSELF.
MAGNIFICATION: x10,000
>>WARNING. NON-STANDARD SYSTEM CONFIGURATION! WARNING.
THE SUIT "SEES" FOR A FULL 360 DEGREES.
WITH SOME CONCENTRATION, IT CAN TAKE THAT IMAGE DATA AND PLASTER IT ALL OVER THE WARSUIT EXTERIOR, IN REAL TIME.
THINK YOU CAN STAY OUT OF SIGHT?
I'LL MANAGE.
CAN'T KEEP THIS UP FOR LONG, BUT HOPEFULLY...
...IT'LL BE ENOUGH TO GET US INSIDE.

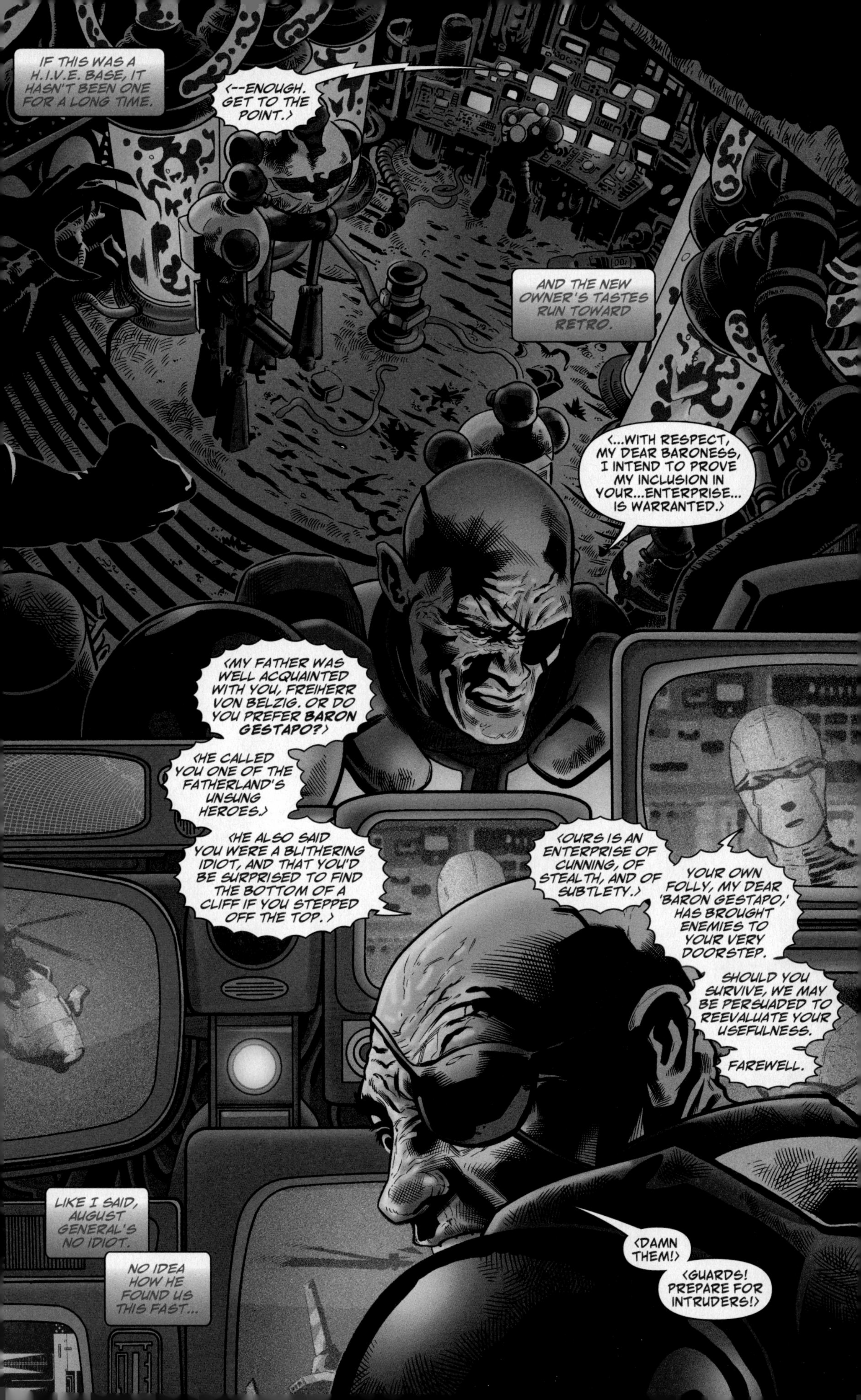
IF THIS WAS A H.I.V.E. BASE, IT HASN'T BEEN ONE FOR A LONG TIME.
<--ENOUGH. GET TO THE POINT.>
AND THE NEW OWNER'S TASTES RUN TOWARD RETRO.
<...WITH RESPECT, MY DEAR BARONESS, I INTEND TO PROVE MY INCLUSION IN YOUR...ENTERPRISE... IS WARRANTED.>
<MY FATHER WAS WELL ACQUAINTED WITH YOU, FREIHERR VON BELZIG. OR DO YOU PREFER BARON GESTAPO?>
<HE CALLED YOU ONE OF THE FATHERLAND'S UNSUNG HEROES.>
<HE ALSO SAID YOU WERE A BLITHERING IDIOT, AND THAT YOU'D BE SURPRISED TO FIND THE BOTTOM OF A CLIFF IF YOU STEPPED OFF THE TOP.>
<OURS IS AN ENTERPRISE OF CUNNING, OF STEALTH, AND OF SUBTLETY.>
YOUR OWN FOLLY, MY DEAR 'BARON GESTAPO,' HAS BROUGHT ENEMIES TO YOUR VERY DOORSTEP.
SHOULD YOU SURVIVE, WE MAY BE PERSUADED TO REEVALUATE YOUR USEFULNESS.
FAREWELL.
LIKE I SAID, AUGUST GENERAL'S NO IDIOT.
NO IDEA HOW HE FOUND US THIS FAST...
<DAMN THEM!>
<GUARDS! PREPARE FOR INTRUDERS!>

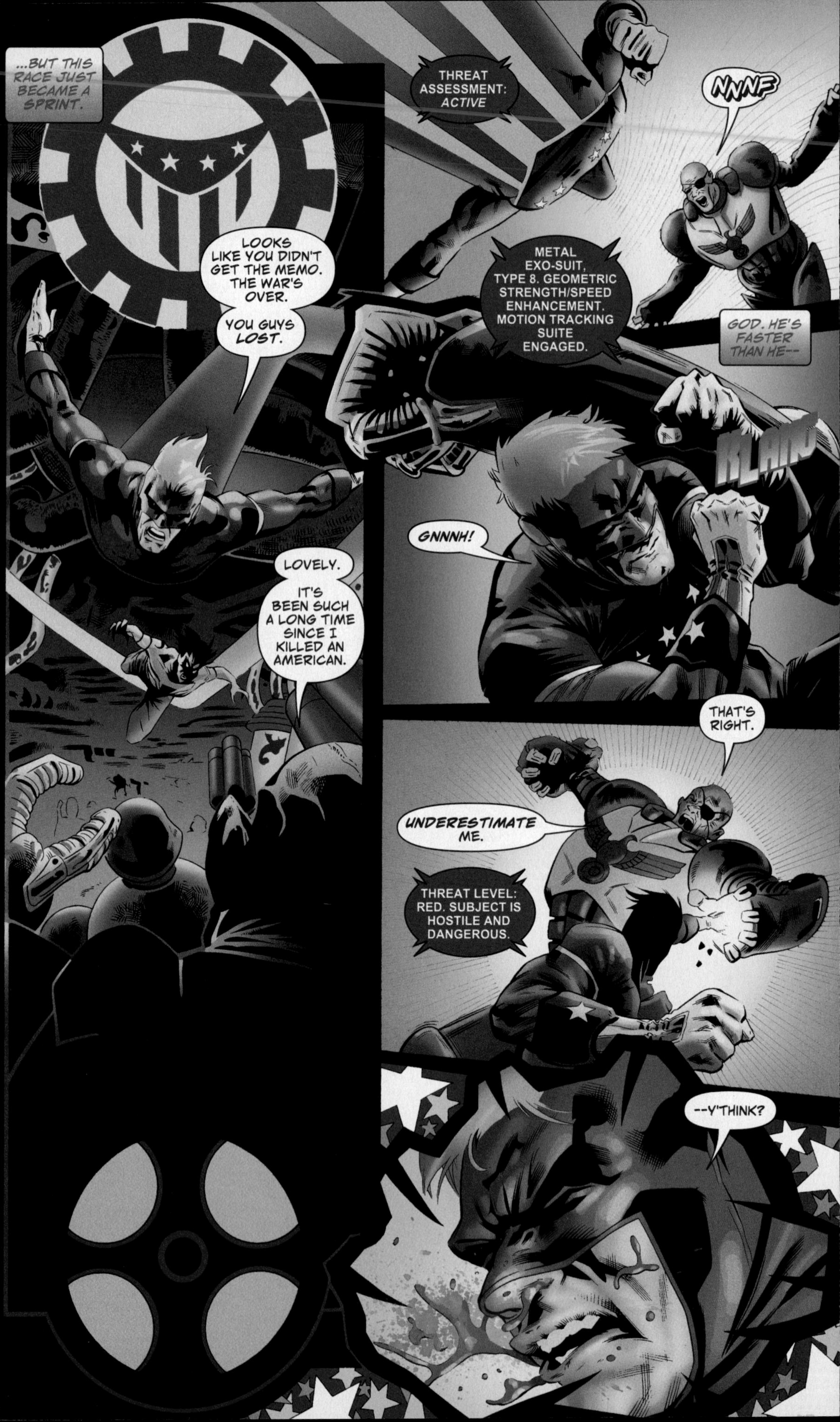

...BUT THIS RACE JUST BECAME A SPRINT.
LOOKS LIKE YOU DIDN'T GET THE MEMO. THE WAR'S OVER.
YOU GUYS LOST.
LOVELY.
IT'S BEEN SUCH A LONG TIME SINCE I KILLED AN AMERICAN.
THREAT ASSESSMENT: ACTIVE
NNNF
METAL EXO-SUIT, TYPE 8. GEOMETRIC STRENGTH/SPEED ENHANCEMENT. MOTION TRACKING SUITE ENGAGED.
GOD. HE'S FASTER THAN HE--
KLANG
GNNNH!
THAT'S RIGHT.
UNDERESTIMATE ME.
THREAT LEVEL: RED. SUBJECT IS HOSTILE AND DANGEROUS.
--Y'THINK?

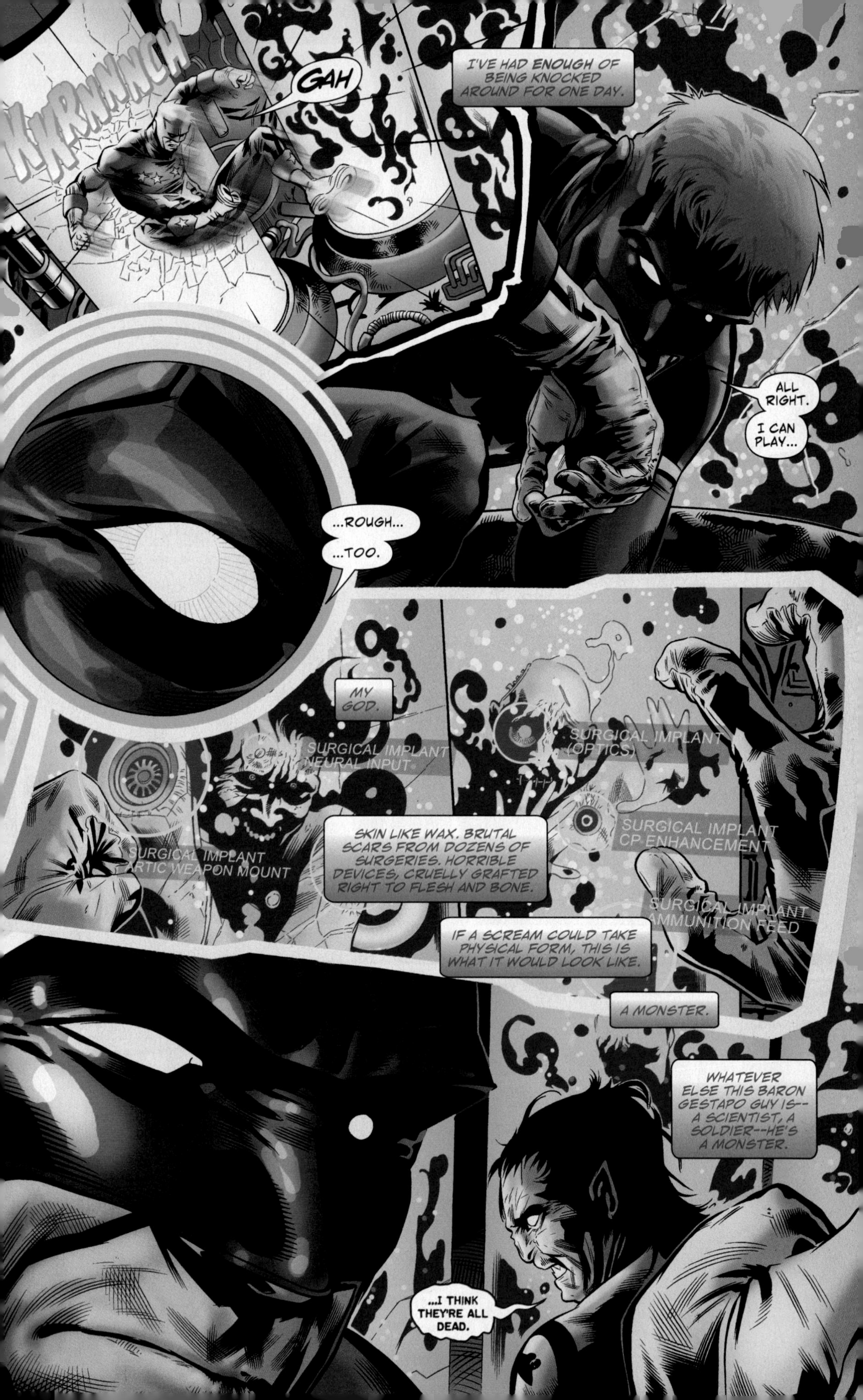
KHRNNNCH
GAH
I'VE HAD ENOUGH OF BEING KNOCKED AROUND FOR ONE DAY.
ALL RIGHT.
I CAN PLAY...
...ROUGH...
...TOO.
MY GOD.
SURGICAL IMPLANT NEURAL INPUT
SURGICAL IMPLANT (OPTICS)
SURGICAL IMPLANT CP ENHANCEMENT
SURGICAL IMPLANT ARTIC WEAPON MOUNT
SKIN LIKE WAX. BRUTAL SCARS FROM DOZENS OF SURGERIES. HORRIBLE DEVICES, CRUELLY GRAFTED RIGHT TO FLESH AND BONE.
SURGICAL IMPLANT AMMUNITION FEED
IF A SCREAM COULD TAKE PHYSICAL FORM, THIS IS WHAT IT WOULD LOOK LIKE.
A MONSTER.
WHATEVER ELSE THIS BARON GESTAPO GUY IS--A SCIENTIST, A SOLDIER--HE'S A MONSTER.
...I THINK THEY'RE ALL DEAD.

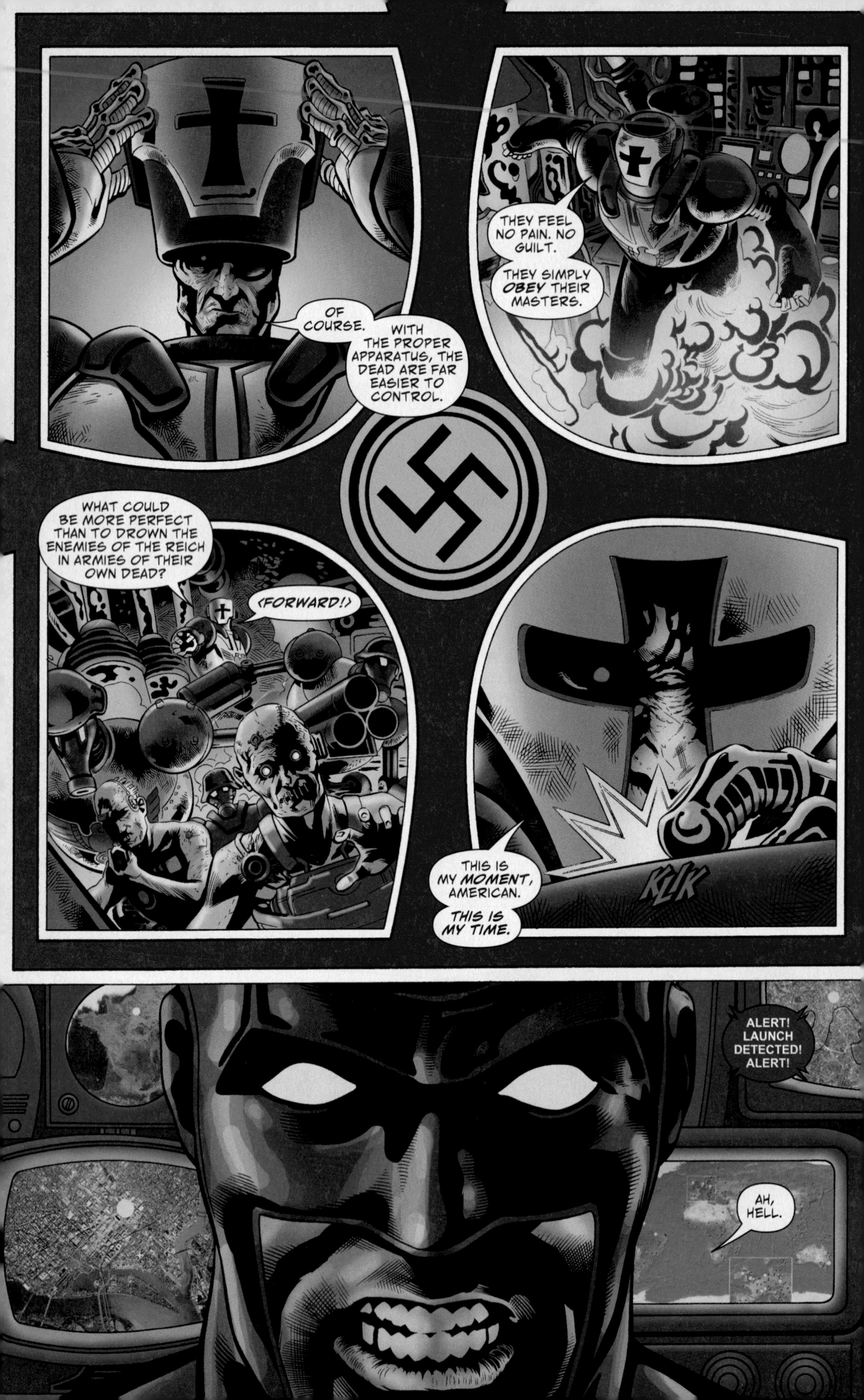
OF COURSE.
WITH THE PROPER APPARATUS, THE DEAD ARE FAR EASIER TO CONTROL.
THEY FEEL NO PAIN. NO GUILT.
THEY SIMPLY OBEY THEIR MASTERS.
WHAT COULD BE MORE PERFECT THAN TO DROWN THE ENEMIES OF THE REICH IN ARMIES OF THEIR OWN DEAD?
<FORWARD!>
THIS IS MY MOMENT, AMERICAN.
THIS IS MY TIME.
KLIK
ALERT! LAUNCH DETECTED! ALERT!
AH, HELL.

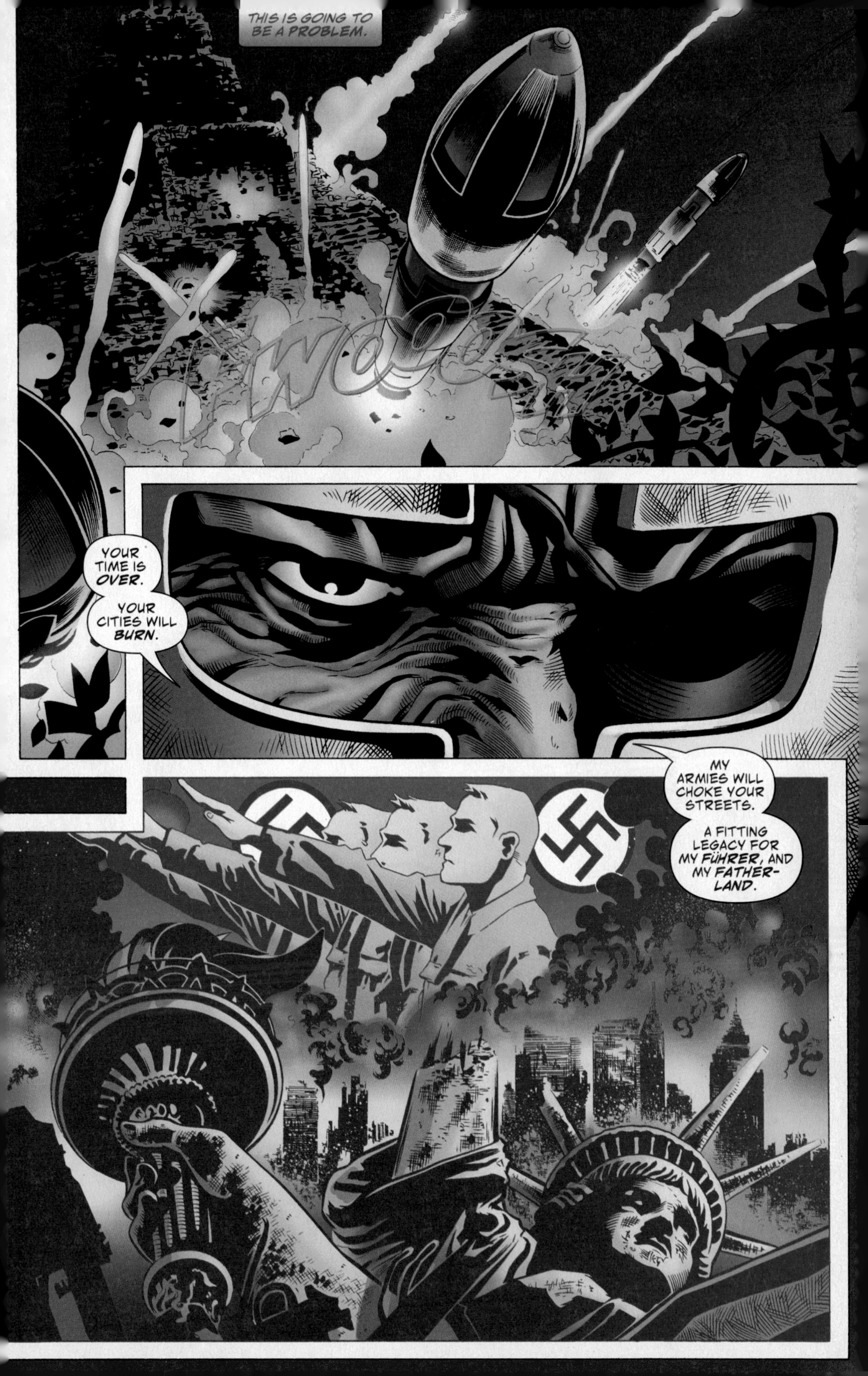
THIS IS GOING TO BE A PROBLEM.
YOUR TIME IS OVER.
YOUR CITIES WILL BURN.
MY ARMIES WILL CHOKE YOUR STREETS.
A FITTING LEGACY FOR MY FÜHRER, AND MY FATHER-LAND.

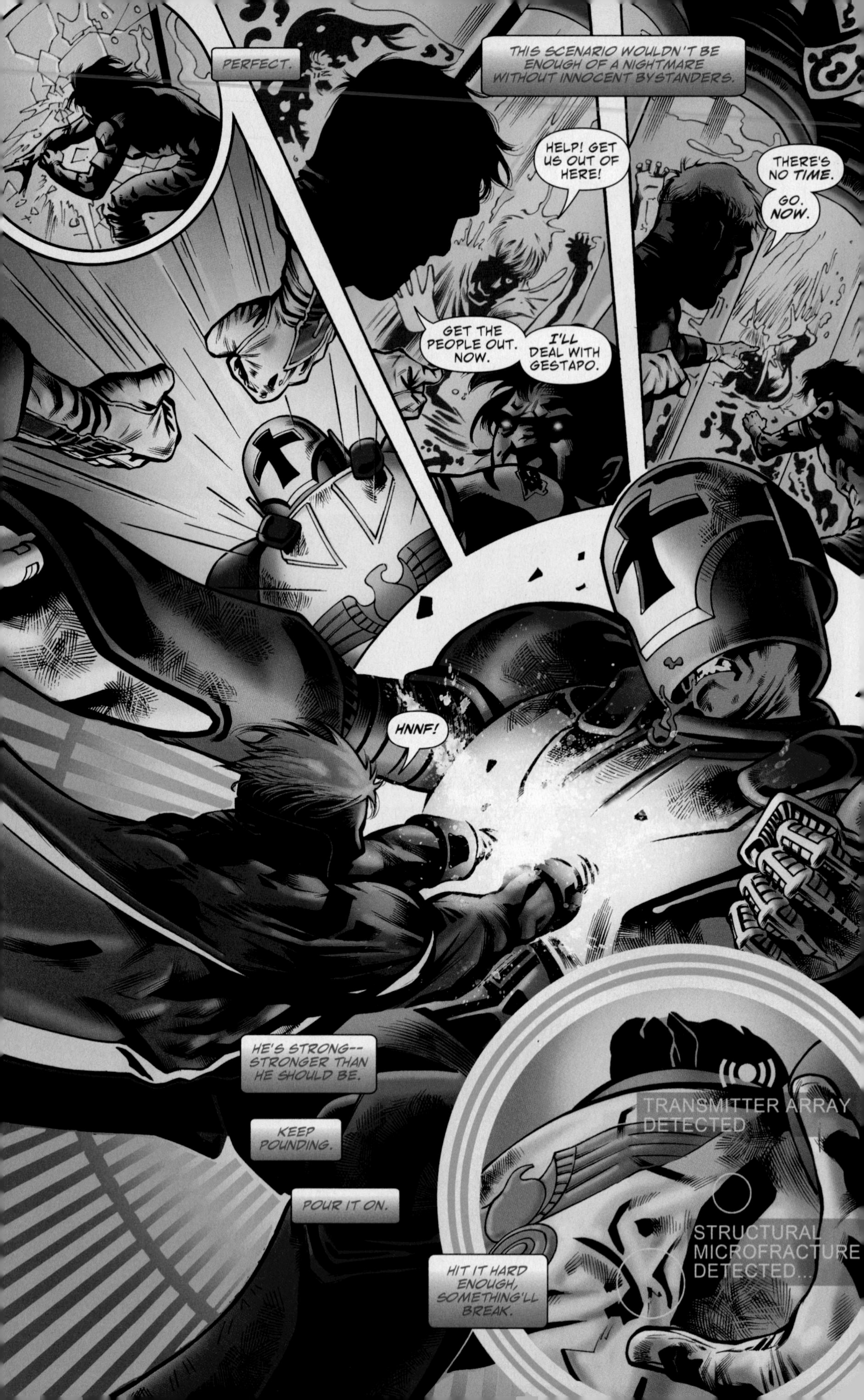

PERFECT.
THIS SCENARIO WOULDN'T BE ENOUGH OF A NIGHTMARE WITHOUT INNOCENT BYSTANDERS.
HELP! GET US OUT OF HERE!
THERE'S NO TIME.
GO. NOW.
GET THE PEOPLE OUT. NOW.
I'LL DEAL WITH GESTAPO.
HNNF!
HE'S STRONG-- STRONGER THAN HE SHOULD BE.
KEEP POUNDING.
POUR IT ON.
HIT IT HARD ENOUGH, SOMETHING'LL BREAK.
TRANSMITTER ARRAY DETECTED
STRUCTURAL MICROFRACTURE DETECTED...

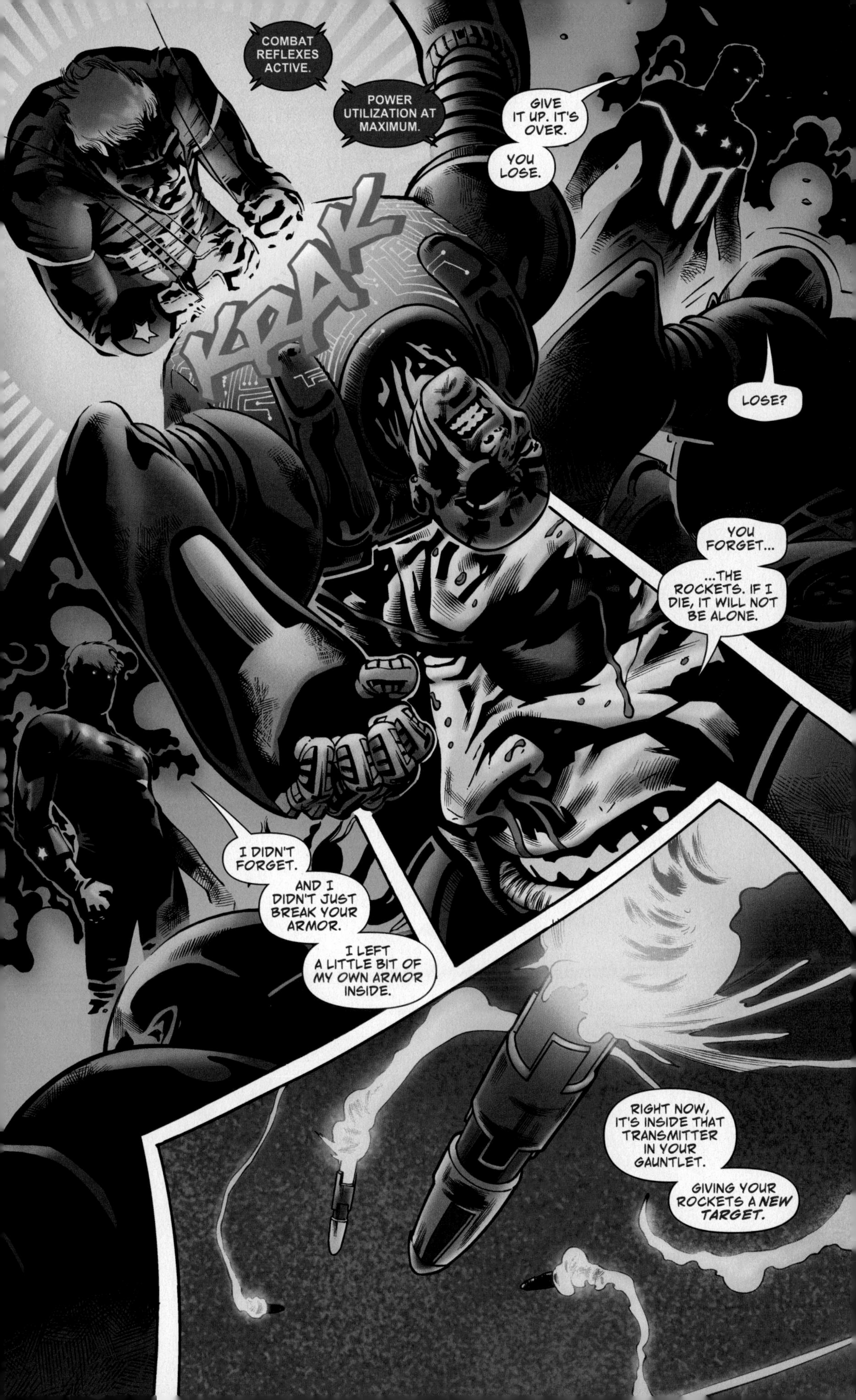
COMBAT REFLEXES ACTIVE.
POWER UTILIZATION AT MAXIMUM.
GIVE IT UP. IT'S OVER.
YOU LOSE.
KRAK
LOSE?
YOU FORGET...
...THE ROCKETS. IF I DIE, IT WILL NOT BE ALONE.
I DIDN'T FORGET.
AND I DIDN'T JUST BREAK YOUR ARMOR.
I LEFT A LITTLE BIT OF MY OWN ARMOR INSIDE.
RIGHT NOW, IT'S INSIDE THAT TRANSMITTER IN YOUR GAUNTLET.
GIVING YOUR ROCKETS A *NEW TARGET*.

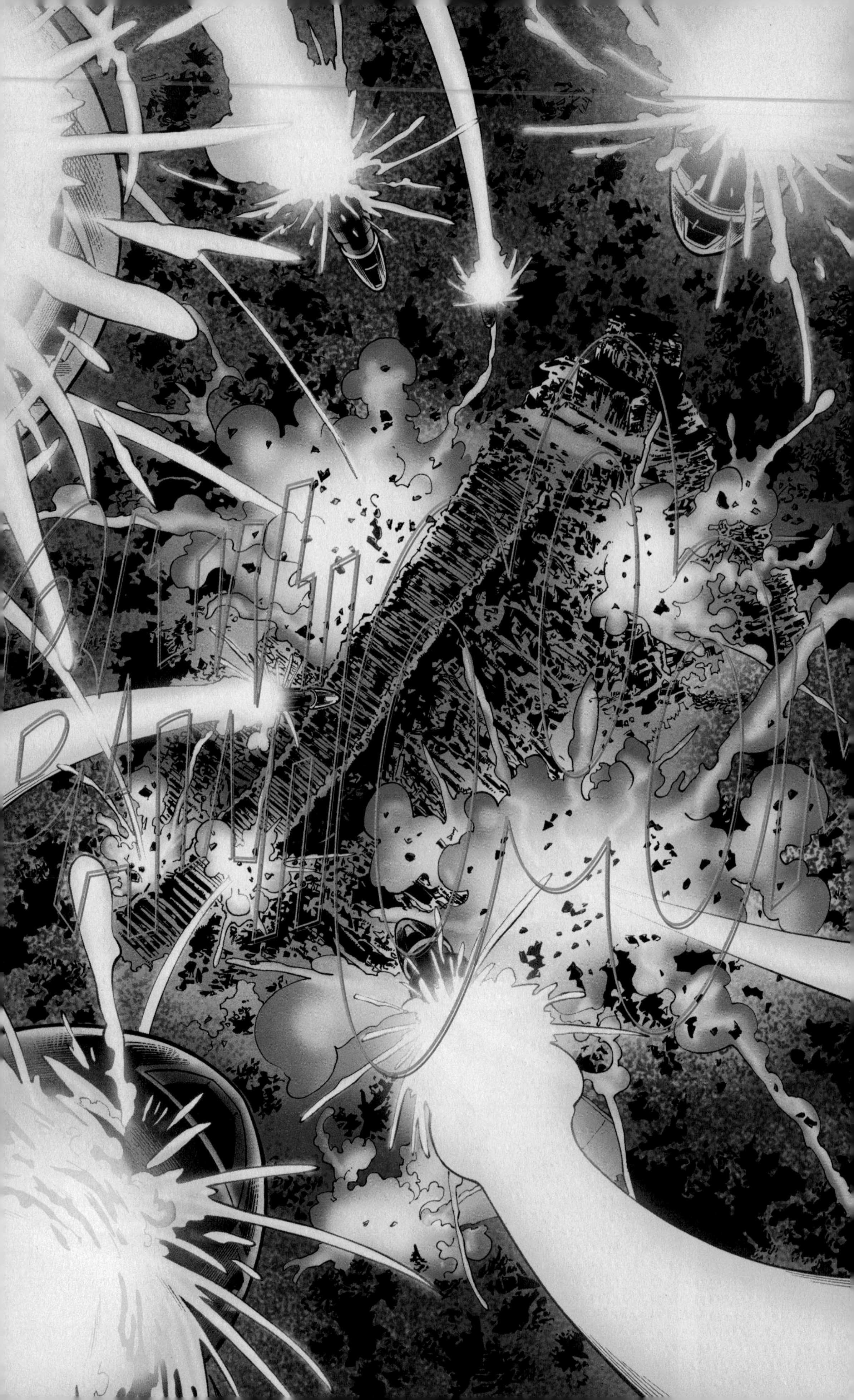

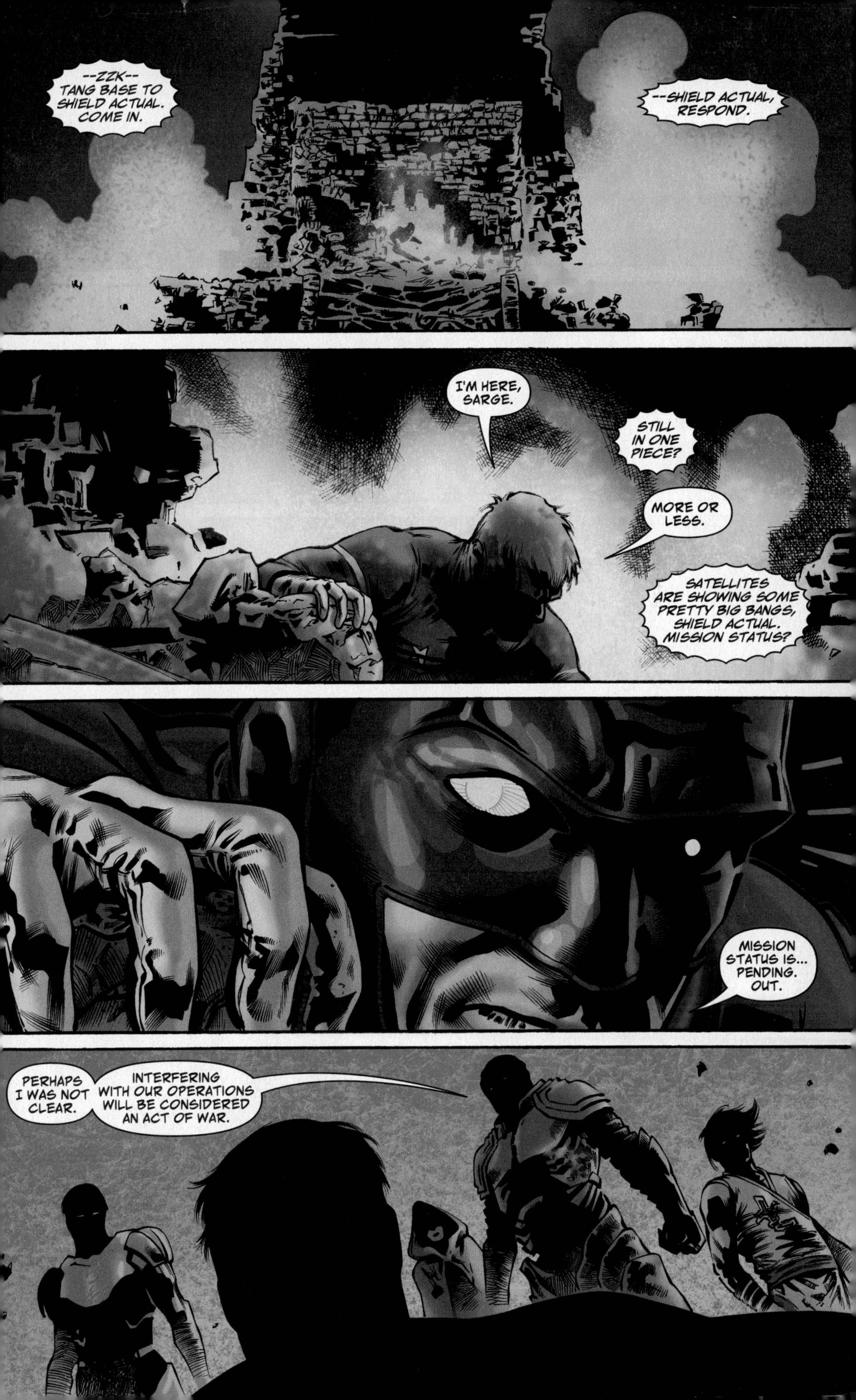
--ZZK-- TANG BASE TO SHIELD ACTUAL. COME IN.
--SHIELD ACTUAL, RESPOND.
I'M HERE, SARGE.
STILL IN ONE PIECE?
MORE OR LESS.
SATELLITES ARE SHOWING SOME PRETTY BIG BANGS, SHIELD ACTUAL. MISSION STATUS?
MISSION STATUS IS... PENDING. OUT.
PERHAPS I WAS NOT CLEAR.
INTERFERING WITH OUR OPERATIONS WILL BE CONSIDERED AN ACT OF WAR.

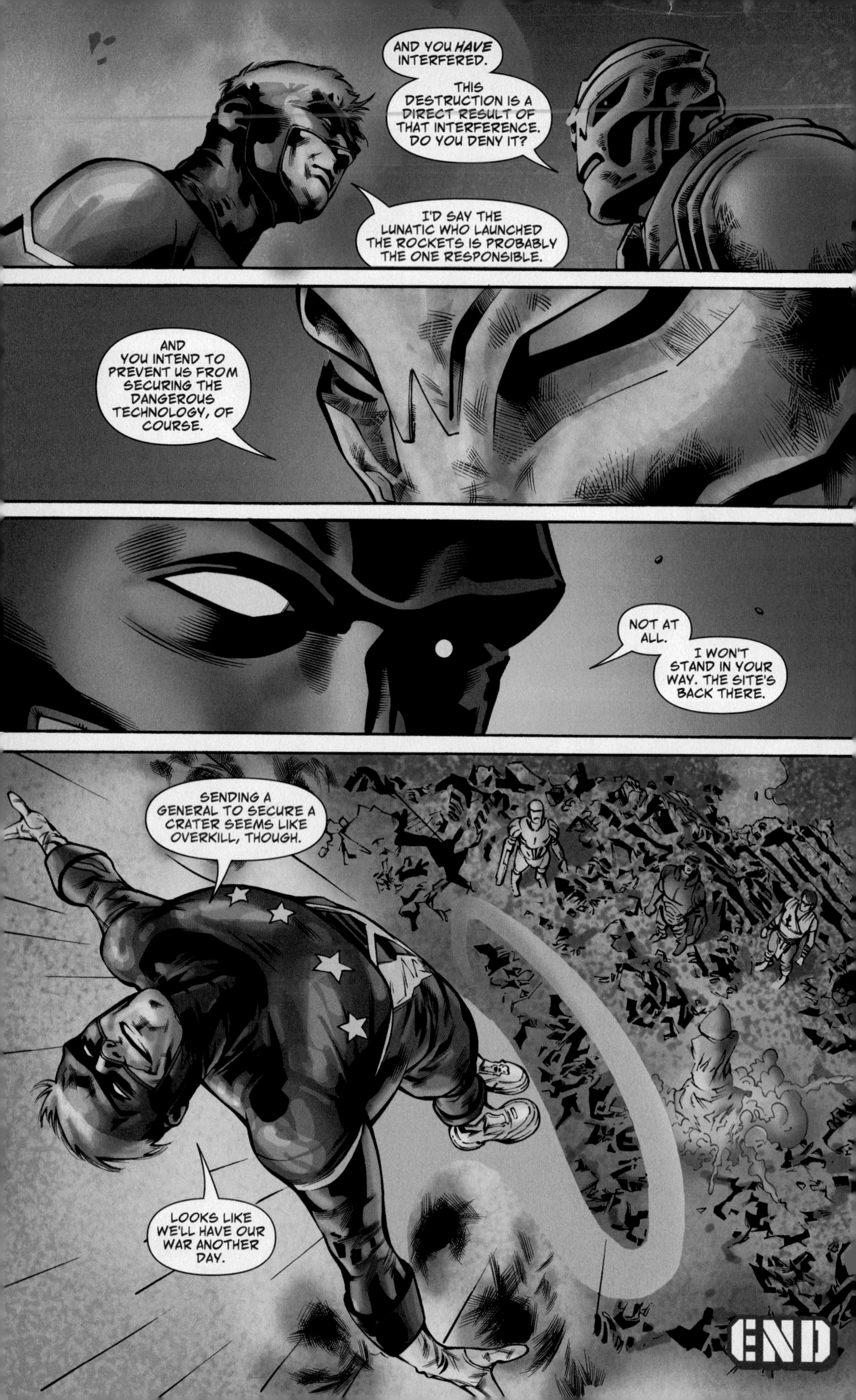
AND YOU HAVE INTERFERED.
THIS DESTRUCTION IS A DIRECT RESULT OF THAT INTERFERENCE. DO YOU DENY IT?
I'D SAY THE LUNATIC WHO LAUNCHED THE ROCKETS IS PROBABLY THE ONE RESPONSIBLE.
AND YOU INTEND TO PREVENT US FROM SECURING THE DANGEROUS TECHNOLOGY, OF COURSE.
NOT AT ALL.
I WON'T STAND IN YOUR WAY. THE SITE'S BACK THERE.
SENDING A GENERAL TO SECURE A CRATER SEEMS LIKE OVERKILL, THOUGH.
LOOKS LIKE WE'LL HAVE OUR WAR ANOTHER DAY.
END